Digital Capitalism

This third volume in Christian Fuchs's Media, Communication and Society book series illuminates what it means to live in an age of digital capitalism, analysing its various aspects, and engaging with a variety of critical thinkers whose theories and approaches enable a critical understanding of digital capitalism for media and communication.

Each chapter focuses on a particular dimension of digital capitalism or a critical theorist whose work helps us to illuminate how digital capitalism works. Subjects covered include: digital positivism; administrative big data analytics; the role and relations of patriarchy, slavery, and racism in the context of digital labour; digital alienation; the role of social media in the capitalist crisis; the relationship between imperialism and digital labour; alternatives such as trade unions and class struggles in the digital age; platform co-operatives; digital commons; and public service Internet platforms. It also considers specific examples, including the digital labour of Foxconn and Pegatron workers, software engineers at Google, and online freelancers, as well as considering the political economy of targeted-advertising-based Internet platforms such as Facebook, Google, YouTube, and Instagram.

Digital Capitalism illuminates how a digital capitalist society's economy, politics, and culture work and interact, making it essential reading for both students and researchers in media, culture, and communication studies, as well as related disciplines.

Christian Fuchs is a critical theorist of communication and society. He is co-editor of the journal *tripleC: Communication, Capitalism & Critique*. He is author of many publications, including the books *Foundations of Critical Theory* (2022), *Communicating COVID-19: Everyday Life, Digital Capitalism, and Conspiracy Theories in Pandemic Times* (2021), *Marxist Humanism and Communication Theory* (2021), *Social Media: A Critical Introduction* (3rd edition 2021), *Communication and Capitalism: A Critical Theory* (2020), *Marxism: Karl Marx's Fifteen Key Concepts for Cultural & Communication Studies* (2020), *Nationalism on the Internet: Critical Theory and Ideology in the Age of Social Media and Fake News* (2020), *Rereading Marx in the Age of Digital Capitalism* (2019), *Digital Demagogue: Authoritarian Capitalism in the Age of Trump and Twitter* (2016), *Digital Labour and Karl Marx* (2014), and *Internet and Society* (2008).

Digital Capitalism

Media, Communication and Society
Volume Three

Christian Fuchs

Routledge
Taylor & Francis Group

LONDON AND NEW YORK

First published 2022
by Routledge
2 Park Square, Milton Park, Abingdon, Oxon OX14 4RN

and by Routledge
605 Third Avenue, New York, NY 10158

Routledge is an imprint of the Taylor & Francis Group, an informa business

© 2022 Christian Fuchs

British Library Cataloguing-in-Publication Data
A catalogue record for this book is available from the British Library

Library of Congress Cataloging-in-Publication Data
Names: Fuchs, Christian, 1976- author.
Title: Digital capitalism / Christian Fuchs.
Description: Abingdon, Oxon ; New York, NY : Routledge, 2022. | Series: Media, communication and society ; volume 3 | Includes bibliographical references and index.
Identifiers: LCCN 2021022153 (print) | LCCN 2021022154 (ebook) | ISBN 9781032119182 (hardback) | ISBN 9781032119205 (paperback) | ISBN 9781003222149 (ebook)
Subjects: LCSH: Digital media--Economic aspects. | Digital media--Social aspects. | Capitalism. | Information technology--Economic aspects.
Classification: LCC HM851 .F829 2022 (print) | LCC HM851 (ebook) | DDC 302.23/1--dc23
LC record available at https://lccn.loc.gov/2021022153
LC ebook record available at https://lccn.loc.gov/2021022154

ISBN: 978-1-032-11918-2 (hbk)
ISBN: 978-1-032-11920-5 (pbk)
ISBN: 978-1-003-22214-9 (ebk)

DOI: 10.4324/9781003222149

Typeset in Univers
by MPS Limited, Dehradun

Contents

Figures

Tables

Acknowledgements

Chapter 2 is a reprint of sections 1, 3, 4.2, 4.3, 4.4, 4.5, 4.6, 4.8, 4.9, 5, and 6 of a journal article. The article is reprinted with permission of the journal *tripleC: Communication, Capitalism & Critique:* Christian Fuchs. 2021. Engels@200: Friedrich Engels in the Age of Digital Capitalism. Introduction. *tripleC: Communication, Capitalism & Critique* 19 (1): 1-14. DOI: https://doi.org/10.31269/triplec.v19i1.1229

Chapter 3 was first published as a journal article. It is reprinted based on a contractual guarantee that allows the author to reuse the article in whole or in part in publications of his own work. Christian Fuchs. 2020. History and Class Consciousness 2.0: Georg Lukács in the Age of Digital Capitalism and Big Data. *Information, Communication and Society*, https://doi.org/10.1080/1369118X.2020.1759670.

Chapter 4 is based on a keynote talk at the conference "Adorno and the Media", Karlsruhe University of Arts and Design, 14 December 2019.

Chapter 6 was first published as a chapter in a collected volume. It is reprinted based on a contractual guarantee that allows the author to reuse the chapter in whole or in part in publications of his own work: Christian Fuchs. 2015. Dallas Smythe and Digital Labor. In *Routledge Companion to Labor and Media*, ed. Richard Maxwell, 51–62. New York: Routledge.

Chapter 7 was first published as a journal article. It is reprinted based on SAGE's Author Archiving and Re-Use Guidelines: Christian Fuchs. 2017. From Digital Positivism and Administrative Big Data Analytics Towards Critical Digital and Social Media Research! *European Journal of Communication* 32 (1): 37–49. DOI: https://doi.org/1 0.1177%2F0267323116682804

Chapter 8 was first published as a chapter in a collected volume. It is reprinted based on a free of charge licence by Informa UK Limited. Christian Fuchs. 2019. Social Media, Big Data, and Critical Marketing. In *The Routledge Companion to Critical Marketing*, eds. Mark Tadajewski, Matthew Higgins, Janice Denegri-Knott and Rohit Varman, 467–481. London: Routledge.

Chapter 9 was first published as a chapter in a collected volume. It is reprinted It is reprinted based on a contractual guarantee that allows the author to reuse the chapter in whole or in part in publications of his own work: Christian Fuchs. 2018. Social Media and the Capitalist Crisis. In *The Media and Austerity: Comparative Perspectives*, eds. Laura Basu, Steve Schifferes and Sophie Knowles, 211–225. Abingdon: Routledge.

Chapter 10 is a shortened version of a journal article that is reprinted based on SAGE's Author Archiving and Re-Use Guidelines. The other parts of this article were reused, revised, and extended in Chapter 10 (Capitalism, Racism, Patriarchy) of the book *Marxist Humanism and Communication Theory* (*Media, Communication and Society Volume One*): Christian Fuchs. 2018. Capitalism, Patriarchy, Slavery, and Racism in the Age of Digital Capitalism and Digital Labour. *Critical Sociology* 44 (4–5): 677–702. DOI: https://doi.org/10.1177%2F0896920517691108

Chapter 11 was first published as a journal article. It is reprinted with permission by *Monthly Review*. Christian Fuchs. 2016. Digital Labor and Imperialism. *Monthly Review* 67 (8): 14–24.

Chapter 12 was first published as a journal article. Reprinted with permission by Taylor and Francis: Christian Fuchs. 2017. The Information Economy and the Labor Theory of Value. *International Journal of Political Economy* 46 (1): 65–89. DOI: https://doi.org/10.1080/08911916.2017.1310475

Part I

Introduction

Chapter One
Introduction: What is Digital Capitalism?

1.1 About this Book

This book deals with the question: what is digital capitalism? It illuminates what it means to live in digital capitalism and presents analyses of a variety of aspects of digital capitalism and engages with the thought of a variety of critical thinkers whose theories and approaches enable a critical understanding of digital capitalism.

The book at hand is the third volume of a series of books titled "Media, Communication & Society". The overall aim of *Media, Communication & Society* is to outline the foundations of a critical theory of communication and digital communication in society. It is a multi-volume book series situated on the intersection of communication theory, sociology, and philosophy. The overall questions that "Media, Communication & Society" deals with are: what is the role of communication in society? What is the role of communication in capitalism? What is the role of communication in digital capitalism?

Digital Capitalism presents and engages with the theoretical approaches of Karl Marx, Friedrich Engels, Georg Lukács, Theodor W. Adorno, Henri Lefebvre, and Dallas Smythe as the foundation for the critical analysis of digital capitalism. The book analyses a variety of digital capitalism's aspects, including digital positivism, administrative big data analytics, critical digital and social media research, what society we live in, everyday life in digital capitalism, the digital culture industry, the role of ideology in digital capitalism, reified consciousness on the Internet, the authoritarian personality on social media, the critical theory of digital labour and the international division of digital labour; the digital labour of Foxconn and Pegatron workers, software engineers at Google and online freelancers; the political economy of targeted-advertising–based

DOI: 10.4324/9781003222149-1

Internet platforms such as Facebook, Google, YouTube, and Instagram; the role and relations of capitalism, patriarchy, slavery, and racism in the context of digital labour; digital alienation, the role of social media in the capitalist crisis, the relationship of imperialism and digital labour, Marx's labour theory of value in the context of information industries, trade unions and class struggles in the digital age, platform co-operatives, digital commons, and public service Internet platforms. *Digital Capitalism* illuminates how a digital capitalist society's economy, politics, and culture work and interact.

The book is organised in the form of 13 chapters, including an introduction and a conclusion. Each chapter focuses on a particular dimension of digital capitalism or a critical theorist whose work helps us to illuminate how digital capitalism works.

The chapters are organised in the form of four parts. Part 1 forms the introduction. Part 2 focuses on theorists and part 3 on themes. Part 4 is the book's conclusion. In part 2, the discussed theorists are Friedrich Engels (chapter 2), Georg Lukács (chapter 3), Theodor W. Adorno (chapter 4), Henri Lefebvre (chapter 5), and Dallas Smythe (chapter 6). The sequence of the chapters in part 2 is organised by ascending birth dates of the discussed theorists. Karl Marx's works are utilised throughout the book, which is why there is not a specific chapter dedicated to his works (for a discussion of Marx in the context of communicative and digital capitalism, see Fuchs 2020b, 2019, 2016b). Part 3 discusses a variety of themes and dimensions of digital capitalism, namely digital positivism (chapter 7), big data (chapter 8), social media in capitalist crises (chapter 9), the connection of capitalism, patriarchy and racism in the digital age (chapter 10), digital labour (chapters 10 and 11), and digital imperialism (chapter 11).

Here are the main questions that each chapter asks:

- Chapter 1: What is digital capitalism?
- Chapter 2: How relevant are Friedrich Engels's works in the age of digital capitalism?
- Chapter 3: How can Georg Lukács' book *History and Class Consciousness* inform the critical analysis of digital capitalism and of ideology in the digital age?
- Chapter 4: How can Theodor W. Adorno's critical theory illuminate how digital capitalism works?
- Chapter 5: How can Henri Lefebvre's three-volume book *Critique of Everyday Life* inform a critical theory of communication? How can it inform a critique of digital capitalism?

- Chapter 6: How can Dallas Smythe's notions of the audience commodity and audience labour inform the analysis of the political economy of targeted-ad–based Internet platforms?
- Chapter 7: What are the features and problems of big data analytics? What are the features of critical digital and social media research?
- Chapter 8: How can we critically analyse and understand social media and big data's political economy?
- Chapter 9: What have been the roles of social media in crises of capitalism?
- Chapter 10: How can understanding the relationship of exploitation and oppression inform the study of digital labour and digital capitalism?
- Chapter 11: What is the relationship of digital labour and imperialism?
- Chapter 12: How can Karl Marx's labour theory of value inform the analysis of the information economy?

There is a number of key thinkers whom you encounter in this book. I want to introduce these thinkers briefly to the reader.

Karl Marx (1818–1883) was a philosopher, economist, sociologist, journalist, and revolutionary socialist. In 1999, he won a BBC online poll that determined the millennium's "greatest thinker" (BBC 1999). His key works include *Economic and Philosophic Manuscripts*, *The Manifesto of the Communist Party* (together with Friedrich Engels), *Grundrisse*, and the three volumes of *Capital*. Karl Marx plays a role throughout this book in all chapters. He is the most important thinker for a critical theory and critique of the political economy of communication (see Fuchs and Mosco 2012, Fuchs 2020a, 2020b, 2016b).

Friedrich Engels (1820–1895) was Marx's closest comrade, collaborator, and friend. He co-authored *The Manifesto of the Communist Party* together with Marx, funded and supported Marx's works, edited volumes two and three of Capital, and made original contributions to critical social theory with works such as *The Condition of the Working Class in England* and *The Origin of the Family, Private Property and the State*. Chapter 2 ("Friedrich Engels in the Age of Digital Capitalism") is dedicated to the analysis of the relevance of Engels's works and especially *The Condition of the Working Class in England* for the analysis of digital capitalism (see also the collected volume "Engels@ 200: Friedrich Engels in the Age of Digital Capitalism", Fuchs 2021a).

Georg/György Lukács (1885–1971) was a philosopher who is often considered the most influential theorist of the 20th century. In his book *History and Class Consciousness* he coined based on Marx the notion of reified consciousness that influenced ideology critique and the development of the Frankfurt School's notion of instrumental reason. *Zur Ontologie des gesellschaftlichen Seins* (*The Ontology of Society's Being*) is Lukács' second masterpiece (see Fuchs 2016a, chapter 2, and Fuchs 2018). Chapter 3 ("*History and Class Consciousness* 2.0: Georg Lukács in the Age of Digital Capitalism and Big Data") is dedicated to the discussion of how History and Class Consciousness can inform the critical analysis of digital capitalism.

History and Class Consciousness has just like Karl Marx's works influenced the development of Marxist humanism, an approach that has an emphasis on dialectical analysis alienation, practices, class struggles, and democratic socialism (see volumes 1 and 2 of my book series Media, *Communication and Society*, of which the volume at hand forms volume 3). In France, Henri Lefebvre has been the most important 20th-century Marxist theorist and Marxists humanist. There are many parallels between Lefebvre and Lukács. Lefebvre was the French Lukács. Henri Lefebvre (1901–1991) was a Marxist-humanist philosopher and sociologist. He can be considered as the most important and most influential French Marxist theorist. He published more than 60 books, including the three-volume *The Critique of Everyday Life* and *The Production of* Space (for an analysis of how The Production of Space matters for a critical theory of communication, see Fuchs 2019). Chapter 5 ("Communication in Everyday (Digital) Life. A Reading of Henri Lefebvre's *Critique of Everyday Life* in the Age of Digital Capitalism") analyses how Henri Lefebvre's three-volume Critique of Everyday Life helps us to critically analyse the analysis of digital capitalism.

Theodor W. Adorno (1903–1969) was a German philosopher and sociologist who together with Max Horkheimer shaped the approach of Frankfurt School critical theory. Among Adorno's most well-known works are *Dialectic of Enlightenment* (written together with Horkheimer), *The Authoritarian Personality*, *Minima Moralia: Reflections from Damaged Life*, *Introduction to the Sociology of Music*, *Hegel: Three Studies*, *The Jargon of Authenticity*, *Negative Dialectics*, and *Aesthetic Theory*. Chapter 4 (Adorno and the Media in Digital Capitalism) analyses how Adorno's works can inform the critical analysis of digital capitalism.

Dallas Smythe (1907–1992) was a Marxist political economist who played an important role in the formation of the academic field of the political economy of communication. Smythe's most influential work has been his essay Communications: Blindspot of Western Marxism, in which he coined the notions of the audience commodity and audience labour that he uses in the analysis of advertising's political economy. These concepts have been revived as the foundation of the analysis of the political economy of targeted advertising on social media platforms. Chapter 6 (Dallas Smythe and Digital Labour) focuses on the question of how Smythe's work can inform the analysis of platforms such as Facebook and what role the concept of digital labour plays in this context (see also Fuchs 2012, 2014a, 2014b, 2015).

One can frequently hear that the thought of Marx and those inspired by him is outdated and is no longer relevant today. Thinkers such as Marx, Engels, Lukács, Adorno, and Smythe were not just analysing the time they live in but also provided concepts that are relevant for the general analysis of capitalism and can therefore be updated for the analysis of digital capitalism. Given that capitalism has taken on peculiar forms in the 21st century, Marxian analysis continues to be of high relevance in the age of digital capitalism.

1.2 This Book's Chapters

Chapter 2 is focused on "Friedrich Engels in the Age of Digital Capitalism". It asks: How relevant are Friedrich Engels's works in the age of digital capitalism? It shows that Engels class-struggle–oriented theory can and should inform 21st-century social science and digital social research. Based on a reading of Engels's works, the chapter discusses how to think of scientific socialism as critical social science today, presents a critique of computational social science as digital positivism, engages with foundations of digital labour analysis, the analysis of the international division of digital labour, updates Engels's *Condition of the Working Class in England* in the age of digital capitalism, analyses the role of trade unions and digital class struggles in the digital age, engages with platform co-operatives, digital commons projects and public service Internet platforms are concrete digital utopias that point beyond digital capital (ism). Engels's analysis is updated for critically analysing the digital conditions of the working class today, including the digital labour of hardware assemblers at Foxconn and Pegatron, the digital labour aristocracy of software engineers at Google, online freelance workers, platform workers at capitalist platform corporations such as Uber, Deliveroo, Fiverr, Upwork, or Freelancer, and the digital labour of Facebook users.

Chapter 3 is titled "History and Class Consciousness 2.0: Georg Lukács in the Age of Digital Capitalism and Big Data". It discusses the relevance of Georg Lukács' 1923 book *History and Class Consciousness* in the context of digital capitalism. It does so by analysing how Lukács' concepts of the dialectic of subject and object, ideology, reification, reified consciousness matter today in the context of big data and digital capitalism. The essay shows that *History and Class Consciousness'* critique of re-ification, ideology, and reified consciousness remains highly topical in the age of digital capitalism and big data. Lukács' analysis allows us to critically analyse how social media, big data, and various other Internet technologies are used as tools of reification. At the same time, Lukács reminds us that only human praxis can establish alternatives.

Chapter 4's title is "Adorno and the Media in Digital Capitalism". The aim of the chapter is to show the relevance of Theodor W. Adorno's critical theory for the analysis of digital capitalism. After an introduction (section 4.1), section 4.2 deals with pre-judices against Adorno. Outright rejection and opposition to Adorno are particularly prevalent in the field of Cultural Studies. Section 4.3 engages with and updates the notion of the culture industry in the age of digital capitalism. It outlines the foundation of the concept of the digital culture industry. Section 4.4 updates Adorno's concept and theory of the authoritarian personality. Drawing on empirical research on how Donald Trump and other right-wing authoritarians use Twitter and other social media, it is shown how authoritarianism is communicated on social media. Section 4.5 deals with the question whether we live in a digital society or digital capitalism. It builds on a similar question that Adorno was asking about industrialism, namely Do we live in an industrial society or in a capitalist society? Taken together, the analysis aims to show the relevance of Adorno's critical theory as part of an update of Marxist theory in the 21st century for the critical analysis of communication and digital capitalism.

Chapter 5's title is "Communication in Everyday (Digital) Life. A Reading of Henri Lefebvre's *Critique of Everyday Life* in the Age of Digital Capitalism". Henri Lefebvre (1901–1991) was one of the most influential French Marxist intellectuals of the 20th century. Chapter 4 asks: How can Henri Lefebvre's *Critique of Everyday Life* inform a critical theory of communication? How can it inform a critique of digital capitalism?

Everyday life is an important category for a dialectical theory of society and com-munication. Lefebvre stresses the dialectical multidimensionality of society and alie-nation, which allows us to distinguish between the economic, political, and the cultural as dialectically interacting and interpenetrating dimensions of society, capitalism, alienation in general, capitalist alienation, and alienation in digital capitalism. Lefebvre reminds us of the predominantly capitalist character of digital technologies. In digital capitalism, we find an ideology that mystifies information and the digital. Computing has the potential to deepen capitalism and class and to advance socialist self-management. Lefebvre's work resonates with the critical theory of digital labour.

Chapter 6's title is "Dallas Smythe and Digital Labour". Dallas Smythe established the notions of the audience commodity and audience labour in 1977 for understanding the political economy of commercial media using advertising as their capital accumulation model. His article has resulted in a foundational debate of Media and Communication Studies that involved Smythe Graham Murdock and Bill Livant. In recent years there has been a very significant rise of references to Smythe's concepts of audience labour/commodification in academic works. This increasing interest has on the one hand to do with a return of a stronger interest in Marx's works and Marxist political economy as well as the rise of social media platforms such as Facebook, YouTube, Twitter, Weibo, Pinterest, Instagram, Blogspot, VKontakte, LinkedIn, Tumblr etc. that use targeted advertising as their capital accumulation model. Explaining how this form of capital accumulation model rises has resulted in the development of the category of digital labour. This chapter presents foundations of how to use Dallas Smythe for under-standing digital labour on advertising-funded social media.

Chapter 7 holds the title "From Digital Positivism and Administrative Big Data Analytics Towards Critical Digital and Social Media Research". It argues for a paradigm shift in the study of the Internet and digital/social media. Big data analytics is the dominant para-digm. It receives large amounts of funding, is administrative and is a form of digital positivism. Critical social media research is an alternative approach that combines critical social media theory, critical digital methods and critical-realist social media research ethics. Strengthening the second approach is a material question of power in academia.

Chapter 8 holds the title "Social Media, Big Data, and Critical Marketing". Its task is to critically understand social media and big data's political economy. It outlines key classical texts (section 8.2), contemporary texts (section 8.3), and future research di-rections (section 8.4) that can help us achieve this goal. The focuses on four classical thinkers and one text by each of them: Dallas Smythe, Karl Marx, Raymond Williams, and Sut Jhally. The chapter also focuses on two key areas of current critical research about social media: digital labour and digital alienation.

Studying social media and big data from a critical marketing perspective is interesting but also complex. It involves multiple dimensions, topics, questions, and approaches. Chapter 8 identifies possible research questions that remain fairly unexplored and could be taken up by PhD students and other scholars.

"Social Media and the Capitalist Crisis" is the title of chapter 9. It focuses on an analysis of social media's roles in the crisis of capitalism. I first present a Marxist analysis of the causes of the ongoing capitalist crisis. It focuses on empirical indicators that measure the development of factors that influence the Marxian rate of profit. The second part discusses the role of targeted social media advertising in the crisis. It focuses on the development of global advertising since the start of the crisis in 2008 and processes of financialisation. The social media industry stands in the context of these developments. The third part discusses ideology in the context of social media. I present empirical results that challenge the idea that contemporary rebellions and revolutions are Twitter revolutions, but stress at the same time that we can also not completely dismiss the role of the Internet in collective action, but rather need a dialectical-realist analysis grounded in empirical social research. I also present some initial empirical findings of the phenomenon of red scare 2.0 in the United Kingdom. It shows how anti-socialist ideology about Jeremy Corbyn is played out and challenged on Twitter. The presentation aims to show how social media are in complex ways embedded into the contradictions of capitalist society, economy, politics and ideology.

Chapter 10's title is "Capitalism, Patriarchy, Slavery, and Racism in the Age of Digital Capitalism and Digital Labour". It asks: How can understanding the relationship of exploitation and oppression inform the study of digital labour and digital capitalism? Chapter 10 combines the analysis of capitalism, patriarchy, slavery, and racism in order to analyse digital labour. The essay presents a typology of differences and common-alities between wage labour, slave labour, reproductive labour, and Facebook labour. It shows that the digital data commodity is both gendered and racialised. It analyses how class, patriarchy, slavery, and racism overgrasp into each other in the realm of digital capitalism. The chapter also introduces the notions of the organic composition of labour and the rate of reproductive labour and shows, based on example data, how to calculate these ratios that provide insights into the reality of unpaid labour in capitalism.

Chapter 11 is focused on "Digital Labour and Imperialism". Lenin's *Imperialism, the Highest Stage of Capitalism*, Bukharin's *Imperialism and World Economy* that were both published in 1917 as well as Rosa Luxemburg's 1913 work *The Accumulation of Capital* spoke of capitalism as imperialism. It was a time of strikes for pay rises, Henry Ford's invention of the first assembly line that laid the foundations for Fordism, World War I, trusts and monopolies, antitrust laws, the October Revolution, the Mexican Revolution, the failed German revolution, etc. It was a time of the extension and deepening of as well as of challenges to capitalism. Chapter 11 first reviews the notion of the role of the international division of labour in classical concepts of imperialism. It then uses these foundations for discussing the role of the international division of labour in the production of information and information technology today and introduces in this context the notion of the international division of digital labour. The overall task is to illuminate the relationship of digital labour and imperialism.

Chapter 12's title is "The Information Economy and the Labour Theory of Value". It discusses aspects of Marx's labour theory of value in the context of the information industries. First, taking the Temporal Single-System Interpretation of Marx's labour theory of value as methodology, the chapter calculates economic demographics at the level of socially necessary labour time and prices of an example case. Second, the chapter questions the assumption that the labour theory of value cannot be applied to the information industries. This chapter tests this hypothesis with an analysis of the development of labour productivity in six countries. Chapter 12 concludes that the labour theory of value is an important tool for understanding the information economy and the peculiarities of the information commodity.

Chapter 13 is the conclusion of the book *Digital Capitalism*. It presents the main findings of the previous chapters and discusses further implications.

1.3 What is Capitalism?

In order to understand what digital capitalism is, we need an understanding of what capitalism is all about. We need to ask: What is capitalism?

Werner Sombart: Modern Capitalism as Entrepreneurial Acquisition

Werner Sombart (1863–1941) was a German sociologist and economist. In 1902, he published the book *Der moderne Kapitalismus* (*Modern Capitalism*). He contributed to the sociology of capitalism. Sombart defines capitalism as an economic system dominated by capital that is focused on the acquisition of money by competition and technological increase of productivity:

> capitalism designates an economic system significantly characterized by the predominance of "capital" [...] The spirit, or the economic outlook, of capitalism is dominated by three ideas: acquisition, competition, and rationality. The purpose of economic activity under capitalism is acquisition, and more specifically acquisition in terms of money. The idea of in creasing

the sum of money on hand is the exact opposite of the idea of earning a livelihood, which dominated all precapitalistic systems, particularly the feudal-handicraft economy. [...] While acquisition constitutes the purpose of economic activity, the attitudes displayed in the process of acquisition form the content of the idea of competition. [...] Economic rationality penetrates gradually into other cultural spheres, reaching even those which are only remotely connected with economic life. [...] capitalist technology must insure a high degree of productivity. [...] The technology characteristic of the capitalist system must also lend itself most readily to improvement and perfection. For constant technical improvements are an important weapon in the hands of the capitalist entrepreneur, who seeks to eliminate his competitor and to extend his market by offering goods superior in quality or lower in price. [...] *The Ideal Entrepreneur* combines the traits of inventor, discoverer, conqueror, organizer, and merchant. (Sombart 2017, 4, 6, 9, 11, 12, 15)

Joseph Schumpeter: Capitalism as Entrepreneurial Creative Destruction

Sombart sees the entrepreneur as the subject of capitalism who invents new economic strategies. Sombart here anticipated the Austrian-American economist Joseph Schumpeter's (1883–1950) stress on the entrepreneur as the subject who innovates capitalism by causing creative destruction. Schumpeter defines capitalism as "that form of private property economy in which innovations are carried out by means of borrowed money, which in general, though not by logical necessity, implies credit creation" (Schumpeter 1939, 216) and where "[c]reative destruction is the essential fact" (Schumpeter 1943/2003, 83).

Sombart's and Schumpeter's definitions of capitalism fetishise and idealise the capitalist as capitalism's subject and are methodologically individualist in character. The economy is reduced to the individual spontaneous activity of the entrepreneur. There is neither a capitalist class nor the working class in these definitions of capitalism. They are devoid of class, labour, surplus-value, surplus-labour, and exploitation – elements that are key for the Marxian understanding of capitalism. Sombart stresses the need to grow capital as a feature of capitalism and that technological innovation is a means for capital growth. Schumpeter has a strong focus on creative destruction via technological innovations.

Max Weber: Capitalism as Calculation of Capital

In the introduction to his book *The Protestant Ethic and the Spirit of Capitalism*, the German sociologist Max Weber (1864–1920) gives a definition of capitalism:

> But capitalism is identical with the pursuit of profit, and forever *renewed* profit, by means of continuous, rational, capitalistic enterprise. [...] We will define a capitalistic economic action as one which rests on the expectation of profit by the utilization of opportunities for exchange, that is on (formally) peaceful chances of profit. [...] Where capitalistic acquisition is rationally pursued, the corresponding action is adjusted to calculations in terms of capital. This means that the action is adapted to a systematic utilization of goods or personal services as means of acquisition in such a way that, at the close of a business period, the balance of the enterprise in money assets (or, in the case of a continuous enterprise, the periodically estimated money value of assets) exceeds the capital, i.e. the estimated value of the material means of production used for acquisition in exchange. [...] The important fact is always that a calculation of capital in terms of money is made, whether by modern book-keeping methods or in any other way, however primitive and crude. Everything is done in terms of balances: at the beginning of the enterprise an initial balance, before every individual decision a calculation to ascertain its probable profitableness, and at the end a final balance to ascertain how much profit has been made. (Weber 1992, xxxi–xxxiii)

Like Sombart, Weber takes from Marx implicitly the notion of accumulation of capital for defining capitalism. But he does not speak of accumulation, but of renewed profit, capitalistic acquisition, and capital excess. Weber's notion of rational action is at the heart of his understanding of capitalism which is why he stresses that capitalists have to make calculations about invested capital and expected returns in order to yield profits. Weber influenced the Frankfurt School's notion of instrumental rationality. His understanding of capitalism falls behind the one of Marx. It lacks a focus on class and exploitation and the labour process that creates commodities and surplus value that are owned by the capitalist class.

The examples of Weber, Sombart, and Schumpeter show that bourgeois definitions of capitalism often are focused in a one-sided manner on capitalists' actions, interests and rationality. Such understandings disregard the class antagonism and capital's exploitation of surplus-value producing labour that, as Marx writes, is the "secret of profit-making" (Marx 1867, 280).

What is Capitalism?

Although Anthony Giddens has thoroughly read Marx, which is why he stresses that capitalism "is a class society" (Giddens 1984, 317) and that the "buying and selling of time, as labour time, is surely one of the most distinctive features of modern capitalism" (Giddens 1984, 144), when it boils down to defining capitalism, the definition he and his colleagues give is devoid of the working class and its exploitation and the focus is on the action of capitalists: capitalism is an "economic system based on the private ownership of wealth, which is invested and reinvested in order to produce profit" (Giddens et al., 2018, 14).

Insofar as they use and define the term capitalism, also neoliberal economists have often understood capitalism as economic order. For example, one of the most famous neoliberals, Milton Friedman, defines capitalism as "organization of the bulk of economic activity through private enterprise operating in a free market" (Friedman 1962 [2002], 4).

Varieties and Commonalities of Capitalism

Hall and Soskice's (2001) varieties of capitalism approach are grounded in institutional political economy. They see the firm as the central actor in capitalism. According to Hall and Soskice, the firm operates in five spheres: (1) the sphere of industrial relations where working conditions are defined, (2) the sphere of relations between firms and their employees, (3) inter-firm relations, (4) the sphere of corporate governance, (5) the sphere of vocational training and education.

Hall and Soskice understand capitalism not just as an economic system, but as an economic system plus its governance and educational relations. Spheres (1), (2) and (3) constitute economic relations, sphere (4) is political in character, and sphere (5) is part of the cultural system of society. Sphere (5) disregards cultural institutions that are important in the definition of meanings, ideologies, and knowledge, and the reproduction of the body and the mind, especially the media system, entertainment, sports, health care, and the academic system. Furthermore, Hall and Soskice do not include systems and spheres shaped by the accumulation logic that stand outside of the economic system into the definition of capitalism. The problem of institutional approaches is that they define actors such as firms as capitalism's central collective actors. They do not give enough attention to the key roles that classes and class struggles play in capitalism.

Hall and Soskice (2001) distinguish between two basic types of capitalism, namely liberal market economies and coordinated market economies:

> In *liberal market economies*, firms coordinate their activities primarily via hierarchies and competitive market arrangements. [...] In *coordinated market economies*, firms depend more heavily on non-market relationships to coordinate their endeavors with other actors and to construct their core competencies. These non-market modes of coordination generally entail more extensive relational or incomplete contracting, network monitoring based on the exchange of private information inside networks, and more reliance on collaborative, as opposed to competitive, relationships to build the compe-tencies of the firm. (Hall and Soskice 2001, 8)

Albert (1993) distinguished between the Anglo-American and the Rhine model of ca-pitalism, which is a differentiation that corresponds to the one made by Hall and Soskice. Esping-Andersen (1990) worked out an early version of the varieties of ca-pitalism approach that defines three political economies that he characterises as "three models of welfare capitalism" (Esping-Andersen 1990, 221): the liberal model, the social-democratic model, and the corporatist-statist model.

What Hall and Soskice define with their typology is a distinction between neoliberal capitalism and Keynesian capitalism. But there have also been other forms of capit-alism, including right-wing authoritarian and fascist forms of capitalism (such as Nazi-Germany), state capitalism with a socialist ideology such as contemporary China, clientelist versions of capitalism, etc.

Critics stress Hall and Soskice's neglect of statist forms of capitalism, the need of allowing for the conceptual existence of hybrid models, and the functionalist and dualist character of Hall and Soskice's approach (Crouch 2005, chapters 1 and 2; Hancké, Rhodes and Thatcher 2007, 7–8; Schmidt 2002; Streeck 2010). Various authors have identified more than two models of capitalism. Schmidt (2002, chapter 3) defines three models of capitalism: market capitalism, coordinated capitalism, and state ca-pitalism. Whitley (1999, chapter 2) defines six types of capitalism: fragmented capit-alism, coordinated industrial district capitalism, compartmentalised capitalism, state-organised capitalism, collaborative capitalism, highly coordinated capitalism. Amable (2003, chapter 3) speaks of five types of capitalism: market-based capitalism (the Anglo-Saxon model), social-democratic capitalism, Asian capitalism, Continental European capitalism, and South European capitalism. He characterises these models

What is Capitalism?

along five dimensions: competition, the wage-labour nexus, the financial sector, social protection, and education. The culture here only plays a role in the form of education, while aspects such as the media system and ideology are missing.

Many varieties of capitalist approaches do not build on Marx. In Hall and Soskice's collected volume *Varieties of Capitalism: The Institutional Foundations of Comparative Advantage*, which is the most widely read and cited book on the varieties of capitalism-approach, Marx and his works are conspicuous by their absence only. What is missing in the varieties of capitalism-approach is a focus on class relations, class struggle, surplus-value, exploitation, commodity fetishism, and ideology critique. Streeck (2016 chapter 9, 2010, 2009) stresses that the varieties of capitalist approaches put too much emphasis on differences. He argues for the study of the dynamic commonalities of capitalism (see also Pontusson 2005).

> Why should national "capitalisms" become and remain different, despite powerful pressures for cross-national convergence emanating from the diffusion of technologies, international competition, border-crossing markets, transnational firms, international organizations, an increasingly global culture, and the like? (Streeck 2010, 17)

Just like globalisation, financialisation and acceleration, consumer culture and commodification, digitalisation is one of the factors that has advanced the convergence of national capitalisms. Digital technologies have the feature to help transcend boundaries, which under capitalist conditions has advanced capitalist societies convergence. In a way, varieties of capitalism approaches share postmodern theory's focus on differences without unity. What is instead needed is more focus on what contemporary societies have in common, a focus on the unity in diversity of societies.

Karl Marx: Capitalism as a Formation of Society (*Gesellschaftsformation*)

Neither classical nor contemporary bourgeois theorists have given a satisfactory definition of capitalism. They all fall far behind Marx's understanding. We need to start with Marx when we want to understand capitalism. Marx spoke of the "capitalist society" (e.g. Marx 1867, 103, 134, 667, 797, 875, 1063) and "the capitalist mode of production" (e.g. Marx 1867, 90, 95, 98, 125, 278, 341, 345, 382, 645, 711). This means that for Marx capitalism is both a type of the economy (*Produktionsweise*, mode of production) and a type of society (*Gesellschaftsformation*, a formation of society/societal formation). Other than Sombart, Weber, Schumpeter, and Giddens, Marx does not limit the notion of capitalism to the economy but assumes that it operates as a dialectic of the economy and society. Wolfgang Streeck argues in this context:

> How to study contemporary capitalism, then? My first answer is: not as an economy but as a society – as a system of social action – and a set of social institutions. [...] A capitalist society, or a society that is inhabited by a capitalist economy, is one that has on a current basis to work out how its *economic social relations,* its specific relations of production and exchange, are, to connect to and interact with its *non-economic social relations.* [...] For this reason.alone, capitalism must be studied, not as a static and timeless ideal type of an economic system that exists outside of or apart from society, but as a *historical social order* that is precisely about the relationship between the social and the economic. (Streeck 2016, 201 & 203)

Streeck (2016, chapter 9) argues that analysing capitalism as a society means analysing it as an economic system, historical social order, culture, polity, and way of life.

Not all Marxist theorists share Marx's view of capitalism as a formation of society. For example, Dobb (1946) sees capitalism as an "economic form" (p. 9), an "economic system" (p. 11), and "a distinctive economic order" (p. 13) where "a leisured class can exploit the surplus labour of others" (p. 17) and that is based on commodity production, labour-power as a commodity, the capitalist class' control of the means of production, and surplus-value (pp. 7–8). Another example is the works of Erik Olin Wright. Wright (2006, 100) defines capitalism as an economic system that combines a) "a class structure characterized by private ownership of the means of production, whereby most people earn their living by selling their labour on a labour market" and b) " economic coordination organized through decentralized market exchange. Capitalism is not simply a 'free market economy'; it is a market economy with a particular form of class relations". Wright (2006, 101) reduces the notion of the capitalist society to "a society with capitalist economic structure", which is not wrong but overlooks that the logic of capitalism is not limited to the economy but also shapes non-economic systems where it takes on emergent properties.

A formation of society (*Gesellschaftsformation*) is the totality of all dialectics of practices and structures and all dialectics of objects and subjects that humans *produce and reproduce* and through which *humans produce and reproduce* their life and relations in a routinised manner in space-time. The formation of society is a fundamental unity and totality of humans' social production processes (see Fuchs 2020a, chapter 5). That such a totality of human life is routinised in space-time means that a formation of society's dialectics of practices and structures are not just produced once, but are again and again recreated (reproduction) based on routines and social roles.

Capitalism as a particular formation of society includes economic relations such as commodity production, markets, capital, labour as well as social, political, legal and cultural relations (Küttler 2008, 238). A formation of society is, according to Marx, a "totality" of "the material conditions of life" (Marx 1859, 262). In society, the material conditions of life is constituted by humans' social production processes; social and societal production and reproduction processes form the materiality of society (see Fuchs 2020a).

For Marx, (1894, 957), a formation of society is "both a production process of the material conditions of existence for human life and a process [...] that produces and reproduces these relations of production themselves". A formation of society is the totality of relations that humans have "towards nature and one another" (p. 957). Social and societal relations and the conditions of human life are the "results and creation" of the social production processes of humans (p. 957). Human production produces and reproduces societal and social relations and human conditions of life (p. 957).

The originality of Marx's notion of *Gesellschaftsformation* is that it is simultaneously both economic and non-economic. Marx analyses the special role of the economy in capitalist society and society in general without reducing the non-economic to the economic whole at the same time ascertaining the trans-economic role of production in all social systems of society so that the economy is in the form of social production sublated in the non-economic spheres, practices and dimensions of society where it takes on emergent qualities.

> The concept of the formation of society (*Gesellschaftsformation*) functions both as a systematic bracket for the analysis of the economy and its effects on all other spheres of life in bourgeois society and as a framework concept for the methodological justification of this procedure in a more general conception of history and society. (Küttler 2001, 591)

Bob Jessop (1997, 2002) takes up Marx's notion of *Vergesellschaftung* (societalisation) for the analysis of capitalism. He argues that the "capitalist economy and its dynamic" are "embedded in a wider nexus of social relations and institutions" and that capitalism is "a complex economic and extra-economic social relation" (Jessop 1997, 565). Societalisation has to do with the way of how the economic and the non-economic are related in society and how social relations are organised. "Societalization refers to the production of 'society effects' within a specific 'time-space envelope': society effects have two dimensions - social cohesion and system (or institutional) integration" (Jessop 1997, 579, footnote 7).

Capitalist logic aims at making accumulation society's principle of societalisation, which is a process of struggle, involving domination, struggles, resistance, and hegemony.

> What bourgeois societalization really involves is the relative subordination of an entire social order to the logic and reproduction requirements of capital accumulation. [...] here is wide variation in how far capitalist market forces (and the associated logic of profit-seeking) come to dominate the overall organization and dynamics of social formations. This raises questions about the conditions under which accumulation can become the dominant principle of societal organization (or societalization). For there are always interstitial, residual, marginal, irrelevant, recalcitrant and plain contradictory elements that escape subordination to any given principle of societalization and, indeed, serve as reservoirs of flexibility and innovation as well as actual or potential sources of disorder. This implies in turn that there is ample scope for conflict over societal projects that privilege radically different organizational principles as well as for conflict over rival projects based on the same principle. (Jessop 2002, 23, 22)

One should revise Jessops's account with respect to the concept of accumulation. Individuals and groups not just accumulate money, but also decision-power, reputation, symbolic power, etc. The imposition of the logic of accumulation on other realms of society, therefore, does not necessarily imply that private ownership, markets and commodities are introduced, although in neoliberal capitalism this has often been the case.

For Marx, the two key features of the capitalist economy are the general production of commodities and the proletariat's production of surplus-value that is appropriated and owned by the capitalist class and transformed into profit by commodity sales that enable the accumulation of capital and the reinvestment of capital:

> Two characteristic traits mark the capitalist mode of production right from the start. *Firstly.* It produces its products as commodities. The fact that it produces commodities does not in itself distinguish it from other modes of

production; but that the dominant and determining character of its product is that it is a commodity certainly does so! [...] The *second* thing that particularly marks the capitalist mode of production is the production of surplus-value as the direct object and decisive motive of production. (Marx 1894, 1019–1020)

For Marx, class antagonism is a key aspect of the capitalist economy. The working class produces in the unpaid part of the working day surplus-value that is not paid for and is appropriated by capital. "In capitalist society, free time is produced for one class by the conversion of the whole lifetime of the masses into labour- time" (Marx 1867, 667). The members of the working class are via capitalism's dull compulsion of the labour market forced to sell their labour-power and produce capital, commodities, surplus-value, and profits for the capitalist class. The capitalist economy is a class system, in which workers produce commodities with the help of means of production that are the private property of members of the capitalist class. These commodities are sold on commodity markets so that profit is achieved and capital can be accumulated.

Class relations where capital exploits labour are a key feature of the capitalist economy. Workers are alienated from the conditions of production in class society because they do not own the means of production and the products of their labour. The logic of accumulation is not limited to the realm of the economy but extends into the political and cultural realms. We can therefore speak of capitalist *society*. Capitalism is a type of society where the mass of humans is alienated from the conditions of economic, political and cultural production, which means that they do not control the conditions that shape their lives, which enables privileged groups' accumulation of capital in the economy, decision-power in politics, and reputation, attention and re-spect in culture. Alienation in the economy means the dominant class' exploitation of the working class' labour. Alienation in non-economic systems means domination, that is, one group's benefits at the expense of other groups via means of control such as state power, ideology, and violence. In capitalism, we find the accumulation of capital in the economy, the accumulation of decision-power and influence in politics, and the accumulation of reputation, attention and respect in culture. The key aspect is not that there is growth, but that there is the attempt of the dominant class and dominant groups to accumulate power at the expense of others who as a consequence have disadvantages. Capitalist society is therefore based on an economic antagonism of exploitation between classes and social antagonisms of domination. Table 1.1 shows the levels and structures of capitalist society.

TABLE 1.1 Levels and structures of capitalist society

	Micro-level	Meso-level	Macro-level
Economic structures	Commodity, money	Companies, markets	Capitalist economy
Political structures	Laws	Parties, government	The capitalist state
Cultural structures	Ideology	Ideology-producing organisations	The capitalist ideological system

Capitalist society is, as Fernand Braudel stresses, "an accumulation of power" (Braudel 1982, 22). It should better be said that capitalism is a system, the totality of the accumulation of power, a "'system' extending over the whole of society" (Braudel 1982, 239). Braudel does, however, not give a clear definition of capitalism and sees no special role of capital and class in contrast to other forms of power in capitalism.

David Harvey's Understanding of Capitalism

My understanding of capitalism resonates with the one by David Harvey. Harvey defines capitalism as a capitalist society, namely as

> any social formation in which processes of capital circulation and accumulation are hegemonic and dominant in providing and shaping the material, social and intellectual bases for social life. Capitalism is rife with innumerable contradictions [...] racialisation and gender discriminations have been around for a very long time and there is no question that the history of capitalism is an intensely racialised and gendered history. [...] although they are omnipresent within capitalism they are not specific to the form of circulation and accumulation that constitutes the economic engine of capitalism. This in no way implies that they have no impact on capital accumulation or that capital accumulation does not equally affect ("infect" might be a better word) or make active use of them. Capitalism clearly has in various times and places pushed racialisation, for example, to extremes (including the horrors of genocide and holocausts). Contemporary capitalism plainly feeds off gender discriminations and violence as well as upon the frequent dehumanisation of people of colour. The intersections and interactions between racialisation and capital accumulation are both highly visible and powerfully present. (Harvey 2014, 7–8)

What is Capitalism?

Capitalist Accumulation

For Harvey, capital accumulation is the central feature of capitalist society that shapes all aspects of this society. It is not clear if he by "accumulation" refers to the accumulation of capital only or, as I argue, the logic of accumulation that originated in the economy but diffused into all realms of capitalism. In a capitalist society, the economy plays a special role because all realms of society are conditioned, shaped, and influenced by the logic of accumulation and by class relations.

Table 1.2 shows how we can make sense of accumulation as a general process and in capitalist society. In capitalism, alienation takes on the form of accumulation processes that create classes and inequalities. Capitalism is based on capitalists' accumulation of capital in the economy, bureaucrats' accumulation of decision-power and influence in the political system, and ideologues', influencers' and celebrities' accumulation of reputation, attention, and respect in the cultural system. Capitalism is an antagonistic system. Its antagonisms (see Table 1.2) drive its development and accumulation. Accumulation is an antagonistic relationship that not just constitutes dominant classes and groups but also subordinated, dominated, and exploited groups such as the working class in the capitalist economy dominated citizens in the capitalist political system, and ideologically targeted everyday people in capitalism's cultural system.

Capitalist society's antagonistic relations that drive accumulation are the source of inequalities and crises, which means that capitalism is an inherently negative dialectical system. As a response to crises, the ruling class and ruling groups require mechanisms they use for trying to keep the dominated class and dominated groups in check so that they do not rebel and revolt. Capitalism, therefore, is also an ideological system where dominant groups use the logic of scapegoating for blaming certain

TABLE 1.2 Accumulation as general process in capitalist society

Realm of society	Central process in general	Central process in capitalist society	Underlying antagonism in capitalist society
Economy	Production of use-values	Capital accumulation	Capitalists vs. workers
Politics	Production of collective decisions	Accumulation of decision-power and influence	Bureaucrats vs. citizens
Culture	Production of meanings	Accumulation of reputation, attention, respect	Ideologues/celebrities/influencers vs. everyday people

groups for society's ills and problems. Scapegoating entails the logic of the friend/ enemy-scheme. And the friend/enemy-scheme can lead to violence, fascism, racism, anti-semitism, and nationalism. Capitalism has barbaric potentials. Crises of capitalism can be fascism-producing crises that turn barbarism from a potentiality of capitalism into an actuality. Only class and social struggles for socialism and democracy can keep capitalism's negative potentials in check.

In a capitalist society, powerful actors control natural resources, economic property, political decision-making, and cultural meaning-making, which has resulted in the accumulation of power, inequalities, and global problems, including environmental pollution as well as the degradation and depletion of natural resources in the nature-society-relation, socio-economic inequality in the economic system, dictatorships and war in the political system, ideology and misrecognition in the cultural system.

Undeniably the outlined model of capitalist society has certain parallels to and has to some degree been influenced by Pierre Bourdieu's (1984) work (see Fuchs 2003, 2008). Bourdieu has generalised Marx's approach and stresses the importance of accumulation processes in the creation of inequality. But he went a step too far and overgeneralised the notions of capital and class so that they are not specific to the capitalist economy but features of contemporary society in general. For Bourdieu, there are economic, political/ social, cultural, and symbolic forms of capital and dimensions of class. In my own ap-proach, class and capital are economic categories. I share Bourdieu's insight that accu-mulation is a key feature of the logic of capitalist society. Bourdieu focused many of his analyses on cultural capital. My approach in contrast is interested in the analysis of society as a capitalist totality, its accumulation processes, antagonisms, and struggles.

Robert L. Heilbroner's Definition of Capitalism

Robert L. Heilbroner (2018; see also 1985) defines capitalism as "a system of social domination" (2018, p. 1380) and a "historical formation with distinctive political and cultural as well as economic properties" (p. 1383) whose "organizing principle is the ceaseless accumulation of capital" (p. 1380) and that is characterised by the accu-mulation of wealth as commodities that takes on the form of the "never-ending me-tamorphosis" M-C-M' (p. 1379) (money capital is invested, which results in the production of commodities that are sold so that more money capital M' that contains a surplus-value and profit is produced), the institution of the private property of the means of production (p. 1379), the institution of the wage-labour-contract (p. 1379) and the "propertyless waged labor force" (p. 1380), the capitalist class that is both an economic and a political force (p. 1379), the division between the two realms of the capitalist economy and the state that interact dialectically (pp. 1381–1382), as well as a culture characterised by the "calculating mind-set" (p. 1382) and "the pre-dominance of a prudent, accountant-like comparison of costs and benefits" (p. 1382) and the separation of scientific, political, economic and moral belief systems so that the "ideology of economics" emerged that removes the "problem of good and evil" from political economy and relegates it to the realm of morality (p. 1383). Further immanent features of capitalism that Heilbroner identifies include its "constant revolutionizing of the techniques of production and its continuous commodification of material life" (Heilbroner 2018, 1384), the global expansion of capitalism so that there is a global search for cheap labour-power, cheap raw materials and markets for the sale of commodities (p. 1385), and economic crisis tendencies (p. 1386).

Heilbroner provides a comprehensive understanding of capitalism as a type of society that is first and foremost informed by Marx. A key feature of capitalism is that in the class relation between capital and labour, capital exploits labour so that the latter produces commodities, profit and surplus-value that are the private property of the capitalist class. In his definition of capitalism, Heilbroner does not give much attention to the notions of class and exploitation.

A key feature of capitalism that Heilbroner does not discuss is the political-ideological tendency of the creation and reproduction of scapegoats that are blamed for capitalism's social ills in order to try to distract attention from the systemic causes of societal problems. It is a consequence of what Horkheimer and Adorno (1947/2002) term the dialectic of the Enlightenment as an important feature of capitalist society, i.e. the tendency of the "self-destruction of enlightenment" (Horkheimer and Adorno 1947 [2002], xvi) in and through capitalism that results in "the reversion of enlightened civilization to barbarism" (p. xix). Capitalism's freedom of private ownership comes into conflict with social freedom (everyone's right to lead a good life). There is a capitalist antagonism between economic and social freedom that is at the heart of capitalism's fascist, racist, anti-Semitic, and nationalist potentials. Auschwitz was a culmination of capitalism's barbaric potentials. Capitalist society's antagonisms create crises that increase the likelihood that capitalist barbarism is transformed from potentiality into actuality. In such situations, accumulation turns via crises into annihilation. Crises of capitalism have the potential to be fascism-producing crises. Only social struggles for socialism, humanism, and democracy can keep capitalism's fascism- and Auschwitz-producing potentials in check. In Heilbroner's key book on the analysis of capitalism's logic, *The Nature and Logic of Capitalism* (Heilbroner 1985), there is no discussion of capitalism's violent, fascist, racist, anti-Semitic, and nationalist potentials and realities. It is important to overcome the *Auschwitz-blindness* of many definitions of capitalism.

Furthermore, one should add to Heilbroner's understanding that in capitalism, individual capitalists are compelled to compete for investment opportunities and the cheapening of resources, that there is a capitalist dialectic of economic competition and monopoly so that competition creates oligopolies and monopolies, and that the political economy of capitalist globalisation not just includes the global search for cheap raw materials, cheap labour and commodity markets but also the global search for opportunities for capital export and investment so that new realms of accumulation are created, and warfare as international and global means for the defence and expansion of capitalism's logic. Furthermore, one should also add to Heilbroner's understanding of capitalism the importance of finance capital that follows the accumulation cycle M-M' in capitalism.

Heilbroner stresses that capitalism is not simply an economic system but a type of society. This is why he speaks of capitalism as a historical formation, social system of domination, "capitalist society" (Heilbroner 2018, 1380), and also as a "social formation" (see Heilbroner 1985, chapter 1). Importantly, Heilbroner stresses that there are economic, political and cultural dimensions of capitalist society. For Heilbroner, the economic logic of capital accumulation determines the roles of the state and of ideology in capitalist society, which means that he reduces politics and culture to the logic of capital accumulation: "All the foregoing aspects of the system can be traced to its inner metabolism, the money–commodity–money circuit" (Heilbroner 2018, 1387). What is missing in Heilbroner's understanding of capitalism is the dialectic of the economic and the non-economic: the logic of accumulation originated in the capitalist economy and has shaped all realms of capitalist society, where the logic of accumulation takes on specific forms that have relative autonomy such as the accumulation of decision-power in capitalist society's state system and the accumulation of reputation and definition-power in capitalist society's cultural system (see Fuchs 2020a).

1.4 What is Digital Capitalism?

The notion of digital capitalism originated in the context of the eulogisation of finance capitalism: The earliest mentioning of the term "digital capitalism" that I was able to trace was in a 1993 article in Forbes magazine, where Forbes then-senior editor Robert Lenzner, a Forbes senior editor, and Forbes reporter William Heuslein wrote the issue's cover story titled "The Age of Digital Capitalism" (Lenzner and Heuslein 1993). The article describes "computerized financial instruments" (Lenzner and Heuslein 1993, 63), derivatives such as options, futures, currency forwards, interest-rates swaps, options on futures and swaps, etc. "Computers make all this magic [of derivatives] possible. [...] Think of all this as an adult Nintendo game with big dollar signs attached" (Lenzner and Heuslein 1993, 63). Digital technologies have played an important role in finance capitalism. Ironically, the financial instruments that Forbes celebrated at the time of the popularisation of the World Wide Web 15 years later played an important role in the global economic crisis that started in 2008.

A bit later, more critical understandings of digital capitalism were developed. Schiller (1999) published the first book that contained the term "digital capitalism" in its title: *Digital Capitalism. Networking the Global Market System*. He sees the Internet as a means of the globalisation of capitalism:

> Networks are directly generalizing the social and cultural range of the capitalist economy as never before. That is why I refer to this new epoch as one of *digital capitalism*. The arrival of digital capitalism has involved radical social, as well as technological, changes. [...] As it comes under the sway of an expansionary market logic, the Internet is catalyzing an epochal political-economic transition toward what I call digital capitalism – and toward changes that, for much of the population, are unpropitious. (Schiller 1999, xiv, xvii)

A variety of publications analysing digital capitalism has been published (see, e.g., Betancourt 2015, Daum 2017, Meier 2019, Pace 2018, Sadowski 2020, Seidl 2021, Staab 2019, Staab and Nachtwey 2016, Wajcman 2015).

Many of such works understand digital capitalism as an economic order. Here are some examples.

Betancourt (2015, 75) understands digital capitalism as "a new type of automated, immaterial production". Daum (2017) characterises digital capitalism as "a new accumulation model". For Pace (2018), digital capitalism is an "economic system" (p. 259) and economic "mode of production" (p. 259) consisting of the digital mediation of particular forms of property, markets, production styles, accumulation styles, and management styles (p. 260). Seidl (2021, 14) understands digital capitalism as "data-driven, and artificial-intelligence-powered business models". Staab (2019) characterises digital capitalism as privatised mercantilism, a specific "praxis of economic action".

In this respect, many works on digital capitalism stand more in the tradition of Sombart, Schumpeter and Weber than Marx because they just like these three authors define capitalism and digital capitalism as an economic system. In contrast, for Marx capitalism is a *Gesellschaftsformation* (formation of society, societal formation) and for the present author digital capitalism is a *dimension* of the capitalist formation of society that emerged in the 20th century and has ever since shaped society. Digital capitalism is not a new totality, not a new formation of society. It is not a new society, but rather a novel feature and dimension of the capitalist formation of society.

Sabine Pfeiffer (2021) understands digital capitalism as a phase of capitalism that she characterises as capitalism of distribution (*Distributivkapitalismus*, 191). She characterises advertising, marketing, transport, storage, planning, and forecasting as distributive forces.

> *I define all technological and organisational measures and activities associated with (securing) the realisation of surplus-value as distributive forces.* Distributive forces thus aim at value realisation – the successful act of selling – and the optimisation of the associated processes that aim to shorten the time between production and sale and minimise the risk for a sale. (Pfeiffer 2021, 159)[1]

According to Pfeiffer, digitalisation has advanced the development of the distributive forces so that capitalism where the distributive forces play a key role has emerged (191). For Pfeiffer, digital capitalism is a capitalism of distribution. Pfeiffer uses the term digital capitalism in a specific economic sense, namely as limited to the economic system and with a focus on the distribution and consumption of commodities. But digitalisation also plays an important role in contemporary capitalism as means of production of surplus-value. Think for example of software such as Microsoft Word and Adobe Photoshop that writers use for creating electronic books and digital images that

What is Digital Capitalism?

---

1 Translated from German: „*Alle mit der Mehrwertrealisierung verbundenen, technologischen und organisatorischen Maßnahmen und Aktivitäten (zur Sicherung) der Wertrealisierung fasse ich als Distributivkräfte.* [...] Die Distributivkräfte zielen also auf die Wertrealisierung – den gelungenen Verkaufsakt – und die Optimierung der damit einhergehenden Prozesse, mit denen die Zeit zwischen der Produktion und dem Verkauf verkürzt und das Risiko für einen Verkauf minimiert werden soll" (Pfeiffer 2021, 159).

are sold as commodities. Adobe and Microsoft sell software licences, which is not an aspect of the distribution of commodities but the production and sale of digital commodities in order to accumulate capital. In 2020, Microsoft was with annual profits of US$ 46.3 billion the world's 13th largest transnational corporation and Adobe with annual profits of US$ 21.2 billion the 418th largest one.[2] What Pfeiffer terms the distributive forces are an important aspect of capitalism, but not the only realm where digitalisation shapes *capitalist society*. Rudi Schmiede (2006, 2015) therefore speaks in the context of digitalisation and capitalism of the informatisation of the economy and society, whereby he understands "the process nature of the penetration of all social dimensions by new contents, forms, and techniques of information" (Schmiede 2006, 352–353).

Speaking of digital capitalism is not a Marxist theory equivalent to analyses of the post-industrial society (Daniel Bell) or the network society (Manuel Castells). The way I conceptualise digital capitalism does not imply that digitalisation is the main feature of contemporary societies. The core characteristic of contemporary societies is that they are capitalist societies. Capitalist society is based on dialectics of many capitalisms, that is of many dimensions of capitalism that develop over time and through restructurations that are implemented as specific responses to crises of capitalist society. Digital capitalism has been a particular dimension of capitalist society in the 20th and 21st centuries.

In the mid-1970s, capitalism experienced a profound multidimensional crisis that resulted in the rise of neoliberal capitalism, a new round of political-economic globalisation, and the advancement of new digital technologies as means of production and communication (Fuchs 2008). The rise of capitalism's digital technological paradigm was a response to the crisis of capitalist society.

Digital capitalism is the dimension of capitalist society where processes of the accumulation of capital, decision-power and reputation are mediated by and organised with the help of digital technologies and where economic, political and cultural processes result in digital goods and digital structures. Digital labour, digital capital, political online communication, digital aspects of protests and social struggles, ideology online, and influencer-dominated digital culture are some of the features of digital capitalism. In digital capitalism, digital technologies mediate the accumulation of capital and power.

---

2 Data source: Forbes 2000 List of the World's Largest Public Companies, year 2020, https://www.forbes.com/global2000/#1439081f335d, accessed on 2 May 2021.

One characteristic of networked computing is that it supports the transcendence of boundaries and helps to produce and reproduce relations. For example, the World Wide Web is a network of interlinked texts, sites, and platforms. At the level of social systems and society, digitalisation enables the production and reproduction of relations between objects and human subjects, between structures and human practices. Digital capitalism as a societal formation neither operates just as a practice nor just as a structure. Digital capitalism is not just a digital practice and not just a digital structure, it is the totality of the dialectics of digital practices and digital structures that take place in capitalist society. For example, Facebook's and Google's server farms are technological structures that store massive amounts of big personal data. Google and Facebook are only social and meaningful through the human practices of searching, clicking, liking, commenting, uploading, etc. These practices produce and reproduce data structures that condition – enable and constrain – further digital practices. Google's and Facebook's profits are based on the valorisation of this dialectic of digital structures and practices so that they exploit their users' digital labour (see Fuchs 2021b, especially chapters 4, 5, 6). Digitalisation affects both the productive forces and the relations of production and the dialectic of forces and relations.

Table 1.3 shows the role of capitalist accumulation in digital capitalism's economic, political and cultural realms.

Accumulation in digital capitalism results in particular forms of the social antagonisms characteristic of capitalism. Table 1.4 gives an overview and examples of these antagonisms. Digital capitalism is an antagonistic society, which means it is a digital class society and a digital form of domination.

Let us have a look at an example from the capitalist economy that shows that digital capitalism is just one dimension of capitalism and that capitalism consists of many interacting capitalisms that form a totality. Table 1.5 shows the share of specific

TABLE 1.3 The role of accumulation in digital capitalism

Realm of society	Accumulation in digital capitalism
Economy	Accumulation of digital capital based on digital commodities
Politics	Accumulation of decision-power in respect to the control of digital knowledge and digital networks
Culture	Accumulation of reputation, attention and respect by the spread of ideologies on and of the Internet

30 Introduction

TABLE 1.4 The antagonisms of digital capitalism

Realm of society	Underlying antagonism in capitalist society	Antagonisms in digital capitalism	Examples
Economy	Capitalists vs. workers	Digital capital vs. digital labour, digital commodity vs. digital commons	Monopoly power of Google, Facebook, Apple, Amazon, Microsoft, etc.
Politics	Bureaucrats vs. citizens	Digital dictators vs. digital citizens, digital authoritarianism/fascism vs. digital democracy	Donald Trump's use of Twitter and other social media
Culture	Ideologues and celebrities vs. everyday people	Digital ideologues vs. digital humans, digital hatred/division/ideology vs. digital friendship in culture.	Asymmetrical attention economy in popular culture on social media: the cultural power of online-influencers such as PewDiePie (>100 million followers)

TABLE 1.5 Share of specific industries in the profits, revenues, and assets of the world's largest 2,000 transnational corporations (data source: Forbes 2000 List of the World's Largest Public Companies, year 2018)

Industry	No. of Companies	Share of Sales	Share of Profits	Share of Assets
Conglomerates	36	2.0%	1.1%	0.9%
Culture & Digital	260	14.6%	17.7%	5.1%
Energy & Utilities	199	14.3%	9.8%	5.7%
Fashion	26	1.0%	0.9%	0.0%
FIRE (finance, insurance & real estate)	634	22.5%	33.7%	74.8%
Food	86	3.6%	5.8%	1.2%
Manufacturing & Construction	352	15.2%	13.1%	5.4%
Mobility & Transport	169	11.6%	9.4%	3.6%
Pharmaceutical & Medical	105	7.2%	4.9%	1.9%
Retail	86	6.9%	2.5%	0.9%
Security	1	0.0%	0.0%	0.0%
Various Services	46	1.1%	1.1%	0.4%

capitalist industries' in the world's 2,000 largest transnational corporations' total sales, profits, and capital assets.

The classification of industries used in Table 1.5 is based on the primary products that corporations produce. For example, corporations that are part of the culture and digital industry primarily produce culture, digital goods, or digital services. The culture and digital industry were conceived of consisting of the following sub-industries for which data was available: advertising, broadcasting & cable, business supplies, casinos & gaming, communications equipment, computer & electronics retail, computer hardware, computer services, computer storage devices, consumer electronics, diversified media, electronics, Internet retail, publishing & printing, recreational products, semiconductors, software & programming, and telecommunications services.

In the data presented in Table 1.5, the culture and digital industry account for 17.7% of the world's largest 2000 corporations' profits. Finance capital controls 33.7% of profits, manufacturing and construction capital 13.1%, and mobility and transport capital 9.4%. These data indicate that the capitalist economy is finance capitalism, digital capitalism, industrial capitalism, mobility capitalism, etc. simultaneously. The dimensions of capitalism are not separate but interact. For example, finance capital in the form of venture capital often supports the "start-up" of digital corporations and thereby gains influence on ownership, management, and governance in the digital industry. And if digital companies become large enough, they often become listed on stock markets and thereby part of finance capital. The example shows how finance capitalism and digital capitalism interact in a dialectical manner.

Also, Ulrich Dolata (2019) warns that one should not characterise digital capitalism as a radically new type of economy or capitalism. He argues that the Internet and digitalisation do

> not constitute a new demarcated *economic sector*—they are much too heterogeneous for that – but offer services that can be economically assigned to traditional sectors and markets such as commerce, advertising, and various service sectors. [...] The technical and socio-economic transformations that have been apparent for some years now do not mark, historically speaking, a starting point or a radical new beginning – as is insinuated with the use of somewhat grandiose-sounding concepts such as digital capitalism, platform capitalism, or digital economics – but rather a new phase within the framework of a socio-technical paradigm shift. (Dolata 2019, 185–186, 194–195)

Companies such as Google (advertising), Facebook (advertising), Amazon (commerce), Netflix and Spotify (entertainment) or Uber (transportation) do not constitute novel sectors of the economy but transform existing ones. One should add that the software business where software licences are sold as commodities is relatively new. The world's largest software companies are Microsoft, Oracle, SAP, VMware, Adobe, and Salesforce. In 2020, they were the world's 13th (Microsoft), 94th (Oracle), 150th (SAP), 403rd (VMWare), 418th (Adobe), and 578th (Salesforce) largest transnational companies. The software industry did not exist before computing became commercially viable. These large software companies were created in 1975 (Microsoft), 1977 (Oracle), 1972 (SAP), 1998 (VMWare), 1982 (Adobe), and 1999 (Salesforce). In the long history of capitalism that according to Immanuel Wallerstein goes back to the 16th century when "our modern world-system came into existence as a capitalist world-economy" (Wallerstein 2004, x) and according to Braudel (1980) had its origins in the *longue durée* (long duration) of commercial capitalism that started in the 12th century in places such as the city-states of Venice, Florence, and Genoa (on the discussion of the history of commercial capitalism, see Banaji 2020 & Melants 2007 & Wood 2002), such companies are relatively novel.

Advertising and entertainment that have been transformed by digital platforms have started to boom in the 20th century as part of Fordist mass production and mass consumption. These industries are a bit older than the software industry, but the culture industry, which Horkheimer and Adorno (1947/2002, 94–136) characterise as the capitalist transformation of culture into exchange-value and ideology, is in the long history of capitalism also still relatively new. What Dolata hints at is that the hype of radical economic novelty that comes along with the rise of digital companies is often ideological in character. It serves as a marketing strategy of large corporations that promise to create a radically new and better society in order to make humans buy their commodities. In reality, digitalisation is based on dialectics of continuity and change in the economy and society.

Shoshana Zuboff (2019, 7) characterises contemporary societies as "surveillance capitalism", a term whereby she understands a "new economic order that claims human experience as free raw material for hidden commercial practices of extraction, prediction, and sales" and a "parasitic economic logic in which the production of goods and services is subordinated to a new global architecture of behavioral modification".

Economic surveillance is certainly an important aspect of the capital accumulation model of many transnational digital corporations such as Facebook. Surveillance scandals such as Edward Snowden's revelations and the Cambridge Analytica scandal have shown how surveillance is an important aspect of the interaction of the power of capitalist corporations that belong to the digital industry and state power. But surveillance is not the only and not the primary feature of capitalism and digital capitalism. There

> are also other important information-based processes that are key features of contemporary capitalism:
> - exploitation of information-producing and digital labour in the realm of class;
> - the governance of information in the realm of political power;
> - the creation of false consciousness in the realm of ideology.
>
> Digital/informational/communicative capitalism is a more suited term than surveillance capitalism. Surveillance is one of the means to advance exploitation, control/domination, and manipulation/ideology in capitalism. (Fuchs 2021b, 168)

The notion of digital capitalism better characterises what is going on in contemporary society than the category of surveillance capitalism. Digital capitalism is a still relatively novel dimension of capitalism and capitalist accumulation processes. It is an important topic of research that requires an interdisciplinary critical approach to social research. The book at hand is a contribution to the foundations of the critical analyses of digital capitalism.

References

Albert, Michael. 1993. *Capitalism Against Capitalism*. London: Whurr.

Amable, Bruno. 2003. *The Diversity of Modern Capitalism*. Oxford: Oxford University Press.

Banaji, Jairus. 2020. *A Brief History of Commerical Capitalism*. Chicago, IL: Haymarket Books.

Betancourt, Michael. 2015. *The Critique of Digital Capitalism: An Analysis of the Political Economy of Digital Culture and Technology*. Brooklyn, NJ: Punctum.

Bourdieu, Pierre. 1984. *Distinction. A Social Critique of the Judgement of Taste*. Cambridge, MA: Harvard University Press.

Braudel, Fernand. 1982. *Civilization and Capitalism 15th-18th Century. Volume II: The Wheels of Commerce*. London: William Collins Sons & Co.

Braudel, Fernand. 1980. *On History*. Chicago, IL: The University of Chicago Press.

Crouch, Colin. 2005. *Capitalist Diversity and Change*. Oxford: Oxford University Press.

Daum, Timo. 2017. *Das Kapital sind wir. Zur Kritik der digitalen Ökonomie*. Hamburg: Edition Nautilus. eBook version.

Dobb, Maurice. 1946. *Studies in the Development of Capitalism*. London: Routledge & Kegan Paul.

Dolata, Ulrich. 2019. Privatization, Curation, Commodification. Commercial Platforms on the Internet*Österreichische Zeitschrift für Soziologie* 44 (supplement 1): 181–197.

Esping-Andersen, Gøsta. 1990. *The Three Worlds of Welfare Capitalism*. Cambridge: Polity Press.

Friedman, Milton. 1962 [2002]. *Capitalism and Freedom, 40thAnniversary Edition*. Chicago, IL: The University of Chicago Press.

Fuchs,Christian. 2021a. Engels@200: Friedrich Engels in the Age of Digital Capitalism. *tripleC: Communication, Capitalism & Critique* 19 (1): 1–194.

Fuchs, Christian. 2021b. *Social Media: A Critical Introduction*. London: Sage. Third edition.

Fuchs, Christian. 2020a. *Communication and Capitalism. A Critical Theory*. London: University of Westminster Press. doi: 10.16997/book45

Fuchs, Christian. 2020. Marxism. Karl Marx's Fifteen Key Concepts for Cultural and Communication Studies. In *Key Ideas in Media & Cultural Studies Series*. New York: Routledge.

Fuchs, Christian. 2019. Henri Lefebvre's Theory of the Production of Space and the Critical Theory of Communication. *Communication Theory* 29 (2): 129–150. Also published as chapter 5 in: Fuchs. C. (2021). *Marxist Humanism and Communication Theory. Media, Communication and Society Volume One*. New York: Routledge.

Fuchs, Christian. 2018. Towards A Critical Theory of Communication with Georg Lukács and Lucien Goldmann. *Javnost – The Public* 25 (3): 265–281. Also published as chapter 6 in: Fuchs. C. (2021). *Marxist Humanism and Communication Theory. Media, Communication and Society Volume One*. New York: Routledge.

Fuchs, Christian. 2016a. *Critical Theory of Communication: New Readings of Lukács, Adorno, Marcuse, Honneth and Habermas in the Age of the Internet*. London: University of Westminster Press. ISBN 978-1-911534-04-4. Open access version: 10.16997/book1

Fuchs, Christian. 2016b. *Reading Marx in the Information Age. A Media and Communication Studies Perspective on Capital Volume 1*. New York: Routledge.

Fuchs, Christian. 2015. *Culture and Economy in the Age of Social Media*. New York: Routledge.

Fuchs, Christian. 2014a. Dallas Smythe Reloaded. Critical Media and Communication Studies Today. In *The Audience Commodity in a Digital Age. Revisiting a Critical Theory of Commercial Media*, eds. McGuigan L. and Manzerolle V, 267–288. New York: Peter Lang.

Fuchs, Christian. 2014b. *Digital Labour and Karl Marx*. New York: Routledge.

Fuchs, Christian. 2012. Dallas Smythe Today – The Audience Commodity, the Digital Labour Debate, Marxist Political Economy and Critical Theory. Prolegomena to a Digital Labour Theory of Value. *tripleC: Communication, Capitalism & Critique* 10 (2): 692–740. doi: 10.312 69/triplec.v10i2.443

Fuchs, Christian. 2008. *Internet and Society. Social Theory in the Information Age*. New York: Routledge.

Fuchs, Christian. 2003. Some Implications of Pierre Bourdieu's Works for a Theory of Social Self-Organization. *European Journal of Social Theory* 6 (4): 387–408.

Fuchs, Christian and Mosco, Vincent. 2012. Marx is Back – The Importance of Marxist Theory and Research for Critical Communication Studies Today*tripleC: Communication, Capitalism & Critique* 10 (2): 127–632. doi: 10.31269/triplec.v10i2.427

Giddens, Anthony. 1984. *The Constitution of Society*. Cambridge: Polity.

Giddens, Anthony, Duneier, Mitchell, Appelbaum, Richard P., and Carr, Deborah. 2018. *Introduction to Sociology*, 11th edn. New York: W. W. Norton

Hall, Peter A. and David Soskice, eds. 2001. An Introduction to Varieties of Capitalism. In *Varieties of Capitalism*, 1–68. Oxford: Oxford University Press.

Hancké, Bob, Martin Rhodes, and Mark Thatcher, eds. 2007. Introduction: Beyond Varieties of Capitalism. In *Beyond Varieties of Capitalism*, 3–38. Oxford: Oxford University Press.

Harvey, David. 2014. *Seventeen Contradictions and the End of Capitalism*. Oxford: Oxford University Press.

Heilbroner, Robert L. 2018. Capitalism. In *The New Palgrave Dictionary of Economics*, 3rd edn, 1378–1389. London: Palgrave Macmillan

Heilbroner, Robert L. 1985. *The Nature and Logic of Capitalism*. New York: W. W. Norton & Company.

Horkheimer, Max and Theodor W. Adorno. 1947 [2002]. *Dialectic of Enlightenment. Philosophical Fragments*. Stanford, CA: Stanford University Press.

Jessop, Bob. 2002. *The Future of the Capitalist State*. Cambridge: Polity Press.

Jessop, Bob. 1997. Capitalism and its Future: Remarks on Regulation, Government and Governance. *Review of International Political Economy* 4 (3): 561–581.

Küttler, Wolfgang. 2008. Kapitalismus. In *Historisch-kritisches Wörterbuch des Marxismus 7/I*, ed. Wolfgang, Fritz Haug, 238–272. Hamburg: Argument.

Küttler, Wolfgang. 2001. Gesellschaftsformation. In *Historisch-kritisches Wörterbuch des Marxismus 5*, ed. Wolfgang, Fritz Haug, 585–598. Hamburg: Argument.

Lenzner, Robert and William Heuslein. 1993. The Age of Digital Capitalism. *Forbes* 151 (7): 62–72.

Marx, Karl. 1894. *Capital Volume III*. London: Penguin.

Marx, Karl. 1867. *Capital Volume I*. London: Penguin.

Marx, Karl. 1859. A Contribution to the Critique of Political Economy. Part One . In *Marx & Engels Collected Works, Volume 29*, 257–417. London: Lawrence & Wishart.

Meier, Werner A. 2019. Towards a Policy for Digital Capitalism? In *Digital Media Inequalities: Policies Against Divides, Distrust and Discrimination*, ed. Trappel Josef, 265–284. Göteborg: Nordicom.

Melants, Eric H. 2007. *The Origins of Capitalism and the "Rise of the West"*. Philadelphia, PA: Temple University Press.

Pace, Jonathan. 2018. The Concept of Digital Capitalism *.Communication Theory* 28 (3): 254–269.

Pfeiffer, Sabine. 2021. *Digitalisierung als Distributivkraft. Über das Neue am digitalen Kapitalismus*. Bielefeld: transcript.

Pontusson, Jonas. 2005. Varieties and Commonalities of Capitalism. In *Varieties of Capitalism, Varieties of Approaches*, ed. David Coates, 163–188. Basingstoke: Palgrave Macmillan.

Sadowski, Jathan. 2020. *Too Smart. How Digital Capitalism is Extracting Data, Controlling our Lives, and Taking Over the World*. Cambridge, MA: The MIT Press.

Schiller, Dan. 1999. *Digital Capitalism. Networking the Global Market System*. Cambridge, MA: The MIT Press.

Schmidt, Vivien A. 2002. *The Futures of European Capitalism*. Oxford: Oxford University Press.

Schmiede, Rudi. 2015. *Arbeit im informatisierten Kapitalismus. Aufsätze 1976-2015*. Baden-Baden: Nomos.

Schmiede, Rudi. 2006. Knowledge, Work and Subject in Informational Capitalism. In *Social Informatics: An Information Society for All? In Remembrance of Rob Kling*, eds. Jacques Berleur, Markku I. Nurminen, and John Impagliazzo, 333–354. New York: Springer.

Schumpeter, Joseph A. 1943. *Capitalism, Socialism & Democracy*. London: Routledge.

Schumpeter, Joseph A. 1939. *Business Cycles: A Theoretical, Historical and Statistical Analysis of the Capitalist Process*. New York: McGraw-Hill.

Seidl, Timo. 2021. *Ideas, Politics, and Technological Change. Essays on the Comparative Political Economy of Digital Capitalism*. PhD dissertation. Florence: European University Institute.

Sombart, Werner. 2017. *Economic Life in the Modern Age*, eds. Nico Stehr and Reiner Grundmann. London: Routledge.

Staab, Philipp. 2019. *Digitaler Kapitalismus. Markt und Herrschaft in der Ökonomie der Unknappheit*. Frankfurt am Main: Suhrkamp. eBook version.

Staab, Philipp and Oliver Nachtwey. 2016. Market and Labour Control in Digital Capitalism. *tripleC: Communication, Capitalism & Critique* 14 (2): 457–474.

Streeck, Wolfgang. 2016. *How Will Capitalism End? Essays on a Failing System*. London: Verso.

Streeck, Wolfgang. 2010. *E Pluribus Unum? Varieties and Commonalities of Capitalism*. MPIfG Discussion Paper No. 10/12. Cologne: Max Planck Institute for the Study of Societies.

Streeck, Wolfgang. 2009. *Re-Forming Capitalism: Institutional Change in the German Political Economy*. Oxford: Oxford University Press.

Whitley, Richard. 1999. *Divergent Capitalisms*. Oxford: Oxford University Press.

Wajcman, Judy. 2015. *Pressed for Time. The Acceleration of Time in Digital Capitalism*. Chicago, IL: The University of Chicago Press.

Wallerstein, Immanuel. 2004. *World-Systems Analysis: An Introduction*. Durham, NC: Duke University Press.

Weber, Max. 1992. *The Protestant Ethic and the Spirit of Capitalism*. London: Routledge.

Wood, Ellen Meiksins. 2002. *The Origin of Capitalism. A Longer View*. London: Verso.

Wright, Erik Olin. 2006. Compass Points: Towards a Socialist Alternative. *New Left Review* 41: 93–124.

Zuboff, Shoshana. 2019. *The Age of Surveillance Capitalism: The Fight for a Human Future at the New Frontier of Power*. New York: Hachette.

Part II

Theorists

Chapter Two
Friedrich Engels in the Age of Digital Capitalism

2.1 Introduction

28 November 2020: Friedrich Engels was born 200 years ago on 28 November 1820. Together with Karl Marx, Engels was the founder of the critique of the political economy. He was a theorist, historian, journalist, philosopher, politician, and entrepreneur who used the money capital he accumulated to support Marx and the international socialist movement. In 2020, capitalism has changed but is still around. Engels's 200th anniversary is a good occasion in order to ask: How relevant are Friedrich Engels's works in the age of digital capitalism? This essay deals with this question.

Engels together with Marx wrote the *Manifesto of the Communist Party*, *The German Ideology*, and *The Holy Family*. Engels also helped out Marx with writing newspaper articles that appeared under Marx's name. And he made a genuine contribution to critical theory with works such as *Anti-Schelling (Schelling and Revelation)*, *Outlines of a Critique of Political Economy*, *The Condition of the Working Class in England*, *The Housing Question*, *Anti-Dühring*, *Socialism: Utopian and Scientific*, *Dialectics of Nature*, *The Origin of the Family, Private Property and the State*, *Ludwig Feuerbach and the End of Classical German Philosophy*. This article discusses the relevance of a variety of Engels's works for the critical analysis of digital capitalism with a special focus on *The Condition of the Working Class in England* because we are interested in the condition of the working class in digital capitalism today.

Section 2.2 outlines a critique of computational social science based on Engels's understanding of scientific socialism. Section 2.3 analyses the digital condition of the working class today. It uses Engels's works, especially his book *The Condition of the Working Class*

DOI: 10.4324/9781003222149-2

in England, for analysing the digital labour of hardware assemblers, Google software engineers, platform workers, and Facebook users. The section also analyses the role of productivity gains achieved by digital automation and robotisation and labour. Section 2.4 discusses working-class struggles in digital capitalism. Section 2.5 draws conclusions.

2.2 Computational Social Science and Scientific Socialism

To speak of "scientific socialism" does not automatically and not necessarily apply a mechanistic and deterministic theory of society that assumes that capitalism automatically breaks down and society is determined by natural economic laws. The scientific understanding of socialism is not a natural science applied society but rather a social science of society (*Gesellschaftswissenschaft*) that stresses the key role of the conscious human being, social practices, social production, and social relations in society. Natural science theories are not necessarily deterministic and mechanistic. The point is that in the social sciences, the positivist tradition treated society based on natural science methods and mathematics, which focuses on pure quantification and assumes that everything can be calculated. The logic of positivism neglects society's qualities and the fact that not everything social and societal is calculable. We cannot properly calculate love, morals, sadness, happiness, (dis)respect, (in)justice, solidarity, etc. Society's social qualities can only be properly analysed by qualitative social research methods. Marx and Engels are not as such opposed to calculation and quantification, but they are critical of computing as means of domination and exploitation that drives capital accumulation and makes the qualities of society disappear behind things and numbers. This critique of quantification as an aspect of capitalist accumulation has been reflected in Georg Lukács' (1971) notion of reification and Max Horkheimer's (1947) notion of instrumental reason.

In the contemporary social sciences, computational social sciences have emerged as a dominant paradigm that attracts lots of attention, support, funding and has increasingly been institutionalised.

David Lazer et al. (2009, 722) define computational social science as a social science that "leverages the capacity to collect and analyze data with an unprecedented breadth and depth and scale" and operates with "terabytes of data". In the textbook *Introduction to Computational Social Science*, Cioffi-Revilla (2014, 2) defines computational social science:

The new field of *Computational Social Science* can be defined as the interdisciplinary investigation of the social universe on many scales, ranging from individual actors to the largest groupings, through the medium of computation. [...] Computational social science is based on an information-processing paradigm of society. (Cioffi-Revilla 2014, 2)

The *Manifesto of Computational Social Science* (Conte et al. 2012) argues that compu-tational social science operates with "massive ICT data" (p. 327), conducts "massive data analysis" (p. 330) that operates "up to the whole world population" (p. 331). It is "a new field of science in which new type of data, largely made available by new ICT applications, can be used to produce large-scale computational models of social phenomena" (p. 333). The *Manifesto* claims that computational social science constitutes "a new era" (p. 327).

Computational social scientists set out to radically transform the social sciences. Computational social science is new positivism. Its methods cannot understand the qualitative features of society such as motivations, norms, moral values, feelings, ideologies, and experiences.

Cioffi-Revilla (2014, 1) explicitly situations computational social science in the context of Auguste Comte's "natural science of social systems, complete with statistical and mathe-matical foundations". Comte was the founder of positivism. Computational social science explicitly stands in the context of positivism. The *Manifesto of Computational Social Science* argues for turning sociology and the social sciences into a natural science: "sociology in particular and the social sciences, in general, would undergo a dramatic paradigm shift, arising from the incorporation of the scientific method of physical sciences" (Conte et al. 2012, 341).

The danger is that computer science colonises the social sciences and leaves no space and time for critical theory, social theory, and philosophy. The main danger of compu-tational social sciences is that this paradigm makes the social sciences uncritical and turns them into administrative sciences (see Fuchs 2017a). Engels warned in a different context of the dangers of positivism. He argues against a mathematical method that is

> reducing qualitative differences to merely quantitative differences [...] As Hegel has already shown *(Encyclopädie,* I, S. 199), this view, this "one-sided mathematical view", according to which matter must be looked upon as having only quantitative determination, but, qualitatively, as identical originally, is 'no other standpoint than that' of the French materialism of the 18th century. It is even a retreat to Pythagoras who regarded quantitative determination as the essence of things. (Engels 1925, 534)

Computational Social Science and Scientific Socialism

For Engels (1925, 469), such reductive approaches are a form of "naïve materialism".

Engels criticises mechanical materialism that does not see and analyse the qualitative and dialectical aspects of the world. Engels in this passage refers to the first part of Hegel's *Encyclopaedia*, where Hegel discusses dialectical logic. The reference is to the discussion of pure quantity as an aspect of quantity. Hegel writes in this passage that

> when we look closely at the exclusively mathematical standpoint that is here referred to (according to which quantity, which is a definite stage of the logical Idea, is identified with the Idea itself) we see that it is none other than the standpoint of *Materialism*. (Hegel 1830 [1991], 159, addition to §99)

He stresses that "freedom, law, ethical life [...] cannot be measured and computed or expressed in a mathematical formula" (Hegel 1830 [1991], 159, addition to §99) and that

> we know very little about these things and the distinction between them, if we simply stick to a 'more or less' of this kind, and do not advance to some grasp of specific determinacy, which is here in the first place qualitative. (Hegel 1830 [1991], 160, addition to §99)

Hegel and Engels remind us that computational social science cannot grasp society's dialectical relations that are not easily quantifiable. It cannot understand, model, calculate freedom, law, moral judgement, love, etc. Its analyses are one-dimensional. Critical social science should certainly adopt and experiment with data-driven methods, but not at the expense of the engagement with and application of critical theory (Fuchs 2017a). Digital data gathered on social media and other data-intensive environments can reveal important aspects of life in contemporary societies. What is needed are not simply new forms of prediction and quantification, but critical, creative and experimental methods that combine aspects of quantitative data with a qualitative understanding of humans' motivations, experiences, interpretations, norms and values (Fuchs 2017a). Whereas Marx and Engels were social scientists who wrote the *Communist Manifesto*, some contemporary social scientists write manifestos for new positivism and many more believe in what such manifestos postulate, which results in the institutionalisation of computational social science and big funding for big data-based methods and project. Big data analytics and computational social science miss the difference between society and nature that Engels points out. The danger is that they reduce society to quantitative data and neglect its indeterminate, open, dialectical qualities.

To speak of "scientific socialism" doesn't automatically and not necessarily apply a mechanistic and deterministic theory of society that assumes that capitalism automatically breaks down and society is determined by natural economic laws. The scientific under-standing of socialism is not a natural science applied society but rather a social science of society (*Gesellschaftswissenschaft*) that stresses the key role of the conscious human being, social practices, social production, and social relations in society. Natural science theories are not necessarily deterministic and mechanistic. The point is that in the social sciences, the positivist tradition treated society based on natural science methods and mathematics, focuses on pure quantification and assumes that everything can be calculated.

The logic of positivism neglects society's qualities and the fact that not everything social and societal is calculable. We cannot properly calculate love, morals, sadness, happiness, (dis)respect, (in)justice, solidarity, etc. Society's social qualities can only be properly analysed by qualitative social research methods. Marx and Engels are not as such opposed to calculation and quantification, but they are critical of computing as means of domination and exploitation that drives capital accumulation and makes the qualities of society disappear behind things and numbers. This critique of quantifica-tion as an aspect of capitalist accumulation has been reflected in Georg Lukács' (1971) notion of reification and Max Horkheimer's (1947) notion of instrumental reason.

Computational social science is a paradigm in the social sciences that propagates math-ematical models of society that use big data and predictive algorithms. Engels's scientific socialism is critical of positivism. Computational social science is a neo-positivism that neglects that qualitative features of society such as motivations, norms, moral values, feelings, ideologies, experiences, love, death, freedom, or (in)justice that cannot be reduced to mere quantities. Computational social science poses the danger of turning the social sciences into administrative, instrumental, positivist research that supports domination and exploitation and is a branch of computer science that has colonised the social sciences.

2.3 The Digital Condition of the Working Class Today

The Condition of the Working Class in England (*CWCE*) is for many Engels's most influential book. In this section, we will discuss the situation of the working class in digital capitalism. Engels's book *The Condition of the Working Class in England* plays an important role as the starting point for such an analysis. The section discusses the relationship of technology and society in Engels's book (section 3.1), digital technology and relative surplus-value production (section 3.2), absolute surplus-value production at

Foxconn (section 3.3), play labour at Google (section 3.4), precarious platform workers (section 3.5), and Facebook labour (section 3.6).

2.3.1 Technology and Society

Some observers, such as McLellan (1993, xviii) argue that the underlying Engels approach in *CWCE* is "a technological determinism that was to remain with Engels all his life". There are indeed some formulations in CWCE that can create such an impression: The "industrial revolution [...] altered the whole civil society" (*CWCE*, 15); the "proletariat was called into existence by the introduction of machinery" (*CWCE*, 29)

But Engels leaves no doubt that capitalist relations of production, that is private property relations, the class relation between capital and labour and the profit imperative, shape the development and application of machinery. He says that capitalism is the cause of misery: The "great central fact" is "that the cause of the miserable condition of the working class is to be sought [...] in *the capitalistic system itself*" (*CWCE*, 314). When discussing machinery, Engels points out that the social conditions under which technology exist are the factors that have a decisive influence on technology's impacts on society: "The consequences of improvement in machinery under our present social conditions are, for the working man, solely injurious, and often in the highest degree oppressive" (*CWCE*, 149).

In *CWCE*, Engels often describes class relations as competition and makes clear that not machines, but the transformation of class relations created the proletariat. Competition — "the battle of all against all" — "created and extended the proletariat" (*CWCE*, 87). Capitalist competition means a class conflict between capital and labour but also competition between capitalists that results in the centralisation of capital and competition between workers, such as between the "power-loom weaver" and "the hand-loom weaver" (*CWCE*, 87).

Engels (1848b, 482) inserted a note to the 1888 edition of the *Manifesto*, saying that by

> bourgeoisie is meant the class of modern Capitalists, owners of the means of social production and employers of wage-labour. By proletariat, the class of modern wage-labourers who, having no means of production of their own, are reduced to selling their labour-power in order to live.

Capital means "the direct or indirect control of the means of subsistence and production" as "the weapon with which this social warfare is carried on" (*CWCE*, 37–38).

The bourgeoisie is the class of property-holders (*CWCE*, 281). The bourgeoise measures "[a]ll the conditions of life [...] by money" (*CWCE*, 282). The decisive aspect of technology in capitalism is that capitalists own technologies as private property that is a means of production used for accumulating capital and the production of surplus value and commodities.

Also in *Outlines of a Critique of Political Economy*, a foundational text of Marx's and Engels's approach, young Engels (1843, 442–443) stresses that science and technology are instruments in the hands of the bourgeoisie:

> In the struggle of capital and land against labour, the first two elements enjoy yet another special advantage over labour – the assistance of science; for in present conditions science, too, is directed against labour. Almost all mechanical inventions, for instance, have been occasioned by the lack of labour-power; in particular Hargreaves', Crompton's and Arkwright's cotton-spinning machines. There has never been an intense demand for labour which did not result in an invention that increased labour productivity considerably, thus diverting demand away from human labour. The history of England from 1770 until now is a continuous demonstration of this. The last great invention in cotton-spinning, the self-acting mule, was occasioned solely by the demand for labour, and rising wages. It doubled machine-labour, and thereby cut down hand-labour by half; it threw half the workers out of employment, and thereby reduced the wages of the others by half; it crushed a plot of the workers against the factory owners, and destroyed the last vestige of strength with which labour had still held out in the unequal struggle against capital.

Marx (1859, 264) characterised the *Outlines* as a "brilliant essay on the critique of economic categories" and directly referred to it several times in *Capital Volume I* (Marx 1867, 168 [footnote 30], 253 [footnote 5], 266–267 [footnote 20], 788 [footnote 15]). In the Outlines, Engels points out that "the mental element of invention, of thought" (Engels 1843, 427), as in the form of science, is part of human labour and the "human, subjective side, labour" (p. 427) of production. In work, the human being is "active physically and mentally" (p. 428). Engels here, on the one hand, points out the dialectic of mental and physical activity in work and on the other hand identified mental work, or what today is often called knowledge or information work, as an important aspect of production.

The assumption that Engels was a technological determinist cannot be sustained. He analysed technology in capitalism as embedded into class relations so that there is capitalist ownership of technology as private property that is utilised as means for the production of surplus value, commodities, and profit.

2.3.2 Digital Technology and Relative Surplus-Value Production

In the *Grundrisse*, Marx (1857 [1858]) introduced the notion of surplus-value, by which he means that during a portion of the work, workers produce unpaid labour that capitalists appropriate and turn into monetary profit. Marx (1867, 645) distinguishes two methods of surplus-value production: "The production of absolute surplus-value turns exclusively on the length of the working day, whereas the production of relative surplus-value completely revolutionises the technical processes of labour and the groupings into which society is divided". Absolute surplus-value production means the lengthening of the unpaid part of the working day. Relative surplus-value production is the increase of productivity so that more value is produced during a certain time period than before. Engels anticipated both concepts in *CWCE*.

Engels gives many concrete examples of the increase of productivity through the introduction of new technologies. In the cotton industry, the invention of the jenny "made it possible to deliver more yarn than heretofore" (*CWCE*, 18). The introduction of the power-loom further increased the productivity of the English cotton industry: "In the years 1771–1775, there were annually imported into England rather less than 5,000,000 pounds of raw cotton; in the year 1841 there were imported 528,000,000 pounds, and the import for 1844 will reach at least 600,000,000 pounds" (*CWCE*, 21). Similar productivity increases could be observed in other industries, for example, the manufacturing of wool: "In 1738 there were 75,000 pieces of woollen cloth produced in the West Riding of Yorkshire; in 1817 there were 490,000 pieces, and so rapid was the extension of the industry that in 1854, 450,000 more pieces were produced than in 1825. In 1801, 101,000,000 pounds of wool (7,000,000 pounds of. it imported) were worked up; in 1855, 180,000,000 pounds were worked up, of which 42,000,000 pounds were imported" (*CWCE*, 22–23).

Engels describes the phenomenon of relative surplus-value production but did not have a theoretical concept naming this process. Marx later introduced based on Engels the concepts of surplus-value and the methods of surplus-value production.

Since the middle of the 20th century, the capitalist invention and the capitalist application of digital production technologies has led to significant increases in productivity. Just like Engels observed the impacts of technologies such as the steam engine and the power loom, today we can observe the effects of the digitalisation of production that has increased productivity.

Table 2.1 shows productivity growth data for the G7-economies. It uses labour productivity growth as a measure of productivity. Labour productivity is a statistical measure of the gross value added (measured in constant US$) produced per hour worked in a particular industry. It calculates labour productivity by diving the total value added in the industry during one year by the total amount of working hours in that industry. The data in Table 2.1 shows the ten-year growth rate of labour productivity. Not all data was available, so some fields have been left undefined. In advanced capitalist countries, labour productivity has more than doubled over a time period of forty years (1970–2010). In the analysed national economies, it takes on average between 26 and 44 years to double the productivity of manufacturing. This was also the time when computing was introduced in manufacturing as a production technology. Capitalist digitalisation has resulted in large productivity growth in manufacturing and other industries.

Industry 4.0 is about technologies that combine the Internet of Things, Big Data, social media, cloud computing, sensors, artificial intelligence and robotics in the production, distribution and use of physical goods. The bourgeoisie has declared the fourth industrial revolution to try to automate the production, distribution, handling, repair, and disposal of industrial goods such as cars (Fuchs 2018c). It hopes to increase the profit rate of the manufacturing industry.

Engels pointed out that the capitalist shaping and use of industrial technologies turned workers into "machines pure and simple" (*CWCE*, 17). The capitalist shaping, development, design, and use of digital technologies has contributed to forms of alienation such as the enslavement of mineworkers who extract the physical resources out of which digital hardware is manufactured, long working hours in the assemblage of hardware and in the software and creative industry, an always-on-work-culture mediated by laptops, phones and tablets as means of production, precarious freelancing in the digital industries, etc.

2.3.3 Absolute Surplus-Value Production at Foxconn

Engels gives a picture of the terrible conditions that members of the working faced in England in the 1840s. One of his examples is the dress-makers in London:

TABLE 2.1   Total annual labour productivity growth in manufacturing in percentage, productivity is measured as labour productivity per unit labour input (in most cases gross value added in constant prices per hour worked), data source: OECD STAN

	1951–1960	1961–1970	1971–1980	1981–1990	1991–2000	2000–2010	2011–2019 (Canada: 2018)	Total (for available time period)	Average annual produc-tivity growth (1970–2010)	Years it takes to double productivity (based on average annual productivity, 1970–2010)
Canada			27.8	26.5	33.0	6.0	14.9	108.2	2.3	43.5
France	47.0	68.5	42.5	38.7	43.5	29.4	9.1	269.6	3.9	25.6
Germany			28.3	16.4	32.4	19.5	9.5	106.0	2.4	41.7
Italy			52.6	32.8	26.4	-0.1	12.6	124.2	2.8	35.7
Japan			49.2	38.7	26.6	38.2		152.6	3.8	26.3
UK			22.5	45.6	30.5	31.9	1.4	132.0	3.3	30.3
USA			19.7	33.6	42.9	46.7		142.9	3.6	27.8
G7			30.1	32.7	34.6	33.9		131.3	3.3	30.3
OECD					20.1	34.6		54.8	2.4	41.7

They employ a mass of young girls – there are said to be 15,000 of them in all – who sleep and eat on the premises, come usually from the country, and are therefore absolutely the slaves of their employers. During the fashionable season, which lasts some four months, working-hours, even in the best establishments, are fifteen, and, in very pressing cases, eighteen a day; but in most shops work goes on at these times without any set regulation, so that the girls never have more than six, often not more than three or four, sometimes, indeed, not more than two hours in the twenty-four, for rest and sleep, working nineteen to twenty-two hours, if not the whole night through, as frequently happens! The only limit set to their work is the absolute physical inability to hold the needle another minute. (*CWCE*, 217)

Here's another example of long working hours that Engels describes:

Other manufacturers were yet more barbarous, requiring many heads to work thirty to forty hours at a stretch, several times a week, letting them get a couple of hours of sleep only, because the night-shift was not complete, but calculated to replace a part of the operatives only. [...] The consequences of these cruelties became evident quickly enough. The Commissioners mention a crowd of cripples who appeared before them, who clearly owed their distortion to the long working hours. This distortion usually consists of a curving of the spinal column and legs. (*CWCE*, 161–162)

What Engels analyses here is the method of absolute surplus-value production. Capitalists have the interest to make workers produce commodities for as many hours per day and per week as possible for as little wage as possible. Long hours and small wages promise high profits.

Absolute surplus-value production is also an important method of surplus-value production in 21st-century digital capitalism. In the period from 1992 until 2019, the number of agricultural workers in China decreased from 350 million to 120 million, the number of manufacturing workers increased from 180 million to 200 million, and the number of service workers went from 120 million to 440 million[1]. Unlike economic development in Western capitalism, where the rise of the service and information industries was accompanied by the shrinking of agriculture and manufacturing, China's capitalism with Chinese characteristics (Harvey 2005, chapter 5) combines industrialisation and informatisation as simultaneous processes.

---

1 Data source: ILO World Employment and Social Outlook, http://www.ilo.org/wesodata

Western transnational digital corporations such as Apple, Dell, HP, and AsusTek make use of Chinese large and comparatively cheap labour force in order to export capital so that digital hardware is assembled in China by workers contracted by suppliers such as Foxconn, Pegatron, Compal Electronics, or Wistron. The goal is to increase profits by minimising labour costs.

Students & Scholars Against Corporate Misbehaviour (SACOM) (2011) reported that workers at the Chinese factories at Foxconn, where iPhones and other hardware is assembled, faced conditions such as military drill, forced and unpaid overtime, fines such as the non-payment of wages, crowded accommodations, low wages, compulsory internships, toxic workplaces, etc. In 2010/2011, 19 young Foxconn workers aged between 17 and 28 attempted to commit suicide by jumping from Foxconn buildings. Most of them died. They could no longer stand the terrible working conditions.

China Labor Watch (2017, 1 & 3) conducted research in order to find out how the working conditions look like in the factories of the Apple suppliers Compal, Foxconn, Green Point, and Pegatron:

> In all of the four factories, weekly working hours surpassed 60 hours and monthly overtime hours surpassed 90 hours, with most overtime amounting to of 136 hours over a month. [...] Workers were required to sign an agreement to voluntarily do overtime, opt out of paying for social insurance and opt out of housing funds. These acts are blatant attempts to evade responsibilities and are clear violations against China's Labor Law. [...] Workers at Pegatron and Green Point were continuously working overtime without compensation. [...] Both excessive working hours and tremendous pressure are severe problems at Foxconn. Since 2010, there have been more than 10 suicides, indicative of the terrible working conditions and rigid management. In September 2016, [a] CLW [China Labour Watch] investigator launched another undercover investigation at Foxconn. [...] Most workers there had accumulated 122 hours of overtime each month [...], far exceeding the legal limit of 36 hours per month as per China's labor laws.

Just like the dress-makers whose labour Engels analysed in the 1840s, 21st-century digital hardware assemblage workers at Foxconn, Pegatron and other suppliers are a largely young and female workforce that is highly exploited. Capitalist hardware corporations try to make workers conduct a high number of weekly working hours for low pay and with unpaid overtime in order to minimise production costs so that these transnational corporations profits can be maximised. The Chinese manufacturing industry is part of a global capitalist system, in which transnational corporations outsource labour to Asia in order to accumulate capital by making use of the method of absolute surplus-value production. China's large working class, whose members often leave rural areas in order to find work in urban manufacturing centres, is transnational corporations' source of cheap and highly exploited labour.

2.3.4 Play Labour at Google

Engels describes a faction of the working class that was relatively privileged. These were workers whose "state of misery and insecurity in which they live now is as low as ever" (*CWCE*, 321). He terms these workers the labour aristocracy, "an aristocracy among the working-class" (engineers, carpenters, joiners, bricklayers) that has "succeeded in enforcing for themselves a relatively comfortable position" (*CWCE*, 321). Lenin (1920, 194) uses the notion of the labour aristocracy for "workers-turned-bourgeois", "who are quite philistine in their mode of life, in the size of their earnings and in their entire outlook". "They are the real *agents of the bourgeoisie in the working-class* movement, the labour lieutenants of the capitalist class".

Software engineers are a digital labour aristocracy. They tend to earn very high wages, which gives them a privileged position. The demand for their labour-power is very high. Although many software engineers are relatively rich money-wise, they are socially poor. They often lack social relations friendships, outside of the office. They spend most of their time in offices such as the Googleplex, where they work long hours. Many software companies want to keep them in the office by providing facilities for sports, entertainment, relaxation, etc. The Googleplex more looks like a playground than an office. In the life of software engineers, labour and play converge. Google workers are playworkers, workers for whom labour feels like play.

Google workers in comparison to ICT manufacturers have much higher wages and privileges, which also means that they are more unlikely to resist, which is, as Engels describes, typical for the labour aristocracy: "they are very nice people indeed nowadays to deal with, for any sensible capitalist in particular and for the whole capitalist class in general" (*CWCE*, 321).

This passage from Friedrich Engels's book *The Condition of the Working Class in England in 1844* describes typical working conditions in the phase of the industrialisation of capitalism: work in factories was mentally and physically highly exhausting, had negative health impacts, and was highly controlled by factory owners and security forces.

The manufacturing labour that Engels analysed in the 1840s was physically highly exhausting. Programming does not require engineers to burn lots of energy. Whereas manufacturing labour feels like toil, Google labour tends to feel like play.

Like at the time of Engels engineers, carpenters, joiners, bricklayers, in digital capitalism software engineers hold qualifications and produce goods that are in high demand and allow achieving relatively high wages and income. The poor workers who Engels portrays in *CWCE* as toiling in industries such as cotton and wool manufacturing, dress-making, etc. were compelled to work long hours by poverty wages and the "silent compulsion of economic relations" (Marx 1867, 899) of the labour market that makes them starve if they don't sell their labour-power. Poverty wages were used as a means of coercion, as a method of absolute surplus-value production. The contemporary digital labour aristocracy also faces the silent compulsion of having to sell their wages. But these wages are very high because they work in a highly productive industry that produces a key commodity – software – that plays an influential role in almost all parts of 21st-century society. Digitalisation transforms all aspects of society, which is why software is in high demand and allows achieving high profits and commodity prices. Those who possess the key skill of knowing how to code software can therefore in turn achieve high wages. Absolute surplus-value production takes on a new form in this industry: software engineers often sign all-inclusive contracts that fix a certain wage-sum per month without extra pay for overtime. In the USA, the Fair US Labor Standards Act (Section 13 [a] 17) enables software corporations such as Google not to pay overtime if there is an hourly wage of at least US$ 27.63. This law legally enacts absolute surplus-value production in the US software industry.

In addition, new management methods that try to blur the distinction between labour-time/spare-time and between workspace/private spaces are often used in software corporations in order to keep the workers in the company for long hours, which makes them work overtime and to experience the long hours they spend in their employers' premises not as alienation, but as play and fun. The result is that they work longer hours that are unpaid. Absolute surplus-value production in key sectors of 21st-century digital capitalism such as the software industry takes on the form of play labour.

The first, second, and third editions of my book *Social Media: A Critical Introduction* contains a chapter about the critique of the political economy of Google (Fuchs 2014, chapter 6; Fuchs 2017b, chapter 6; Fuchs 2021, chapter 5). For this chapter, I analysed online forums, where Google workers report on their working conditions. I updated this analysis for each edition (2014, 2017, 2021). The working conditions at Google stayed constant during this time: Google employees enjoy the content of their job, the perks such as free food and working for a high-reputation brand, but complain about the lack of work-life balance. When asked about working conditions at Google, the typical Google software engineer says that "work/life balance is nearly non-existent" and one must be prepared to "work all day and night long" (Fuchs 2021, chapter 5).

Google employees enjoy the idea of working in a high-reputation company, tend to find their work tasks interesting, like the perks such as free food, but tend to complain about the long working hours, a lot of overtime, and the lack of work-life balance. Lack of work-life balance at companies such as Google makes a playful work environment that turns spare-time into unpaid labour-time.

Luc Boltanski and Ève Chiapello (2005) speak in this context of the "new spirit of capitalism". The new spirit of capitalism is a management method and management ideology. It promises labour that is characterised by

> autonomy, spontaneity, rhizomorphous capacity, multitasking (in contrast to the narrow specialization of the old division of labour), conviviality, openness to others and novelty, availability, creativity, visionary intuition, sensitivity to differences, listening to lived experience and receptiveness to a whole range of experiences, being attracted to informality and the search for interpersonal contacts. (Boltanski and Chiapello 2005, 97).

Such promises "are taken directly from the repertoire of May 1968" (Boltanski and Chiapello 2005, 97). The new spirit of capitalism is a work culture of creativity, play, and fun that capital uses as a new, sophisticated method of absolute surplus-value production that blurs establish distinctions and demarcations of space and time in the economy. Inspired by Boltanski and Chiapello, Eran Fisher summarises these changes in the following way:

> It is therefore best understood in terms of the eradication of the distinctions between these components: between companies and the network, producers and consumers, producers and users, labor and fun, forces of production and the production process, and so forth. These established industrial demarcations (and more specifically, part and parcel of the Fordist phase of capitalism) are now overturned with the emergence of network production. (Fisher 2010, 140)

Figure 2.1 shows a typical Google job-ad. It advertises a variety of jobs such as software engineer, designer, business strategist, marketing, sales support, policy and privacy manager, etc. in Googleplex, the company headquartered in Mountain View, California. Google in this ad lauds itself for proving worker "[o]nsite benefits like fitness and wellness centers", "a group cooking class", "coffee tasting", riding "a gBike to one of our cafés". The business philosophy is that "taking care of Googlers is good for us all". The point is that these benefits that promise fun, relaxation and entertainment are "onsite": They keep Googlers at the Google premises and turn leisure time into labour time. When workers attend yoga and fitness classes, cooking classes, cafés etc. at the workplace, then the reproduction of their labour-power takes place at the workplace so that there is no clear spatial and temporal demarcation of labour time and relaxation. The three images in the job ad symbolise the blurring of space and time at Google: coding, chatting with colleagues in a café, and relaxation in a garden are presented as integral parts of work at Google. Googlers do not leave the workplace for leisure time but stay at the Google workplace. The blurring boundaries between workspace and playground and between work time and leisure time result in an increase of unpaid labour-time. For Google workers, lifetime becomes Google time and value-creating labour-time. What Google means by saying that "taking care of Googlers is good for us all" is that providing a playful work environment is a method of exploitation by absolute surplus-value production that is good for Google's profits.

FIGURE 2.1 A google ad for jobs at the Googleplex, source: https://careers.google.com/locations/mountain-view/?hl=en, accessed on 11 July 2020

2.3.5 Precarious Platform Workers

Digital capitalism has also given rise to platform workers. These are workers who mostly are freelancers and use apps and Internet platforms for finding work. Examples are the Uber and DiDi taxi driver, the Deliveroo biker who delivers food, and the online freelancer who uses platforms such as Fiverr, Upwork, or Freelancer for finding work. All of these platforms have in common that they are large capitalist corporations that own a proprietary software programme that platform workers use in order to find customers. The platform is a key means of production that is privately owned by digital corporations. Without access to this platform, freelancers cannot find customers. They depend on this means of production. Formally speaking they are self-employed, but in reality, they are workers who are exploited by digital platforms that control the key means of production as private property and capital. For each service organised via the platform, the capitalist platform corporation typically charges a share of the service price. It makes a profit by renting out its platform to freelancers who produce a service commodity that is sold to customers that are found via the platform's algorithms. Platform capitalists typically advertise their platforms as enabling flexible work that allows workers to earn lots of money. Figures 2.2 and 2.3 show two examples.

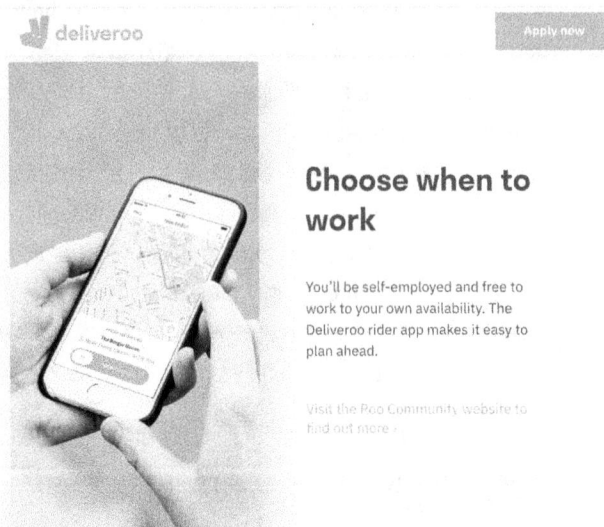

deliveroo

Apply now

Choose when to work

You'll be self-employed and free to work to your own availability. The Deliveroo rider app makes it easy to plan ahead.

Visit the Roo Community website to find out more >

FIGURE 2.2 Deliveroo's self-presentation as a platform that enables workers' freedom, source: https://deliveroo.co.uk, accessed on 11 July 2020

The Digital Condition of the Working Class Today

Make money when you want

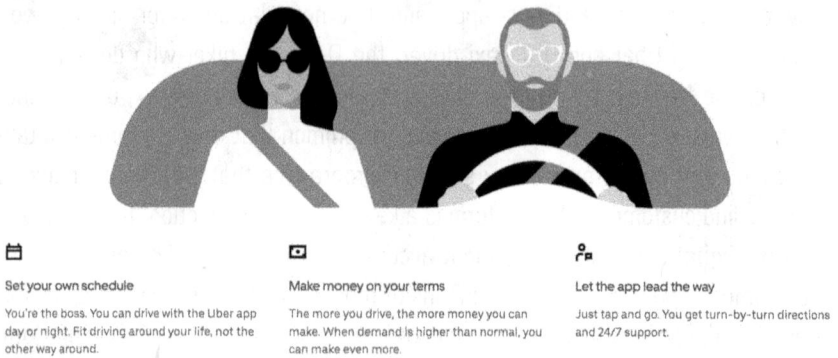

Set your own schedule

You're the boss. You can drive with the Uber app day or night. Fit driving around your life, not the other way around.

Make money on your terms

The more you drive, the more money you can make. When demand is higher than normal, you can make even more.

Let the app lead the way

Just tap and go. You get turn-by-turn directions and 24/7 support.

FIGURE 2.3 Uber's self-presentation as a platform that enables workers' freedom, source: https://www.uber.com/at/en/drive/, accessed on 11 July 2020

The common narrative of these self-presentations is that freelancer platforms enable and support workers' freedom to be their own boss and determine their work times themselves, and in doing so earn lots of money. The reality is that platform workers are very often highly exploited, precarious workers who work long hours to survive (see Fuchs 2021, chapters 11 and 12; Fuchs 2017b, chapter 10).

Platform workers are often piece-workers. They are not paid by the hour, but for each completed service, each piece of work. Karl Marx (1867) dedicates chapter 21 in *Capital Volume 1* to piece-wages (see also Fuchs 2016, chapter 21). He characterises piece-work and piece-wages as the most fruitful source of reductions on wages, and of frauds committed by the capitalists" (Marx 1867, 694). Platform labour is a contemporary form of piece-labour and piece-wages in digital capitalism that aims at platform capitalists' reduction of investment costs for maximising profits. If platforms such as Uber had to pay its drivers per hour, it might make much less profit than it does when charging a percentage share of the piece price. Platform capitalism is a dimension of digital capitalism that advances highly precarious labour.

In *CWCE*, Engels describes the working conditions of needlewomen, who were paid per piece. They were low-paid and conducted highly tiresome labour.

> With the same cruelty, though somewhat more indirectly, the rest of the needle-women of London are exploited. The girls employed in stay-making have a hard, wearing occupation, trying to the eyes. And what wages do they

get? I do not know; but this I know, that the middleman who has to give security for the material delivered, and who distributes the work among the needle-women, receives 1½d. per piece. (*CWCE*, 218)

In a digital capitalist society, transnational digital corporations such as Uber, Deliveroo, Fiverr, or Upwork are the contemporary middlemen that exploit digital pieceworkers.

2.3.6 Facebook Labour

In the book *The Origin of the Family, Private Property and the State*, Engels (1892, 131–132) gives a definition of materialism:

> According to the materialist conception, the determining factor in history is, in the last resort, the production and reproduction of immediate life. But this itself is again of a twofold character. On the one hand, the production of the means of subsistence, of food, clothing and shelter and the implements required for this; on the other, the production of human beings themselves, the propagation of the species.

Materialism in society is the insight that social production is the key factor of all societies and social realms. What Engels's passage allows us to understand is that social production as the foundation of society is not limited to the office and the factory, but extends into all realms of society, including the family. Engels's formulation has been influential on and led to discussions in Marxist and socialist feminism (e.g. Barrett 1980, 48–49, 131–132; Eisenstein 1979; Federici 2012, 1; Fraser and Jaeggi 2018, 32; Gimenez 1987; Haug 2015; Leacock 2008, 13–29; Notz 2020; Rowbotham 1973, 47; Sayers, Evans and Redclift 1987; Vogel 1996).

Although there is besides agreement lots of criticism of Engels's formulation, its importance lies in the stress that reproductive labour such as housework is a very important aspect of capitalism. It allows a focus on the economic dimension of the household where labour-power is reproduced. Rejecting interpretations that Engels separates gender oppression from class, Martha Gimenez (1987) argues that Engels's formulation should be interpreted dialectically. "Dialectically, that is the meaning of Engels's term, 'twofold'. To speak of the twofold nature of production is to refer, at the *metatheoretical level*, to its fundamental moments or aspects" (Gimenez 1987, 40). Gimenez argues that Engels stresses that class and gender oppression have different and united dynamics that are interacting, interconnected and entangled through (re)production and labour.

A key insight from Engels's *The Origin of the Family, Private Property and the State* for understanding digital labour is that labour extends beyond the factory and the office. The political economist of communication Dallas W. Smythe (1977) stresses that audience labour is labour that produces attention for advertisements. Consumers are audience workers who create the value of the advertisement (see Fuchs 2012). Targeted-advertising–based Internet platforms such as Google and Facebook make a profit based on the analysis of users' online behaviour, which results in the collection of big data, which allows them to target ads (see Fuchs 2017a, 2021). Users of Google and Facebook are unpaid digital workers, who produce Google and Facebook's value. They produce social relations, content, data, and meta-data that is appropriated by Google and Facebook and used for targeting and selling ads. Audience and user labour are like housework unpaid forms of productive, value-generating labour that operate beyond wage-labour. But housework and user labour are also quite different (for a discussion of commonalities and differences of wage-labour, slave-labour, housework, and user labour, see Fuchs 2018a). Housework produces and reproduces labour power. It is reproductive labour. Audience and user labour operate as part of the entertainment as reproductive labour in the household. But the audience and user labour also operate outside the home in a variety of social spaces via the use of mobile phones, laptops, tablets, etc. They facilitate the sale of commodities and the realisation of surplus value, that is the generation of profit by commodity sale. Housework makes labour-power saleable on the labour commodity. User and audience labour contribute to the reproduction of labour-power via advertising-financed entertainment. These two forms of labour help selling goods on commodity markets by creating the value of ads.

Engels's *The Origin of the Family, Private Property and the State* has laid the foundation for the critical comprehension of the extension of the notion of productive labour beyond wage-labour and of the extension of the factory and the office into the household and onto the Internet.

2.3.7 Section Summary

Digital capitalism is based on an international division of digital labour, where a variety of workers is exploited under a variety of working conditions in different countries and working spaces so that transnational digital corporations accumulate capital. Engels in *CWCE* outlines concepts and analyses that can inspire digital labour analysis in the 21st century. He shows how capital uses technology as a method of relative surplus-value production. In digital capitalism, digital technologies constitute a technological paradigm that advances new forms of automation and rationalisation of labour that have resulted in significant productivity increases so that more capital can be accumulated in less time. Engels also points out the inhumane consequences of absolute surplus-value production, that is, the lengthening of the working day. In digital capitalism, absolute surplus-value production takes on the form of highly exploitative Taylorist work organisation in Chinese hardware assemblage factories owned by companies such as Foxconn or Pegatron, where workers toil long hours to produce the profits of transnational digital corporations such as Apple, Dell, or HP.

In digital capitalism, one also finds a form of absolute surplus-value production in software and other companies that employ highly skilled and highly paid engineers, who are incentivised to spend long hours and their life in office complexes such as the Googleplex where the boundaries between labour/play, working time/leisure time, office/home, workers/friends and family blur. The result is that the digital labour aristocracy works very long hours and has high wages but suffers from social poverty, that is, a lack of work/life balance, friendships and social life outside of the workplace. Digital platform workers are what Engels and Marx characterised as piece-wage workers. Engels's stress on reproductive labour in *The Origin of the Family, Private Property, and the State* reminds us that in capitalism there are unremunerated unpaid forms of labour, such as housework and Facebook usage, that create commodities such as labour-power and advertising space. In digital capitalism, we find digital houseworkers who are unpaid and highly exploited (see Jarrett 2016).

The international division of digital labour means transnational digital corporations' global outsourcing of labour in order to maximise profits. The question arises what potentials there are for working-class struggles against exploitation in digital capitalism. The next section addresses this issue.

2.4 Working-Class Struggles in Digital Capitalism

CWCE's chapter 8 "Labour Movements" analyses the role of working-class struggles in capitalism. In this chapter, Engels identifies and analyses different types of working-class struggles: (a) crime, (b) the destruction of machinery, (c) trade unions, and (d) political movements.

Engels stresses that there are different ways of how workers react to their exploitation. "To escape despair, there are but two ways open to him [the worker]; either inward and outward revolt against the bourgeoisie or drunkenness and general demoralization. And the English operatives are accustomed to take refuge in both", which resulted in "hundreds of uprising against machinery and the bourgeoisie" (*CWCE*, 149). At the time when Engels wrote *CWCE*, the struggles of the working class were particularly focused on the introduction of the ten hours working day. Engels, again and again, refers to these struggles (*CWCE*, 179, 182–185, 242, 313). Such struggles resulted in the introduction of the Ten Hours Bill 1847 that limited the working day for women and teenagers to a maximum of ten hours.

Engels sees crime as a purely individual reaction and the destruction of machinery as limited to one single dimension of capital's rule. He propagates the unity of economic-class struggles and political-class struggles. He argues for the "union of Socialism with Chartism, the reproduction of French Communism in an English manner". In digital capitalism, there is a large number of different cybercrimes, the crime that is committed using digital technologies such as the Internet (see Wall 2007 for an overview discussion of cybercrime). Many Internet users every day receive spam and online scams via e-mails, which are the most widely spread forms of cybercrime. Such forms of cybercrime are not the reactions of a disenfranchised working class, but highly profitable capitalist businesses.

Machine breaking means the resistance against the introduction of machinery and "revolts against machinery" (*CWCE*, 222). In industrialising England, machine breaking was known as "Luddism", a movement named after its founder Ned Ludd. "This form of opposition also was isolated, restricted to certain localities, and directed against one feature only of our present social arrangements" (*CWCE*, 222). In the book *The Making of the English Working Class,* the Marxist historian E. P. Thompson (1966) makes a more positive assessment of the Luddite movement than Engels (see also Fuchs 2016, 2000–2004). He writes that Luddism was not a blind attack on machinery as end-in-itself, but a well-organised movement that attacked the machines of capitalists that laid-off workers (Thompson 1966, 564). Luddism was a working-class struggle for "a democratic community, in which industrial growth should be regulated according to ethical priorities and the pursuit of profit be subordinated to human needs" (Thompson 1966, 552).

In digital capitalism, one can, again and again, hear suggestions and see initiatives that call for stopping to use of digital technologies. An example is digital detoxing, the conscious choice to stop using digital technologies for certain periods of time. The problem with such strategies is that they often are technophobic and techno-deterministic. They see digital technologies as such as the cause of stress, health problems, depression, loneliness, etc. They abstract from the capitalist, class and power relations that shape contemporary digital technologies. Digital detox retreats have turned into a new form of capital accumulation, where stressed digital workers pay for switching off their phones and laptops for a weekend or a week. For example, the three-day digital detox retreat at The Detox Barn in Suffolk (UK) costs £415 per person "for three nights (Friday – Monday) including all meals, two yoga sessions, smoothie demos, guided country walks and guided meditation".[2] Deceleration, digital detox and digital Luddism are capital accumulation strategies. They advance the very cause of the stress and problems that digital workers suffer – capitalism.

Engels "was the first socialist to highlight the importance of trade unions to the struggle for socialism, and this fundamental insight was the concrete corollary of his historical humanism" (Blackledge 2019, 42). Trade unions aim at raising wages and "protecting the single working man against the tyranny and neglect of the bourgeoisie" (*CWCE*, 223). The strike is the union's main method of struggle by which they harm capitalists whose capital is "idle as long as the strike lasted, and his machinery would be rusting" (*CWCE*, 225). The capitalist antagonism between capital and labour is one about the control of the means of production and working time. The capitalist wants to make the workers conduct as much unpaid labour-time as possible, whereas the workers have the interest to control all of their labour-time themselves and not to be controlled by capitalists and managers. A strike disrupts labour time. Workers stop working. Necessary and surplus labour time are both zero. No value is created. No commodities are produced. Capitalists make no profit.

Engels writes about the emergence of a "New Unionism" (CWCE, 324), new trade unions of unskilled workers. These trade unions differed from the old unions of skilled workers focused on wage increases because unskilled workers often faced un-employment and no wages at all. In digital capitalism, we need digital trade unions that support digital workers in uniting in struggles against digital capital.

Digital socialism begins and develops through the class struggles of digital workers. The working class has changed. There are a lot of digital workers in an international

Working-Class Struggles in Digital Capitalism

---

2 https://queenofretreats.com/retreats/the-detox-barn-suffolk-uk/, accessed on 12 July 2020.

digital division of labour. Class struggles in the 21st century must look different than in the 19th and 20th centuries, as the forms and places of work have changed. Many freelancers work in the digital industry. They are not capitalists, but members of the working class. Most of them only own a computer as a means of production, no monetary capital. They do not hire other workers either. They work sporadically and precariously. And they are very difficult to reach and organise in trade unions. Co-working spaces provided free or cheaply by unions create spaces where digital workers come together and can be social spaces and starting points for union organising.

Traditional trade unions have problems with the representation and organisation of atypical workers such as freelancers. Some unions do not even intend to represent freelancers because they consider them to be capitalists. As the world of work has changed, trade unions and their strategies must change if they want to advance the interests of the working class. It is of particular importance that trade unions as well as left, socialist and communist parties and movements deal with precarious work, domestic work, unemployment, consumer work, public work, Facebook user work, digital work, digital surveillance, etc. and defend and represent these forms of work.

With the convergence of production and consumption, some consumer issues have become labour rights issues. Trade unions and left, socialist and communist parties and movements should therefore consider digital consumer issues as labour rights issues and start to join forces with consumer protection associations.

The unions have lost influence and power, which means that the power of capital has been strengthened in class struggles. If the labour movement and trade unions do not succeed in engaging and organising on issues such as digital work, domestic work, unpaid work, freelance work, crowdsourcing, platform work, consumer work, work of Internet users, privacy, digital surveillance, consumer protection, slave labour, etc., and if they do not see these issues as key to labour struggles, these movements commit suicide. To challenge the power of global capital requires the global networking of the working class and the internationalisation of trade unions, left movements, socialist parties and trade union membership.

Class struggles are of course already taking place in digital capitalism. One example is the strike by Uber-riders. They are digital workers exploited by the Uber corporation, which controls the Uber app as a means of production. In a lawsuit in Britain, it was confirmed that Uber drivers have the legal status of workers.

Worker self-control means that the workers gain control over the app and its source code. For example, if the digital courier workers unionise with software engineers, an alternative app could be created. A strike by digital workers at Uber, Deliveroo, etc. would then consist of, for example, using the union app for one week instead of the capitalist app and damaging the capitalist companies during this period, for example, to push through demands for a minimum wage of 15 Euros per hour for platform workers. Such a strike is a new form of class struggle in and against digital capital.

In digital capitalism, strikes need to add new digital dimensions of struggles in order to be effective. On the one hand, given that lots of news consumption and everyday communication take place via social media, unions and labour movements should be present on social media and should mobilise and organise via social media and communicate their goals using hashtags, video platforms, social networking sites, messenger apps, blogs, memes, digital images, digital animations, etc. On the other hand, digital corporations such as Google, Facebook, and Amazon accumulate capital online, which is why digital strikes against such companies should make use of user-boycotts, which helps to disrupt these corporations profit-making and allows putting pressure on them when making demands. An example of the digital strike is Adbuster's #OccupySiliconValley, a one-day digital strike against Facebook, Amazon, Apple, and Google that took place in September 2018. It called on users not to use these platforms for one day. Given that online usage of platforms such as Facebook and Google is not just consumption but also labour, a Facebook- and Google-boycott is also a labour strike. The digital workers put their eyeballs to rest or direct them elsewhere, which disrupts digital value creation. The campaign call read:

> Big Tech competes for one thing: our attention. They exploit our basic human instincts in the pursuit of unprecedented financial and cultural control. [...] You can turn September 17th into DO NOTHING DAY [....] Partake in a one-day embargo against tech altogether. [...] On September 17th, each one of us, in our own sweet way, will participate in a global takedown of Big Tech! [...] Make the Internet ours again.[3]

With respect to political struggles, Engels was a supporter of the Chartist movement, a political reform movement that struggled for suffrage and was associated with the English working-class movement. Engels writes that the Chartists "wish to put a proletarian law in the place of the legal fabric of the bourgeoisie" (*CWCE*, 235). Chartism was for Engels a "class movement" that aimed at "Chartist democracy"

Working-Class Struggles in Digital Capitalism

---

3 http://abillionpeople.org/occupy-silicon-valley/, accessed on 11 July 2020.

(*CWCE*, 242). Already in this early work by Engels, it becomes evident that he did not understand communism as a totalitarian state but as a democratic socialist society. Consequently, Marx and Engels in the Manifesto of the Communist Party spoke of communism as "the struggle for democracy"[4] (Marx and Engels 1848a, 481).

The struggle for the reduction of the working day is the practical combination of economic and political struggles. In England, the 1847 Ten Hours Bill was the result of the combination of the socialist, the union and the Chartist movement. In the 1860s, the First International, in which Marx and Engels were key figures, formulated the demand of "eight hours work as the legal limit of the working day" (International Working Men's Association 1868, 5).

In 1919, the International Labour Organization passed the Hours of Work (Industry) Convention and in 1930 the Hours of Work (Commerce and Offices) Convention that defines the standard working week as not exceeding 48 hours per week and eight hours a day. In 2020, 52 countries had passed the first convention and 30 the second. Given there are 193 member states of the United Nations, it is evident that only a rather low number of countries have signed these international conventions. The prevalence of temporary work, zero-hours contracts, part-time work, freelance labour, etc. shows that labour-time remains a key dimension of the class antagonism between capital and labour in the 21st century.

In 2020, the digital productive forces are developed to a high degree so that labour-time could be significantly reduced and everyone could work fewer hours but lead a better life. But digital technologies are embedded into what Marx and Engels termed the antagonism between the productive forces and the relations of production.

In the *Communist Manifesto*, they speak of the "revolt of modern productive forces against modern conditions of production" in capitalist society "that has conjured up such gigantic means of production and of exchange" and "is like the sorcerer, who is no longer able to control the powers of the nether world whom he has called up by his spells" (Marx and Engels 1848b, 489). In digital capitalism, the antagonism between the digital productive forces and capitalist relations of production takes on the form of an antagonism between digital capital and the digital commons. On the one hand, there are new forms of capital accumulation in the digital industries that combine a variety of digital commodities and digital labour. On the other hand, there are new

---

4 Translation from German: "die Erkämpfung der Demokratie"

forms of the digital commons – such as not-for-profit online platforms, non-commercial news media, Wikipedia, the free and open-source software, non-commercial Creative Commons, platform co-operatives, the free software movement, radical open access, etc. – that go beyond digital capital and practically question capital accumulation. The antagonism between the digital machines and class relations has advanced the radical asymmetrical distribution of labour-time. Whereas some workers are highly stressed, have no leisure time and work very long hours, others are unemployed, underemployed, or precarious workers. The productive forces enable a substantial reduction of the standard working day that allows a more symmetrical distribution of labour time and a good life for all. Establishing a reduction of the working week without wage cuts requires class struggles for radical reforms of labour legislation. Just like the labour movement struggled for first for the ten-hours- and then for the eight-hours-working day, in digital capitalism, we need struggles for the five-hours-working day and a four-day-working week with full wage compensation. Such struggles point towards a post-scarcity society, in which digital technologies are used to minimise necessary labour time and maximise free time and the good life for all.

Writing in 1845, Engels says that a "mass of Acts for enclosing and cultivating commons is passed at every session of Parliament" (*CWCE*, 287). Communism "does away with all class antagonisms" (*CWCE*, 301). In the early phase of capitalism, common land was enclosed and peasants were forced into wage labour. Marx (1867) terms this phase of primitive accumulation. But primitive accumulation never ended. It continues in the form of imperialism, attempts of capital to make use of violence and other means for turning non-commodified spheres of society and nature into realms of capital accumulation. That is why digital capital seeks to colonise non-capitalist spaces such as the digital commons and turn them into spheres of digital capital accumulation. Engels pointed out that non-capitalist alternatives are possible and needed. For example, in the realm of media and education, he argues that radical media and education are important intellectual means of struggle. He saw the Chartist newspaper *Northern Star* as "The only sheet which reports all the movements of the proletariat" (*CWCE*, 232). He stressed the importance of educational institutions such as the Chartist institutions where "the children receive a purely proletarian education, free from all the influences of the bourgeoisie" and one finds "reading-rooms" with "proletarian journals and books" (*CWCE*, 245).

We need concrete utopias of digital socialism. I see two potentials: On the one hand, the renewal of the movement of co-operatives and self-managed companies in the

Working-Class Struggles in Digital Capitalism

form of platform co-operatives, that is, Internet platforms that are self-managed by users and digital workers. On the other hand, the creation of public Internet platforms through a network of public service media.

Examples of platform co-operatives are the music platform Resonate, Fairbnb (an alternative to Airbnb), Taxiapp (an alternative to Uber), the photo platform Stocksy and the cooperation platform Loomio (Fuchs 2021, chapters 12, 14, and). Many platform co-operatives do not make it from concept to reality and many soon disappear again. Those that do exist usually remain small and insignificant, so they cannot challenge the digital capital. The Marxist social scientist Marisol Sandoval (2019) analyses how some of the platform co-operatives use the capitalist language and logic of "shareholders", "profits", "investments", "creators", "entrepreneurs", "innovation", etc., thus displacing radical politics.

Socialism is neither an app nor a platform. It cannot be downloaded from the Internet or clicked on a mobile phone. It is not enough to organise platforms as co-operatives. In order to survive and create a better society, platform co-operatives must politicise themselves and act as part of radical social movements that fight collectively and politically against capitalism and for socialism. Socialism is not an app and not a platform, but a political movement. Sandoval (2016a, 2016b, 2019) argues that platform co-operatives should play an important role in this movement and that we need class struggle co-operatives. By class-struggle co-operatives, Sandoval means that co-operatives become parts of socialist movements fighting for redistribution, capital taxation and socialism. They are part of what Bhaskar Sunkara (2019) calls class-struggle social democracy, whereby social democracy is to be understood in the sense of Luxembourg as a democratic socialist movement and party.

In order to prevent new fascism, it is necessary to defend and renew democracy. Public media should play an important role in this. They are non-capitalist because they are not profit-oriented. And they can only act critically and as public media, if they are not controlled by the state, that is they are not state media. The strengthening of non-capitalist media is an aspect of the class struggle in so far as the power of the capitalist media is pushed back. But today we see that right-wing forces are attacking the public media and would like to abolish them. One strategy against this is the renewal of the public media in the Internet age.

There are initiatives like Public Open Space (https://public-open-space.eu) and discussions about the need for public media and international networks of public media as operators of public Internet platforms. For example, a public YouTube, jointly operated by the BBC, ARD, ORF, etc., on which the archive material of the public media is offered with Creative Commons licenses for remixing for non-commercial purposes (Fuchs 2017c, 2018b, 2018d). Or a new edition of the legendary debate format Club 2 of the Austrian Broadcasting Corporation (ORF) in the form of an Internet-based Club 2.0, in order to counter the lack of debate culture that prevails in mediatised, digital capitalism. The principle of Club 2 was that it was a live discussion without censorship, without advertising and with open air time. Club 2 was a public sphere.

In today's highly accelerated capitalism there is hardly any time and space for complex arguments and debates. The acceleration logic of capital has also colonised culture, leading to the acceleration and boulevardisation of the public sphere. More and more experiences are squeezed into short time spans, leaving hardly any time for reflection and reflected discussion. The result is the boulevardisation of the media. Reality TV is one example of this. In my opinion, Hartmut Rosa (2013) correctly points out the alienated aspects of acceleration. It is crucial in this respect to see that acceleration under capitalism is driven by the logic of accumulation.

Club 2.0 is the digital public sphere in the age of user-generated content and social media (Fuchs 2017c, 2018b, 2018d). We need to strengthen and update the independence of public media from the state and capital and empower them to act as operators of digital platforms on the Internet and to use these platforms for further developing public service media's remits.

Concrete utopias of digital socialism need concrete initiatives and projects that should be part of broader movements and struggles for socialism and the rescue and strengthening of the commons and the public sphere.

In *CWCE*, Engels gave significant attention to working-class struggles. One can draw important lessons from Engels's insights for the analysis of digital working-class struggles. Engels stresses the importance of trade unions, strikes, and radical political reforms as aspects of class struggles. In digital capitalism, we need new forms, strategies and methods of trade unions and class struggle. 21st-century society trade unions need to take serious housework, freelancers, the unemployed, platform labour and other forms of digital labour, the tendency of production and consumption to converge, digital surveillance, etc. In digital capitalism, many consumer rights issues are labour rights issues. In digital capitalism, strikes need to add new digital dimensions of struggles in order to be effective. There are two implications: First, class struggles and strikes should make use of digital platforms as means of organisation, mobilisation and communication. Second, strikes should also take place online and disrupt value production on digital platforms in order to exert digital power against digital capital. Engels stresses that questions of labour time are an important aspect of working-class struggles. In 21st-century digital capitalism, the digital productive forces are so highly developed that the struggle for a five hour-working day and a four hour-working week is a realistic and necessary demand for improving the quality of life of the working class that today suffers from the precarity caused by the antagonism between the digital productive forces and the capitalist relations of production. Engels stressed the need for alternatives to capital and capitalism. In a digital society, platform co-operatives, digital commons projects and public service Internet platforms are concrete digital utopias that point beyond digital capital(ism). Such projects and demands to implement and support them should be part of struggles for a good life for all and 21st-century socialism.

2.5 Conclusion

Engels 200th anniversary is an excellent occasion for the analysis of life and the conditions of the working class in digital capitalism. This article contributed to this task by dealing with the question: How relevant are Friedrich Engels's works in the age of digital capitalism?

This paper showed that Friedrich Engels's works remain highly relevant in 21st-century society and can inform the critical analysis of digital capitalism, technology and society, computational social science, digital positivism, digital labour, digital labour struggles, and the digital commons.

It is a mistake to assume that Engels is to blame for Stalinism and was the first vulgariser of Marx. But it is also an error to assume that his works are flawless. There are problematic, deterministic formulations in his works. But by and large, he has stressed the importance of class struggles in and against capitalism and that the basic social law of society is that humans make their own history based on and shaped by given conditions. Engels did not formulate a theory of the automatic collapse of capitalism. Scientific socialism is not a natural science theory of society, but an anti-positivist dialectical social analysis the uses the dialectics of subject/object, agency/structures, practices/conditions, experience/reason, empirical research/social theory, chance/necessity, discontinuity/continuity, disorder/order, diversity/unity, individual/society, local/global, spontaneity/organisation, etc.

Let us summarise the main findings of this article:

- ● **Scientific socialism:**

Scientific socialism doesn't mean that society is governed by mechanical laws, but that socialist research studies society based on the combination of critical social theory and critical empirical social research. For Engels just like for Marx, there is a difference between natural dialectics and societal dialectics. The basic law of society is that humans make their own history under given conditions. In class society, class and social struggles are the processes, by which humans make their own history.

- ● **The critique of computational social science as digital positivism:**

In the contemporary social sciences, computational social sciences have emerged as a dominant paradigm that attracts lots of attention, support, and funding. Engels understood scientific socialism as a critique of positivism. Computational social science is digital positivism that poses the danger of turning the social sciences into administrative, instrumental, positivist research that supports domination and exploitation. It neglects that qualitative features of society such as motivations, norms, moral values, feelings, ideologies, experiences, love, death, freedom, or (in)justice that cannot be reduced to quantities and computation.

- ● **The international division of digital labour:**

Digital capitalism is based on an international division of digital labour, where a variety of workers is exploited under a variety of working conditions in different countries and working spaces so that transnational digital corporations accumulate capital. The international division of digital labour means transnational digital corporations' global outsourcing of labour in order to maximise profits. Engels in *The Condition of the Working Class in England* outlines concepts and analyses that can inspire digital labour analysis in the 21st century.

- ● **The antagonism between the digital productive forces and the capitalist relations of production:**

Engels shows how capital uses technology as a method of relative surplus-value production. In digital capitalism, digital technologies constitute a technological paradigm that advances new forms of automation and rationalisation of labour that have resulted in significant productivity increases so that more capital can be accumulated in less time. Digital capitalism is shaped by the antagonism between the digital productive forces and the capitalist relations of production. In 21st-century digital capitalism, the digital productive forces are so highly developed that the struggle for a five hour-working day and a four hour-working week is a realistic and necessary demand for improving the quality of life of the working class that today suffers from the precarity caused by the antagonism between the digital productive forces and the capitalist relations of production. Engels stresses that questions of labour time are an important aspect of working-class struggles.

- **The exploitation of digital labour:**

Engels points out the inhumane consequences of absolute surplus-value production, that is, the lengthening of the working day. In digital capitalism, absolute surplus-value production takes on the form of highly exploitative Taylorist work organisation in Chinese hardware assemblage factories owned by companies such as Foxconn or Pegatron, where workers toil long hours to produce the profits of transnational digital corporations such as Apple, Dell, or HP. In digital capitalism, one also finds a form of absolute surplus-value production in software and other companies that employ highly skilled and highly paid engineers, who are incentivised to spend long hours and their life in office complexes such as the Googleplex where the boundaries between labour/play, working time/leisure time, office/home, workers/friends and family blur. The result is that the digital labour aristocracy works very long hours and has high wages but suffers from social poverty, i.e. a lack of work/life balance, friendships and social life outside of the workplace. Digital platform workers are what Engels and Marx characterised as piece-wage workers.

- *The Condition of the Working Class in England:*

In *CWCE*, Engels gave significant attention to working-class struggles. One can draw important lessons from Engels's insights for the analysis of digital working-class struggles.

- **Trade unions in the digital age:**

Engels stresses the importance of trade unions, strikes, and radical political reforms as aspects of class struggles. In digital capitalism, we need new forms, strategies and methods of trade unions and class struggle. 21st-century society trade unions need to take serious housework, freelancers, the unemployed, platform labour and other forms of digital labour, the tendency of production and consumption to converge, digital surveillance, etc. In digital capitalism, many consumer rights issues are labour rights issues.

- **Digital working-class struggles:**

In digital capitalism, strikes need to add new digital dimensions of struggles in order to be effective. There are two implications: First, class struggles and strikes should make use of digital platforms as means of organisation, mobilisation and communication. Second, strikes should also take place online and disrupt value production on digital platforms in order to exert digital power against digital capital.

- **Alternatives to digital capitalism:**

Engels stressed the need for alternatives to capital and capitalism. In a digital society, platform co-operatives, digital commons projects and public service Internet platforms are concrete digital utopias that point beyond digital capital(ism). Such projects and demands to implement and support them should be part of struggles for a good life for all and 21st-century socialism.

In *The Housing Question*, Engels (1872, 324–325) argues:

> And it is precisely this industrial revolution which has raised the productive power of human labour to such a high level that – for the first time in the history of mankind – the possibility exists, given a rational division of labour among all, of producing not only enough for the plentiful consumption of all members of society and for an abundant reserve fund, but also of leaving each individual sufficient leisure so that what is really worth preserving in historically inherited culture – science, art, forms of intercourse, etc. – may not only be preserved but converted from a monopoly of the ruling class into the common property of the whole of society, and may be further developed.

Computing has helped to create foundations for a highly productive post-scarcity socialist society, where wealth for all is possible and culture is the common property of the whole of society. Writing in the 19th century, Engels wrote of science, art (and more general forms of intercourse) as aspects of culture that in socialism benefit all. Today, he would also include digital technologies such as the Internet and would demand the creation of digital commons. If Engels were alive today, he would criticise all digital capital accumulation models and argue that digital technologies shouldn't be capital and commodities but common properties available without payment to the whole of society and benefiting everyone. Engels would certainly support the creation of a public service and commons-based Internet (see Fuchs 2021, chapters 14 and 12).

Refrences

Barrett, Michèle. 1980. *Women's Oppression Today. Problems in Marxist Feminist Analysis.* London: Verso.

Blackledge, Paul. 2019. *Friedrich Engels and Modern Social and Political Theory.* Albany, NY: State University of New York Press.

Boltanski, Luc and Ève Chiapello. 2005. *The New Spirit of Capitalism.* London: Verso.

China Labor Watch. 2017. *A Year of Regression in Apple's Supply Chain. Pursuing Profits at the Cost of Working Conditions.* New York: China Labor Watch.

Cioffi-Revilla, Claudio. 2014. *Introduction to Computational Social Science. Principles and Applications.* London: Springer.

Conte, Rosaria et al. 2012. Manifesto of Computational Social Science. *The European Physical Journal Special Topics* 214: 325–346.

Eisenstein, Zillah. 1979. Developing a Theory of Capitalist Patriarchy and Socialist Feminism. In *Capitalist Patriarchy and the Case for Socialist Feminism*, ed. Zillah Eisenstein, 5–40. New York: Monthly Review Press.

Engels, Friedrich. 1925. Dialectics of Nature. In *Marx & Engels Collected Works (MECW) Volume 25*, 311–588. London: Lawrence & Wishart.

Engels, Friedrich. 1892. The Origin of the Family, Private Property and the State. In the Light of the Researches by Lewis H. Morgan. In *Marx & Engels Collected Works (MECW) Volume 26*, 129–276. London: Lawrence & Wishart.

Engels, Friedrich. 1872. The Housing Question. In *Marx & Engels Collected Works (MECW) Volume 23*, 317–391. London: Lawrence & Wishart.

Engels, Friedrich. 1843. Outlines of a Critique of Political Economy. In *Marx & Engels Collected Works (MECW) Volume 3*, 418–443. London: Lawrence & Wishart.

Federici, Silvia. 2012. *Revolution at Point Zero: Housework, Reproduction, and Feminist Struggle.* Oakland, CA: PM Press.

Fisher, Eran. 2010. *Media and the New Capitalism in the Digital Age. The Spirit of Networks.* New York: Palgrave Macmillan.

Fraser, Nancy and Rahel Jaeggi. 2018. *Capitalism: A Conversation in Critical Theory.* Cambridge: Polity.

Fuchs, Christian. 2021. *Social Media: A Critical Introduction*, 3rd edn. London: Sage.

Fuchs, Christian. 2020b. Everyday Life and Everyday Communication in Coronavirus Capitalism. *tripleC: Communication, Capitalism & Critique* 18 (1): 375–399. doi: 10.31269/triplec.v18i1.1167

Fuchs, Christian. 2018a. Capitalism, Patriarchy, Slavery, and Racism in the Age of Digital Capitalism and Digital Labour. *Critical Sociology* 44 (4–5): 677–702.

Fuchs, Christian. 2018b. Digitale Demokratie und Öffentlich-Rechtliche Medien. In *ORF Public Value Studie 2017/2018: Der Auftrag: Demokratie*, 94–138. Wien: ORF. Available at: https://zukunft.orf.at/show_content.php?sid=147&pvi_id=1986&pvi_medientyp=t&oti_tag=studie

Fuchs, Christian. 2018c. Industry 4.0: The Digital German Ideology. *tripleC: Communication, Capitalism & Critique* 16 (1): 280–289. doi: 10.31269/triplec.v16i1.1010

Fuchs, Christian. 2018d. *The Online Advertising Tax as the Foundation of a Public Service Internet*. London: University of Westminster Press. doi: 10.16997/book23

Fuchs, Christian. 2017a. From Digital Positivism and Administrative Big Data Analytics Towards Critical Digital and Social Media Research. *European Journal of Communication* 32 (1): 37–49.

Fuchs, Christian. 2017b. *Social Media: A Critical Introduction*, 2nd edn. London: Sage

Fuchs, Christian. 2017c. Towards the public service Internet as alternative to the commercial Internet. In *ORF Texte No. 20 – Öffentlich-Rechtliche Qualität im Diskurs*, 43–50. Vienna: ORF.

Republication: Fuchs, Christian. 2018. Towards the public service Internet as alternative to the commercial Internet. In *Public Open Space: Zur Zukunft öffentlich-rechtlicher Medien*, eds. Konrad Mitschka and Klaus Unterberger, 301–307. Vienna: Facultas.

Fuchs, Christian. 2016. *Reading Marx in the Information Age. A Media and Communication Studies Perspective on "Capital Volume I"*. New York: Routledge.

Fuchs, Christian. 2014. *Social Media: A Critical Introduction*, 1st edn. London: Sage

Fuchs, Christian. 2012. Dallas Smythe Today – The audience Commodity, the Digital Labour Debate, Marxist Political Economy and Critical Theory. Prolegomena to a Digital Labour Theory of Value. *tripleC: Communication, Capitalism & Critique* 10 (2): 692–740.

Fülberth, Georg. 2018. *Friedrich Engels*. Köln: PapyRossa.

García-Hodges, Ahiza, Jo Ling Kent, and Ezra Kaplan. 2020. Amazon Warehouse in Minnesota Had More Than 80 COVID-19 Cases. *NBC News*. Available at: https://www.nbcnews.com/tech/tech-news/amazon-warehouse-minnesota-had-more-80-covid-19-cases-n1231937 (accessed on 24 June 2020).

Gimenez, Martha. 1987. Marxist and Non-Marxist Elements in Engels's views on the oppression of women. In *Engels Revisited. New Feminist Essays*, eds. Janet Sayers, Mary Evans and Nanneke Redclift, 37–56. London: Tavistock.

Harvey, David. 2005. *A Brief History of Neoliberalism*. Oxford: Oxford University Press.

Haug, Frigga. 2015. Gender relations & the Marx within feminism. In *Marxism and Feminism*, ed. Shahrzad Mojab, 33–101. London: Zed.

Hegel, Georg Wilhelm Friedrich. 1830 [1991]. *The Encyclopaedia Logic (with the Zusätze). Part I of the Encyclopaedia of the Philosophical Sciences with the Zusätze*. Indianapolis, IN: Hackett.

Hobsbawm, Eric J. 1969. *Introduction. In Friedrich Engels: The Condition of the Working Class in England: From Personal Observation to Authentic Sources*, 7–17. London: Panther.

Horkheimer, Max. 1947. *Eclipse of Reason*. New York: Continuum.

Hunt, Tristam. 2009. *Marx's General. The Revolutionary Life of Friedrich Engels*. New York: Metropolitan Books.

International Working Men's Association. 1868. *Resolutions of the Congress of Geneva, 1866, and the Congress of Brussels,1868*. London: Westminster Printing Company.

Jarrett, Kylie. 2016. *Feminism, Labour and Digital Media: The Digital Housewife*. New York, NY: Routledge.

Kopf, Eike. 2017. *Marxismus ohne Engels?* Köln: PapyRossa.

Krätke, Michael. 2020. *Friedrich Engels oder: Wie ein "Cotton-Lord" den Marxismus erfand*. Berlin: Dietz.

Kurz, Heinz D. 2000. Der junge Engels über die "Bereicherungswissenschaft", die "Unsittlichket" von Privateigentum und Konkurrenz und die "Heuchelei der Oekonomen". In *Arbeiten am Widerspruch – Friedrich Engels zum 200. Geburtstag*, eds. Rainer Lucas, Reinhard Pfrim and Hans-Dieter Westhoff, 65–120. Marburg: Metropolis.

Lazer, David et al. 2009. Computational Social Science. *Science* 323: 721–723.

Leacock, Eleanor Burke. 2008. *Myths of Male Dominance. Collected Articles on Women Cross-Culturally*. Chicago, IL: Haymarket Books.

Lenin, Vladimir Ilyich. 1920. *Preface to the French and German Editions of 'Imperialism, the Highest Stage of Capitalism'*. In *Lenin Works Volume 22*, 189–194. London: Lawrence & Wishart.

Levine, Norman. 2018. Engels' Co-option of Lenin. In *The Palgrave Handbook of Leninist Political Philosophy*, 161–199. Basingstoke: Palgrave Macmillan.

Levine, Norman. 2006. *Divergent Paths. Hegel in Marxism and Engelism. Volume 1: The Hegelian Foundations of Marx's Method*. Oxford: Lexington Books.

Levine, Norman. 1975. *The Tragic Deception. Marx Contra Engels*. Oxford: Oxford University Press.

Lukács, Georg. 1971. *History and Class Consciousness*. London: Merlin.

Marx, Karl. 1857/1858. *The Grundrisse*. London: Pengui.

Marx, Karl. 1867. *Capital. Volume* I. London: Penguin.

Marx, Karl. 1863. Marx to Engels. In *Marx & Engels Collected Works (MECW) Volume 41*, 466–469. London: Lawrence & Wishart.

Marx, Karl. 1859. A Contribution to the Critique of Political Economy. Preface. In *Marx & Engels Collected Works (MECW) Volume 29*, 261–265. London: Lawrence & Wishart.

Marx, Karl. 1852. The Eighteenth Brumaire of Louis Bonaparte. In *Marx & Engels Collected Works (MECW) Volume 11*, 99–197. London: Lawrence & Wishart.

Marx, Karl. 1844. Ökonomisch-philosophische Manuskripte aus dem Jahr 1844. In *Marx Engels Werke (MEW) Band 40*, 465–588. Berlin: Dietz.

Marx, Karl and Friedrich Engels. (1848a). Manifest der Kommunistischen Partei. In *Marx Engels Werke (MEW) Band 4*, 459–493. Berlin: Dietz. S. 462–463.

Marx, Karl and Friedrich Engels. 1848b. The Manifesto of the Communist Party. In *Marx & Engels Collected Works (MECW) Volume 6*, 477–519. London: Lawrence & Wishart.

Marx, Karl and Friedrich Engels. 1845. The Holy Family, or Critique of Critical Criticism. Against Bruno Bauer and Company. In *Marx & Engels Collected Works (MECW) Volume 4*, 5–211. London: Lawrence & Wishart.

Mayer, Gustav. 1935. *Friedrich Engels. A Biography.* London: Chapman & Hall.

McLellan, David. 1993. Introduction. In Friedrich Engels: *The Condition of the Working Class in England*, ix–xx. Oxford: Oxford University Press.

Notz, Gisela. 2000. Auseinandersetzung mit Friedrich Engels' "Ursprung der Familie ..." ... und was er uns heute noch zu sagen hat. In *Arbeiten am Widerspruch – Friedrich Engels zum 200. Geburtstag*, eds. Rainer Lucas, Reinhard Pfrim and Hans-Dieter Westhoff, 397–416. Marburg: Metropolis.

Rosa, Hartmut. 2013. *Social Acceleration. A New Theory of Modernity.* New York: Columbia University Press.

Rowbotham, Sheila. 1973. *Woman's Consciousness, Man's World.* Harmondsworth: Penguin.

Sandoval, Marisol. 2019. Entrepreneurial Activism? Platform Cooperativism Between Subversion and Co-optation. In *Critical Sociology*, doi:10.1177/0896920519870577

Sandoval, Marisol. 2016a. Fighting Precarity with Co-operation? Worker Co-operatives in the Cultural Sector. *New Formations* 88: 51–68.

Sandoval, Marisol. 2016b. What Would Rosa Do? Co-operatives and Radical Politics. *Soundings: A Journal of Politics and Culture* 63: 98–111.

Sayers, Janet, Mary Evans and Nanneke Redclift, eds. 1987. *Engels Revisited. New Feminist Essays.* London: Tavistock.

Schmidt, Alfred. 1971. *The Concept of Nature in Marx.* London: NLB.

Stalin, Joseph V. 1945. Dialectical and Historical Materialism. In *History of the Communist Party of the Soviet Union*, 105–131. Moscow: Foreign Languages Publishing House.

Students & Scholars Against Corporate Misbehaviour (SACOM). 2011. *iSlave Behind the iPhone: Foxconn Workers in Central China.* Available at: https://sacom.hk/wp-content/uploads/201 8/10/2011-iSlave-Behind-the-iPhone-Foxconn-Workers-in-Central-China.pdf (accessed on 21 October 2019).

Sunkara, Bhaskar. 2019. *The Socialist Manifesto: The Case for Radical Politics in An Era of Extreme Inequality.* London: Verso.

Smythe, Dallas W. 1977. Communications: Blindspot of Western Marxism. *Canadian Journal of Political and Social Theory* 1 (3): 1–27.

Thompson, Edward P. 1966. *The Making of the English Working Class.* New York: Vintage Books.

Vogel, Lise. 1996. Engels's *Origin*: Legacy, Burden and Vision. In *Engels Today. A Centenary Appreciation*, ed. Christopher J. Arthur. Basingstoke: Macmillan. 129–151.

Wall, David S. 2007. *Cybercrime: The Transformation of Crime in the Information Age*. Cambridge: Polity.

Zimmermann, Clemens. 2020. Die Lage der arbeitenden Klasse in England. In *Friedrich Engels: Ein Gespenst geht um in Euopa. Begleitband zur Engelsausstellung 2020*, ed. Lars Bluma, 70–83. Remscheid: Bergischer Verlag.

Chapter Three
History and Class Consciousness 2.0: Georg Lukács in the Age of Digital Capitalism and Big Data

3.1 Introduction

This chapter asks: what elements of Georg Lukács' *History and Class Consciousness* can inform the foundations of a critical theory of communication in the age of digital capitalism? To provide an answer, the article proceeds in the following manner: section 3.2 analyses ideology and reified consciousness. Section 3.3 draws attention to the relationship between journalism and reification. Section 3.4 discusses the reification of communication technologies. Some conclusions are drawn in section 3.5. Based on a reading of Lukács, the chapter wants to show Lukács' analysis can be used for critically analysing contemporary forms of digital communication.

Dannemann (2017) argues that we today "require an updating of Lukács' phenomenology of reification" in "our brave new digital world" that considers contemporary reification's "peculiar rationality and irrationality", "technical dimensions and human particularity". The chapter at hand understands itself as a contribution to this task.

3.2 Ideology and Reified Consciousness

Reification

Reification is *HCC*'s key category. With it, Lukács describes and analyses capitalism's structural effects on human subjectivity and especially consciousness. The notion of reification derives from Marx's concept of commodity fetishism.

DOI: 10.4324/9781003222149-3

"The essence of commodity-structure" is that "a relation between people takes on the character of a thing and thus acquires a 'phantom objectivity', an autonomy that seems so strictly rational and all-embracing as to conceal every trace of its fundamental nature: the relation between people" (Lukács 1971, 83; henceforth referred to as *HCC*). Lukács here refers to a passage in Marx's *Capital Volume 1* (chapter 1, section 1.1), where Marx describes commodities as having a "phantom-like objectivity" (Marx 1867, 128). With the metaphor of the commodity as a ghost, Marx expresses that the commodity's value appears in the money form and the commodity's price, but its substance – the average labour-time that workers have to expend in class relations for the production of the commodity – remains hidden.

Lukács' notion of reification and Marx's concept of alienation have in recent debates featured prominently within philosophy and critical social theory. For example, Rosa (2013) interprets acceleration as a process of alienation. Jaeggi (2014) argues that reification means that human subjects are prevented from appropriating the world and the self. Honneth (2007) is one of the critical theorists who have in recent times worked most directly on actualising Lukács' concept of reification. He argues that reification means society's disrespect and lack of giving recognition to human beings. Building on Lukács and Honneth, Fuchs (2020) has identified exploitation, political oppression, and ideology as economic, political and cultural forms of oppression. This argument is in line with recent works by Harvey (2018), who points out that alienation is a universal process that takes not just place in class relations but in many realms of society. Taken together, these authors show that reification means humans face conditions under which they cannot control these conditions, humans' and society's potentials cannot be realised, and where certain groups instrumentalise others in order to realise partial interests. This understanding of reification is in line with Lukács' outline of reification in *HCC*. His theory remains an important point of reference in 21st-century critical theories of society.

Ideology as Reified Class Consciousness

Class consciousness is "the appropriate and rational reactions 'imputed' [zugerechnet] to a particular typical position in the process of production" (*HCC*, 51). Imputed/ascribed/attributed class consciousness (*zugerechnetes Klassenbewußtsein*) is objective class consciousness (*HCC*, 323). Objective class consciousness is defined by the subject's role in the production process, it is not simply empirical consciousness, but an "objective possibility" of consciousness – the "thoughts and feelings which men would have in a particular situation if they were *able* to assess both it and the interests arising from it in their impact on immediate action and on the whole structure of society" (*HCC*, 51). False consciousness is consciousness that "by-passes the essence of the evolution of society and fails to pinpoint it and express it adequately" (*HCC*, 50).

Ideology has in capitalist society a double nature:

1) Capitalism has an inherent fetishist character because producers and consumers do not experience the entire social relations and process of commodity production in its totality so that the thing-status of the commodity and money hides the underpinning class relations and makes capitalism appear as a natural and infinite system without alternatives;

2) Naturalisation is an important feature of ideologies in general, an important ideological strategy that makes domination appear necessary, timeless, inevitable, and infinite in order to justify and legitimate oppression. For Lukács, ideology is a necessary legitimating feature of capitalism. The "veil drawn over the nature of bourgeois society is indispensable to the bourgeoisie itself. [...] the need to deceive the other classes and to ensure that their class consciousness remain amorphous is inescapable for a bourgeois regime" (*HCC*, 66).

Just like there is the labour of producing ideology conducted by managers, consultants, bourgeois scientists, intellectuals and journalists, etc, there is the ideology of labour: according to Lukács, the ideology of Calvinism is constitutive for "bourgeois reified consciousness with its things-in-themselves in a mythologised but yet quite pure state" (*HCC*, 192).

Ideology partly operates with the reification of language. Lukács quotes Marx from the *German Ideology* and remarks in a footnote: "Marx goes on to make a number of very fine observations about the effects of reification on language. A philological study from the standpoint of historical materialism could profitably begin here" (*HCC*, 209, footnote 16). Marx argues in the passage mentioned by Lukács that capitalism's "relations of buying and selling" penetrate and shape language:

> For example, *propriété* – property [*Eigentum*] and characteristic feature [*Eigenschaft*]; property – possession [*Eigentum*] and peculiarity [*Eigentümlichkeit*]; "*eigen*" ["one's own"] – in the commercial and in the individual sense; *valeur*, value, *Wert*; commerce, Verkehr; *échange*, exchange, *Austausch*, etc., all of which

are used both for commercial relations and for characteristic features and mutual relations of individuals as such. (Marx and Engels 1845/46, 231)

The reified society also brings about reified language. Indicative of this phenomenon is the presence of reified language in the Oxford Dictionary: for example, it defines communication as the "imparting or exchanging of information by speaking, writing, or using some other medium".[1] Exchange is a social relation, in a specific amount of a commodity is exchanged for a particular amount of another commodity: x commodity A = y commodity B (Marx 1867, 163). In communication, you do not expect an "exchange" of 10 words for 10 words. Indeed, one person might utter a sentence consisting of ten words and another person might answer with just one word or a sentence consisting of 20 words. Language is in general, not a commodity, although its objectification can be turned into commodities, as the case of a book that is sold for a particular amount of money shows. The example shows that the commodity form in capitalism not just reifies social relations, but as part of reified social relations also reifies communication and language that mediate the production and reproduction of social relations.

In the English language, "exchange" stems from the Latin word *excambiare*, the Anglo-Norman word *eschanger*, and the Old French verb *eschangier*[2]. During the rise of Mercantilism in the 16th century, "exchange" was established as a common word for the "[p]ractice of merchants or lenders meeting to exchange bill of debt" and "building for mercantile business".[3] Fetishism makes the particular appear as general. Communication is a general feature of all societies, whereas exchange only exists in societies shaped by class, markets, and divisions of labour. The linguistic conflation of exchange as commodity trade and exchange as communication creates the impression that markets are a general necessary feature of all societies. As a consequence of capitalist fetishism's impact on language, the Oxford Dictionary defines exchange simultaneously as a "short conversation or an argument" and "the trading of a particular commodity or commodities", a "system or market in which commercial transactions involving currency, shares, etc. can be carried out", and the "changing of money to its equivalent in the currency of another country".[4]

Lukács wrote *History and Class Consciousness* longest chapter "Reification and the Consciousness of the Proletariat" in 1923. Given that Nazis had not yet come to power

---

1 https://en.oxforddictionaries.com/definition/communication
2 https://en.wiktionary.org/wiki/exchange
3 https://www.etymonline.com/word/exchange
4 https://en.oxforddictionaries.com/definition/exchange

and just five years had passed since the Russian Revolution, Lukács was at this point of time rather optimistic about the potentials of proletarian revolutions. He argues that the bourgeoisie has necessary false consciousness, whereas the proletariat does not automatically have revolutionary consciousness, but has the possibility to see through fetishism. Lukács' political optimism is for example present in formulations such as the ones that the "consciousness of the proletariat is still fettered by reification" (*HCC*, 76) or capitalism keeps "the bourgeoisie imprisoned within this immediacy while forcing the proletariat to go beyond it" (*HCC*, 164).

In the immediate years after the Russian Revolution, optimistic assessments of the proletariat's actuality were certainly more justified than in the years between 1933 and 1945 or today. But *HCC* overall avoids overstressing the actuality of the proletariat's revolutionary consciousness and puts more stress on the proletariat's reified consciousness. Lukács, therefore, speaks of an "ideological crisis of the proletariat in which proletarian ideology lags behind the economic crisis" (*HCC*, *p.*305). Reification is "the necessary, immediate reality of every person living in capitalist society" (*HCC*, 197). "The danger to which the proletariat has been exposed since its appearance on the historical stage was that it might remain imprisoned in its immediacy together with the bourgeoisie" (*HCC*, 196). The proletariat can fail "to take this step" of becoming "the identical subject-object of history whose praxis will change reality". Capitalism constitutes at the same time potentials for the "quantitative increase of the forms of reification" and the "undermining of the forms of reification" (*HCC*, 208).

Revolutionary consciousness is no automatism, the proletariat "can be transformed and liberated only by its own actions" (*HCC*, 208). "History is at its least automatic when it is the consciousness of the proletariat that is at issue" (*HCC*, 208). "Above all the worker can only become conscious of his existence in society when he becomes aware of himself as a commodity" (*HCC*, 168).

Lukács argues that there are three sources of the "bourgeoisification of the proletariat" (*HCC*, 310, *Verbürgerlichung* in the German original): the emergence of privileged sections of the working class (*HCC*, 304–305), the effects of capitalism's structures of reification on consciousness (*HCC*, 310), and the taming influence of reformist social democratic parties and unions. Revisionist social democracy is an ideology with which "the proletariat falls victim to all the antinomies of reification" (*HCC*, 197). For Lukács, the communist party plays an important role in the development of proletarian class consciousness. "The struggle of the Communist Party is focused upon the class consciousness of the proletariat" (*HCC*, 326).

Right-Wing Authoritarianism and New Nationalisms Online: Reified Consciousness on the Internet

Since the new world economic crisis started in 2008, the predominant reaction has not been the strengthening of the political left, but the rise of new nationalism and right-wing authoritarianism (Fuchs 2018a). In many parts of the world, far-right, nationalist ideology finds crucial support among blue-collar workers. Morgan and Lee analysed the relation of voting behaviour and the occupational structure in the USA's 1,142 geographical units (defined by the American Community Survey). The working class was in this analysis defined as consisting of lower-grade service workers, skilled manual workers, unskilled manual workers, farmers, agricultural workers, and individuals without occupation whose highest educational attainment is a high school diploma. The analysis found that

> Trump's gains in 2016, relative to Romney's more generic performance as a near-loss Republican candidate in 2012, were most substantial in areas with the largest percentages of eligible voters who can be identified as members of the white working class. (Morgan and Lee 2018, 239)

> A complementary areal analysis of 1,142 geographic units shows that Trump's gains in 2016 above Romney's performance in 2012 are strongly related to the proportions of the voting population in each geographic unit that was white and working class. This strong relationship holds in the six states that Trump flipped, and it varies little across other types of states. […] the results […] of our analysis support the claim that Trump's appeal to the white working class was crucial to his victory. (Morgan and Lee 2018, 240)

Similar developments of far-right, nationalist politicians and parties succeeding in elections can be found in many countries. In many cases, blue-collar workers strongly support these types of politics (see Fuchs 2018a), which is an indication that since 2008, there has been an intensification and extension of the tendency that nationalist ideology reifies blue-collar workers consciousness: a significant share of this part of the working class succumbs to the ideology that not class relations and capitalism, but immigrants, refugees and other nations are the cause of inequality and social problems. Nationalist and racist ideologies present a constructed conflict between nations and constructed conflicts between cultures as stratifying divisions in order to distract attention from the class conflict between capital and labour that has in the past decades resulted in rising profit and capital shares (the share of profits and capital in the gross domestic product) at the expense of the wage share (the share of wages in the gross domestic product) (Fuchs 2018a).

Social media such as Facebook and Twitter are key communication tools of contemporary right-wing politics. In the past couple of years, analyses of the right-wing use of the Internet have become more important (see e.g. Ernst et al. 2017; Müller and Schulz 2019; Stier et al. 2017), which is a consequence of the global proliferation of what Lukács termed reified consciousness. Nationalists communicate four aspects of right-wing authoritarianism over online media: top-down leadership, nationalism, the friend/enemy-scheme, and the need for militant measures against the constructed enemies (Fuchs 2018a).

Let us have a look at an example: Breitbart is a far-right online news portal that frequently features nationalist propaganda and has supported Donald Trump. Its former executive chairman Steven Bannon was the chief executive officer of Trump's presidential campaign and the Trump-executive's White House Chief Strategist from January until August 2017. But the relations between Trump and Breitbart are older than that. On 11 July 2014, Breitbart published an article by Trump titled "A Country That Cannot Protect its Borders Will Not Last". Trump wrote in this article:

> USMC [United States Marine Corps] Sgt. Tahmooressi sacrificed for our country, and while Obama is welcoming illegals, our Marine is locked in a Mexican jail. Mexico is allowing tens of thousands to go through their country and to our very stupid "open door" at the Mexican border. Frankly, Sgt. Tahmooressi is the only person who can't come into our country! [...] It's clear to me that a country that cannot protect its borders will not last. What about the people at home? We are not caring for our own. [...] We cannot, as a nation, continue this way. The underlying fear now is that Obama has planned it that way. [...] The problem is easy to solve with leadership. We don't have leadership in any capable capacity. It is a sad time for America. (Trump 2014)

In order to promote his piece, Trump shared a link to it on Twitter (see Figure 3.1). The background to this article is that former Marine Corps sergeant Andrew Tahmooressi was jailed in Mexico after he illegally crossed the border with three loaded guns in his car. All four elements of right-wing authoritarian ideology are present in Trump's piece:

- The friend/enemy-scheme: Trump constructs a national conflict between Mexico and the USA. Mexico is said to allow illegal immigrants to cross into the USA and to jail American soldiers. The channelling of immigrants and the jailing of a former soldier, who was put into prison not in his role as soldier, but as a private individual allegedly violating Mexican law, are presented as Mexican practices that harm US citizens;

- Nationalism: Trump constructs a national "we"-identity of US citizens that is directed against Mexico by speaking of "our country", "our Marine", "our own" interest, or "we as a nation". Trump presents us/them-difference, where "we" US-Americans are opposed to Mexicans and "their country";

- Militarism: Trump speaks of "our Marine" who "is locked in a Mexican jail" in order to argue that US soldiers are individuals of highest honour because they take up arms to enforce US interests. Trump in general idolises soldiers and the military. In his ideology, the soldier is the ideal type of a human being. Whereas he considers US state violence as appropriate, he decries the use of Mexican law against US citizens, implying that it is unjust to prosecute US soldiers for breaking Mexican laws. Trump fuses militarism with nationalism and racist prejudices in order to create the impression that there is a national conflict between Mexico and the USA;

- Strong leadership: Finally, Trump argues that Illegal immigration and the alleged destruction of the US nation ("a country that cannot protect its borders will not last") is due to Obama's alleged weak leadership ("We don't have leadership in any capable capacity") and "open door"-policy "at the Mexican border". Trump implicitly suggests that he himself would be a strong leader ("The problem is easy to solve with leadership") and thereby anticipated his own candidacy in the 2016 US presidential election.

In order to be effective, ideologies need to be reproduced in the form of a constant flow of tabloid news, scandals, revelations, etc. Right-wing forces make use of social media for spreading the ideologies of top-down leadership, nationalism, the friend/enemy-scheme, and militarism/law & order-politics. Social media is a suited medium for spreading fake news and far-right propaganda because it is brief and superficial, operates at high speed, can reach a vast number of potential users in a short time by making postings spread in a networked information space, supports the amplification of emotions in the form of "likes" and other emoticons, and appeals to individuals' interest in sensationalism. The tabloid-like structure of Twitter, Facebook, and YouTube supports the online spread of right-wing ideology. Capitalist social media have tolerated right-wing propaganda because vast flows of content and data promise higher profits from targeted ads. Social media is not the cause of

FIGURE 3.1   Donald Trump promotes a Breitbart-piece he wrote on Twitter

the proletariat's reified consciousness in the contemporary world, but it is one of the communication tools that right-wing demagogues employ for spreading their ideologies. The very cause of the rise of the far-right is that capitalist politics have backfired and created a negative dialectic, in which the freedom of the market has intensified fears and inequalities that express themselves in support for far-right ideologies, politicians, movements, and parties. Of course, also democrats and left-wing activists use social media for trying to challenge far-right ideology and communicate different stories and worldviews. But without a doubt, right-wing authoritarian ideology has contributed to a sustained reification of the proletariat's consciousness so that the rootedness of social problems in capitalism's very structure is veiled.

Anti-fascists and anti-racists contest right-wing authoritarianism online. There are not just the likes of Breitbart on social media, but also groups and individuals such as Hope Not Hate (around 100k followers on Twitter), Democratic Socialists of America (around 250k Twitter-followers), Black Lives Matter (around 350k Twitter-followers), National Association for the Advancement of Colored People (around 450k Twitter-followers), etc. that challenge racism and right-wing extremism and run online campaigns. An example is the International Day Against Fascism and Antisemitism (9 November) that uses hashtags such as #SpeakUpNow, #FightFascism, #9November, #DayAgainstFascism, and #DayAgainstAntisemitism.

The next section will based on *HCC* discuss the relationship of journalism and reification and will relate *HCC* to digital phenomena such as social media, online fake news, targeted advertising, algorithms, and political bots.

Ideology and Reified Consciousness

3.3 Journalism and Reification

Lukács on Journalism

Ideology does not exist independent from human beings but must be constantly produced and reproduced in social relations. Lukács mentions bourgeois journalists as producers of ideology. By "bourgeois" journalists, we mean journalists who create stories that reify capitalism and domination with the help of various ideological strategies. Bourgeois journalism is a particular type of ideological labour, labour that creates ideological news stories.

Lukács argues that physical workers experience reification relatively directly. Their labour "directly possesses the naked and abstract form of the commodity, while in other forms of work this [reification] is hidden behind the façade of 'mental labour', of 'responsibility', etc." (*HCC*, 172). "The more deeply reification penetrates into the soul of the man who sells his achievement as a commodity the more deceptive appearances are (as in the case of journalism)" (*HCC*, 172). Journalists' love of their work and their ethos as democracy's fourth estate that guarantees freedom of expression and opinion and tries to make power transparent and tries to prevent the abuse of power, can easily veil their status as wage-workers.

In *HCC*, Lukács remarks in one passage: "The journalist's 'lack of convictions', the prostitution of his experiences and beliefs is comprehensible only as the apogee of capitalist reification" (*HCC*, 100). As a result, the news produced by bourgeois journalism often reifies capitalism and domination. In a footnote to the passage just cited, Lukács (*HCC*, 210, footnote 24) refers to an essay by Béla Fogarasi (without mentioning its title). Fogarasi (1891–1959) was like Lukács a member of the Hungarian Communist Party. They were both members of the "Sunday Circle", an intellectual discussion group that existed from 1915 until 1918 in Budapest. Fogarasi's (1921/1983) essay "Tasks of the Communist Press", to which Lukács refers, was published in 1921.

The essay distinguishes between the capitalist and the communist press and argues that the capitalist press is "an ideological weapon in the class struggle" (p. 149) utilised by the bourgeoisie in order to dominate "the ideology of the ensemble of classes" (p. 149).

> What the capitalist press seeks is to shape the structure of the reader's consciousness in such a way that he will be perpetually unable to distinguish

between true and false, to relate causes and effects, to place individual facts in their total context, to rationally integrate new knowledge into his perspective. (Fogarasi 1921/1983, 150)

Fogarasi implicitly applies Lukács' critique of reified consciousness to the capitalist press. In the capitalist press, the focus is often not on the dialectic of totality, particularity, and individuality, but merely on individual, isolated pieces of news. According to Fogarasi, strategies of the capitalist press include to report a multitude of isolated facts that shall quench the readers' thirst for knowledge, de-politicisation, and sensationalism that work systematically in the service of distraction, and pseudo-objectivity. In contrast, the communist press tries to advance the consciousness of society as totality and of the relation of single events with each other and broader contexts, the unmasking of the capitalist press, and the participation of readers as producers of reports.

Fogarasi not just applied Lukács' concepts of reification and the totality to journalism, but also in 1921 anticipated Benjamin's (1934, 777) idea of turning "consumers [...] into producers" and "readers or spectators into collaborators" as well as Brecht's (1932, 42) idea of a radio that lets "the listener speak as well as hear". Fogarasi's essay also points out aspects of ideology in the media that resonate with Lukács notions of ideology and reified consciousness.

The next two sub-sections will show that Lukács' analyses of news and journalism as reified consciousness remain topical in the contemporary age of the Internet, social media, and fake news.

The New Spirit of Capitalism

In contemporary capitalism, creative workers' love of the content of their labour and the high degree of self-determination has become a new ideology that veils the fact that those, who can do what they love, often do so under precarious conditions. Boltanski and Chiapello (2005) speak in this context of the "new spirit of capitalism". The new spirit of capitalism is a management ideology that promises to workers to conduct labour that features "autonomy, spontaneity, rhizomorphous capacity, multi-tasking (in contrast to the narrow specialization of the old division of labour), conviviality, openness to others and novelty, availability, creativity, visionary intuition, sensitivity to differences, listening to lived experience and receptiveness to a whole range of experiences, being attracted to informality and the search for interpersonal contacts" – qualities that "are taken directly from the repertoire of May 1968" (Boltanski and Chiapello 2005, 97).

The new spirit of capitalism promises to knowledge workers less alienated labour, by which they can live the life of an artist, celebrity, or journalist. A range of studies has shown that knowledge workers in media industries see their labour as highly creative, self-determined and self-fulfilling, but that it is at the same time often highly precarious[5] Gill (2011) summarises the results of such studies by identifying ten features of cultural and media labour: such labour is often characterised by (1) love of the work, (2) the entrepreneurial aspiration to innovate and pioneer, (3) is often short-term, precarious and insecure, (4) is characterised by low pay and (5) long hours, (6) requires that workers constantly develop their knowledge and skills, (7) is based on DIY learning and (8) informality, (9) features inequalities relating to gender, age, class, race, ethnicity and disability, and (10) deprives workers of the time and resources necessary to plan their future.

Cultural and media labour *appears* to be less reified and alienated than manual labour, but is often organised as precarious freelancing that does not provide adequate social, job, and income security. The ideology of conducting labour that is creative and innovative can reify the consciousness of cultural workers so that they do not see themselves as workers, but entrepreneurs, are hostile to unionisation, see precarity as their individual fault and not a class relation imposed by capitalism, etc. The new spirit of capitalism is a new ideology that reifies labour by creating the appearance of de-alienation and at the same time imposes highly individualised working conditions that undermine social and income security. It is a new form of alienation that appears to be unalienated. Whether workers' reaction to this new ideology is reified or non-reified consciousness, depends among several factors on the question whether they can be collectively politically organised and develop critical consciousness that lets them see through the capitalist reality behind the false appearances.

Especially young precarious workers in the cultural sector have tried to fight back against neoliberalism by reinvigorating the cooperative movement. Cultural co-operatives are self-managed companies that are collectively owned and governed by their workers (see http://cultural.coop/) (Sandoval 2016). In the realm of the Internet, there have been experiments with platform co-operatives (Scholz and Schneider 2016).

---

5 For an overview see the contributions in Maxwell (2016).

The Age of Online Fake News

Advertising-funded media focus on sensationalism and entertainment in order to attract and sell audiences and tend to feature pro-capitalist and conservative worldviews. Google, Facebook, and Twitter use targeted advertising, which allows to personalise and individualise ads with the help of digital surveillance and big data analytics. The Cambridge Analytica scandal has shown how the targeted ad-based model of digital capitalism collides with democracy: in 2013, University of Cambridge neuroscientist Aleksandr Kogan began to use Facebook's developer platform in order to conduct a personality quiz. As a result, personal data of around 90 million users was collected and sold to Cambridge Analytica, a company whose vice-president was Steve Bannon. Cambridge Analytica used the data for targeting users with fake news in election campaigns, which has been widely seen as the attempt to manipulate democracy. In the light of Cambridge Analytica, critical studies of online fake news and post-truth online have proliferated (see e.g. Duffy et al. 2019; Humprecht 2019; Carlson 2020). Facebook has as a consequence come under public scrutiny in 2018 because it seems to have known about the use of its targeting mechanism for anti-democratic activities. Targeted online advertising allows large corporations to manipulate and colonise the public sphere by using their advertising budgets for targeting users with corporate and political propaganda. In the online world, native advertising and branded content make it difficult to discern advertising from editorial content, which undermines journalistic autonomy.

Selective sourcing that benefits elites and the capitalist class constitutes a news filter. Online communication other than mass media is based on a decentralised communication infrastructure, where in principle everyone can produce and disseminate information. In the online world, the power hierarchy and class structuration shift from the production of content to the production of visibility and attention. Corporations, celebrities, traditional and new elites dominate online visibility and online attention (see Fuchs 2017, 122–128). For example, in July 2018 Luis Fonsi's music video "Despacito" was with 5 billion and 368 million views the most accessed YouTube video of all time.[6] Universal Music Latin Entertainment, a division of the Universal Music Group that is owned by Vivendi, is the publisher of Fonsi's song and video, which shows that big multimedia corporations play a dominant role on YouTube. Given that corporate social media are advertising-based,

6 https://www.youtube.com/watch?v=kJQP7kiw5Fk, accessed on 29 July 2018.

attention can be purchased as a commodity, which benefits wealthy corporations and individuals.

Fake news is as old as the tabloid press, but in the online world fake news can spread quickly, can be individually targeted, and it is often hard to distinguish if online behaviour in the context of fake news is conducted by humans or algorithms. Right-wing movements try to make use of social media for spreading their propaganda and challenging socialist and liberal political positions and worldviews online. They not just use bots and traditional lobbying methods online, but often also resort to threats, bullying, and hate speech.

Bourgeois media often, but not exclusively spread ideology. In section three, we have already seen an example of how nationalist and xenophobic ideology is spread online. Ideology on the Internet tends to be visual and tabloidised. It makes use of strategies such as simplification, the use of only a few words, emotionalisation, scandalisation, polarisation, banalisation, manipulation, fabrication, etc. User-generated ideology means that the labour of producing ideology is not confined to professional ideologues, but has penetrated everyday life. Ideologies are sensational, populist, simplistic, emotional, and directly address particular groups. Algorithms amplify the views of those who gain high levels of attention. As a consequence, we find the online tendency of the algorithmic amplification of online ideologies.

The actions of corporations, celebrities, and political elites result in the colonisation of the public sphere. These processes also operate in the online world and on social media, where targeted advertising, algorithms, big data, political bots, fake online news, digital surveillance, and other mechanisms are used and result in the corporate and political stratification of the Internet.

Fake news has been challenged by developments such as fact-checking organisations and the quest for building a public service Internet that consists of non-commercial platforms that do not have a for-profit imperative but want to benefit the public by reliable news, information, and educational resources that are provided online and engage users (Fuchs 2018a, 2018b).

In the next section, we will see that communication technologies are not just a medium for the communication and challenging of reified thought, but also form an object of reification. Lukács' work will be used for showing how one can analyse ideologies of the Internet and digital media.

3.4 The Reification of Communication Technologies

Lukács on Intellectual Workers

In the essay *"Intellectual Workers" and the Problem of Intellectual Leadership*, written in 1919, Lukács (2014, 12–18) argues that intellectual workers do not form a separate class. Those "who, like manual workers, are able to participate in production only by means of their labour power (white-collar workers, engineers, etc.)" differ

> sharply from those whose intellectual work is only an accessory to their bourgeois status (major share-holders, factory owners). The class distinction between these two groups is so clear to the objective observer that it is impossible to bring them together under one heading, as the class of "intellectual workers". (Lukács 2014, 12)

"Those 'intellectual workers' who participate in production therefore belong (*with an unclear class consciousness, at best*) to the same class as the manual workers" (Lukács 2014, 13). Intellectual workers are not "a *homogeneously structured class*, since even within their ranks a clear division into oppressors and oppressed" (Lukács 2014, 13) can be found.

Knowledge Workers in the Information Society

In discussions of the "information society" (Webster 2014), a distinction among the agricultural sector, the manufacturing sector, and the service sector is frequently made. As part of this division, information and knowledge workers are often said to form a distinct group within the service sector. The problem of this argument is, as Lukács indicates, that managers who sustain the control of workers and represent the capitalist interest are said to share the same position in the production process as productive knowledge workers, who directly create commodities that are sold in order to yield profit.

Today, the class character of knowledge workers has become even more complex because many creative workers have the status of freelancers: they sell their labour via one-time contracts and do not have the capital necessary to employ others. Freelancing is especially prevalent among knowledge workers such as data inputters, software and web developers, designers, translators, writers, personal assistants, editors, and proofreaders. Such workers sell their labour-power and yield profit for others. As long as a freelancer does not form a business that besides him- or herself also employs others, there is no doubt that s/he is part of the working class. Journalists are either wage-workers or, increasingly, freelancers. Their position in the production process on the one hand makes them part of the working class. But journalists, consultants, and others who serve, as Lukács writes, "material, ideological and power interests" (Lukács 2014, 13) by justifying capitalist interests in their writings, are just like managers part of the ruling class. Only the critical journalists, who investigate capitalism critically, is fully part of the working class and not part of the ruling class.

Fake news has been challenged by developments such as fact-checking organisations and the quest for building a public service Internet that consists of non-commercial platforms that do not have a for-profit imperative but want to benefit the public by reliable news, information, and educational resources that are provided online and engage users (Fuchs 2018a, 2018b).

Lukács' Critique of Technological Fetishism in the Age of Big Data Capitalism

There are not just ideologies that are communicated with the help of technologies, but also ideologies of technologies. In respect to digital technologies, we do not just find ideologies on the Internet, but also ideologies of the Internet. Lukács does not use the term "technological fetishism", but describes how technologies are turned into fetish objects. He speaks of "the exploitation for particular human ends (as in technology, for example) of [...] fatalistically accepted and immutable laws" (*HCC*, 38). Technological fetishism distorts the machine's "true objective nature by representing its function in the capitalist production process as its 'eternal' essence" (*HCC*, 153).

In the age of digital capitalism, digital technologies such as the Internet, social media platforms, the mobile phone, big data technologies, the Internet of Things, cloud computing, industry 4.0/industrial Internet, etc. are often treated as technological fetishes in bourgeois thought. Let us consider an example. The business press is in general a good source for observing the newest trends in bourgeois ideology.

In May 2017, *The Economist* ran a cover story under the title "The World's Most Valuable Resource is no Longer Oil, but Data": "A NEW commodity spawns a lucrative, fast-growing industry. [...] A century ago, the resource in question was oil. Now similar concerns are being raised by the giants that deal in data, the oil of the digital era" (*The Economist* 2017). Google, Amazon, Apple, Facebook, and Microsoft are "titans" that "look unstoppable". "The giants' success has benefited consumers. Few want to live without Google's search engine, Amazon's one-day delivery or Facebook's newsfeed". "Algorithms can predict when a customer is ready to buy, a jet-engine needs servicing or a person is at risk of a disease". *Fortune* published an interview on big data with Intel's CEO Brian Krzanich. He said: "Oil changed the world in the 1900s. It drove cars, it drove the whole chemical industry. [...] Data, I look at it as the new oil. It's going to change most industries across the board" (Gharib 2018). Artificial Intelligence-based data is "not just gonna change business, it's gonna change every person on this planet's life in some positive way". "I think if you go and talk to the employees, they've never seen the company on this level of pace of change and competitiveness. But I don't think you can ever stand still and say that it's fast enough in this technology world".

These examples show some typical features of technological fetishism:

- Autonomy: Technology is presented as being autonomous from society's power structures. Technology is not situated in society as totality. In the two examples, there is predominantly a focus on how new technologies such as big data technologies and Artificial Intelligence positively change society without a focus on how they are embedded into class structures, exploitation, and domination;
- Subjectivity: Technology and not humans are presented as a subject that acts ("Oil changes", etc., Data is "going to change most industries", AI "changes every person on this planet's life"). The purpose of this strategy is to reify technological developments as inevitable, unchangeable, unavoidable and irreversible by presenting them as independent from human will and action;
- Revolution: Technological developments are presented as revolutionary, as taking place rapidly and as changing everything ("Data" as the "new oil", "data, the oil of the digital era", "this level of pace of change" is never "fast enough in this technology world"). The goal of this strategy of presentation is that humans do not question undoing certain technologies or aspects of them;
- Technology as one-dimensional cause, digital determinism: Technology is said to be the cause of changes in society ("it's gonna change every person on this planet's life in some positive way"). Power structures and social contradictions are disregarded;
- Technological optimism/pessimism: Changes in society that stand in the context of technology are said to be either purely positive (technological optimism) or purely negative (technological pessimism). In the examples, it is for example claimed that big data "has benefited consumers. Few want to live without" it. Or

The Reification of Communication Technologies

that algorithms can predict when a person is "at risk of a disease" and "change every person's [...] life in some positive way". There is no talk about actual or potential harms such as algorithmic surveillance, algorithmic discrimination, disadvantages arising from errors and false predictions, etc.

Lukács' Critique of Quantification

In *HCC*, Lukács develops a critique of the logic of quantification that he sees at the heart of reified thought and bourgeois consciousness. It lies in the "nature of capitalism to" reduce "the phenomena to their purely quantitative essence, to their expression in numbers and numerical relations" (*HCC*, 6). Capitalism uses the sciences in order to assess and optimise investments, labour-time, capital accumulation, commodities, power, etc. Capitalism is the society of accumulation that is based on the logic of capital, which is transferred into different realms of society, such as politics and culture, in order to accumulate not just money, but also decision-power and definition-power. In order to accumulate, you need to assess existing quantities as foundation for identifying strategies of how to increase them. At the end of the process, the result is quantified in order to identify strategies of what to do when the accumulation process starts all over again. Capitalism has to develop ever newer forms of rationalisation and new methods of production in order to increase productivity, reduce costs and accumulate capital. The history of capitalist technology is therefore a history of rationalisation and the development of ever newer methods of quantification.

> If we follow the path taken by labour in its development from the handicrafts via co-operation and manufacture to machine industry we can see a continuous trend towards greater rationalisation, the progressive elimination of the qualitative, human and individual attributes of the worker. (*HCC*, 88)

Modern philosophy has developed together with technologies of rationalisation (*HCC*, 113). Lukács argues that reification's reduction of totalities to partialities is not limited to the economy, but also affects bureaucracy, the state, the law, and culture (*HCC*, 98–100).

The logic of computing is reductionist and anti-dialectical: "The methodology of the natural sciences which forms the methodological ideal of every fetishistic science and every kind of Revisionism reject the idea of contradiction and antagonism in its subject matter" (*HCC*, 10). Mathematical logic cannot see "the whole system at once" (*HCC*, 117). It reduces explanations to basic principles (reductionism) and believes in the exact predictability and calculability of the world (determinism) (*HCC*, 117). Lukács (*HCC*, 89–90) quotes Marx in order to show capitalism's fetishism of quantification: "Time is everything, man is nothing; he is, at the most, time's carcase. Quality no longer matters. Quantity alone decides everything; hour for hour, day for day" (Marx 1847, 127). Lukács writes: "Thus time sheds its qualitative, variable, flowing nature; it freezes into an exactly delimited, quantifiable continuum filled with quantifiable 'things' (the reified, mechanically objectified 'performance' of the worker, whole separated from his total human personality)" (*HCC*, 90). In the essay *The Question of Educational Work* (first published in 1921), Lukács (2014, 91–92) argues that the bourgeois belief in the power of quantification and the natural sciences was reflected in the mechanical determinism advanced by both bourgeois economics and revisionist social democracy. Critical thought, in contrast, has to do "away completely with all forms of fatalism" (Lukács 2014, 93). It stresses human qualities such as the capacity of humans to change the world.

Freelancers not just face a peculiar form of exploitation, but have also self-organised in order to resist precarity. As a result, unions such as the Freelancer's Union and the Independent Workers' Union have been created that put an emphasis on being platforms for self-organised struggles of freelancers and other non-traditional workers.

Lukács' Critique of Quantification Revisited: the Critique of Big Data Analytics

Big data analytics is the newest methodological trend of quantification in almost all academic fields. It is a method that gathers large amounts of data and applies algorithms and mathematical analysis (such as correlation analysis) to this data in order to identify patterns, relations, correlations and predict behaviour that allows "to monitor, manage, and control citizens" (Mosco 2017, 8). As a reaction to the rise of big data, a series of critical studies of big data analytics and its implications for society has emerged (see e.g. Andrejevic 2014; Beer 2018; Boyd and Crawford 2012; Couldry and Mejias 2019; Chandler and Fuchs 2019; Van Dijck et al. 2018).

Big data analytics' fetishism of quantification has led uncritical tech enthusiasts such as the former editor of the neoliberal *Wired* magazine Anderson (2008) to argue that big data results in the "end of theory": "With enough data, the numbers speak for themselves [...] [When] faced with massive data, this [traditional] approach to science – hypothesize, model, test–is becoming obsolete. [...]".

Big data positivism's quantitative methodology disregards the qualitative aspects of the analysis of society, such as ethics, morals, critique, theory, emotions, affects, motivations, worldviews, interpretations, political assessments, power, social struggles, or contradictions. The danger is that big data analytics advances uncritical, instrumental knowledge that serves dominant interests in the execution of capitalist rule and domination. Another danger of big data analytics is that the social sciences and humanities are colonised by a combination of computer science and business studies that tries to root out critical thinking and critical theory by instrumental big data reason. Big data analytics is one of the newest developments in the history of tools of reification that Lukács analyses and criticises.

Chen et al.'s (2012) article is one of the most cited articles that contain "big data" in the title[7]. The authors identify big data analytics as "business intelligence and analytics (BI&A) 3.0" that follows after the two stages of BI&A 1.0 (statistical analysis and data mining applied to structured data collected through enterprise systems) and BI&A 2.0 (text and web analytics applied to unstructured web contents).

> [B]ig data and big data analytics have been used to describe the data sets and analytical techniques in applications that are so large (from terabytes to exabytes) and complex (from sensor to social media data) that they require advanced and unique data storage, management, analysis, and visualization technologies. (Chen et al. 2012, 1166)

The authors argue that big data analytics will have "big impact" (Chen et al. 2012, 1168) on society. They list purely positive impacts in the realms of the economy, politics, science and technology, health and wellbeing, and security and public safety that include "increased sale and customer satisfaction", the improvement of "transparency, participation, and equality", increased "scientific impact", "[i]mproved healthcare quality", and "[i]mproved public safety and security". Chen, Chiang, and Story's article is typical for mainstream research on big data: it is the expression of highly reified thought that argues that pure quantification as represented by big data analytics will radically transform society and only have positive impacts that will improve life in society in many respects. Possible negative consequences are not analysed and discussed, which is the consequence of the abstraction of the analysis from society as totality and its social relations of power.

---

7 ISI Web of Knowledge: search conducted on July 29, 2018: With 863 citations, the article was the second most cited work containing "big data" in the title.

Big data analytics tends to forget about class and domination. Its fetishism of quantification sees society as a thing constituted by large quantities of data and disregards the social qualities that make up society. Big data analytics is what Lukács describes as a "fetishistic science" that disregards "contradiction and antagonism" (*HCC*, 10) and the totality.

Big data analytics is certainly a major trend in research and academia. Its digital positivism has, however, been challenged by approaches such as critical digital and social media studies, critical digital sociology, and critical digital humanities (Fuchs 2017; Lupton 2015; Berry and Fagerjord 2017).

3.5 Conclusion

We can summarise this chapter's key results:

- In *HCC*, Lukács conceives of society based on a dialectic of subject and object that avoids the pitfalls of voluntarist spontaneism and mechanist fatalism. In later works, he clarified the mediating role of language and communication in the dialectic of subject and object: communication is the mediating process in the dialectic of subject of object that produces and reproduces social relations. There is a dialectic of work and communication (communication at work, the work of communication);

- Lukács shows in *HCC* that the reification of consciousness has objective foundations in capitalism's commodity structures and forms an element of ideologies that justify capitalism by naturalising structures and practices of domination. In contemporary capitalism, social media have become a medium of communication, where reified thought is communicated and challenged. Especially the communication of right-wing authoritarian ideologies and its elements of strong leadership, nationalism, the friend-enemy-schema, and militarism is prevalent on corporate social media such as Twitter, Facebook, and YouTube;

- Cultural and media labour constitutes a new form of reification: by fostering creativity and self-determined labour, it appears as and creates an aura of non-alienated labour that deflects attention from the fact that such labour is often highly insecure and precarious;

- Private ownership/profit-orientation, advertising, and ideology operate in new ways in the realm of social media and on the Internet, which results in the colonisation of the online public sphere by the interests of corporations, celebrities, and political elites;

- Lukács' critique of reification entails a critique of technological fetishism and the logic of quantification. In digital capitalism, this analysis matters in several respects, including the critique of digital determinism and digital positivism;
- Digital determinism fetishises digital technologies by presenting them as autonomous subjects that bring about revolutionary technological changes of society that are either purely positive or purely negative;
- Big data analytics is one of the newest developments in the history of tools of reification that Lukács analyses and criticises. Big data analytics is a form of digital positivism and fetishistic science that disregards qualities, contradictions, and totalities. It advances uncritical, instrumental knowledge that serves dominant interests by being used as a tool of reification.

History and Class Consciousness' critique of reification, ideology, and reified consciousness remains highly topical in the age of digital capitalism and big data. Lukács' analysis allows us to critically analyse how social media, big data, and various other Internet technologies are used as tools of reification. Those new technologies are deeply embedded into capitalist and dominative structures does however not imply that there are no alternative potentials and no alternative forces at work in the realm of digital technologies. Lukács opposed deterministic analyses, which implies that although exploitation and domination are ubiquitous in capitalism, there is always the possibility for critical consciousness and critical action (praxis).

In reified computing and technology, the instrumental logic of quantification, capital, and bureaucracy subsumes human activities and destroys solidarity. At the same time, modern technology has created new potentials for co-operation and socialisation. Computing operates at different levels. A socialist framework of society and technology does not need to abolish computing but needs to transform its design so that technologies are human-centred, humans in collective processes control the design and use of technology, and quantification is subsumed under the logic of human-centredness. For example, socialist design does not mean to abolish social media, but to make them truly social so that privacy violations, intransparent algorithms, targeted advertising, individualism, and the accumulation of reputation are no longer design principles and are substituted by privacy-friendliness, direct human communication, collective production, co-operation, solidarity, creative commons and transparency and the openness of algorithms as design principles.

Digital technologies such as the Internet are today also used by activists for challenging exploitation and domination (Fuchs 2014). Digital commons projects such as

Wikipedia and alternative online media (e.g. Democracy Now! and Alternet) challenge the capitalist shaping of digital technologies. Furthermore, there are potentials for public service Internet platforms and platform co-operatives that challenge the logic of the corporate digital giants (Fuchs 2018b). These are attempts to create a non-reified, commons-based and public and commons-based digital media landscape. One crucial lesson we can learn from Lukács is that revolutionising the digital media landscape so that the capitalist Internet can be transcended towards a commons-based Internet can neither be achieved by technology nor by single individuals, but only by critically conscious humans who organise themselves as political collectives and engage in class struggles that transform technology and society. Only human praxis can create a commons-based Internet and a socialist society.

Lukács stresses that the creation of workers' councils is a form of class struggle that "spells the political and economic defeat of reification" (*HCC*, 80). In the digital age, where users are producers and there is a variety of digital workers, the creation of platform co-operatives that are owned by workers and users as well as public service Internet platforms that are publicly owned are part of the struggle of the working class against digital capital's power. In addition, we today find the use of social media and apps as communicative weapons in social struggles. Examples are the use of social media in various Occupy movements (Fuchs 2014) and in the Chinese working class' struggles against corporations such as Foxconn (Qiu 2016). Another important realm of class struggle in digital capitalism is the demands of gig economy workers for better working conditions that are voiced with the help of the Internet (see e.g. Cant 2020; Ravenelle 2019; Woodcock 2019). Digital media today are not just tools of reification, but also tools of class struggles by which the contemporary digital proletariat has the opportunity to perfect "*itself by annihilating and transcending itself, by creating the classless society through the successful conclusion of its own class struggle*" (*HCC*, 80).

References

Anderson, Chris. 2008. The End of Theory: The Data Deluge Makes the Scientific Method Obsolete. *Wired Magazine* 16 (7), 23 June 2008.

Andrejevic, Mark. 2014. The Big Data Divide. *International Journal of Communication* 8: 1673–1689.

Benjamin, Walter. 1934. The Author as Producer. In *Walter Benjamin: Selected Writings Volume 2, Part 2, 1931-1934*, 768–782. Cambridge, MA: Belknap Press.

Beer, David. 2018. Envisioning the Power of Data Analytics. *Information, Communication & Society* 21 (3): 465–479.

Berry, David M. and Anders Fagerjord. 2017. *Digital Humanities: Knowledge and Critique in a Digital Age*. Cambridge: Polity.

Boltanski, Luc and Chiapello, Ève. 2005. *The New Spirit of Capitalism*. London: Verso.

Boyd, Danah and Kate Crawford, K. 2012. Critical Questions for Big Data. *Information, Communication & Society* 15 (5): 662–679.

Brecht, Bertolt. 1932. The Radio as a Communications Apparatus. In *Bertolt Brecht on Film & Radio*, 41–46. London: Bloomsbury.

Cant, Callum. 2020. *Riding for Deliveroo: Resistance in the new economy*. Cambridge: Polity.

Carlson, Matt. 2020. Fake News as an Informational Moral Panic. *Information, Communication & Society* 23 (3): 374–388.

Chandler, David and Christian Fuchs, eds. 2019. *Digital Objects, Digital Subjects. Interdisciplinary Perspectives on Capitalism, Labour and Politics in the Age of Big Data*. London: University of Westminster Press. 10.16997/book29

Chen, Hsinchun, Roger H. L. Chiang, and Veda C. Storey. 2012. Business Intelligence and Analytics: From Big Data to Big Impact. *MIS Quarterly* 36 (4): 1165–1188.

Couldry, Nick and Ulises A. Mejias. 2019. *The Costs of Connection*. Stanford, CA: Stanford University Press.

Dannemann, Rüdiger. 2017. Georg Lukács Theory of Reification and the Idea of Socialism. *Contours Journal* 8, http://www.sfu.ca/humanities-institute/contours/issue8/theory/3.html

Duffy, Andrew, Edson Tandoc, and Rich Ling. 2019. Too Good to be True, Too Good to Share: The Social Utility of Fake News. *Information, Communication & Society* 23 (13): 1965–1979.

Ernst, Nicole et al. 2017. Extreme Parties and Populism. *Information, Communication & Society* 20 (9): 1347–1364.

Fogarasi, Bela. 1921. Aufgaben der kommunistischen Presse. *Kommunismus: Zeitschrift der Kommunistischen Internationale für die Länder Südosteuropas* 2 (25/26): 845–854.

Fuchs, Christian. 2020. *Communication and Capitalism. A Critical Theory*. London: University of Westminster Press.

Fuchs, Christian. 2018a. *Digital Demagogue. Authoritarian Capitalism in the Age of Trump and Twitter*. London: Pluto Press.

Fuchs, Christian. 2018b. *The Online Advertising Tax as the Foundation of a Public Service Internet*. London: University of Westminster Press. 10.16997/book23

Fuchs, Christian. 2017. *Social Media. A Critical Introduction*, 2nd edn. London: Sage.

Fuchs, Christian. 2014. *OccupyMedia! The Occupy Movement and Social Media in Crisis Capitalism*. Winchester: Zero Books.

Gharib, Susie. 2018. Intel CEO Says Data is the New Oil. *Fortune Online*, June 7, 2018. https://fortune.com/2018/06/07/intel-ceo-brian-krzanich-data/ (accessed 23 July 2021).

Gill, Rosalind. 2011. "Life is a Pitch": Managing the Self in New Media Work. In *Managing Media Work*, ed. Mark Deuze, 249–262. London: Sage.

Harvey, David. 2018. Universal Alienation. *tripleC: Communication, Capitalism & Critique* 16 (2): 424–439.

Honneth, Axel. 2007. *Disrespect: The Normative Foundations of Critical Theory*. Cambridge: Polity.

Humprecht, Edda. 2019. Where "Fake News" Flourishes. *Information, Communication & Society* 22 (13): 1973–1988.

Jaeggi, Rahel. 2014. *Alienation*. New York: Columbia University Press.

Lukács, Georg. 2014. *Tactics and Ethics, 1919-1929*. London: Verso.

Lukács, Georg. 1971. *History and Class Consciousness (HCC)*. London: Merlin.

Lupton, Deborah. 2015. *Digital Sociology*. London: Routledge.

Marx, Karl. 1867. *Capital Volume I. MECW Volume 35*. London: Lawrence & Wishart.

Marx, Karl. 1847. The Poverty of Philosophy. In *MECW Volume 6*, 105–212. London: Lawrence & Wishart.

Marx, Karl and Friedrich Engels. 1845/46. The German Ideology. In *Marx & Engels Collected Works (MECW) Volume 5*, 19–539, London: Lawrence & Wishart.

Morgan, Stephen L. and Jiwon Lee. 2018. Trump Voters and the White Working Class. *Sociological Science* 5: 234–245.

Mosco, Vincent. 2017. *Becoming Digital: Toward a Post-Internet Society*. Bingley: Emerald.

Müller, P. and Schulz, A. (2019). Alternative media for a populist audience? *Information, Communication & Society*, 10.1080/1369118X.2019.1646778

Qiu, Jack L. 2016. *Goodbye iSlave: A Manifesto for Digital Abolition*. Urbana, IL: University of Illinois Press.

Ravenelle, Alexandra J. 2019. *Hustle and Gig: Struggling and Surviving in the Sharing Economy*. Oakland, CA: University of California Press.

Rosa, Hartmut. 2013. *Social Acceleration: A New Theory of Modernity*. New York: Columbia University Press.

Sandoval, Marisol. 2016. What Would Rosa Do? Co-Operatives and Radical Politics. *Soundings*, *63*, 98–111.

Scholz, Trebor and Nathan Schneider, eds. 2016. *Ours to Hack and Own. The Rise of Platform Cooperativism, a New Vision for the Future of Work and a Fairer Internet*. New York: OR.

Stier, Sebastian et al. 2017. When Populists Become Popular. *Information, Communication & Society* 20 (9): 1365–1388.

The Economist. 2017. The World's Most Valuable Resource is no Longer Oil, But Data. *The Economist*, 6 May 2017.

Trump, Donald J. 2014. A Country that Cannot Protect Its Borders Will Not Last. *Breitbart*, 11 July 2014. https://www.breitbart.com/politics/2014/07/11/must-get-tough-on-border/ (accessed 3 December 2019).

Van Dijck, José, Poell, Thomas, and Martijn de Waal. 2018. *The Platform Society*. New York: Oxford University Press.

Webster, Frank. 2014. *Theories of the Information Society*. Abingdon: Routledge.

Woodcock, Jamie. 2019. *Marx at the Arcade: Consoles, Controllers, and Class Struggle*. Chicago, IL: Haymarket.

Chapter Four
Adorno and the Media in Digital Capitalism

4.1 Introduction

In 2019, there was the 50th anniversary of Theodor W. Adorno's death. On this occasion, there have been new publications by and about Adorno and events asking how relevant Adorno is today. This chapter was presented as a keynote talk at one of these events, namely at the conference "Adorno and the Media" that took place on 13 December and 14 in Karlsruhe University of Arts and Design and its Center for Art and Media (ZKM). The chapter asks: how relevant is Adorno for the critical understanding of digital capitalism? It situates Adorno in the context of contemporary media and communication study, especially the analysis of the interaction of digital media and society.

Section 4.2 focuses on why dismissals and vilifications of Adorno are wrong. Building on Adorno, section 4.3 analyses the digital culture industry. Section 4.4 deals with digital authoritarianism, a phenomenon that it is highly relevant in times when authoritarians such as Donald Trump have almost 70 million followers on Twitter. Section 4.5 asks Adorno whether we live in a capitalist or a digital/informational society.

4.2 Adorno's Demonisation

There is a lack of engagement with Adorno in communication, media, and cultural studies, where Adorno is regularly demonised and dismissed with one-line prejudices

DOI: 10.4324/9781003222149-4

that ignore the complexity and totality of his works. The typical argument goes like this: "Adorno was a pessimist who saw humans as passively manipulated. He considered instrumental society to be without alternative and thought political change was hopeless. His theory is false and outdated".

Here are some examples from cultural studies. David Morley (2019) claims that the Frankfurt School "guys were past their sell by date when Jeremy Corbyn was a nipper". John Fiske (1989, 183) argues that the "Frankfurt School have no room in their scenario for resistant or evasive practices" and represent "a left-wing elitism". Henry Jenkins (2006) writes that Adorno "doesn't know anything about popular culture, he's never consumed any popular culture – in fact, it seems like he's never even spoken to anybody who's ever consumed any popular culture!". Du Gay et al. (1997, 87) argue that Horkheimer and Adorno's culture industry hypothesis, "citizens are turned into a passive mass of consumers" and "all is false and inauthentic". Storey (2006, 55) claims that the "Frankfurt School perspective on popular culture is essentially a discourse from above on the culture of other people". Hesmondhalgh (2019, 30) writes that "there is a constant sense in Adorno and Horkheimer that the battle has already been lost, that culture has been already subsumed".

Such prejudices keep students, scholars, and citizens from engaging with Adorno. They are false in at least three respects. First, Adorno did not despise popular culture as such, but its commodity form. He pointed out the critical role of the clown in popular culture (Adorno 1996) and was a "fan" of the clown of all clowns – Charlie Chaplin. In the *Culture Industry*-chapter of the *Dialectic of the Enlightenment*, positive elements of popular culture are visible. For example, Adorno writes that "traces of something better persist in those features of the culture industry by which it resembles the circus" (Horkheimer and Adorno 2002, 114). Adorno's fondness of Chaplin, the figure of the clown, and the circus shows that he was not opposed to entertainment as such. He rather despised capitalism and therefore the commodity form.

Second, Adorno wasn't a determinist and fatalist. He stressed the antagonistic character of culture and saw active potentials of resistance and liberation. For example, he wrote about the culture industry's antagonisms:

> In its attempts to manipulate the masses the ideology of the culture industry itself becomes as internally antagonistic as the very society which it aims to control. The ideology of the culture industry contains the antidote to its own lie. No other plea could be made for its defence. (Adorno 1991, 181)

He also argued that audiences consume and accept the culture industry's products "with a kind of reservation" so that "it is not quite believed in", "the integration of consciousness and free time has not yet completely succeeded", "the real interests of individuals are still strong enough to resist, within certain limits, total inclusion", "a society, whose inherent contradictions persist undiminished, cannot be totally integrated even in consciousness", "a chance of maturity (*Mündigkeit*)" remains (Adorno 1991, 196–197).

Third, Adorno didn't see capitalist society and the culture industry as having no alternatives, which means that he wasn't a political and cultural pessimist. Adorno stressed the potentials for alternative media. He stresses that television/*Fernsehen* literally means to watch into the distance. True television would enable humans to watch into society's future. Therefore,

> to keep the promise still resonating within the word [television], it must emancipate itself from everything within which it – reckless wish-fulfilment – refutes its own principle and betrays the idea of Good Fortune for the smaller fortunes of the department store. (Adorno 1998, 57)

Adorno argued for the use of TV in anti-fascist education in order to reach "the nerve centres" of the authoritarian personality (Adorno 1967, 24). Adorno certainly would have supported the Maximilian-Kolke-Werk's project that has since 2010 organised meetings of young journalists and media studies students with survivors of the Nazis' extermination camps. The students create and publish videos, interviews, written and audio reports, blog postings, etc. that they spread via various media, including social media such as YouTube. Adorno would welcome using social media and user-generated content platforms for anti-fascist education but would advice against combining such content with ads.

Adorno was a public intellectual who effectively used broadcast media for discussing contemporary political issues. He especially gave lectures on the radio and participated in discussions broadcast on radio and television. Today, there are Adorno-CDs and many Adorno broadcasts are available on YouTube.

Adorno's works are complex and multi-layered. They are of key importance today for understanding contemporary society, including the interaction of capitalism and digital technologies. The next section, therefore, gives based on Adorno attention to the digital culture industry.

Adorno's Demonisation

4.3 The Digital Culture Industry

The culture industry is a particularly capitalist form of mediation where culture and the economy interlock and culture is mediated by the commodity form. As a consequence, the culture industry "is interested in human beings only as its customers and employees and has in fact reduced humanity as a whole, like each of its elements, to this exhaustive formula" (Horkheimer and Adorno, 2002, 118). "[U]se value in the reception of cultural assets is being replaced by exchange value" (128).

The culture industry subjects human meaning-making to the commodity form in multiple respects:

- Cultural workers sell their labour-power in order to produce culture;
- Culture takes on the form of cultural commodities;
- Advertising propagates the sale of commodities;
- Consumer culture advances an environment and lifestyles of commodity consumption.

In digital capitalism, the commodity form dominates everyday life in digital culture as a multitude of digital commodities. Table 4.1 gives an overview of commodities in the digital culture industry. In the digital culture industry, digital labour-power, digital content, online services, computing hardware, access to digital networks, digital ads, access to digital resources, and digital content libraries are sold as commodities. There are also capital accumulation models that combine the sale of various digital commodities.

The digital culture industry faces 11 problems (Fuchs 2020a, 2020b): there is (1) the exploitation of *digital labour*, (2) *digital surveillance*; (3) transnational digital corporations' *monopoly power*, (4) a *digital attention economy* where corporations and celebrities control lots of online visibility, voice and attention; (5) a digital commerce culture where the dominant social media platforms are *digital tabloids* dominated by tabloid entertainment and advertising. Political and educational content ("public service content") is minority content. (6) *Digital acceleration* results in information flows and communication that are processed at very high speed on social media. The attention span given to information is very short. (7) There is a *lack of time and space* for complex and deep analysis and discussion.

(8) There are *unsocial/individualistic social media* focused on the accumulation of attention and agreement to individual profiles and postings as well as *anti-social social*

TABLE 4.1 Commodities in the digital culture industry

Model	Commodity	Example
Digital labour model	Labour-power	Miners who extract minerals out of which components are created, Foxconn assemblage workers, software engineers, crowd workers/ platform workers, online freelancers, e-waste workers
The digital content as commodity model	Digital content, digital code, software	Microsoft, Adobe, Oracle, SAP, Electronic Arts (computer games)
Digital finance model	Financial services sold online	eBanking, PayPal, Google Checkout, Amazon Payments, cryptocurrency, and digital currency exchanges (e.g. Bitstamp, Coinbase, Coinmama, Kraken)
Hardware model	Computing hardware	Apple, HP, Dell, Fujitsu, Lenovo
Network model	Access to digital networks	Telecommunications and Internet service providers: AT&T, Verizon, China Mobile, Deutsche Telecom, Orange, BT
The online advertising model	Targeted ads	Google, Facebook, Twitter
The online retail model	Various commodities ordered online	Amazon, Alibaba, Apple iTunes, eBay,
The sharing economy-pay per service model	Services organised via an online platform	Uber, Upwork, Deliveroo
The sharing economy-rent on rent model	Renting of goods via an online platform	Airbnb, Hiyacar, Drivy
Digital subscription model	Access to a collection of digital resources	Netflix, Spotify, Amazon Prime, Apple Music
Mixed models	Combination of various digital commodities	Spotify, online newspapers, Apple

media that pose a threat to democracy. In the Cambridge Analytica scandal, Cambridge Analytica paid Global Science Research for conducting fake online personality tests in order to obtain personal Facebook data of almost 90 million users (first assumed to be 50 million) that were used for targeting political ads and fake news during election campaigns. The scandal showed how anti-social social media combine far-right ideology, digital capitalism, and the neoliberal mode of regulation: far-right activists use all means necessary for manipulating information. Online corporations see data generation as a way of achieving profits. The lack of legal regulation of corporate social media platforms invites data and content commodification that does not care about whether targeted ads sell fascism or chocolate cookies.

(9) In the age of new nationalism and new authoritarianism, a culture has emerged that results in the publication and spread of *false online news*, *post-truth politi*cs where

citizens distrust facts, and the emotionalisation of politics. (10) In *automated algo-rithmic politics*, automated computer programmes ("bots") replace human activities, post information, make "likes", etc. As a consequence, it has become more difficult to identify if information and dis/agreements stem from humans or machines. (11) On the Internet, there are *fragmented publics* that take on the form of filter bubbles.

These 11 tendencies have resulted in a public sphere that is characterised and divided by economic, political, and cultural power asymmetries

Targeted online advertising is the capital accumulation model that dominates the Internet and social media platforms. Adorno stresses the importance of advertising in the culture industry: "Culture is a paradoxical commodity. It is so completely subject to the law of exchange that it is no longer exchanged. [...] it merges with the advertisement" (Horkheimer and Adorno 2002, 131). He argues that advertising is the culture industry's "elixir of life" (131). In the digital culture industry, advertising has taken on a new form.

Smythe (1977) analysed advertising's political economy. He stresses that in advertising-funded media, it is not the content that is the commodity. It is the "time of the audiences, which is sold to advertisers" (3). He argues that audiences of advertising-funded media conduct audience labour that produces the audience com-modity. The larger the number of viewers, listeners, readers of such media, the higher ad rates can be set.

On social media, the audience commodity takes on a peculiar form. It is a big data commodity created by digital labour: users of produce online attention, big data, and online social relations that are the foundations of targeted ads. Whereas audiences produce meanings of content, users of Google, Facebook, YouTube, Twitter, Instagram, etc. also produce big data, content, and social relations. They are prosumers (producing consumers). There is constant real-time surveillance of online behaviour that is used for targeting ads. Ads are personalised. Predictive algorithms predict users' interests in commodities. Ad prices are often set based on algorithmic auctions that use the pay per view- or the pay per click-mode. Facebook and Google are not communications companies, but the world's largest advertising agencies.

Marx pointed out that commodity fetishism means that the commodity form and the money form conceal the "social character of private labour and the social relations between the individual workers, by making those relations appear as relations be-tween material objects, instead of revealing them plainly" (Marx 1867, 168–169). The commodity hides the social relations that produce it. It thereby empties out the meaning of commodities. Advertising uses this void and fills it with commodity ideology. The social media commodity inverts commodity fetishism. The commodity character of Facebook data is hidden behind the social use-value of Facebook, that is the social relations and functions enabled by platform use. The object status of users, that is the fact that they serve the profit interests of Facebook, is hidden behind the social networking enabled by Facebook. Social activity veils digital labour and its digital commodity. What some call the sharing economy is in fact platform capitalism. A true "sharing society" has to "begin by really sharing what it has, or all its talk of sharing is false or at best marginal" (Williams 1983, 101).

Adorno created foundations of a theory of the authoritarian personality and fascism. After the new world economic crisis 2008, new forms of nationalism and authoritarianism proliferated. Their proponents have also made use of digital authoritarianism, that is the use of the Internet and social media for spreading authoritarian ideology. Thinking about the relevance of Adorno today must therefore encompass thinking about digital authoritarianism.

4.4 Digital Authoritarianism

The digital humanities and computational social science are the dominant approaches in the empirical analysis of social media. They focus on big data analytics, that is the quantitative analysis of vast amounts of data collected online. The danger of big data analytics is that the "convergence of social-scientific methods toward those of the natural sciences is itself the child of a society that reifies people" (Pollock and Adorno 2011, 20). In neoliberal capitalism, first the business school's logic colonised the university. Today, computer science in combination with the logic of the business school has started to colonise the social sciences and humanities.

Critical digital and social media research is the alternative to big data analytics (Fuchs 2019, 2017). It combines critical theory, qualitative empirical research, and political praxis. Critical social media discourse analysis is a form of critical digital and social media research that is focused on the analysis of online ideology (Fuchs 2020a, 2018). It allows us to conduct analyses that focus on the question: how is nationalism and authoritarianism communicated online and on social media? Such analyses can be grounded in the theory of the authoritarian personality.

Fromm (1936) argues that authoritarian societies, including capitalism, foster sado-masochistic personalities (117–118) who feel pleasure in both submission to authority

Right-Wing Authoritarianism (RWA)
Individual ⇔ Group ⇔ Institution ⇔ Society
RWA's social role: Deflection of attention from structures
of class, capitalism and domination

FIGURE 4.1 A model of right-wing authoritarianism

and the subjection of underdogs/scapegoats. In their book *The Authoritarian Personality*, Adorno et al. (1950) developed the F scale that measures the authoritarian personality. There were four versions that consisted of 78, 60, 45, and 40 questions organised along nine dimensions. For qualitative research, a comprehensive model of right-wing authoritarianism that has four dimensions can be developed (Figure 4.1).

Right-wing authoritarianism is an ideology and organisational model of society. It integrates top-down leadership, nationalism, the friend/enemy-scheme, and militant patriarchy. Top-down leadership is right-wing authoritarianism's organisational principle. Nationalism forms its internal identity that is bounded by defining outside enemies who are seen as not belonging to and threatening the nation. Militant patriarchy advocates law-and-order policies and violence as means for solving conflicts.

Taken together, right-wing authoritarianism is an ideology that distracts attention from the complex problems of society's problems and the role that class plays in society.

A critical social media discourse analysis of Donald Trump's tweets allows us to show the importance of Adorno's theory today (see Fuchs 2018 for an in-depth analysis).

4.4.1 Top-Down Leadership

First, let us have a look at the dimension of top-down leadership. The relative use of first-person singular pronouns ("I", "me") over first-person plural pronouns ("We", "Us") in American English is 0.173, which means that on average the use of the first-person singular is 17.3% higher in written American English than the use of the first-person plural (Uz 2014). I conducted an analysis of pronouns of 1,815 tweets by Donald Trump (see Table 4.2). First-person singular pronouns were 28% more frequent than first-person plural pronouns, which provides indications that Trump has a narcissistic personality.

Twitter is a me-centred medium that lives through the accumulation of followers, likes and re-tweets. The custom of liking and re-tweeting on Twitter appeals to Trump's narcissism. Trump makes use of Twitter for broadcasting 280-character long sound bites about what he likes and dislikes.

An analysis of the elimination scenes in 201 episodes of reality TV programme *The Apprentice* with Donald Trump as host showed that in 47.3% of eliminations of candidates Trump used the argument "You have no leadership capacities!" (Fuchs 2018, 183–190). Reality TV and Twitter are Trump's preferred two contemporary

TABLE 4.2   Occurrences of pronouns in the Trump-Twitter-dataset, source: Fuchs 2018, 210

First-person singular pronouns	Absolute frequency	First-person plural pronouns	Absolute frequency
"I"	363	"We"	252
"I'll"	4	"We'll"	1
"I'm"	3	"We're"	4
"I've"	4	"We've"	3
"Me"	188	"Us"	57
	$\Sigma = 562$		$\Sigma = 317$

Trump's relative use of first-person singular over first-person plural pronouns: $(562 - 317) / (562 + 317) = 0.2787$

Digital Authoritarianism

formats of public communication. Both support narcissism and that Trump can present himself as a strong leader. Trump conducts first-person singular politics via Twitter.

The great little man is according to Adorno "a person who suggests both omnipotence and the idea that he is just one of the folks" (Adorno 1951, 142). Trump constructs himself as the great little man on Twitter and reality TV. Trump's demagogic, aggressive, attack-oriented, offensive, proletarian language, and style make him appear as a great little man who is on top, but at the same time is an ordinary person. He acts as a politician just like he acts as a reality TV entertainer. He brings populism in the form of popular culture and authoritarianism into politics. Trump appeals to the working class by his direct, rude manners, behaviour, and language. He is a billionaire who likes McDonald's culture. The focus on the latter distracts attention from the antagonism between billionaires and workers. In reality, Trump is not working-class but someone who appeals to the working class but is a rich billionaire whose interests are opposed to working-class interests. Trump is a figure for projection that allows collective narcissism that results in the "enlargement of the subject: by making the leader his ideal he loves himself, as it were, but gets rid of the stains of frustration and discontent which mar his picture of his own empirical self" (Adorno 1951, 140).

4.4.2 Nationalism

Second, nationalism is an important feature of right-wing authoritarianism. Let us have a look at a video that Trump posted on Twitter (Figure 4.2).

In the video, Trump says about the American Labor Day:

> The American worker built the foundation for the country we love and have today. But the American worker is getting crushed. Bad trade deals like NAFTA and TPP, such high and inexcusable taxes and fees on small businesses that employ so many good people. This Labor Day, let's honour our American workers, then men and women who proudly keep America working. They are the absolute best anywhere in the world. There is nobody like 'em. I'm ready to make America work again and to make America great again. That's what we are going to do on November 8.

There are four ideological features of Trump's tweet:

1) Trump constructs the US-Americans as a mythic collective;
2) He claims that there is a unified national interest of US capital and US labour;

FIGURE 4.2   Nationalist tweet by Trump, source: https://twitter.com/realdonaldtrump/status/7727988095083 72480

3) He identifies other nations such as Mexico and China as enemies of the USA that threatens its national interest;

4) He constructs political-economic conflict as a conflict of nations and disregards actual class conflicts.

In reality, US capital exploits labour both inside and outside of the USA. Trump's nationalism distracts attention from the class antagonism. Adorno helps us to understand nationalism by arguing that demagogues make use of the logic of repressive egalitarianism as featured in nationalist ideology. "They emphasize their being different from the outsider but play down such differences within their own group and tend to level out distinctive qualities among themselves with the exception of the hierarchical one" (Adorno 1991, 146).

Nationalism constructs national identity. It is inherently repressive because it defines the nation's inner identity against outside enemies. It makes use of the friend/enemy-scheme.

4.4.3 The Friend/Enemy-Scheme

Let us have a look at a tweet by Boris Johnson (Figure 4.3):

This tweet implies works with a combination of the topos of numbers, the topos of weighing down, and the topos of danger (Reisigl and Wodak 2001, 77–79): it is claimed

Digital Authoritarianism

FIGURE 4.3 Tweet by Boris Johnson about immigration, source: https://twitter.com/borisjohnson/status/11 98905666905100289, posted on 25 November 2019

that a Labour Party government would vastly increase immigration ("uncontrolled", "unlimited"). The formulation of a "huge pressure" on housing and public services implies that immigrants are a danger that weighs down the social system. Immigrants are constructed as outsiders who only have a negative function and threaten the nation's welfare and social cohesion. It is not mentioned that they also pay taxes, pay for housing, etc. The NHS wouldn't exist without immigrant nurses and doctors because there is a shortage of both. The friend/enemy-scheme here plays the ideological role of distracting attention from the neoliberal politics of Thatcher, the Conservatives, and New Labour whose austerity politics have limited and cut investments into public services and have resulted in various privatisations, including of council housing. Johnson promises tough immigration laws in the form of an "Australian-style points-based system".

The friend/enemy-scheme not just takes on the form of racism and xenophobia, but is frequently also expressed as the scapegoating of political opposition and investigative media. Figure 4.4 shows an example.

In his ideological logic, Trump identifies himself with the US people. It is a frequent claim of populists that they alone authentically and absolutely Represent the people and the nation. Based on this logic criticism of Trump is presented as anti-American and directed against the American people. Trump, therefore, presents media that have reported critically about him, namely New York Times, NBC, ABC, CBS, and CNN, as "the enemy of the American People!".

Donald J. Trump @
@realDonaldTrump

The FAKE NEWS media (failing @nytimes, @NBCNews, @ABC, @CBS, @CNN) is not my enemy, it is the enemy of the American People!

10:48 PM · Feb 17, 2017 · Twitter for Android

46.6K Retweets **145.3K** Likes

FIGURE 4.4 Tweet by Donald Trump, source: https://twitter.com/realdonaldtrump/status/832708293516632065, posted on 17 February 2017

Trump claims that criticisms of him are "fake news" although he himself has spread false stories such as the one that Barack Obama a Kenyan Muslim who never attended Columbia University, the one that Hillary Clinton was very ill and therefore couldn't have served as US president, etc. (see Holloway 2017).

Adorno explains the ideological logic of the friend/enemy-scheme:

> So, the group to which they count themselves – and it does not matter which people it is – is presented as being endowed with all kinds of good qualities and is counted among those who can be saved, while the others that they reject as negative and whom they either have to psychologically foreclose or at least do not want to have there, are considered as the wretched. This is the outgroup or at least the minority in their own area with which they are currently dealing. (Adorno 1960, 253–254, translation from German)

Right-wing authoritarians construct out-groups such as illegal immigrants, Mexico, China, Muslims, oppositional politicians, and critics. They are presented as threatening the greatness of the nation. According to Adorno, identification with the leader and hatred against the out-group allows emotional release (Adorno 1975, 16–20). Such a release of aggression encourages "excess and violence" (17). Violence is the fourth characteristic of right-wing authoritarianism.

4.4.4 Violence and Law-and-Order Politics

Donald Trump frequently expresses his admiration of the US army on Twitter and considers armament and nuclear weapons as appropriate means of political communication (see the examples in Figure 4.5).

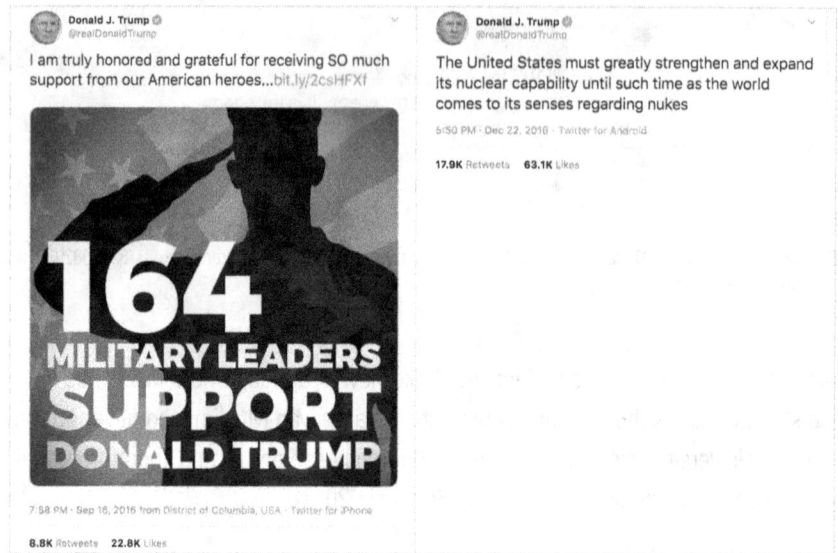

FIGURE 4.5 Donald Trump on military affairs, sources: https://twitter.com/realDonaldTrump/status/776842 647294009344, https://twitter.com/realdonaldtrump/status/811977223326625792?lang=en

Trump sees violence as an appropriate means for solving conflicts. He is a militarist who worships soldiers and the army. Armies fetishise male military strength. As a consequence, militarism is closely entwined with patriarchy. In militarist and patriarchal ideology, to the male soldier as an ideal citizen who takes up arms to defend the nation corresponds the female role model of the housewife who gives birth to and brings up new soldiers. Trump expresses his belief in violent retaliation: "When somebody screws you, screw them back in spades. [...] When someone attacks you publicly, always strike back. [...] Go for the jugular so that people watching will not want to mess with you" (Trump and Zanker 2007, 199).

As a teenager, Donald Trump attended New York Military Academy, which partly explains why he is so fond of the army and hierarchies. From a psychoanalytical perspective, one can speculate about whether a feeling of a lack of parental love may have resulted in love of the army and military drill as attempted flight and compensation mechanism.

Adorno argues that there is a logic that connects the friend/enemy-scheme to violence: the right-wing authoritarian "cannot help feeling surrounded by traitors, and so continuously threatens to exterminate them" (Adorno 1975, 78). Trump sees war, violence, weapons, and guns as a generally appropriate means of handling conflicts. The "model of the military officer" is "transferred to the realm of politics" (Adorno 1975, 49). Love to the leader is an "emotional compensation for the cold, self-alienated life of most people" (Adorno 1975, 37). In Trump's world, survival, toughness, strength, and the willingness to fight, lead and compete are moral norms. Any "reference to love is almost completely excluded", and the "traditional role of the loving father" is replaced "by the negative one of threatening authority" (Adorno 1991, 137).

Adorno helps us to critically understand top-down leadership, nationalism, the friend/enemy-scheme, and militant patriarchy as principles of right-wing authoritarianism and as ideological moments that distract attention from the complexity of society's problems and from their aspects of capitalism and class. Next, we will have a look at how Adorno helps us to answer the question of whether we live in an information/digital society or digital capitalism.

4.5 Digital Society or Capitalism?

The main question of the information society debate is: in what kind of society do we live? Is it an information and digital society? Or a capitalist society? Or something different?

Theodor W. Adorno (1968/2003) argued that the "fundamental question of the present structure of society" is "about the alternatives: late capitalism or industrial society" (111). He asked if society was a capitalist society or an industrial society. Today, Adorno's question can be reposed in a slightly altered form: do we live in capitalism or an information/digital society?

The information society debate's dominant narrative is that a radically new society has emerged. For example, Daniel Bell (1974) spoke of the emergence of a post-industrial information society that "is based on services" in "health, education, research, and government" and where what "counts is not raw muscle power, or energy, but information" (15). This is a subjectivist view with a focus on radical change: for Bell, information/knowledge work constitutes "a vast historical change" (37).

Adorno gave an answer to the question of whether society was at the time he lived capitalist or industrial:

> In terms of critical, dialectical theory, I would like to propose as an initial, necessarily abstract answer that contemporary society undoubtedly is an

industrial society according to the state of its *forces* of production. Industrial labor has everywhere become the model of society as such, regardless of the frontiers separating differing political systems. It has developed into a totality because methods modelled on those of industry are necessarily extended by the laws of economics to other realms of material production, administration, the sphere of distribution, and those that call themselves culture. In contrast, however, society is capitalist in its *relations* of production. People are still what they were in Marx's analysis in the middle of the nineteenth century […] Production takes place today, as then, for the sake of profit (Adorno 1968/2003, 117).

Paraphrasing Adorno, we can give a similar answer to the question "Do we live in a capitalist or digital/information society?". Contemporary society is an information society according to the state of its *forces* of production. In contrast, however, contemporary society is capitalist in its *relations* of production. People are still what they were in Marx's analysis in the middle of the 19th century. Production takes place today, as then, for the sake of profit and for achieving this end it to a certain extent makes use of knowledge and information technology in production.

In 2018, 26.5% of the world population in employment lived on less than US$3.10 (PPP).[1] The United Nations considers them as working poor. According to ILO estimates, in the year 2018, there were 3.3 billion employed people in the world.[2] The absolute number of poor employees was around 875 million. Together, these workers earned less than US$990 billion per year, whereas the total revenues of the world's largest information corporations[3] were 2.2 times as large as the total sum of these poverty wages. Whereas a small number of companies yields huge profits, billions of humans have to live in poverty. Digital society is first and foremost a global class society.

Let us have a look at a data example that deepens the engagement with the question of what character contemporary society has. Table 4.3 gives an overview of the size, share of sales, profits, and assets of the world's largest 2,000 transnational corporations. The data are ordered by industries.

1 Data source: UNDP. 2018. *UNDP Human Development Indices and Indicators 2018 Statistical Update*. New York: UNDP.
2 Data source: ILO Statistics, https://www.ilo.org/ilostat, accessed on 18 May 2019.
3 Data source: Forbes 2000 List of the World's Largest Public Companies, year 2018.

TABLE 4.3 Share of specific industries in the profits, revenues, and assets of the world's largest 2,000 transnational corporations (data source: Forbes 2000 List of the World's Largest Public Companies, year 2018)

Industry	No. of companies	Share of sales (%)	Share of profits (%)	Share of assets (%)
Conglomerates	36	2.0	1.1	0.9
Culture & digital	260	14.6	17.7	5.1
Energy & utilities	199	14.3	9.8	5.7
Fashion	26	1.0	0.9	0.0
FIRE (finance, insurance & real estate)	634	22.5	33.7	74.8
Food	86	3.6	5.8	1.2
Manufacturing & construction	352	15.2	13.1	5.4
Mobility & transport	169	11.6	9.4	3.6
Pharmaceutical & medical	105	7.2	4.9	1.9
Retail	86	6.9	2.5	0.9
Security	1	0.0	0.0	0.0
Various services	46	1.1	1.1	0.4

Let us have a closer look at the structure of the structural distribution of profits of the world's 2,000 largest corporations according to the data in the table. Finance capital controls 33.7% of these corporations' profits, the culture and digital industry 17.7%, manufacturing and construction 13.1%, energy and utilities 9.8%, and the mobility and transport sector 9.4%.

These data show that it is an exaggeration to claim that digital capitalism is capitalism's dominant moment. There are multiple, intersecting, and interacting capitalisms. Capitalism's "individual sectors [...] are themselves economically intertwined" (Horkheimer and Adorno 2002, 96). Digital capitalism is linked to finance capitalism via venture capital investments into digital start-ups and the listing of digital corporations on stock markets. Digital and cultural capitalism requires energy inputs, which links to classical resources and hyper-industrial capitalism. Global communication advances the increased transportation of people and goods, which is why the digital/culture industry and the mobility/transport industries are interacting. Contemporary capitalism is at the same time finance capitalism, digital capitalism, hyper-industrial capitalism, mobility capitalism, etc. All of these dimensions interpenetrate.

Adorno's insight that we need to look at society from the perspectives of the productive forces and the relations of production is complicated by what Marx termed the antagonism between the productive forces and the relations of production. There is an

Digital Society or Capitalism?

antagonism between the informational, networked productive forces and the digital and informational class relations. This relation is antagonism between digital capital and the digital commons. It becomes evident in phenomena such as intellectual property rights VS. digital gifts/non-commercial Creative Commons, for-profit open access VS. non-profit open access, ad-funded for-profit Internet platforms VS. non-profit Internet platforms, capitalist platforms VS. platform co-operatives, etc.

Digital capitalism at the same time deepens exploitation and creates new foundations for autonomous realms that transcend the logic of capitalism. Marx argued that the "material conditions for the existence" of "new superior relations of production" mature "within the framework of the old society" (Marx 1857/58, 263). With digitalisation, "the commodity becomes increasingly transparent" (Negri 2017, 25), "there begin to emerge sectors that are increasingly sensitive to the autonomy of social cooperation, to the self-valorisation of proletarian subjects" (Negri 2017, 25).

4.6 Conclusion

Scholars in media/communication/cultural studies have often vilified Theodor W. Adorno, which has hampered engagement with the complexity of his works and theory. This chapter has shown some aspects of why Adorno is relevant today for a critical understanding of digital capitalism. Based on Adorno, it has outlined the following aspects:

- Digital capitalism is based on a complex culture industry;
- We are experiencing the rise of authoritarian capitalism. Right-wing authoritarians use the Internet to communicate nationalism, leadership ideology, the friend/enemy-logic, and militarism;
- Contemporary society is a digital society at the level of the productive forces and a capitalist society at the level of the relations of production;
- There is an antagonism between the digital commons and digital capital.

Capitalism entails the tendency of the "self-destruction of enlightenment" (Horkheimer and Adorno 2002, xvi). We today experience a surge of new nationalism and new authoritarianism. Far-right movements and new nationalisms are the "wounds, the scars of a democracy that, to that day, has not yet lived up to its own concept" (Adorno

1968/2020, 9). They are the result of the negative dialectic of neoliberal capitalism and the new imperialism.

The commodification of everything, entrepreneurialism, privatisation, deregulation, financialisation, globalisation, deindustrialisation, outsourcing, precarisation, and the new individualism have backfired. These are developments that have extended and intensified inequalities and crisis tendencies, which created a fruitful ground for new nationalism, right-wing extremism, and new fascism.

How can nationalism and right-wing authoritarianism be counteracted? Adorno stresses that one should point out that authoritarianism's consequences mean disasters for everyone, including war: one should "warn the potential followers of right-wing extremism about its own consequences, to convey to them that this politics will lead its own followers to their doom too" (Adorno 1968/2020, 17).

Adorno also mentions that reason and facts should be used to counter "fake news" and "post-truth". Anti-fascism and anti-nationalism should not "fight lies with lies", but "counteract it with the full force of reason, with the genuinely unideological truth" (Adorno 1968/2020, 49–50).

Horkheimer and Adorno (2002, 60) speak about the "ambiguity of laughter":

> If laughter up to now has been a sign of violence, an outbreak of blind, obdurate nature, it nevertheless contains the opposite element, in that through laughter blind nature becomes aware of itself as such and thus abjures its destructive violence.

Authoritarianism online and offline is emotional and irrational, which is why authoritarians often do not listen to rational arguments. Making fun of right-wing authoritarianism should be part of its deconstruction.

Contemporary digital technologies such as social media should be used for advancing the anti-fascist strategies that Adorno had in mind, namely reminders about authoritarian capitalism's consequences, rational arguments opposing it, and satire that deconstructs its logic.

Adorno's theory allows us to understand why neoliberalism has backfired and turned into authoritarian capitalism. These changes are mediated by and expressed in digital means of communication. The struggle for defending and extending the democratic public sphere is key to resisting authoritarian capitalism.

Conclusion

References

Adorno, Theodor W. 1998. *Critical Models. Interventions and Catchwords*. New York: Columbia University Press.

Adorno, Theodor W. 1996. Chaplin Times Two. *Yale Journal of Criticism* 9 (1): 57–61.

Adorno, Theodor W. 1991. *The Culture Industry*. Abingdon: Routledge.

Adorno, Theodor W. 1975. The Psychological Technique of Martin Luther Thomas' Radio Addresses. In *Soziologische Schriften II.1*, 11–141. Frankfurt am Main: Suhrkamp.

Adorno, Theodor W. 1968/2020. *Aspects of the New Right-Wing Extremism*. Cambridge: Polity.

Adorno, Theodor W. 1968/2003. Late Capitalism or Industrial Society? The Fundamental Question of the Present Structure of Society. In *Can One Live After Auschwitz?*, ed. Rolf Tiedemann, 111–125. Stanford, CA: Stanford University Press.

Adorno, Theodor W. 1967. Education After Auschwitz. In *Can One Live After Auschwitz? A Philosophical Reader*, ed. Rolf Tiedemann, 19–33. Stanford, CA: Stanford University Press.

Adorno, Theodor W. 1960. Die autoritäre Persönlichkeit. In *Theodor W. Adorno: Vorträge 1949-1968*, ed. Michael Schwarz, 239–264. Frankfurt am Main: Suhrkamp.

Adorno, Theodor W. 1951. Freudian Theory and the Pattern of Fascist Propaganda. In *The Culture Industry*, 132–157. Abingdon: Routledge.

Adorno, Theodor W., Else Frenkel-Brunswik, Daniel J. Levinson and R. Nevitt Sanford. *The Authoritarian Personality*. New York: Harper & Brothers.

Bell, Daniel. 1974. *The Coming of Post-Industrial Society. A Venture in Social Forecasting*. London: Heinemann.

Du Gay, Paul, Stuart Hall, Linda Janes, Hugh Mackay and Keith Negus. 1997. *Doing Cultural Studies: The Story of the Sony Walkman*. London: Sage.

Fiske, John. 1989. *Reading the Popular*. London: Routledge.

Fromm, Erich. 1936. Sozialpsychologischer Teil. In *Studien über Autorität und Familie*, 77–135. Lüneburg: zu Klampen.

Fuchs, Christian. 2020a. *Nationalism on the Internet. Critical Theory and Ideology in the Age of Social Media and Fake News*. New York: Routledge.

Fuchs, Christian. 2020b. *Social Media: A Critical Introduction*. London: Sage.

Fuchs, Christian. 2019. What is Critical Digital Social Research? Five Reflections on the Study of Digital Society. *Journal of Digital Social Research* 1 (1): 10–16.

Fuchs, Christian. 2018. *Digital Demagogue: Authoritarian Capitalism in the Age of Trump and Twitter*. London: Pluto.

Fuchs, Christian. 2017. From Digital Positivism and Administrative Big Data Analytics Towards Critical Digital and Social Media Research! *European Journal of Communication* 32 (1): 37–49.

Hesmondhalgh, David. 2019. *Cultural Industries*, 4th edn. London: Sage.

Holloway, Kali. 2017. 14 Fake News Stories Created or Publicized by Donald Trump. *Alternet*, 12 January 2017. https://www.alternet.org/media/14-fake-news-stories-created-or-publicized-donald-trump/

Horkheimer, Max and Theodor W. Adorno. 2002. *Dialectic of Enlightenment. Philosophical Fragments*. Stanford, CA: Stanford University Press.

Jenkins, Henry. 2006. Behind the Scenes: Beautiful Things in Popular Culture (Part One), https://henryjenkins.org/2006/09/behind_the_scenes_beautiful_th.html

Marx, Karl. 1867. *Capital Volume 1*. London: Penguin.

Marx, Karl. 1857/1858. Economic Manuscripts of 1857/58. In *Marx & Engels Collected Works, Volume 29*. London: Lawrence & Wishart.

Morley, David. 2019. Comment on the Article "We Need A Public Service Internet – State-Owned Infrastructure is Just the Start", https://theconversation.com/we-need-a-full-public-service-internet-state-owned-infrastructure-is-just-the-start-127458

Negri, Antonio. 2017. *Marx and Foucault*. Cambridge: Polity.

Pollock, Friedrich and Theodor W. Adorno. 2011. *Group Experiment and Other Writings*. Cambridge, MA: Harvard University Press.

Reisigl, Martin and Ruth Wodak. 2001. *Discourse and Discrimination: Rhetorics of Racism and Antisemitism*. London: Routledge.

Smythe, Dallas W. 1977. Communications: Blindspot of Western Marxism. *Canadian Journal of Political and Social Theory* 1 (3): 1–27.

Storey, John. 2006. *Cultural Theory and Popular Culture. An Introduction*. 4th edn. Harlow: Pearson Education.

Trump, Donald and Bill Zanker. 2007. *Think Big: Make It Happen in Business and Life*. New York: Harper.

UNDP. 2018. *UNDP Human Development Indices and Indicators 2018 Statistical Update*. New York: UNDP.

Uz, Irem. 2014. Individualism and First Person Pronoun Use in Written Texts Across Languages. *Journal of Cross-Cultural Psychology* 45 (10): 1671–1678.

Williams, Raymond. 1983. *Towards 2000*. London: Chatto & Windus.

Chapter Five

Communication in Everyday (Digital) Life. A Reading of Henri Lefebvre's *Critique of Everyday Life* in the Age of Digital Capitalism

---

5.1 Introduction

Henri Lefebvre (1901–1991) was one of the most influential French Marxist intellectuals of the 20th century. He was a Marxist-humanist theorist who was not just a major critical of capitalism, but also a critic of structuralism and Stalinism. He was an interdisciplinary critical theorist who focused on topics social as everyday life, social space, the city, alienation, ideology, dialectical philosophy, society, nationalism, fascism, Karl Marx, Lenin, social movements, the state, modernity, language, the Paris Commune, globalisation, aesthetics, rural life, existentialism etc. Lefebvre published more than 70 books.

The Production of Space (*La production de l'espace*) is Lefebvre's (1974/1991) most widely read and cited book (for a discussion of this book's relevance for a critical theory of communication see). *Critique of Everyday Life* (*Critique de la vie quotidienne,CEL*) is a three-volume book in which Lefebvre outlines a critical theory of society and everyday life in capitalism (Lefebvre 1991, 2002, 2008, 2014). Lefebvre saw *CEL* as "his principal contribution to Marxism" (Elden 2004, 110). Lefebvre "is the quintessential critical theorist of everyday life" (Gardiner 2000, 71). *CEL* is a "non-statist Marxism that concretely addresses problems of human existence" (Shields 1999, 17). The first volume (*CEL1*) was published in French in 1947, the second one (*CEL2*) in 1961, the third one (*CEL3*) in 1981. *Everyday Life in the Modern World* is an accompanying volume published in 1968 in French (Lefebvre 1971). Although less read

DOI: 10.4324/9781003222149-5

than *Production of Space*, *CEL* is a very rich dialectical, Marxist and humanist work and a major contribution to 20th-century social theory.

This chapter asks: How can Henri Lefebvre's *Critique of Everyday Life* inform a critical theory of communication? How can it inform a critique of digital capitalism?

Section 5.2 focuses on Lefebvre's concept of society. Section 5.3 discusses the role of communication in everyday life. Section 5.4 analyses the role of communication in capitalism. Section 5.5 draws the reader's attention to the communication of ideology. Conclusions are drawn in section 5.6.

5.2 Lefebvre's Concept of Society

5.2.1 Practices and Structures

Lefebvre outlines a dialectical concept of structure. Structures are "(relative) stabilities, defined and relatively constant contours, regularities, form which are born and survive, which produce and which reproduce, at the heart of innumerable interactions" (*CEL2*, 162). Structures exist everywhere. They enable and constrain and are the result of the interactions of moments and elements. In society, such interactions are communication flows between humans who stand in social relations to each other.

Lefebvre was a critical of structuralism and structuralists such as Lévi-Strauss, Saussure, Barthes, Althusser, and so forth. The problem of structuralism is that it "proceeds by privileging structure absolutely" and substantifying structure (*CEL2*, 176). It "totalizes structure" (186). Structures' plasticity, negations, and their inner contradictions are marginalised (176). Structuralism "loses touch with historicity", dialectical development, and processes (177). It "reifies actions" and is therefore a form of reification and alienation (177).

Lefebvre sees totality as a dialectical aspect of structure. Immanent in every totality and every process of totalisation is the potential for negation, the "breaking of totality" (*CEL2*, 183). He sees dialectical negation as more fundamental than totality (186). Lefebvre argues that a totality is made up by the dialectical interaction of need, work, and pleasure (189–193). Work satisfies and transforms human needs. The human being is a human of need, a human at work, and a human of pleasure (192). Humans have biological and social needs, transform the world and satisfy their needs through practices, and are beings that strive towards satisfaction and enjoyment so that they lead a pleasurable life.

Lefebvre characterises functionalism as a version of structuralism that reduces everything to a function and cannot think of anything as not having a function. Functionalism "eliminates critical thought" and is a "technocratic ideology" (199). Functionalism is an extreme form of what Horkheimer (1947/2004) characterises as instrumental reason. It is a mode of thinking that suggests that everything is an instrument of something else. Functionalism is an extreme form of what Lukács (1971) terms reified consciousness. It reduces the world to the status of things and instruments. Lefebvre (*CEL2*) writes that everyday life has no function (199), which is why functionalism cannot explain it. Functionalism is an ideology of control that has no place for the unforeseen and the marginal (202). Lefebvre's critique implies that functionalism is an intellectual form of totalitarianism.

Lefebvre (*CEL2*, 232–244) stresses the importance of practices in everyday life and society. He distinguishes between ideological practices, specific practices related to professions and skills, inventive/creative practices, repetitive practices, political practices, knowledge practices, partial revolutionary practices, and total revolutionary practices. Lefebvre stresses that practices are not just economic production but extend into all realms of society, including politics, culture, and technology. For Lefebvre, practices constitute totality. He therefore says that praxis is the "total field" (276).

5.2.2 Base/Superstructure, Material/Non-Material, Economic/Non-Economic

There are formulations in *Critique of Everyday Life* that make it appear like Lefebvre like orthodox Marxism assumes that that the economy forms the material base and politics and culture the non-material superstructure. He speaks of "the economic base (the productive forces) and the apex (the ideological and political superstructures)" (*CEL2*, 34). The everyday is "totality in action, it encompasses the base and the superstructure, as well as the interactions between them" (45).

Lefebvre speaks of "material production" and "non-material" production (236), "economic (material) production" (237). "Praxis encompasses both material production and 'spiritual' production" (237). He also writes that services are "non-material" forms of production in realms such as advertising, distribution, education, health, leisure, training, or transportation (236).

But it is also evident that Lefebvre is critical of the base/superstructure-model. He speaks of "the simplified scheme: '*economic base – political superstructure*'" as "impoverished" thought that "characterizes the Stalinist interpretation of Marxism" (*CEL1*, 52). This is also why Lefebvre speaks of "so-called" base and superstructure and often refers to both terms with quotation marks. For example, Lefebvre argues that "symbols, culture, representations and ideologies" are "so-called 'superstructural' elements" that "react on the 'base'" (*CEL2*, 237). He speaks of "ideologies and 'superstructures'" (236), "'base' or 'foundation'" (10).

For Lefebvre, social practices are the decisive aspect of society and everyday life. Social practices extend into all realms of society. The "superstructures are linked to society as a whole, to social practice as a whole" (*CEL1*, 57). The logical implication is that the physical production is not simply a base to which culture and politics can be reduced. Culture and politics are material and economic because they are produced and reproduced. There are political, cultural, ideological, intellectual, and so forth workers. In *Volume 3*, Lefebvre argues that the importance of bureaucracy, information production and information technology explodes the Stalinist distinction between base and superstructure:

> The traditional Marxist thesis makes the relations of production and productive forces the "base" of the ideological and political superstructures. Today — that is to say, now that the state ensures the administration of society, as opposed to letting social relations, the market and blind forces take their course — this thesis is reductionist and inadequate. (*CEL3*, 123)

> Information is produced. It is consumed. Information technology confirms the outmoded character of the classical Marxist contrast between base and superstructure. Information is not — or not merely — a superstructure, since it is an — exchangeable — product of certain relations of production. What was regarded as superstructural, like space and time, forms part of production, because it is a product that is bought and sold. (*CEL3*, 144)

Lefebvre advances several important arguments why the orthodox separation of the economy and culture is untenable:

- Computing as convergence technology: Networked computer technologies are convergent means of production, distribution, and consumption of information. Computing transcends the traditional separation between production as economic and consumption as cultural.
- Knowledge work: Information technology is characteristic of the knowledge age, where knowledge work that produces information has become an important

feature in the economy. Knowledge work transcends the boundary between the economy and culture. It produces cultural products within the economy.

- The culture industry: In the culture industry, culture is produced as commodity. Examples are music, films, entertainment, live performances, advertising, sports events, video games, software, magazines, branding, etc. The cultural commodity means the economisation and commodification of culture so that no boundary can be drawn between the economy and culture.

Lefebvre questions the separation of economy/culture and base/superstructure. The economy operates as the production of ideas in culture. Culture operates as knowledge goods and knowledge work in the economy. Culture is material, economic, and non-economic (Williams 1977, Fuchs 2020). For Lefebvre, human beings' practices that constitute everyday life "*are* the soil" (CEL3, 123) of society. Everyday life is society's foundation[1]. In the book *Dialectical Materialism*, Lefebvre (2009, 73) argues that humans' "practical relations" are their "concrete conditions of existence". Human practices are social and societal and form society's foundation.

Lefebvre, however, assumes that information is "an immaterial product" (*CEL3*, 56). The separation of intangible products of mental work from matter is part of the orthodox dualism that Lefebvre questions. If the mind and its products and the products of mental work are immaterial, then there must be two substances in the world, matter and spirit. The question what the world is fundamentally made of can be based on a dualist ontology with two substances not be adequately explained. The assumption that there are two substances – the material and the immaterial – cannot explain what the world's ground is and opens up philosophy to spiritualism and esotericism that assume that the world is determined by spiritual forces.

The next section discusses the role of communication in everyday life.

5.3 Communication in Everyday Life

The critique of everyday life analyses how humans live, "how badly they live, or bow they do not live at all" (*CEL2*, 18). It aims at informing the transformation of society and

---

1 Shmuely (2008) points out the parallels between the works of Raymond Williams and Henri Lefebvre, including the cultural materialist interpretation of society that transcends the orthodox-Marxist base/superstructure-model.

people's lives. It is a praxis that wants to contribute to the establishment of "a decentralized socialism" (130). The critique of everyday life "attacks alienation in all its forms, in culture, ideology, the moral sphere, and in human life beyond culture, beyond ideology, beyond the moral sphere" (63). Lefebvre argues that in phases of fundamental societal change, "everyday life is suspended, shattered or changed" (109). For example, as a result of a general strike against government measures that degrade working conditions, the practices of everyday life such as commuting, shopping, and working come to a halt and alternative messages that are normally not being heard in everyday life are publicly communicated through demonstrations, public gatherings, media presence, and so forth. Everyday life is the "vital element in which the working classes" are active and that is controlled by the bourgeoisie (1971, 39).

Everyday life refers to social practices within the totality of society (*CEL2*, 31), humans' "lived experience" (*CEL1*, 49), everyday relations between humans. The focus on experience and class experience is a parallel between the approaches of Lefebvre and E. P. Thompson (1978). Thompson points out that lived experience involves affects, beliefs, consciousness culture, feelings, ideas, ideology, interests, instincts, law, morals, myth, needs, norms, obligations, science, thought, and values (see Fuchs 2019). Everyday life is an "intermediate and mediating *level*" of society (*CEL2*, 45). It mediates society's dialectics, such as the dialectic of repetition and monotony/creativity, banality/profoundness, need/desire, pleasure/pain, satisfaction/privation, fulfilment/emptiness, work/non-work, possible/impossible, random/certain, achieved/potential, cyclic time/linear time, alienation/disalienation, society/individual, private life/public life, etc. The critique of everyday life studies the "differences, dualities, oppositions and conflicts" that humans face (47).

Lefebvre argues for a multidimensional theory of society that operates with a variety of levels. He identifies three dimensions of everyday life: natural forms of necessity, the economic realm of the appropriation of objects and goods, and the realm of culture (*CEL2*, 62). So Lefebvre sees nature, the economy, and culture as three important realms of everyday life. What is missing is the realm of politics, where humans take collective decisions that are binding for all and take on the forms of rules.

Inspired by Lefebvre, we can identify three levels of society (see Table 5.1): the micro-level of individuals and groups, the meso-level of organisations, and the macro-level of the subsystems of society. Each of these levels has economic, political, and cultural dimensions. The economic, the political, and the cultural are distinct, interacting dimensions of society. Table 5.1 outlines what type of structures we find at society's various levels.

TABLE 5.1 Levels of society

	Micro-level	Meso-level	Macro-level
Economic structures	Use-values	Economic organisations & institutions	Economic subsystem of society
Political structures	Rules	Political organisations & institutions	Political subsystem of society
Cultural structures	Collective meanings, recognition	Cultural organisations & institutions	Cultural subsystem of society

TABLE 5.2 Lefebvre's distinction between the lived and the living (sources: *CEL2*, 166, 216–218)

The lived (le vécu)	The living (le vivre)
Individuals	Groups
Experience	Context, horizon
Practices	Structures
Present	Presence

Lefebvre argues that in society and at all of its levels and in all its dimensions, we find dialectics of social practices and social structures. There is a dialectic of practices and structures in society. Lefebvre's theory of society opposes the one-sidedness of both structuralism that fetishises structures and methodological individualism that fetishises individual thought and behaviour. A core aspect of his concept of everyday life that allows him to ground a dialectical theory of society is the dialectic of the lived and the living.

Lefebvre distinguishes between the lived (le vécu) and the living (le vivre) as two levels of everyday life (see Table 5.2). Based on Lefebvre, I have constructed a model of everyday life that adds to Lefebvre's theory the role of communication in everyday life as the process that mediates between the lived and the living. Figure 5.1 visualises this model.

The lived is the level of practices and individuals. The living is the level of structures and trans-individuality. At the level of lived reality, humans produce social objects through communicative practices. They do so under the conditions of the living, i.e. structural conditions that enable and constrain human practices, production, and communication. The notion of the communicative practice means that to "speak is to

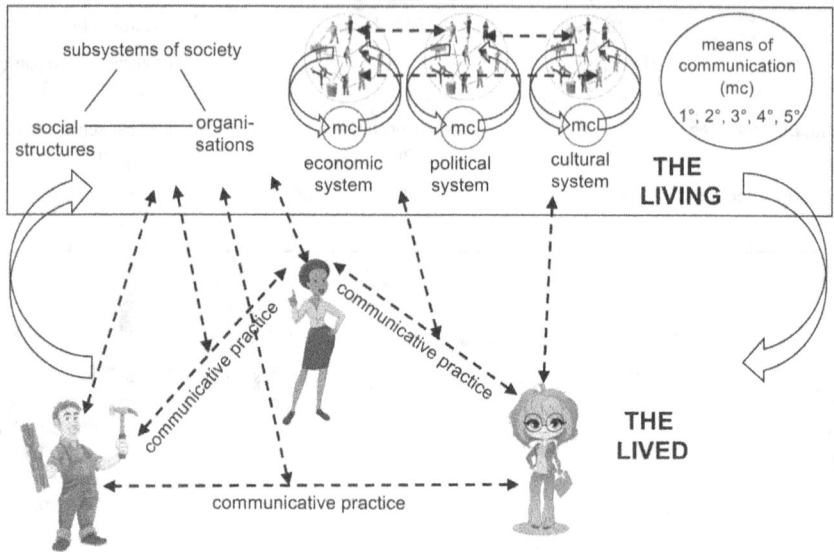

FIGURE 5.1 Everyday life and communication

act" (*CEL2*, 282). Practices are communicative and communication is a human practice. When we communicate, we influence ourselves and others.

The level of living life consists of an interaction of social structures, organisations, and the subsystems of society. All structures, groups, organisations, institutions, systems, and subsystems have economic, political, and cultural dimensions. In many social systems, one of these dimensions is dominant so that we can differentiate between economic, political and cultural structures/organisations/subsystems of society (compare Table 5.1). At the level of lived life, humans relate to each other through communicative practices. These communicative practices are the foundations of the production, reproduction, and differentiation of economic, political, and cultural structures/organisations/subsystems that condition human practices. There is a dialectic of the living and the lived in any society. This is a dialectic of human subjects and social objects.

Lefebvre stresses that in communication there are two subjects but that there is always the presence of the third (*CEL2*, 150–156). We talk about others and communication takes place in social contexts where others shape our everyday life and everyday communication. Communication also has the potential to change social structures which impacts the everyday life of others. There are parallels between

Lefebvre's focus on the tridimensionality of everyday life and communication and Jean-Paul Sartre's (1960/2004) argument that a human relation is a "ternary relation" (374) where the "unity of a dyad can be *realised* only within a totalisation performed from outside by a third party" (115), by a "human mediator" (106) (see also Fuchs 2021a for an analysis of Sartre's contribution to critical communication theory).

Language is dialectically related to communications. Whereas communication is a process and human practice, language is a structure and means. There is dialectic of means of communication and communicative practices. Lefebvre stresses that language is a "means of action and communication" (*CEL2*, 165), that it mediates the lived/living-dialectic (166), and that it is a social fact that "plays a part in all social facts" (170). Language is "the active element of every social phenomenon. It helps to bring it into being and to fix it" (170). Although language helps to fix the social and society, it is itself not a static, fixed structure but evolves because it is made and changed by humans. "Language is a work, the work of a society" (257). What Lefebvre expresses by saying that language is a work is that it is the historical result of humans' communicative practices and social relations. Humans work in society and thereby also collectively work on the development of language.

There are different forms of language such as written language, spoken language, visual language, abstract/formal languages, and so forth. Language is often a very structural concept devoid of its connection to communication and therefore to human practices and the human being. In contrast, the notion of the means of communication stresses the mediation of structures ("means") and practices ("communication"). Table 5.3 gives an overview of five types of the means of production.

The means of communication are structures that operate at the level of the living. Communicative practices are a dimension of the lived. Seen from the point of view of information and communication, the dialectic of the lived and the living is a dialectic of the means of communication and communicative practices. Communication is a dialectic of means and practices of communication. It involves a double dialectic: Communication's internal dialectic is a dialectic of communicative practices and means of communication. Communication's external dialectic means that communication has a mediating role in society. It mediates the dialectic of society and the individual, the dialectic of structures and individual practices, the dialectic of society's objects and subjects.

In volume two of *Critique of Dialectical Reason*, Lefebvre (*CEL2*, 276–314) introduces the notion of the semantic field. My own interpretation and understanding are that

TABLE 5.3 Five types of the means of communication

	Role of mediation by technology	Examples
Primary communication technologies	Human body and mind, no media technology is used for the production, distribution, reception of information	Theatre, concert, performance, interpersonal communication
Secondary communication technologies	Use of media technology for the production of information	Newspapers, magazines, books, technologically produced arts and culture
Tertiary communication technologies	Use of media technology for the production and consumption of information, not for distribution	CDs, DVDs, tapes, records, Blu-ray disks, hard disks
Quaternary communication technologies	Use of media technology for the production, distribution and consumption of information	TV, radio, film, telephone, Internet
Quinary communication technologies	Digital media prosumption technologies, user-generated content	Internet, social media

semantic field is the space where the dialectic of communicative practices and means of communication takes place. The semantic field has to do with (individual and social) consciousness (296), experience, knowledge, practices (299). It involves signals, signs (representations) such morphemes and the word (verbal and visual sign), language consisting of signs and syntactic and grammatical rules, symbols such as religious symbols (e.g. the cross) that operate at the level of affects, spontaneity and emotions; images, signification, expression, sense. All communication uses images. "The deepest communication of all is achieved through images" (289)

Lefebvre criticises that structural linguistics has shattered "the living (dialectical) unity" of language (*CEL2*, 293). It would reduce the semantic field to the sign. Behaviourism such as Pavlov's theory would reduce the semantic field to signals. Signification is the process of making meaning of a sign. Lefebvre sees it as a fixed and stable process that is attached to the sign. Expression is in contrast a creative process that involves the voice, gestures, and the face and has a certain level of unexpectedness. "Expression is speech. Signification is language as form" (293). Lefebvre says that a dialectical contradiction between signification and expression shapes the semantic field. This contradiction constantly results in the production of sense, the goal, orientation and direction of dialogue. Sense is the sublation of the contradiction between signification and expression.

Lefebvre argues that since the rise of industrialism, signals have invaded everyday life and have tried to programme everyday life (*CEL2*, 300). Lefebvre associates signals with the instrumental reason of quantification and computability. He imagines that cyberneticians could create "a gigantic machine" that processes signals and tries to regulate and control everyday life (300). Lefebvre anticipated discussions about digital surveillance and big data capitalism (see Fuchs 2021b).

The next section discusses everyday life and everyday communication in capitalism.

5.4 Everyday Life and Communication in Capitalism

5.4.1 Alienation

Alienation is Marx's most general category of critique. Whereas for Hegel contradiction is alienation, for Marx alienation is a type of social contradiction (*CEL1*, 70). It involves both exploitation and domination, the economic and the non-economic (see Fuchs 2018). It is not just specific for capitalism but for all dominative and class societies. Lefebvre (*CEL2*, 206–216) provides a definition of alienation: Alienation stops groups from "fully 'appropriating' the conditions in which they exist and keep them *below their possibilities*" (209). Alienation dehumanises human (*CEL1*, 180). Lefebvre argues there are many forms of alienation, not just economic alienation (*CEL1*, 52–83; *CEL2*, 206–216) but also, for example, social, political, ideological, or philosophical alienation (*CEL1*, 249). For Lefebvre, alienation is a process and reification a state. Reification is the result of and condition that shapes alienation. Alienation stands in a dialectical relation to disalienation. "The worst alienation is when the alienation itself is non-conscious (or unrecognized)" (*CEL2*, 208). Reification "both defines and disguises all alienations" (209). Lukács (1971) terms unrecognised alienation reified consciousness of the proletariat.

Based on Lefebvre's insight that there are multiple levels of society and alienation, we can identify three types of alienation: exploitation (economic alienation), domination (political alienation), and ideology (cultural alienation). All three forms have in common that not humans cannot control their conditions of existence that shape their lives. A privileged group with partial interests controls these conditions and derives benefit at the expense of everyday people. Table 5.4 opposes alienated societies to humanistic societies. It summarises the three types of alienation and relates them to the social character. The social character is a common type of social action and psychological disposition characteristic for a particular social group (Fromm 1965). Alienated societies are class and dominative societies. Humanist societies are non-dominative and post-class societies. Socialism is a humanism. True humanism is socialism.

Table 5.5 shows that alienation is an antagonistic social relation between human groups. Table 5.6 gives an overview of reification practices, alienated structures, co-operation practices, and humanistic structures. There is an antagonism between re-ification and co-operation and between alienation and humanism.

TABLE 5.4 The authoritarian and the humanistic character in the economy, politics, and culture

	Form of alienation	Dominant social character in alienated societies	Dominant social character in humanist societies
Economy	Exploitation	The exploiter	The commoner
Politics	Domination	The dictator	The democrat
Culture	Ideology	The ideologue/demagogue	The friend

TABLE 5.5 Three types of alienation as antagonistic social relations

Realm	Form of alienation	Alienating subjects	Alienated subjects
Economy	Exploitation	Dominant class of exploiters	Exploited class
Politics	Domination	Dictator, dictatorial group	Excluded groups and individuals
Culture	Ideology	Ideologues	Disrespected groups and individuals

TABLE 5.6 Alienation and disalienation in society

	Reification practices, alienated structures	Co-operation practices, humanistic structures
Economy	Exploitation: private property	Self-management: commons
Politics	Domination: dictatorship	Participation: democracy
Culture	Disrespect: ideology, demagoguery	Love: friendship

5.4.2 Accumulation

Lefebvre is not just interested in a general theory of society but has established a dialectical theory that is an interaction of a general social theory and a critical theory of capitalism. Capitalism is not just an economic system but a social formation, a type of society.

Lefebvre (*CEL2*, 315–339) distinguishes between accumulative and non-accumulative aspects of nature and society. The one's key aspect is their growth and increase of quantity, the other's key feature is quality and that non-accumulative systems cannot grow in a quantitative sense. For example, you can improve your moral values qualitatively but one cannot quantitatively increase morality. For Lefebvre, morality, sensitivity, sensory perception, sensuality, spontaneity, art, emotions and affects have a non-accumulative character. He sees a danger in attributing an accumulative character to them. Human spontaneity and creativity would thereby be undermined. He argues that there is a dialectic of accumulative and non-accumulative processes. For example, the brain stores, remembers, and forgets knowledge (331).

For Marx, accumulation is not a general process of society and humankind that consists in growth. Accumulation is rather a logic that is specific for capitalism. Accumulation implies uneven development, inequality, concentration of control and ownership. Accumulation of capital implies labour's non-ownership of capital. Marx (1867) argues that capital entails that "the product belongs to the capitalist and not to the worker" (731), that surplus-value is "the legitimate property of the capitalist" (731), and that the worker has to sell labour-power (731). Capitalism is "divorcing the producer from the means of production" (Marx 1867, 875). Labour is in capitalism "*absolute poverty* [...] as total exclusion of objective wealth" (Marx 1857/58, 296). Inequality is built into the accumulation of capital:

> Accumulation of wealth at one pole is, therefore, at the same time accumulation of misery, the torment of labour, slavery, ignorance, brutalisation and moral degradation at the opposite pole, i.e. on the side of the class that produces its own product as capital. (799)

The "increasing concentration of the social means of production in the hands of individual capitalists [...] grows directly out of accumulation, or rather is identical with it" (Marx 1867, 776). "Accumulation [...] presents itself [...] as increasing concentration of the means of production, and of the command over labour" (Marx 1867, 776–777).

Lefebvre's general sociological use of the term splits of non-ownership, inequality, concentration, and crisis from the concept of accumulation. He sees these phenomena as external to accumulation, whereas for Marx they are immanent to capital accumulation. Lefebvre's terminology risks fetishising capital accumulation as a natural process of society. For Lefebvre, the problem is accumulation that results as part of class society in inequality. For Marx, inequality is part of the definition of accumulation. There is a difference between growth as general natural and social process and accumulation as logic of increasing quantity that shapes capitalism.

Lefebvre clearly sees that surplus production beyond the realm of necessity exists in all societies that aim at increasing productivity. "A society without surplus product, in which labour allows for nothing more than the survival of its workers, will quickly disappear" (*CEL2*, 320). Scientific-technological progress is always connected to the question of how to create surplus. In capitalism, surplus-value production becomes and end in itself that serves the capitalist class' interests. The capitalist class owns the means of production, surplus-value, capital, profit, commodities, and compels the working class to sell its labour-power as commodity. In all class societies the ruling class owns the surplus product. The capitalist economy is specific in that workers are compelled to sell their labour-power and produce commodities, surplus-value and profit that are owned by the capitalist class. Lefebvre argues that in capitalist society, the accumulation of capital comes along with the accumulation of rationality and knowledge in culture and political action in bureaucracies (327). Lefebvre stresses that in capitalist society, the logic of accumulation extends beyond the economy into society at large.

Uneven development, the atomisation of the individual, and the segregation of individuals into groups with polarised interests in respect to the division of labour, education, influence, and so forth are the consequences of capitalist accumulation. Lefebvre argues that capitalism implies an uneven development of everyday life so that general upheaval benefits the ruling class and creates a "backward sector" where humans are exploited and oppressed (*CEL2*, 316). Lefebvre sees uneven development as a central feature of capitalism. He does, however, not see it, as Marx does, as identical with accumulation (Marx 1867, 776).

From Marx, we can take the insight that the logic of accumulation includes the alienation of workers from the control of the means of production, commodities, capital, surplus-value, and their own lives. From Lefebvre, we can take the insight that in capitalist society, accumulation is both an economic and a non-economic process.

In my own model that is based on these insights, society is the totality of social production processes. We can distinguish between social production in the economy, politics, and culture. In capitalism, we find the accumulation of capital in the economy, the accumulation of decision-power and influence in politics, and the accumulation of reputation, attention, and respect in culture. The key aspect is not that there is growth, but that there is the attempt of the dominant class and dominant groups to accumulate power at the expense of others who as a consequence have disadvantages. Capitalist society is therefore based on an economic antagonism of exploitation between classes and social antagonisms of domination.

Based on Marx and Lefebvre, we can outline some systematic aspects of capitalist society. Table 5.7 applies Table 5.1 to capitalist society. It shows what forms structures take on the various levels of capitalist society.

Table 5.8 shows how we can make sense of accumulation as general process and in capitalist society. In capitalism, alienation takes on the form of accumulation processes that create classes and inequalities. Capitalism is based on capitalists' accumulation of capital in the economy, bureaucrats' accumulation of decision-power and influence in the political system, and ideologues', influencers', and celebrities' accumulation of reputation, attention, and respect in the cultural system. Accumulation is an antagonistic relation that not just constitutes dominant classes and groups but also subordinated, dominated, and exploited groups such as the working class in the capitalist economy, dominated citizens in the capitalist political system, and ideologically targeted everyday people in capitalism's cultural system.

TABLE 5.7 Structures in capitalist society

	Micro-level	Meso-level	Macro-level
Economic structures	Commodity, money	Companies, markets	Capitalist economy
Political structures	Laws	Parties, government	The state
Cultural structures	Ideology	Ideology-producing organisations	Ideological system

TABLE 5.8 Accumulation as general process in capitalist society

Realm of society	Central process in general	Central process in capitalist society	Underlying antagonism in capitalist society
Economy	Production of use-values	Capital accumulation	Capitalists VS. workers
Politics	Production of collective decisions	Accumulation of decision-power and influence	Bureaucrats VS. citizens
Culture	Production of meanings	Accumulation of reputation, attention, respect	Ideologues/influencers/celebrities VS. everyday people

Everyday Life and Communication in Capitalism

TABLE 5.9 Alienation and disalienation/humanism in the context of knowledge and communication

Realm of society	Alienated knowledge and communication	Disalienated/humanistic knowledge and communication
Economic system	Knowledge and communication as private property, commodities, exploitation of knowledge labour, means of communication as private property	Knowledge and communication as commons, co-ownership and co-production in self-managed knowledge-creating companies
Political system	Dictatorial control of knowledge and communication processes	Participatory knowledge and democratic communication, public service media
Cultural system	Ideological knowledge and communication	Socialist humanist knowledge and communication, citizen media

TABLE 5.10 The role of accumulation in communicative capitalism and digital capitalism

Realm of society	Accumulation in capitalist society in respect to knowledge and communication	Accumulation in digital capitalism
Economy	Accumulation of capital based on knowledge commodities	Accumulation of digital capital based on digital commodities
Politics	Accumulation of decision-power in respect to the control of knowledge and communication	Accumulation of decision-power in respect to the control of digital knowledge and digital networks
Culture	Accumulation of reputation, attention and respect by the spread of ideologies such as individualism, nationalism, racism, etc.	Accumulation of reputation, attention and respect by the spread of ideologies on and of the Internet

Alienation also plays a role in the context of knowledge and communication. In capitalism, communication is "instrument and content" (Lefebvre 1971, 116–117). Lefebvre argues that in capitalism, active groups with active communication practices are replaced by "formal communication, means thus becoming ends and form content", ideologies (1971, 120), and "emptiness filled with signs" (1971, 135). Table 5.9 gives an overview of alienated and disalienated knowledge and communication. Table 5.10 shows a) the role of capitalist accumulation in respect to knowledge and communication and b) accumulation in digital capitalism[2].

Accumulation in communicative capitalism and digital capitalism results in particular forms of the social antagonisms characteristic for capitalism. Table 5.11 gives an overview of these antagonisms.

2 Studies of the Internet that have been influenced by Lefebvre include, for example, Bakardjieva, 2005; Nunes 2006; Poster 2006, part III.

TABLE 5.11 The antagonisms of communicative capitalism and digital capitalism

Realm of society	Underlying antagonism in capitalist society	Antagonisms in communicative capitalism	Antagonisms in digital capitalism
Economy	Capitalists VS. workers	Knowledge capital VS. knowledge labour	Digital capital VS. digital labour
Politics	Bureaucrats VS. citizens	Knowledge-based dictatorship VS. knowledge-based citizenship	Digital dictators VS. digital citizens
Culture	Ideologues, influencers and celebrities VS. everyday people	Ideologues VS. humans	Digital ideologues VS. digital humans

Reading Lefebvre's *Critique of Everyday Life* is an occasion and inspiration for thinking about the role of alienation in capitalism, communicative capitalism, and digital capitalism. In the next section, we will discuss another important dimension of a critical theory of communication, namely, ideology.

5.4.3 Digital Capitalism

Especially in *CEL*'s third volume that was published in French in 1981, Lefebvre gives attention to computing. At this time, personal and home computing was on the rise in France. In 1978, Nora and Minc (1980) published a report to the French President titled "The Computerization of Society". It shaped France's information society policy and prepared the introduction of the Minitel system, an early online service comparable to the WWW that used telephone lines, in the early 1980s. Lefebvre explicitly refers to this report in his discussion of "Information Technology and Daily Life" in *CEL*'s third volume (*CEL3*, part 2, chapter 6, 138 & 148/154 [footnote 8]).

Lefebvre argues that the "scientific and technological revolution" (*CEL3*, 9, 24, 84) was one of the factors that transformed the capitalist mode of production. Lefebvre here implicitly refers to Radovan Richta's report *Civilization at the Crossroads. Social and Human Implications of the Scientific and Technological Revolution* (Richta et al. 1969). Richta was a Czech philosopher, who in his report pointed out how computing transforms both capitalism and socialism. He saw on the one hand the deepening of class society as one dimension of computing in society and on the other hand the advancement of potentials for democratic socialism (see Boucas 2020; Fuchs 2020, chapter 7). Lefebvre sees on the one hand the potentials of computing to deepen class contradictions and on the other hand its potential to make "the end of work possible (in the long run)" (*CEL3*, 91). "Digitally controlled machines, as well as computer and remote control of complex processes, could replace repetitive, dangerous operations" (*CEL3*, 98).

Computers are things whose immense speed of computation exceeds human capacities. This focus on quantification resonates with the interest of the capitalist class to accumulate ever more capital in ever less time and with the bureaucracy to process lots of data about citizens in order to advance the administered society. Scientists and engineers are fascinated by the idea of playing God, for which the computing is an excellent field of research and development. Capitalist media require constant news and spectacles in order to create attention. Computing promises radical changes, which is why the media are interested in new digital technologies. The thing-character, speed, dualistic logic of computing impresses dominant groups, which results in the diffusion of digital ideology in everyday life in digital capitalism. Representatives of such groups "anticipate miracles" (*CEL3*, 143) from digital technologies. Lefebvre speaks of "the information ideology" (146–150) as the "myth of freedom realized by information technology" (91). He questions that computing "will generate its effects *automatically*, since it involves automation" (91). Computer scientists make "optimistic prophecies" (136).

The notion of digital ideology is an update of his notion to 21st-century digital capitalism. Today, such prophecies about computing, the Internet, mobile phones, social media, cloud computing, the Internet of things, industry 4.0, and ever more emergent digital technologies are widespread in daily life. You only need to open a newspaper to find them. I did so on the day when I wrote these lines. One of the first articles I found in the tech section of online news platforms was titled "The World's First 3D-Printed Neighborhood Is Being Built in Mexico for Families Living on $3 a Day" (Zdanowicz 2019). The piece was published in *CNN Online*'s tech section. The author claims that 3D-printing houses is so cheap and fast that the "technology holds promise for affordable housing". It suggests that housing could be created for the homeless. "The technology is there and the application to building homes for those in need brings a lot of hope for the future". The article disregards that building homes not just requires materials but also space that is predominantly privately owned and sold as commodity on financialised housing markets. 3D-printing is itself prone to be subsumed under capital. Those who control 3D-printing technologies can also control put price tags on designs and printers. The article presents 3D-printing as technological fix to the social problems of homelessness and housing crises. It disregards these problems' rootedness in capitalism and class.

Digital ideology conveys the impression that computing with necessity brings about certain changes of society that cannot be undone or stopped. As a consequence, digital ideology with its fetishistic aura of novelty, speed, and pseudo-radicalness distracts attention from class, exploitation, domination, and other social relations. "Information ideology possesses the dubious merit of prophetically heralding the new society: post-industrial, post-capitalist and even post-socialist" (C*EL3*, 147–148). Lefebvre reminds us that despite its aura of novelty the production of information involves "profits for those who are in charge of production" (144). In 2019, there were six information technology and media companies among the world's largest 20 transnational corporations[3]: Apple (#6), AT&T (#12), Samsung Electronics (#13), Microsoft (#16), Alphabet/Google (#17), Verizon Communication (#20). The digital world is first and foremost digital capitalism.

Lefebvre argues that information and communication have always been central for the organisation of capitalism and markets. Think, for example, about the communication of prices and available products. He says that "for many centuries, information as such did not appear on the market" and that what is "novel about the contemporary world is that there is a world market in information, which positively 'drives' the other markets, through advertising, propaganda, the transmission of positive knowledge, and so on" (*CEL3*, 145). The importance of informational and digital capitalism, where information and the digital are commodities, is a relatively recent dimension of capitalism.

Lefebvre says there is a split in society between the expelled such as the unemployed and precarious workers and those who are "well-integrated into circuits and networks focused around so-called 'high-tech production (nuclear energy, computer science, the arm industry, etc.)" (*CEL3*, 86). In 21st-century digital capitalism, there is on the one hand a split between digital capital and digital labour and on the other hand between a well-positioned digital labour aristocracy and precarious digital workers. Think, for example, on the one side of the software engineer with very high wages working for Google in Silicon Valley and on the other side the call-centre agent or the low-paid hardware assembler working for Foxconn in China. Digital capitalism is a deeply divided class society (see Fuchs 2014). Lefebvre argues that the bourgeoisie has made intellectuals and technicians "partners in its system", so that "the new middle class and the new bourgeoisie" (*CEL3*, 120) occupy city life and the working class is displaced.

---

3 Data source: Forbes 2000 List of the World's Largest Public Companies, year 2019, https://www.forbes.com/global2000

Lefebvre reminds us of the antagonistic character of technology in an antagonistic society. The question is if and how information technology is shaped in ways and shaping ways that advance capitalism or socialist self-management, where social groups control their "conditions of existence, of living and surviving" (*CEL3*, 153)

Based on Lefebvre's *CEL*, the next section deepens the engagement with the notion of ideology

5.5 The Communication of Ideology

There are representations of everyday life that take on the form of culture, knowledge, and ideologies (*CEL2*, 60–61). The critique of everyday life reveals the ideological character of such representations. It studies both the "empirical modality for the organization of human life" and the "representations which disguise this organization" (138). For Lefebvre (*CEL1*), Marxism is "a critical knowledge of everyday life" (148) that tears away "the veil of ideologies" (147), especially it is a critique of individualism, mystifications, mystified consciousness, money, needs, labour, and bourgeois freedom (148–175).

Lukács (1971) argues that "the daily life of bourgeois society" is shaped by "unthinking, mundane reality" (101), where the human being's existence is "reduced to an isolated particle and fed into an alien system" (90) and where reality "appears to be unmediated" (*Schein der Unmittelbarkeit* [literally: appearance of immediacy], 163). Lefebvre (*CEL1*, 152) argues that fetishism and alienation in capitalism create individualism and private consciousness, individuals who are "deprived of truth" and are "separated from […] concrete human social reality, deprived of a consciousness of the practical, historical and social whole.

The fetishism of capitalism's immediacy confronts human beings in everyday life. Everyday life is full of commodities, money, capital, and other things. Class relations and relations of dominations disappear behind the immediacy of things. Capitalist society, exploitation, and domination thereby appear to be normal and natural. Capitalist society makes humans forget their own historicity. The "fetish of the pure objectivity of economic relations obscures the fact that they are really relations between" humans (Lukács 1971, 240). While Merrifield (2006, 150–151) stresses the differences between Lefebvre and Lukács, Gardiner (2000, 79) and Trebitsch (1991, xvii-xix) point out the similarities. Lukács and Lefebvre were both influenced by Hegel's dialectical philosophy and Marx's theory of alienation. They are both Hegelian, praxis-oriented Marxist philosophers. Denying the parallels that undoubtedly exist between these two thinkers is a disservice to strengthening Hegelian, humanist Marxism today, an approach to which both Lukács and Lefebvre contributed.

The critique of ideology and fetishism in everyday life is a common feature of the theories of Lefebvre and Lukács. Both established critical analyses of ideology, fetishism, alienation and gave significant attention to praxis and social struggles. Both thinkers have an interest in showing how critique and class struggle can undo fetishistic, reified consciousness and fetishism as such. Lefebvre and Lukács contributed both major insights to the development of Marxist humanism. For Lefebvre, Marxist humanism means to create and struggle for conditions where not simply possession of objects is important but that humans enjoy "the'richest' relationship of joy or happiness with the 'object' – which can be a thing or a living being or a human being or a social reality" (*CEL1*, 156). Lukács points out that Marxist humanism means the total development of humanity, society, and human potentials, which implies the creation of a socialist democracy:

> It is therefore the purpose of socialist democracy to penetrate the totality of human existence and to present its social nature as the product of the activity and participation of all men, stretching from everyday life to the most important question of society. (Lukács 1988, 102)

Lefebvre and Lukács share Marx's understanding of socialism and humanism as "the real *appropriation* of human essence by and for man" (Marx, 1844, 296) so that the human being becomes a total human being that realises its full potentials (Marx, 1844, 299).

For Lefebvre (*CEL2*), ideology is "utilitarian and fetishist practice, which manipulates things" (243). Ideology is empirical consciousness that separates things from "activity and social relations" (243). It takes that which exists for granted and does not recognise its historical character (243). "It champions fetishism as valid consciousness" (243). Ideology is "fetishism in general" (*CEL3*, 53). Ideologies "are made of understanding and interpretation [...] of the world plus a certain amount of illusion, and might bear the name of 'culture'" (1971, 31). Ideology is part of culture. It is a form of culture. It is illusionary culture and the culture of illusion.

Empirical consciousness is Lefebvre's term for what Lukács characterises as reified consciousness. Reified consciousness disregards "contradiction and antagonism"

(Lukács 1971, 10) and the totality. It fetishises "quantifiable 'things'" (Lukács 1971, 90) such as capital, money, and commodities. Lefebvre stresses that commodity logic is "bound up with the general language of quantification" (*CEL3*, 56) that "quantification has conquered society in its entirety" (131) and that the "qualitative has *virtually* disappeared" (131) in everyday life.

Lukács and Lefebvre are both critics of positivism. They oppose dialectical thought to the positivist ideology. Positivism neglects and denies contradictions and the negative. In digital capitalism, digital positivism has emerged as a new ideology that fetishises big data and computing (Fuchs 2017). In this ideology, the collection of massive amounts of data and computing technology in general are seen and presented as the solutions to economic, political, and cultural problems. Digital positivism abstracts from alienation and the antagonisms of capitalist society.

Especially the second volume of *Critique of Everyday Life* tries to show how everyday life is manipulated by advertising, the capitalist media, and the capitalist press. There are strong parallels between Lefebvre's critique, Debord's (1967) critique of the spectacle, Horkheimer and Adorno's (2002) critique of the culture industry, and Marcuse's (1964/1991) critique of one-dimensional man (see also Merrifield 2006, 25–26, 30–36; Schmidt 1972). For example, Lefebvre's insight that the leisure and culture industry create "organized leisure and culture" (*CEL3*, 82) that is homogeneous, fragmented, and hierarchised (*CEL3*, part 1, chapter 8) resonates with Horkheimer and Adorno's (2002, xi, xii) insight that the culture industry creates an "administered world". For Lefebvre, socialism in contrast to capitalist everyday life means the strengthening of the right to difference, equality in difference, and unity (*CEL3*, part 1, chapter 8). Taken together, this means he argues for a programme of unity in diversity as opposed to unity without diversity and diversity without unity.

Lefebvre speaks of "the manipulation of the consumer and of his needs by advertising and propaganda" (*CEL2*, 146) and says that new technologies and consumer capitalism have colonised everyday life (11). He extends the notion of alienation from labour to leisure (*CEL1*, 39) He points out that "'consumer society' manipulates needs; the masters of production are also the masters of consumption, and they also produce the demands for which and according to which they are supposed to be producing" (*CEL2*, 223). There is not a self-regulating market driven by demand and supply but a capitalist system that the capitalist class consciously controls and manipulates in order to accumulate capital. Capitalist leisure is dominated by images and films that promise to distract and "*compensate* for the difficulties of everyday life" (*CEL1*, 33), especially those that exist in respect to labour. The culture industry produces illusory reverse images that create a "false world" that presents itself as true and tries to replace "real unhappiness by fictions of happiness" (*CEL1*, 35).

In the age of digital capitalism, a significant share of everyday life time is spent on social media platforms such as YouTube, Facebook, Instagram, and Twitter. In 2020, the average Internet user aged between 16 and 64 years spent 6 hours and 43 minutes per day on the Internet, 3 hours and 18 minutes watching television, 2 hours and 24 minutes on social media, 1 hour and 26 minutes listening to music on an online streaming platform, and 1 hour and 10 minutes playing video games (We Are Social 2020, 31). In April 2020, the most-watched YouTube video of all times was Luis Fonsi's music video "Despacito"[4]. Social media is primarily about entertainment, advertising, and commerce. The difference to the traditional culture industry is that users actively search, browse, and click for content that is quickly consumed, is very short, and is processed and distributed at very high speed. Compensation and distraction online take place in a more active manner than in the mass media, with a high volume of produced, distributed, and consumed content that is processed at very high speed; with little time spent on a single cultural unit such as a tweet, a Facebook posting, a YouTube video, or an Instagram image than in the traditional mass media; and with interactive possibilities for user-generated content, likes, and comments.

Lefebvre criticises capitalist television as a form of ideology. Television in capitalism "allows every household to look at the spectacle of the world" is a form of "non-communication", "non-participation", and "receptive passivity"; it presents everyday life as "unusual or picturesque and overloading it with meaning" (*CEL2*, 76).

> Using highly sophisticated techniques, mass communications bring master-pieces of art and culture to everyone; [...] Modern techniques make taste more sophisticated, raise the level of culture, instruct, educate, and bring an encyclopaedic culture to the people. At the same time, they make their audience passive. They make them infantile. They "present" the world in a particular mode, the mode of spectacle and the gaze, with all the ambiguity we have already noted and which we continue to emphasize: non-participation in a false presence. (223–224)

In his discussion of advertising, Lefebvre argues that in capitalism, everyday time

4 https://en.wikipedia.org/wiki/List_of_most-viewed_YouTube_videos, accessed on 29 April 2020.

becomes "both homogeneous and dispersed. Work time falls into line with family-life time and leisure time, if not vice versa" (*CEL2*, 79). There are certain parallels here between Lefebvre and Dallas Smythe's (1977) argument that in advertising, audiences are workers who produce an audience commodity that advertisers sell to clients. The consumption of advertising takes place in everyday life and during all daytime. Everyday spaces such as the home where leisure time and family-life time take place are the factories where advertising capital exploits audiences as workers who create attention to ads. In the age of Facebook, audience labour has taken on a new form. Facebook, YouTube, and other Internet platforms that are based on targeted ads exploit users' digital labour that creates online content, attention, data, meta-data, social relations, and attention (Fuchs 2021b). Users' and audiences' leisure time is labour time that creates advertising companies' profits. There is today a general tendency that labour time absorbs leisure time so that humans work long hours from a variety of places, including the home, cafés, public spaces, means of transportation, the Internet, the mobile phone, and so forth. The blurring of the boundaries between labour/leisure, the office/the home, production/consumption, labour/play, public/private, and so forth has resulted from the capitalist colonisation of everyday life so that the logic of profit, accumulation, capital, and labour determines ever more spaces and time of human life.

Lefebvre argues that everyday life is the place where exploitation takes place. He argues that consumer capitalism extends alienation and exploitation from the economy into culture:

> According to this theory, daily life replaces the colonies. Incapable of maintaining the old imperialism, searching for new tools of domination, and having decided to bank on the home market, capitalist leaders treat daily life as they once treated the colonized territories: massive trading posts (supermarkets and shopping centres); absolute predominance of exchange over use; dual exploitation of the dominated in their capacity as producers and consumers. (*CEL3*, 26)

Lefebvre's argument that consumer capitalism means the exploitation of producers and consumers resonates with the contemporary development in digital capitalism that on the capitalist Internet, consumers of information become producers of information who produce online content and social relations. Google and Facebook exploit consumers of the Internet who are, while consuming targeted-ad based online platforms, producers of these companies' surplus-value.

As examples of how to challenge ideology, Lefebvre (*CEL1*, 10–28) discusses Charlie Chaplin's humour, the estrangement effect/distancing effect (*Verfremdungseffekt*) in

FIGURE 5.2 An Apple subvertisement, source: https://www.flickr.com/photos/53359511@N00/256232830, CC-BY licence, created by Brian Fitzgerald

Brecht's epic theatre, and Roger Vailland's writings. These are strategies of making audiences aware of alienation by estranging the estranged aspects of everyday life. Adbusters is an example of dialectical ideology critique from the contemporary age of digital capitalism that Lefbvre would certainly approve of. Adbusters (https://www.adbusters.org/) is a collective that criticises capital and consumer culture by radically affirming the logic of advertising and commodity consumption. It criticises commodity culture through the language and use of commodity culture. Examples are subvertisements, critiques of advertisements that take on the format of ads and are spread online. Figure 5.2 shows an example subvertisement. It builds on a popular Apple ad that presents consumers of Apple hardware as hip, modern, and future-oriented. The subvertisement uses the same aesthetic but adds an e-waste pile in order to criticise Apple's complicity in waste production.

5.6 Conclusion

This chapter has shown that Henri Lefebvre's *Critique of Everyday Life* can inform a critical, dialectical, humanist theory of communication and society in respect to several aspects: the relationship of the economy and culture, communication in everyday life, communication in capitalism, and the communication of ideology.

5.6.1 The Relationship of the Economy and Culture

Lefebvre argues that the rise of information technology undermines the orthodox and Stalinist assumption that there is an economic base and a cultural and political superstructure. The economy operates as the production of ideas in culture. Culture operates as knowledge goods and knowledge work in the economy. Culture is material, economic, and non-economic. Lefebvre partly uses himself the language of base and superstructures and speaks of the immaterial character of culture, which contradicts his criticism of Marxist orthodoxy.

5.6.2 Communication in Everyday Life

Lefebvre is a critic of structuralism, who stresses the importance of practices in society. Everyday life refers to social practices within the totality of society. It is a dialectic of structures and practices, of what Lefebvre terms the living (le vivre) and the lived (le vécu). Everyday life is an important category for a dialectical theory of society and communication. What we need to add to Lefebvre's theory is the role of communication as the process of the production of sociality that mediates the dialectic of the individual and society, individual practices/thought and social structures, the lived and the living. Lefebvre introduces the notion of the semantic field. The semantic field is the space where the dialectic of communicative practices and means of communication takes place.

5.6.3 Communication in Capitalism

Lefebvre stresses the dialectical multidimensionality of society and alienation, which allows us to distinguish between the economic, political, and the cultural as dialectically interacting and interpenetrating dimensions of society. He points out that alienation and accumulation extend beyond the economy into society at large. We can identify three types of alienation: exploitation (economic alienation), domination (political alienation), and ideology (cultural alienation). In capitalism, alienation takes on the form of capital accumulation in the economy, the accumulation of decision-power in the political system, and the accumulation of reputation in the cultural system. It creates inequalities and therefore exploited and oppressed groups and classes, of which the working class is the largest and most important one. Based on, among others, Lefebvre, Marx, and Lukács, a critical theory of communication can be grounded in a critical theory of alienation and capitalism. There are economic, political, and cultural dimensions of the alienation of communication. In digital capitalism, alienation takes on the economic form of the antagonism between digital labour and digital capital, the political form of the antagonism between digital dictators and digital citizens, and the cultural form of the antagonism between digital ideologues and digital humans.

Lefebvre reminds us of the predominantly capitalist character of digital technologies. In digital capitalism, we find ideology that mystifies information and the digital. Computing has potentials to deepen capitalism and class and to advance socialist self-management. It shapes and is shaped by society.

5.6.4 The Communication of Ideology

For Lefebvre, the critique of everyday life is also a critique of ideology. Lefebvre's concept of empirical consciousness parallels Lukács' notion of reified consciousness. Both are today relevant for the critique of digital positivism. Lefebvre's critique of consumer capitalism shares many features of the works of Max Horkheimer, Theodor W. Adorno, Herbert Marcuse, and Guy Debord. For Lefebvre, everyday life is a colony of capitalism where uneven development takes place in multiple forms. Lefebvre's insight that consumer capitalism not just exploits workers in the factory and the office but extends exploitation into leisure time and consumption resonates with Dallas Smythe's concept of audience labour and the theory of digital labour that sees users of targeted-ad based Internet platforms as digital workers who are exploited by digital capital.

Henri Lefebvre's *Critique of Everyday Life* is an important influence for the foundations of a critical theory of communication in general and a critical theory of communication in and beyond digital capitalism.

References

Bakardjieva, Maria. 2005. *Internet Society: The Internet in Everyday Life*. London: Sage.

Boucas, Dimitris. 2020. Theory, Reality, and Possibilities for a Digital/Communicative Socialist Society. *tripleC: Communication, Capitalism & Critique* 18 (1): 48–66.

Debord, Guy. 1967. *The Society of the Spectacle*. London: Rebel Press.

Elden, Stuart. 2004. *Understanding Henri Lefebvre. Theory and the Possible*. London: Continuum.

Fromm, Erich. 1965. The Application of Humanist Psychoanalysis to Marx's Theory. In *Socialist Humanism: An International Symposium*, ed. Erich Fromm, 207–222. Garden City, NY: Doubleday.

Fuchs, Christian 2021a. Jean-Paul Sartre as Social Theorist if Communication. A Theoretical Engagement with "Critique of Dialectical Reason". In *Christian Fuchs: Marxist Humanism and Communication Theory. Media, Communication and Society Volume One*, 177–204. London: Routledge.

Fuchs, Christian. 2021b. *Social Media: A Critical Introduction*. London: Sage. Third edition.

Fuchs, Christian. 2020. *Communication and Capitalism. A Critical Theory*. London: University of Westminster Press.

Fuchs, Christian. 2019. Revisiting the Althusser/E. P. Thompson-Controversy: Towards a Marxist Theory of Communication. *Communication and the Public* 4 (1): 3–20.

Fuchs, Christian. 2018. Universal Alienation, Formal and Real Subsumption of Society Under Capital, Ongoing Primitive Accumulation by Dispossession: Reflections on the Marx@200-Contributions by David Harvey and Michael Hardt/Toni Negri. *tripleC: Communication, Capitalism & Critique* 16 (2): 454–467.

Fuchs, Christian. 2017. From Digital Positivism and Administrative Big Data Analytics Towards Critical Digital and Social Media Research! *European Journal of Communication* 32 (1): 37–49.

Fuchs, Christian. 2014. *Digital Labour and Karl Marx*. New York: Routledge.

Gardiner, Michael E. 2000. *Critiques of Everyday Life*. London: Routledge.

Horkheimer, Max. 1947/2004. *Eclipse of Reason*. London: Continuum.

Horkheimer, Max and Theodor W. Adorno. 2002. *Dialectic of Enlightenment. Philosophical Fragments*. Stanford, CA: Stanford University Press.

Lefebvre, Henri. 2014. *Critique of Everyday Life: The One-Volume Edition*. London: Verso.

Lefebvre, Henri. 2009. *Dialectical Materialism*. Minneapolis, MN: University of Minnesota Press.

Lefebvre, Henri. 2008. *Critique of Everyday Life. Volume III: From Modernity to Modernism*. London: Verso.

Lefebvre, Henri. 2002. *Critique of Everyday Life. Volume II: Foundations for a Sociology of the Everyday*. London: Verso.

Lefebvre, Henri. 1991. *Critique of Everyday Life. Volume I: Introduction*. London: Verso.

Lefebvre, Henri. 1974/1991. *The Production of Space*. Malden, MA: Blackwell.

Lefebvre, Henri. 1971. *Everyday Life in the Modern World*. New York: Harper & Row.

Lukács, Georg. 1971. *History and Class Consciousness*. London: Merlin.

Lukács, Georg. 1988. *The Process of Democratization*. Albany, NY: State University of New York Press.

Marcuse, Herbert. 1964/1991. *One-Dimensional Man. Studies in the Ideology of Advanced Industrial Society*. Abingdon: Routledge. Second edition.

Marx, Karl. 1867. *Capital Volume I*. London: Penguin.

Marx, Karl. 1857/58. *Grundrisse*. London: Penguin.

Marx, Karl. 1844. Economic and Philosophic Manuscripts of 1844. In *Marx & Engels Collected Works (MECW)*, 229–346. London: Lawrence & Wishart.

Nora, Simon and Alain Minc. 1980. *The Computerization of Society: A Report to the President of France*. London: MIT Press.

Nunes, Mark. 2006. *Cyberspaces of Everyday Life*. Minneapolis, MN: University of Minnesota Press.

Merrifield, Andy. 2006. *Henri Lefebvre: A Critical Introduction*. New York: Routledge.

Poster, Mark. 2006. *Information Please. Culture and Politics in the Age of Digital Machines*. Durham, NC: Duke University Press.

Richta, Radovan et al. 1969. *Civilization at the Crossroads. Social and Human Implications of the Scientific and Technological Revolution*. White Plains, NY: International Arts and Sciences Press Inc.

Sartre, Jean-Paul. 1960/2004. *Critique of Dialectical Reason. Volume 1: Theory of Practical Ensembles*. London, England: Verso.

Schmidt Alfred. 1972. Henri Lefebvre and Contemporary Interpretations of Marx. In *The Unknown Dimension: European Marxism since Lenin*, eds. Dick Howard and Karl E. Klare, 322–341. New York: Basic Books.

Shields, Rob. 1999. *Lefebvre, Love and Struggle. Spatial Dialectics*. London: Routledge.

Shmuely, Andrew. 2008. Totality, Hegemony, Difference. Henri Lefebvre and Raymond Williams. In *Space, Difference, Everyday Life*, eds. Kanishka Goonewardena, Stefan Kipfer, Richard Milgrom and Christian Schmid, 212–230. New York: Routledge.

Smythe, Dallas. 1977. Communications: Blindspot of Western Marxism. Canadian *Journal of Political and Society Theory* 1 (3): 1–28.

Thompson, Edward P. 1978. *The Poverty of Theory & Other Essays*. London: Merlin.

Trebitsch, Michel. 1991. Preface. In Henri Lefebvre: Critique of Everyday Life. Volume 1: Introduction, ix–xxviii. London: Verso.

We Are Social. 2020. *Digital 2020. Global Digital Overview*. London: We Are Social.

Williams, Raymond. 1977. *Marxism and Literature*. Oxford: Oxford University Press.

Zdanowicz, Christina. 2019. The World's First 3D-Printed Neighborhood Is Being Built in Mexico for Families Living on $3 a Day. *CNN Online*, 12 December 2019, https://edition.cnn.com/2019/12/12/business/worlds-first-3d-printed-neighborhood-trnd/index.html

Chapter Six
Dallas Smythe and Digital Labour

6.1 Introduction

Dallas Smythe (1977) established the notions of the audience commodity and audience labour in 1977 for understanding the political economy of commercial media using advertising as their capital accumulation model. His article has resulted in a foundational debate of Media and Communication Studies that involved Smythe (1977, 1978), Graham Murdock (1978) and Bill Livant (1979). In recent years there has been a very significant rise of references to Smythe's concepts of audience labour/commodification in academic works (see also Fuchs 2012b). This increasing interest has on the one hand to do with a return of a stronger interest in Marx's works and Marxist political economy as well as the rise of social media platforms such as Facebook, YouTube, Twitter, Weibo, Pinterest, Instagram, Blogspot, VKontakte, LinkedIn, Tumblr, and so forth that use targeted advertising as their capital accumulation model (Fuchs 2012b, 2014a, 2014c). Explaining how this form of capital accumulation model rises has resulted in the development of the category of digital labour[1].

6.2 Audience Labour

The analysis and critique of advertising played a special role in Dallas Smythe's works. He conducted studies of advertising time on commercial television and found that advertising "occupies about one of every five minutes of big city television program time and about of every four minutes of smaller-city program time" (Smythe 1994, 66).

---

1 For an overview see the contributions in Scholz (2013).

DOI: 10.4324/9781003222149-6

Smythe criticised critical and administrative scholars for focusing narrowly on commercial media in terms of messages, information, images, meaning, entertainment, orientation, education, manipulation, and ideology (Smythe 1977, 1).

Smythe asked the question who produces the commodity of the commercial, advertising-financed media. He said that "audiences and readerships" (Smythe 1977, 3) are the workers of the commercial media. They create the "demand for advertised goods" and by consuming media reproduce "their own labor power" (Smythe 1977, 3).

Dallas Smythe's notion of audience labour challenged the idea that one can only be exploited if one earns a wage in a factory. He opened up the notion of exploitation for the age of consumer culture. His notion also challenges the idea that the home and the private sphere are insulated against exploitation, an insight that he shares with Marxist feminism that since the 1970s has stressed the importance of considering reproductive labour as value-generating and therefore exploited by capital. Mariarosa Dalla Costa and Selma James challenged the orthodox-Marxist assumption that reproductive work is "outside social productivity". (Dalla Costa and James 1972, 30; see also Eisenstein 1979, Mies 1986)".

Orthodox-Marxist criticisms of Marxist feminism echo the polemical criticism that Michael Lebowitz and others marshalled against Smythe. Michael Lebowitz argues that Smythe's approach is only a "Marxist-sounding communications theory" (Lebowitz 1986, 165). Marxism would assume that

> surplus value in capitalism is generated in the direct process of production, the process where workers (having surrendered the property rights over the disposition of their labour-power) are *compelled* to work longer than is necessary to produce the equivalent of their wage. Perhaps it is for this reason that there is hesitation in accepting the conception that audiences work, are exploited, and produce surplus value – in that it is a paradigm quite different to the Marxist paradigm. (Lebowitz 1986, 167)

Media capitalists would compete "for the expenditures of competing industrial capitalists", help to "increase the commodity sales of industrial capitalists" and their profits would be "a share of the surplus value of industrial capital" (Lebowitz 1986, 169). Smythe's audience commodity approach would advance an "entirely un-Marxian argument with un-Marxian conclusions" (Lebowitz 1986, 170). In relation to Sut Jhally and Bill Livant's approach that is building on the one of Smythe, Richard Maxwell (1991, 40) argues that "Jhally and Livant misapplied certain propositions in the theory of value to a realm which may be relatively autonomous from the discipline of wage-labor" and that "wage-labor" is "the necessary element of labour control and exploitation in the trans-valuation of televiewing". Related approaches have argued that not the audiences of commercial media are exploited, but the statisticians working for audience rating companies (Bolin 2011, Meehan 1984).

The immediate theoretical and political consequences Lebowitz's logic of argumentation are the following ones:

1) Commercial media are subsumed to industrial capital.
2) Slaves, house workers and other unpaid workers are not exploited.
3) The wage and non-wage work performed under the command of media capital is unproductive work. Media companies cannot exploit workers because they create products and services that are part of the circulation sphere of capitalism.

Graham Murdock (1978) pointed out in the Blindspot Debate that the audience commodity is just one of several political economies of the media besides the sale of content and a strong public service tradition in Europe. He also stressed that corporate media have an ideological role in capitalism. In his 2014 reflection on his debate with Dallas Smythe, Murdock (2014) argued that the notion of the audience commodity would be of crucial relevance for understanding exploitation in the digital age. The digital media landscape would however not just be shaped by commodification, but have huge potentials for the emergence of digital commons. Graham Murdock points out the importance of re-considering the notions of the audience commodity and audience labour in the context of digital media, which points towards the necessity of the category of digital labour for understanding the political economy of advertising-financed digital media.

6.2.1 Digital Labour

The digital labour debate has in its first phase focused on understanding the value creation mechanisms on corporate social media such as Facebook, YouTube, and Twitter. Authors have, for example, discussed the usefulness of Karl Marx's labour theory of value (Arvidsson and Colleoni 2012, Fuchs 2010, Fuchs 2012c), how the notion of alienation shall be used in the context of digital labour (Andrejevic 2012), or if and how Dallas Smythe's notion of audience labour can be used for understanding digital labour (for an overview discussion see Fuchs 2012b, 2014c). The general task has been how to best understand and conceptualise that users under real-time far-reaching conditions of commercial surveillance create a data commodity that is sold to advertising clients and who exactly creates the value that manifests itself in social media corporations' profits. Studying digital labour is now in a second stage, where it gives attention to theorising digital labour in all its forms.

An important question that has arisen within the digital labour debate is if it suffices to focus on the social media world and to limit the notion of digital labour to paid or unpaid work in the online realm (or even narrower to limit the term to users' unpaid labour on social media). We access social media on laptops and mobile phones that tend to be assembled in China. Hon Hai Precision (also known as Foxconn) is a Taiwanese company that was the 139th largest company in the world in 2014[2]. According to the CNN Global 500 2012 list[3], Foxconn was the fifth largest corporate employer in the world in 2012. In 2011, Foxconn had enlarged its Chinese workforce to a million, with a majority being young migrant workers who come from the countryside (SACOM 2011). Foxconn assembles, e.g. the iPad, iMac, iPhone, Kindle, various consoles (by Sony, Nintendo, Microsoft). When 17 Foxconn workers attempted to commit suicide between January and August 2010 (most of them "successfully"), the topic of bad working conditions in the ICT assemblage industry became widely known. This circumstance was followed up with a number of academic works that show that workers' everyday reality at Foxconn includes low wages, working long hours, frequent work shift changes, regular working time of over 10 hours per day, lack of breaks, monotonous work, physical harm caused by chemicals such as benzene or solder paste, lack of protective gear and equipment, forced use of students from vocational schools as interns (in agreement with the school boards) that conduct regular assembly work that does not help their studies, prison-like accommodations with 6–22 workers per room, yellow unions that are managed by company officials and whom the workers do not trust, harsh management methods, a lack of breaks, prohibitions that workers move, talk or stretch their bodies, workers that had to stand during production, punishments, beatings and harassments by security guards, disgusting food (Chan 2013; Chan, Pun and Selden 2013, Pun and Chan 2012, Qiu 2012; Sandoval 2013, 2014). The Foxconn example shows that the existence and usage of digital media not just depends on the labour of software engineers and content producers. Digital labour covers a broad range of labour working under different conditions, including slave miners

2 Forbes 2000, 2014 list: http://www.forbes.com/global2000/, accessed on August 18, 2014.
3 http://money.cnn.com/magazines/fortune/global500/2012/full_list/, accessed on October 29, 2013.

working in African conflict mines, smelters, hardware assemblers, software engineers, digital media content producers, eWaste workers, or users of commercial digital media.

Given the complex, networked, and transnational reality of labour required for the existence and usage of digital media, a concept of digital labour is needed that can reflect these realities. One needs to go beyond cultural-idealist approaches that only focus on user-generated content and see how content production is grounded in in-dustrial and agricultural labour and how the appropriation of nature in this respect interacts with culture. For adequately studying digital labour and digital media in general, a cultural-materialist approach is needed (Fuchs 2013, 2013a; Fuchs and Sandoval 2014; Maxwell and Miller 2012). Given these preliminary assumptions, one can provide a definition of digital work and digital labour (see Fuchs 2014a, 2015; Fuchs and Sandoval 2014; Fuchs and Sevignani 2013):

- Digital work is all activity that creates digital media or uses them for creating use-values that satisfy human needs.
- Digital labour is alienated digital work: it is alienated from itself, from the instruments and objects of labour and from the products of labour. Alienation is alienation of the subject from itself (labour-power is put to use for and is controlled by capital), alienation from the object (the objects of labour and the instruments of labour) and the subject-object (the products of labour).

The digital labour debate has been accompanied a resurgent interest in Dallas Smythe's concept of audience labour and audience commodification for explaining the role of targeted advertising on social media (see Fuchs 2012b). In this context notions such as prosumer labour (Fuchs 2010, 2014c, 2015) have been used.

Prosumer labour on social media differs in a number of respects from audience labour in broadcasting:

- Creativity and social relations: Broadcasting audiences produce meanings of programmes, whereas social media prosumers not just produce meanings but also content, communications with other users, and social relations.
- Surveillance: Broadcasting requires audience measurements, which are approximations, in order to sell audiences as commodities. Social media corporations monitor, store, and assess all online activities of users on their platforms and also on other platforms. They have very detailed profiles of users'

activities, interests, communications, and social relations. Constant real-time surveillance of users is an inherent feature of prosumers labour on capitalist social media. Personal data are sold as a commodity. Measuring audiences has in broadcasting and print traditionally been based on studies with small samples of audience members. Measuring and monitoring user behaviour on social media is constant, total, and algorithmic (Allmer 2014; Allmer, Fuchs, Kreilinger and Sevignani 2014; Fuchs 2012a; Fuchs and Sevignani 2013).

- Targeted and personalised advertising: Advertising on capitalist social media can therefore more easily target user interests and personalise ads, whereas this is more difficult in commercial broadcasting.
- Algorithmic auctions: Algorithms organise the pricing of the user data commodity in the form of auctions for online advertising spaces on the screens of a specific number of users. The ad prices on social media vary depending on the number of auctioneers, whereas the ad prices in newspapers and on radio and TV are set in a relatively fixed manner and are publicly advertised. User measurement uses predictive algorithms (if you like A, you may also like B because 100,000 people who like A also like B)

6.3 Digital Labour and Productive Labour

The digital labour debate has been accompanied by the question how feasible Karl Marx's labour theory of value is for understanding digital labour. And often-overlooked aspect is that this theory is a theory of time in capitalism and that digital labour needs therefore to be situated in the temporalities of capitalism (see Fuchs 2014b). One criticism brought forward against those who argue that users of corporate social media platforms that use targeted advertising are exploited has been that advertising as part of the sphere of circulation that only realises but does not create value, and that users' activities are one or several of the following (see, e.g. Bolaño and Vieira, 2015; Comor 2014, Huws 2014, Reveley 2013, Rigi and Prey 2015; for a reply to these not always original arguments that tend to simply over and over repeat and re-iterate Michael Lebowitz' view, see: Fuchs 2015): unproductive, no labour at all, less productive, a consumption of value generated by paid employees in sectors and companies that advertise on social media, or an expression of a system where what appears as profits are rents derived from the profits of advertisers. These opinions are not new but just a reformulation of Lebowitz's criticism of Smythe.

The crucial category used in such discussions is Marx's notion of productive labour. There are passages, where Marx argues that only wageworkers who produce surplus-value and capital that is accumulated is productive labour. For example:

> Every productive worker is a wage-labourer, but not every wage-labourer is a productive worker. Whenever labour is purchased to be consumed as a use-value, as a service and not to replace the value of variable capital with its own vitality and be incorporated into the capitalist process of production - whenever that happens, labour is not productive and the wage-labourer is no productive worker. (Marx 1867, 1041)

Or:

> Productive labour, therefore, can be so described when it is directly exchanged for money as capital, or, which is only a more concise way of putting it, is exchanged directly for capital, that is, for money which in its essence is capital, which is destined to function as capital, or confronts labour-power as capital. The phrase: labour which is directly exchanged for capital, implies that labour is exchanged for money as capital and actually transforms it into capital. (Marx 1862/1863, 396–397)

Marx's thoughts on this topic are, however, inconsistent, so there cannot be one "true" interpretation of what productive and unproductive labour is. The interpretation of productive labour that I follow is one that stresses the notion of the *Gesamtarbeiter* (collective worker).

Marx stresses that work is not an individual process. The more co-operative and networked work becomes, which is the consequence of the technification of capitalism and the rise of knowledge in production, the more relevant becomes Marx's third understanding of productive labour: productive labour as labour of the collective worker. The notion of the collective worker becomes ever more important with the development of fixed constant capital and productivity (Marx 1857/1858, 707). Marx has set out this concept both in *Capital, Volume 1*, and the *Results of the Immediate Production Process*. He argues that all work is productive that is "an organ of the collective labourer, and to perform any one of its subordinate functions" (Marx 1867, 644) and that with the development of co-operation an "ever increasing number of types of labour are included in the immediate concept of productive labour" so that "the aggregate worker" creates "an aggregate product which is at the same time a quantity of goods" (Marx 1867, 1040).

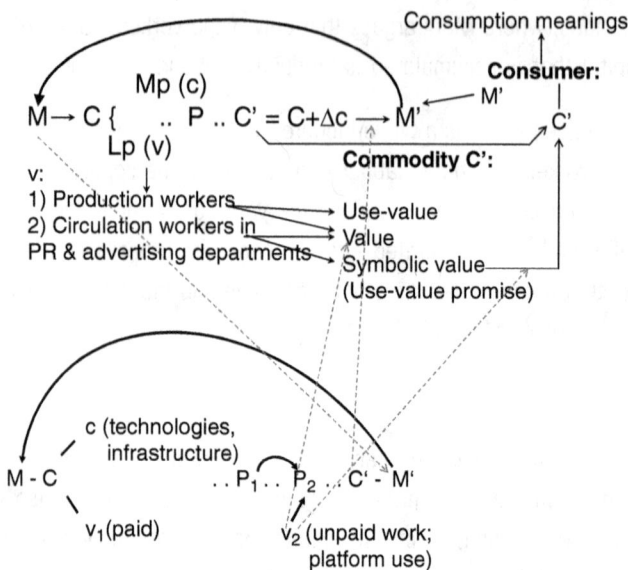

FIGURE 6.1 The economic relationship of Facebook and its advertising clients

Figure 6.1 visualises the economic relationships of Facebook (and other corporate social media platforms using targeted advertising) and its advertising clients.

A commodity has a use-value, value, and symbolic value. A company's production workers create the basic use-value that satisfies human needs. These activities take an average combined number of labour hours. Labour is the substance of value, labour time its measure and magnitude. In order to sell its commodity, a company tries to give positive meanings to it and to communicate these meanings to the public's members whom it tries to convince that this goods or service can enhance their lives and that they should therefore buy this commodity and not a comparable one offered by another company. Most commodities have, independent from their physical or informational nature, a cultural component that is created by cultural labour. The cultural dimension of a commodity is necessary ideological: it appeals to consumers' imagination and wants to make them connote positive images and feelings with the idea of consuming this commodity.

The creation of a commodity's symbolic ideology is a value-creating activity but not a use-value-generating activity. The use-value of a commodity can be physical and/or informational: we have cars for satisfying the need of driving from A to B, we listen to music for satisfying our aesthetic desires, and so forth. The exchange-value of a commodity is the relationship in which it is exchanged with another commodity, normally money: x commodity A = y commodity B (money). Symbolic value establishes a link and mediates between use-value and exchange-value, it helps accomplishing the exchange in which consumers obtain use-values and capitalists money. Wolfgang Fritz Haug (1986) speaks in this context of the commodity's use-value promise: The sales and advertising ideology associated with a commodity promises specific positive life enhancement functions that the commodity brings with it and thereby conceals the commodity's exchange-value behind promises. The symbolic commodity ideology promises a use-value beyond actual consumption, an imaginary surplus and surplus enjoyment. These promises are detached from the actual use-value and are therefore a fictitious form of value.

Saying that the cultural labour of branding, public relations, and creating commodity advertisements creates symbolic value is not detached from the notion of economic value. Rather value here precisely means that for the creation of this symbolic dimension of the commodity labour time is invested. It is therefore no wonder that almost all larger companies have their own public relations departments or outsource public relations and advertising to other companies. Paying the circulation workers employed in such departments or companies needs to be planned and calculated into the price of commodities.

Consumers give specific meanings to the commodities they buy and consume. They thereby construct consumption meaning and in doing so can react to use-value promises in different ways:

1) They can share these ideologies and buy the commodities because they hope the promise is an actual use-value;
2) they can deconstruct the use-value promise as ideology and refuse buying the commodity;
3) they can deconstruct the use-value but nonetheless buy the commodity for other reasons.

For communicating commodity ideologies to consumers, companies need to buy advertisement spaces in commercial media. Commercial media link commodity ideologies to consumers, they "transport" ideologies to consumers, although it is unclear and not determined how the latter react and if the confrontation with commodity ideologies results in actual purchases. Facebook and other corporate social media are advertising companies that sell advertising space and user data as commodities to clients who want to present commodity ideologies to users and hope that the latter buy their commodities. Facebook has paid employees that organise the development, maintenance, and provision of its software platform. On December 31, 2012, Facebook had 4619 paid employees.[4] But Facebook cannot sell advertising space without its users. Without them, it would be a dead platform that would immediately cease to exist. Between March and June 2013, more than a billion people, roughly 43% of all internet users, had accessed Facebook.[5,6]

But are Facebook users productive workers? They are certainly not less important for Facebook's capital accumulation than its paid employees because without users Facebook would immediately stop making profits and producing commodities. Facebook's commodity is not its platform that can be used without charges. It rather sells advertising space in combination with access to users. An algorithm selects users and allows individually targeting ads based on keywords and search criteria that Facebook's clients identify. Facebook's commodity is a portion/space of a user's screen/profile that is filled with ad clients' commodity ideologies. The commodity is presented to users and sold to ad clients either when the ad is presented (pay-per-view) or when the ad is clicked (pay-per-click). The user gives attention to his/her profile, wall, and other users' profiles and walls. For specific time periods parts of his/her screen are filled with advertising ideologies that are with the help of algorithms targeted to his/her interests. The prosumer commodity is an ad space that is highly targeted to user activities and interests. The users' constant online activity is necessary for running the targeting algorithms and for generating viewing possibilities and attention for ads. The ad space can therefore only exist based on user activities that are the labour that create the social media prosumer commodity.

Facebook clients run ads based on specific targeting criteria, e.g. 25–35-year-old men in the USA who are interested in literature and reading. What exactly is the commodity in this example? It is the ad space that is created on a specific 25–35-year-old man's screen interested in e.g. Shakespeare while he browses Facebook book pages or other pages. The ad is potentially presented to all Facebook users who fall into this category,

4 Facebook Inc., SEC Filings, Form 10-K 2012, http://www.sec.gov/Archives/edgar/data/1326801/000132680113 000003/fb-12312012x10k.htm
5 Data source: http://www.alexa.com
6 According to http://www.internetworldstats.com/stats.htm, the latest available world population count was 2 405 518 376 on June 3rd, 2013.

which amounted to 27,172,420 on 3 June 2013. What is the value of the single ad presented to a user? It is the average labour=usage time needed for the production of the ad presentation. Let's assume these 27,172,420 million users are on average 60 minutes per day on Facebook and in these 60 minutes 60 ads are presented to them on average. All the time they spend online is used for generating targeted ads. It is labour time that generates targeted ad presentations. We can therefore say that the value of a single ad presented to a user in this example is one minute of labour/usage/prosumption time.

So Facebook usage is labour. But is it productive labour? Marx sees transportation labour that moves a commodity in space-time from location A to location B, which takes a certain labour time x, as productive labour: What

> the transport industry sells is the actual change of place itself....The productive capital invested in this industry thus adds value to the products transported, partly through the value carried over from the means of transport, partly through the value added by the work of transport. (Marx 1885, 226–227)

The value generated by transporting a commodity from A to B is therefore x hours. The symbolic ideology of a commodity first needs to be produced by special ad and public relations employees and is in a second step communicated to potential buyers. *Advertising therefore involves production and transportation labour.* Advertising production does not create a physical commodity but an ideological dimension of a commodity – a use-value promise that is attached to a commodity as meaning. Advertising transport workers do not transport a commodity in physical space from A to B, they rather organise a communication space that allows advertisers to communicate their use-value promises to potential customers. Facebook's paid employees and users are therefore 21st-century equivalents of what Marx considered as transport workers in classical industry. They are productive workers whose activities are necessary for "transporting" use-value promises from companies to potential customers. Marx associated transport with communication as comparable forms of work. On Facebook and other social media platforms, transportation labour is communication labour.

Dallas W. Smythe (1981, 4) argued that it is a specific feature of audience labour that audiences "work to market [...] things to themselves". Facebook users constantly work and constantly market things to themselves. Their usage behaviour constantly generates data that are used for targeting ads. All Facebook usage is productive labour, with the exception of those cases, where users block advertising with the help of ad block software, which probably only a minority does. Facebook usage labour adds value to the commodity that is sold by Facebook's ad clients. Practically this means that a lot of companies want to advertise on Facebook and calculate social media advertising costs into their commodity prices. Nielsen (2013) conducted a survey among advertisers and advertising agencies. Seventy-five percent of the advertisers and 81% of the agencies that participated in the survey indicated that they buy targeted ads on social media. This shows the importance of social media for advertising today.

The production workers of Facebook's clients produce use-value and value. Their public relations and advertising employees (or the workers in the companies to which this labour is outsourced) produce value and a use-value promise as symbolic value. Facebook users produce the value and the communication of this use-value to themselves. They are productive workers. That they create value means that their labour time objectifies itself in commodities: the ad clients' employees objectify their labour in the commodity that is marketed to Facebook users, whereas Facebook users objectify their labour in the prosumer commodity that is sold to Facebook's clients. User labour is thereby also objectified in the commodity that is marketed and potentially sold to users themselves.

6.4 Conclusion

I have in this chapter revisited Smythe's notion of the audience commodity and audience labour in light of the corporate social media industry that uses targeted advertising. A prevalent criticism is that Facebook users are not paid and therefore do not create value but only consume the value created by paid employees in companies that advertise on Facebook. I have argued against this idea that Marx has a broader notion of productive labour that is based on the notion of the Gesamtarbeiter (collective worker). On Facebook, the boundaries between production and consumption blur and consumption becomes the production of use-values both for the users (information and sociality) and advertisers (user data). Facebook users are ideological transport workers that transport advertising ideologies by their network usage to themselves.

Conceptualising somebody as unproductive is not just an analytical term, it is also a slur and quite emotive. Nobody wants to be called unproductive as it carries the connotation of being useless and parasitic. Saying that Facebook users do not create value and that Facebook is a rentier that consumes the value produced by wage-workers employed by other companies politically implies that users are unimportant in class struggles in the digital age. Wageworkers in the non-digital economy are seen as the true locus of power. Hence, recommended political measures to be taken focus on how to organise these workers in unions, parties, or other organisations and struggles for higher wages and better wage-labour conditions. Users and Facebook are seen as being outside the locus of class struggle or only as something that unions and parties can also use in wage-labour struggles.

Facebook users are productive transport workers who communicate advertising ideologies that make use-value promises. Their activities are productive labour. Politics for the digital age need to consider users as political subjects. Unions, organisations of the Left, and struggles are nothing that should be left to wageworkers but need to be extended to digital media users. Pirate Parties have understood this circumstance better than the orthodox wage-labour fetishistic parts of the Left, but they have not well understood that the exploitation of digital labour is connected to the commodi-fication of the commons that include the communication commons and that as a consequence internet politics need to be connected to the critique of the political economy of capitalism as a whole. So whereas the orthodox part of the Left tends to dismiss users as politically unimportant and to neglect internet politics, Pirate Parties see users as the only political subjects.

The only feasible political way forward is to create unions and organisations of users that are connected and part of a broader political Left. For doing so, the orthodox part of the Left needs to overcome its ignorance of and technophobic biases against the internet and users need to perceive themselves as being ripped off by internet com-panies. We need social media unions and a fusion of Pirate Parties and left-wing parties.

Facebook users are productive workers means that they have the power to bring corporate social media to a standstill. If users go on strike, then Facebook immediately loses money. If Facebook's wageworkers go on strike, the platform is still online and can be further operated for exploiting users. Users are economically powerful because they create economic value. Organising a collective Facebook strike or shifting to alternative non-commercial platforms is a refusal of digital labour. Besides union-isation and online strikes, also policy-oriented measures are feasible in order to strengthen the protection of users from capitalist exploitation. Ad block software is a tool that deactivates advertisings on the websites a user visits. It can either be used as

Conclusion

add-on to web browsers or is automatically integrated into a browser. Using ad block software is digital class struggle: it disables Facebook and others' monetisation of personal data by blocking targeted ads. Think of a legal requirement that makes ad block the standard option in all web browsers: users are empowered because commodification of data is not the standard but an opt-in chosen by the users if they turn off the ad blocker. A useful complementary legal measure is to require all internet platforms to deactivate targeted and other forms of advertising and to make users opt-in if they want to enable such mechanisms.

Class struggles need to extend from factories and offices to Google, Facebook, and Twitter. The theory of digital labour is an ally of users, whereas those approaches that want to reassure us that users are unproductive do not side with the interest of users and denigrates them as unimportant in class struggles. Representatives of the Old Left want to have their factory struggles back without realising that Facebook is a new factory.

References

Allmer, Thomas. 2014. *(Dis)like Facebook? Towards A Dialectical and Critical Theory of Digital and Social Media.* London: Routledge.

Allmer, Thomas, Christian Fuchs, Verena Kreilinger, and Sebastian Sevignani. 2014. Social Networking Sites in the Surveillance Society: Critical Perspectives and Empirical Findings. In *Media, Surveillance and Identity. Social Perspectives*, eds. André Jansson and Miyase Christensen and André Jansson, 49–70. New York: Peter Lang.

Andrejevic, Mark. 2012. Exploitation in the Data Mine. In *Internet and Surveillance. The Challenges of Web 2.0 and Social Media*, eds. Christian Fuchs, Kees Boersma, Anders Albrechtslund, and Marisol Sandoval, 71–88. New York: Routledge.

Arvidsson, Adam, and Eleanor Colleoni. 2012. Value in Informational Capitalism and on the Internet. *The Information Society* 28 (3): 135–150.

Bolaño, César R. S. and Eloy S. Vieira. 2015. The Political Economy of the Internet: Social Networking Sites and a Reply to Fuchs. *Television & New Media* 16 (1): 62–71.

Bolin, Göran. 2011. *Value and the Media. Cultural Production and Consumption in Digital Markets.* Farnham: Ashgate.

Chan, Jenny. 2013. A Suicide Survivor: The Life of a Chinese Worker. *New Technology, Work and Employment* 28 (2): 84–99.

Chan, Jenny, Ngai Pun, and Mark Selden. 2013. The Politics of Global Production: Apple, Foxconn and China's New Working Class. *New Technology, Work and Employment* 2 (2): 100–115.

Comor, Edward. 2014. Value, the Audience Commodity, and Digital Prosumption: A Plea for Precision. In *The Audience Commodity in a Digital Age. Revisiting A Critical Theory of Commercial Media*, eds. Lee McGuigan and Vincent Manzerolle, 245–265. New York: Peter Lang.

Dalla Costa, Mariarosa and Selma James. 1972. *The Power of Women and the Subversion of Community*. Bristol: Falling Wall Press.

Eisenstein, Zillah. 1979. "Developing a Theory of Capitalist Patriarchy and Socialist Feminism. In *Capitalist Patriarchy and the Case for Socialist Feminism*, ed. Zillah R. Eisenstein, 5–40. New York: Monthly Review Press.

Fisher, Eran. 2012. How Less Alienation Creates More Exploitation." *tripleC: Communication, Capitalism & Critique* 10 (2): 171–183.

Fuchs, Christian. 2015. *Culture and Economy in the Age of Social Media*. New York: Routledge.

Fuchs, Christian. 2014c. *Social Media: A Critical Introduction*. London: Sage.

Fuchs, Christian. 2014b. Digital Prosumption Labour on Social Media in the Context of the Capitalist Regime of Time. *Time & Society* 23 (1): 97–123.

Fuchs, Christian. 2014a. *Digital Labour and Karl Marx*. New York: Routledge.

Fuchs, Christian and Marisol Sandoval. 2014. Digital Workers of the World Unite! A Framework for Critically Theorising and Analysing Digital Labour. *tripleC: Communication, Capitalism & Critique* 12 (2): 486–563.

Fuchs, Christian. 2013. Theorising and Analysing Digital Labour: From Global Value Chains to Modes of Production." *The Political Economy of Communication*1 (2): 3–27.

Fuchs, Christian and Sebastian Sevignani. 2013. What Is Digital Labour? What Is Digital Work? What's Their Difference? And Why Do These Questions Matter For Understanding Social Media?" *tripleC: Communication, Capitalism & Critique* 11 (2): 237–293.

Fuchs, Christian. 2012c. With or Without Marx? With or Without Capitalism? A Rejoinder to Adam Arvidsson and Eleanor Colleoni. *tripleC: Communication, Capitalism & Critique: Journal for a Global Sustainable Information Society* 10 (2): 633–645.

Fuchs, Christian. 2012b. Dallas Smythe Today – The Audience Commodity, The Digital Labour Debate, Marxist Political Economy and Critical Theory. Prolegomena to a Digital Labour Theory of Value. *tripleC: Capitalism, Communication & Critique* 10 (2): 692–740.

Fuchs, Christian. 2012a. Critique of the Political Economy of Web 2.0 Surveillance. In *Internet and Surveillance. The Challenges of Web 2.0 and Social Media*, eds. Christian Fuchs, Kees Boersma, Anders Albrechtslund, and Marisol Sandoval, 31–70. New York: Routledge.

Fuchs, Christian. 2010. *Labor* in Informational Capitalism and on the Internet." *The Information Society* 26 (3): 179–196.

Haug, Wolfgang Fritz. 1986. *Critique of Commodity Aesthetics*. Cambridge: Polity Press.

Huws, Ursula. 2014. The Underpinnings of Class in the Digital Age: Living, Labour and Value. *Socialist Register* 50: 80–107.

Lebowitz, Michael A. 1986. Too Many Blindspots on the Media." *Studies in Political Economy* 21: 165–173.

Livant, Bill. 1979. The Audience Commodity: On the 'Blindspot' Debate." *Canadian Journal of Political and Social Theory* 3 (1): 91–106.

Marx, Karl. 1885. *Capital. Volume II*. London: Penguin.

Marx, Karl. 1867. *Capital. Volume I*. London: Penguin.

Marx, Karl. 1862/1863. *Theories of Surplus Value. Part 1*. London: Lawrence & Wishart.

Marx, Karl. 1857/1858. *Grundrisse*. London: Penguin.

Maxwell, Richard. 1991. The Image is Gold: Value, the Audience Commodity, and Fetishism. *Journal of Film and Video* 43 (1-2): 29–45.

Maxwell, Richard and Toby Miller. 2012. *Greening the Media*. Oxford: Oxford University Press.

Meehan, Eileen. 1984.Ratings and the Institutional Approach. A Third Answer to the Commodity Question. *Critical Studies in Mass Communication* 1 (2): 216–225.

Mies, Maria. 1986. *Patriarchy & Accumulation on a World Scale. Women in the International Division of Labour*. London: Zed Books.

Murdock, Graham 2014. Commodities and Commons. In *The Audience Commodity in a Digital Age. Revisiting a Critical Theory of Commercial Media*, eds. Lee McGuigan and Vincent Manzerolle, 229–244. New York: Peter Lang.

Murdock, Graham. 1978. Blindspots about Western Marxism. A Reply to Dallas Smythe. *Canadian Journal of Political and Social Theory* 2 (2): 465–474.

Nielsen. 2013. *Paid Social Media Advertising. Industry Update and Best Practices 2013*. New York: Nielsen.

Pun, Ngai and Jenny Chan. 2012. Global Capital, the State, and Chinese Workers: The Foxconn Experience. *Modern China* 38 (4) 383–410.

Qiu, Jack Lunchuan. 2012. Network Labor: Beyond the Shadow of Foxconn. In *Studying Mobile Media: Cultural Technologies, Mobile Communication, and the iPhone*, eds. Larissa Hjorth, Jean Burgess and Ingrid Richardson, 173–189. New York: Routledge.

Reveley, James. 2013. The Exploitative Web: Misuses of Marx in Critical Social Media Studies. *Science & Society* 77 (4): 512–535.

Rigi, Jako and Robert Prey. 2015. Value, Rent, and the Political Economy of Social Media. *The Information Society* 31 (5): 392–406.

Sandoval, Marisol. 2013. Foxconned Labour as the Dark Side of the Information Age: Working Conditions at Apple's Contract Manufacturers in China. *tripleC: Communication, Capitalism & Critique* 11 (2) 318–347.

Sandoval, Marisol. 2014. *From Corporate to Social Media. Critical Perspectives on Corporate Social Responsibility in Media and Communication Industries*. London: Routledge.

Scholz, Trebor, ed. 2013. *Digital Labor: The Internet as Playground and Factory*. New York: Routledge.

Smythe, Dallas W. 1994. Reality as Presented by Television. In *Counterclockwise. Perspectives on Communication*, 61–74. Boulder, CO: Westview Press.

Smythe, Dallas W. 1981. *Dependency Road*. Norwood, NJ: Ablex.

Smythe, Dallas W. 1978. Rejoinder to Graham Murdock. *Canadian Journal of Political and Social Theory* 2 (2): 120–129.

Smythe, Dallas W. 1977. Communications: Blindspot of Western Marxism. *Canadian Journal of Political and Social Theory* 1 (3): 1–27.

Students & Scholars against Corporate Misbehaviour (SACOM). 2011. *iSlave Behind the iPhone. Foxconn Workers in Central China.*, SACOM (website), https://sacom.hk/wp-content/uploads/2011/09/20110924-islave-behind-the-iphone.pdf

Part III

Themes

Chapter Seven

From Digital Positivism and Administrative Big Data Analytics Towards Critical Digital and Social Media Research

---

7.1 Introduction

Social media has become a popular term used for specific Internet platforms, especially social networking sites, blogs, microblogs, wikis, and user-generated content-sharing sites. The term "web 2.0" preceded the one of social media. The publisher Tim O'Reilly introduced it in 2005 (O'Reilly 2005a, 2005b). He claimed that the Internet had become an "architecture of participation" (O'Reilly 2005b). Five years later, he reflected on the term and also referred to the "social web" (O'Reilly and Battelle 2010). This chapter reflects on the dominant paradigm in digital media studies. It argues for a paradigm shift from big data analytics towards critical digital media studies.

Why has there been so much talk about social media in recent years? In 2000, the Internet economy's financial bubble burst, which resulted in the so-called dot.com crisis. In and after a crisis, industry representatives try to restore investors' confidence. O'Reilly's organisation of the *Web 2.0 Summit* in the years 2004–2011 and the branding of the web 2.0 concept can be seen as such attempts.

Social media is a big business. Today, the video-sharing site YouTube is the world's second most used web platform and the social networking site Facebook the third most

DOI: 10.4324/9781003222149-7

used one.[1] Google renamed itself to Alphabet Inc. It owns and operates YouTube. With annual profits of US$ 17 billion, Alphabet was in 2016 the world's 27th largest transnational corporation. Facebook had annual profits of US$ 3.7 billion in 2015, and in 2016 it was the world's 188th largest transnational corporation.[2] Alphabet and Facebook are the world's largest advertising agencies. Other social media corporations, such as Twitter and Weibo, have struggled to make profits, which shows that targeted advertising is a high-risk realm of capital accumulation. Only a small share of the presented targeted ads results in clicks and profits. Companies' expectations about targeted ads are, however, fairly high. Social media capitalism is based on a techno-fetishistic ideology, which assumes that the Internet has been revolutionised, has become "participatory", and that profits can today be clicked (Fuchs 2014d).

The myth of novelty has been accompanied by the myth that social media has radically transformed media use from passive reception to active participation and constant creativity. The *Occupy Media! Survey* showed that 81.9% of the participating activists watched YouTube videos at least four times per month as the source of political information, but only 28.5% created at least one political YouTube video per month themselves (Fuchs 2014b, 73 and 79). Although social media has bottom-up production potentials that make their affordances somewhat different from those of broadcasting, the reality is that the vast majority tends to use such media more like a television than an user-generated content platform. Only a minority of users is highly active and creative. Social media is both a tool of consumption and "prosumption". The most followed and active social media creators are not everyday users but the public re-lations teams of celebrities (Fuchs 2014c). Social media's potentials differ from their actuality, which is an expression of the power asymmetries of time, skills, motivation, money, influence, attention, reputation, and visibility in contemporary class societies.

Analysing the Internet and social media has become an important dimension of media and communication research. In this contribution, I provide some critical reflections on the status of social media research and argue for a critical turn and paradigm shift. This chapter proceeds by first presenting the dominant paradigm and then looking at theoretical-ontological, epistemological/methodological, and ethical dimensions of a possible alternative paradigm.

---

1 Data source: alexa.com, accessed on 29 May 2016.
2 Data source for both Alphabet and Facebook: Forbes 2000, 2016 list, www.forbes.com/global2000/list, accessed on 29 May 2016.

7.2 Digital and Social Media Research's Mainstream: Positivist Big Data Analytics

A study of 27,340 Internet Studies published between 2000 and 2009 and indexed in the Social Sciences and the Arts and Humanities Citation Index found that only 31% cited theoretical works (Peng et al. 2013). There is a tendency in Internet Studies to engage with theory only on the micro- and middle-range levels that theorise single online phenomena but neglect the larger picture of society as a totality (Rice and Fuller 2013). Such theories tend to be atomised. They just focus on single phenomena and miss society's big picture.

The same study found that 59% of the conducted research used quantitative methods (Tai-Quan et al. 2013). A new trend in quantitative Internet Studies is big data analytics that has a focus on collecting large amounts of data from social media platforms and analysing it in a predominantly quantitative manner. The new media research guru Lev Manovich has argued that Internet Studies should be turned into the large-scale computational analysis of online data. He terms this approach Cultural Analytics (Manovich 2009) and Software Studies.[3] Web Science has a strong focus on computational analysis, and mathematical methods have also been the foundation of the approach of Web Science that understands itself explicitly as a merger of physical science and computer science (Berners-Lee et al. 2006, 3). The obsession with quantification, the use of computation in the social sciences, and big data have also manifested itself as a preoccupation with attempts to develop new digital methods in both the humanities and social sciences: "Digital Humanities" often understands itself as humanities computing (Terras et al. 2013). The Collaborative Social Media Observatory, a strategic £1.5 million science and computer science investment project funded in the United Kingdom by institutions such as the Economic and Social Research Council (ESRC), the Engineering and Physical Sciences Research Council, the UK Department of Health, and others in the years 2012–2015, understands "social media research" explicitly as big data analytics, namely the analysis of "aggregate information in 'big social data' repositories, such as collective sentiment scores for sub-groups of twitter users".[4]

In the United Kingdom, the Arts and Humanities Research Council's (AHRC) strategic theme "Digital Transformations" received an injection of government funding

3 http://lab.softwarestudies.com
4 http://www.cs.cf.ac.uk/cosmos/ethics-resource-guide/

specifically to boost big data research, which resulted in 2014 in funding of 21 big data research projects with a total funding sum of £4.7 million,[5] meaning that a very large part of projects funded via the AHRC Digital Transformations theme have been explorations and uses of big data.

These developments are not limited to the United Kingdom. In the EU Horizon 2020 Work Programme for 2016–2017, social science calls "Europe in a Changing World – Inclusive, Innovative and Reflective Societies", data, big data, and open data were key buzzwords. For example, the funding line "Policy-development in the age of big data" invites submissions of projects that focus on "using data analytics to generate new insights, increasing predictive power, and identifying unexpected patterns and relationships that can help inform policy making". The Trans-Atlantic Platform for the Social Sciences and Humanities's *Digging into Data Challenge* is a partnership of 18 research councils in the following 12 countries: Argentina, Brazil, Canada, Chile, Finland, France, Germany, Mexico, the Netherlands, Portugal, the United Kingdom, and the United States. It funds international projects that focus on developing new "techniques of large-scale digital data analysis",[6] using modelling and simulation techniques and combining multiple data sources. Such funding initiatives privilege quantitative, computational approaches over qualitative, interpretative ones.

Big data analytics' trouble is that it often does not connect statistical and computational research results to a broader analysis of human meanings, interpretations, experiences, attitudes, moral values, ethical dilemmas, uses, contradictions, and macro-sociological implications of social media. There is a danger that a de-emphasis of philosophy, theory, critique, and qualitative analysis advances what Paul Lazarsfeld (2004 [1941]) termed administrative research, research that is predominantly concerned with how to make technologies and administration more efficient and effective. Paraphrasing Jürgen Habermas (1971), we can say that there is a danger that digital positivism advances an "absolutism of pure [digital, quantitative] methodology" (p. 5), forgets about academia's educational role, falls short of fully understanding "the meaning of knowledge" (p. 69) in the information society at large, and is an "immunization of the [Internet] sciences against philosophy" (p. 67).

Vincent Mosco (2014, 2016) calls the ideology of big data analytics "digital positivism" and "cloud sublime". Big data is "a myth, a sublime story about conjuring wisdom not

5 http://www.ahrc.ac.uk/research/fundedthemesandprogrammes/themes/digitaltransformations/bigdata/
6 http://diggingintodata.org/file/1036/download?token=fqylXiET

from the flawed intelligence of humans, with all of our well-known limitations, but from the pure data stored in the cloud" (Mosco 2014, 193). The "hot new profession of data scientist knows only quantitative approaches" (Mosco 2014, 197). Digital positivism's limit is that it remains stuck in the narrowness of the Lasswell formula, focusing its research on the following question: who communicates what to whom on social media with what effects? It forgets users' subjectivity, experiences, norms, values, and interpretations, as well as the embeddedness of the media into society's power structures and social struggles. We need a paradigm shift from administrative digital positivist big data analytics towards critical social media research. Critical social media research combines the critical social media theory, critical digital methods, and critical-realist social media research ethics.

Challenging big data analytics as the mainstream of digital media studies requires us to think about theoretical (ontological), methodological (epistemological), and ethical dimensions of an alternative paradigm.

7.3 Theory: Karl Marx and Critical Digital and Social Media Theory

Social media research is predominantly focused on quantitative case studies that lack grounding in social theory. Most approaches in Internet Studies that consider themselves to have theory foundations are limited to providing definitions of key categories or are purely micro-theoretical. They ignore the embeddedness of communication processes into society as totality. They are not grounded in theories of society, which provide models that allow asking the following fundamental questions: what is society? How should we understand structures, agency, power, social dynamics, social history, and so on? What is capitalism and modernity? In what kind of society do we live today? What is the role of communication in society in general, capitalist society, and contemporary society? Studying digital and social media could take inspiration by the tradition going back to Karl Marx and other critical theorists.

Social media emerged in a situation of deep societal crises. The world economic crisis continues to have negative social effects. It has turned into a political crisis of Europe and the world. We have seen the intensification of nationalism, racism, authoritarianism, and elements of fascism. The mood is not unlike the prelude to a world war. Global society furthermore confronts a series of global problems that threaten its existence. Given conditions of exploitation, domination, warfare, violence, and inequalities, we need not just social/sociological theory but critical theories of society.

Most definitions of social media are enumerative (for a list of example definitions, see Fuchs 2017, chapter 2). They lack an understanding of communication theory and the social. The term "social media" takes on different meanings depending on what concept of the social is foregrounded. Example understandings of the social are Émile Durkheim's concept of social facts, Max Weber's categories of social action and social relations, Ferdinand Tönnies' notion of community, or Karl Marx's understanding of the social as social problems and social co-production that implies the need for social ownership (Fuchs 2017, chapter 2).

Given that we live in a stratified global class society that is full of social problems and inequalities, I consider the tradition of theories of society that go back to Karl Marx as the most suited framework for the social sciences and humanities, including the study of media, communication, and digital/social media (Fuchs 2008, 2011, 2014a, 2014c, 2015a, 2016a, 2016b). There are at least six elements in Marx's works that are of key relevance for understanding communications today (Fuchs 2016b; Fuchs and Mosco 2016a, 2016b):

1) Praxis communication: Marx was not just a critical political economist but also a critical journalist and polemicist, whose writing style can inspire critical thought today;

2) Global communication: Marx stressed the connection of communication technology and globalisation. In an age, where there are lots of talk about both the Internet and globalisation, we should remind ourselves that technology-mediated globalisation has had a longer history;

3) Dialectical philosophy: Marx elaborated a critical theory of technology that is based on dialectical logic. Dialectical philosophy can help us to avoid one-sided analyses of the media (Fuchs 2014c);

4) Class analysis: Marx stressed the relevance of the connection of labour, value, commodities, and capital. He analysed modern society as a class society. Focusing on class today can counter the positivism of analyses of society as information society, network society, knowledge-based society, post-industrial society, and so on;

5) Crisis and social struggles: Marx described class struggle and crisis as factors in the historical dynamics of class societies. Class structures and struggles are in complex ways reflected on and entangled into mediated communication;

6) Alternatives: Marx envisioned alternatives to capitalism and domination. Given capitalist crisis and monopoly control of social media today, it is important to envision alternatives to capitalism and capitalist social media.

Marxian concepts that matter for the understanding of digital/social media, include dialectics, capitalism, commodity/commodification, surplus value, exploitation, alienation, class, globalisation, ideology/ideology critique, class struggle, commons, the public sphere, communism, and aesthetics (Fuchs 2012).

Marx certainly did not describe 21st-century society, although his analysis was very anticipatory. Marxian categories are historical and dialectical themselves, which means that for analysing a specific period of society, one needs to work out the dialectical continuities and changes of social phenomena. Marx opened his main work *Capital* with the analysis of the commodity: "The wealth of societies in which the capitalist mode of production prevails appears as an 'immense collection of commodities'" (Marx 1867, 125). On targeted-advertising-based social media, the commodity takes on a peculiar form: users create and re-create sociality as use value that is as data sold in commodity form to targeted advertisers. Users thereby become digital workers (Fuchs 2014a, 2015a).

Marx is certainly not the only relevant critical social theorist who matters for understanding social media. The critical study of social media should be based on a broad range of critical theories of society. The crisis of capitalism and the devastating social and political effects of austerity and neoliberalism have made evident that political economy can no longer be ignored in the study of society. This does not mean that the economy determines society but rather that all social phenomena have an economy and are economic and non-economic at the same time (Fuchs 2015a).

Marx's critical ontology of society is one of social co-production, in which humans produce the social under particular social relations. In class societies, co-production is embedded into alienated social relations. If we assume that those who co-produce the social have the right to collectively control their products, then the implication for social media platforms is that they are incompletely social: private ownership of social media corporations should be replaced by forms of collective ownership, that is, public social media and commons-based social media. One can, for example, envision an alternative YouTube run by a network that is operated by public service broadcasters, on which all programme archives are made available with Creative Commons licences. And one can envision an alternative Facebook that is decentralised, owned, and

controlled by the community of users and funded by a combination of user contributions and a participatory media fee (Fuchs 2015b).

The rise of big data and social media has resulted in particular transformations of
academia. Deborah Lupton (2015) has, in this context, coined the notion of digital
sociology. She argues that digital sociology consists of (a) professional digital practice
so that sociologists employ "digital tools as part of sociological practice – to build
networks, construct an online profile, publicize and share research and instruct students" (p. 15); (b) the investigation of the use of digital technology; (c) digital data
analysis, which has also been characterised as the rise of digital methods (Rogers
2013); and (d) critical digital sociology, the fourth aspect of digital sociology. Lupton
(2015) defines critical digital sociology as the "reflexive analysis of digital technologies
informed by social and cultural theory" (p. 16).

All forms of social analysis reflect society in complex ways. Critical digital sociology is
a particular reflexion of and on digital technologies' role in society. It is a theoretical
approach grounded in critical and Marxist theory that tries to understand capitalism
and domination as well as their possible alternatives. But one should note that there is
a contradiction between critical sociology as digital sociology's fourth dimension and
big data analytics that is part of Lupton's third dimension of digital sociology.

7.4 Epistemology and Methodology: Critical Digital Methods

Sociology wants to better understand society by a dialectic of social theory and applied
social research methods. Positivism reduces the analysis of society to empiricism and
lacks critical theory's capacity of contextualising social phenomena in the dynamics,
dialectics, and history of power structures. Big data analytics' positivism results in
often very superficial analyses that highlight major topics, users or social relations in
large amounts of data gathered from Twitter, Facebook, and other social media
platforms. It fails to understand users' motivations, experiences, interpretations,
norms, and values. We need critical digital methods as alternative to digital positivism.

It has, for example, been common to study contemporary revolutions and protests (such
as the 2011 Arab Spring) by collecting large amounts of tweets and analysing them.
Such analyses can, however, tell us nothing about the degree to which activists use
social and other media in protest communication, what their motivations are to use or

not to use social media, what their experiences have been, what problems they encounter in such uses, and so on. If we only analyse big data, then the one-sided
conclusion that contemporary rebellions are Facebook and Twitter revolutions is often
the logical consequence (see Aouragh 2016; Gerbaudo 2012). Digital methods do not
outdate but require traditional methods in order to avoid the pitfall of digital positivism. Traditional sociological methods, such as semi-structured interviews, participant
observation, surveys, content and critical discourse analysis, focus groups, experiments, creative methods, participatory action research, statistical analysis of sec-
ondary data, and so on, have not lost importance. We do not just have to understand
what people do on the Internet but also why they do it, what the broader implications
are, and how power structures frame and shape online activities.

The Occupy Media! Survey (Fuchs 2014b) is a good example for a study that in contrast
to big data analytics takes the broader context into account. It empirically studied the
political economy, contradictions, and power dynamics of contemporary activists' political communication. I conducted a survey among activists ($N = 418$). Eighty-five
percent of the respondents used face-to-face communication at least once a month for
trying to mobilise others to attend protests, 74.4% used Facebook for this purpose
during the same time period, 70.2% sent personal e-mail, 63.1% called people on the
phone, 53.8% used e-mail lists, 50.3% texted people, 48.0% made use of Twitter, and
14.1% of YouTube. Face-to-face communication, Facebook, e-mail, phone, SMS, and
Twitter are the most important media that occupy activists employ for trying to mobilise others for protests. Activists use multiple media for mobilisation-oriented
communication. These include classical interpersonal communication via phones, e-
mail, face to face, and private social media profiles as well as more public forms of
communication, such as Facebook groups, Twitter, and e-mail lists.

Correlation analysis showed that there is a mutual positive influence of protest mobilisation communication that is conducted face-to-face or on Facebook. The survey
data provided empirical indications that contemporary protests are not social media
rebellions, and that at the same time digital and social media are also not irrelevant in
these protests.

Critical digital methods do not just mean the use of more established methods for
studying digital media's contradictions in society. Digital media can also be used as
tools of critical research themselves. One aspect is creative methods, in which one
asks participants to use social media in order to generate data about society's problems for analysis. An example for studying precarious labour in the culture industries,

Epistemology and Methodology: Critical Digital Methods

one can ask participants to take a picture of their everyday working life that visualises the main problem they have to face, to share it on an image blog, and to accompany it by a 100-word long description of the problem. The result is not just rich data but also the possibility to, in a second step, make the participants interact with each other, which gives the method a more relational dimension.

Besides conducting qualitative social research with social media users in order to learn about their experiences, interpretations, and perspectives, critical digital methods should not completely discard tools for digital data collection and analytics, but take their use into a new direction. Critical digital methods should certainly engage in collecting and analysing samples of data from social media platforms with the help of tools and services, such as DiscoverText, Tweet Archivist, Netvizz, NodeXL, Gephi, NCapture/NVivo, Sodato, Import.io, InfoExtractor, Google Web Scraper, TAGS, SocioViz, and so on[7].

Critical digital methods, however, do not simply apply large-scale quantitative analysis to these data but use smaller samples ("small data" as opposed to "big data") that are analysed with the help of qualitative methods (critical visual analysis, critical discourse analysis, qualitative text/content analysis, etc.) and interpreted with the help of critical theory. The focus can, for example, be on key topics or the most followed, liked, or re-tweeted users. In some cases, analysing single users' postings may be most appropriate; in other cases, focusing on a specific time period, discourse topic, particular group, specific characteristic, and so on may be most suited.

One important aspect of critical social media research is the study of not just ideologies of the Internet but also ideologies on the Internet. Critical discourse analysis and ideology critique as research method have only been applied in a limited manner to social media data. Majid KhosraviNik (2013) argues in this context that "critical discourse analysis appears to have shied away from new media research in the bulk of its research" (p. 292). Critical social media discourse analysis is a critical digital method for the study of how ideologies are expressed on social media in light of society's power structures and contradictions that form the texts' contexts.

Discourses tend to be intertextual and interdiscursive (Reisigl and Wodak 2001, p. 39). They interlink various texts, discourses, and contexts. Social media data are therefore not independent from other media but tend to be multimodal and connected with texts

---

7 See http://socialmediadata.wikidot.com and https://wiki.digitalmethods.net/Dmi/ToolDatabase for overviews.

in traditional media. An example is that many political tweets tend to link to articles in the online versions of mainstream newspapers. Studying social media therefore does not substitute the study of other media but often requires studying various media's interconnection. Discourses are texts that stand in particular societal, political-economic, historical, and cultural contexts. Understanding them requires taking a holistic point of view, that is, to situate them in history and society. This means that interpretation, explanation, evaluation, and critique of discourses require theories of society (Fairclough 2015). This, for example, means that when a case study of fascist ideology online is conducted, the critical theory and history of fascism will guide the analysis, and a new contribution to theory construction will emerge from the analysis.

7.5 Critical-Realist Social Media Research Ethics

Critical digital methods challenge digital positivism. In this context, also ethical questions arise. All critical theories are inherently ethico-political. They reject the assumption that academic knowledge can be value neutral, and argue that all social construction of knowledge reflects power and norms and is therefore political. One of the critical theory's tasks is to lay open and criticise the ideologies inherent in specific knowledge. Critical theory's own knowledge is aimed at contributing to a better understanding of society's power contradictions and how to overcome them in order to create a better world.

But there is not just the role of ethics in research but also the ethics of conducting research. Research ethics concern issues, such as privacy, anonymity, informed consent, and the sensitivity of data. Given that social media is part of society's tendency to liquefy and blur the boundaries between the private and the public, labour/leisure, production/consumption (Fuchs 2015a, chapter 8), research ethics in social media research is particularly complex. The complexity and confusion resulting from Internet research are, for example, evident in the British Sociological Association's Statement of Ethical Practice. It is very unspecific about Internet research ethics, arguing that one should "take special care when carrying out research via the Internet" and be "familiar with ongoing debates on the ethics of Internet research" (British Sociological Association, 2002, §41). Zimmer and Proferes (2014) analysed 382 academic works that studied Twitter data. One hundred and sixty-eight (44.0%) analysed more than 100,000 tweets, and 216 more than 10,000 (56.5%). Only 4% (16) discussed ethical aspects.

Social media research ethics face a contradiction between big data positivism and research ethics fundamentalism. Big data positivists tend to say, "Most social media data is public data. It is like data in a newspaper. I can therefore gather big data without limits. Those talking about privacy want to limit the progress of social science". This position disregards any engagement with ethics and has a bias towards quantification. The ethical framework *Social Media Research: A Guide to Ethics* (Townsend and Wallace 2016) that emerged from an ESRC-funded project tries to avoid both extremes and to take a critical-realist position: it recommends that social scientists neither ignore nor fetishise research ethics when studying digital media.

Research ethics fundamentalists in contrast tend to say,

> You have to get informed consent for every piece of social media data you gather because we cannot assume automatic consent, users tend not to read platform's privacy policies, they may assume some of their data is private and they may not agree to their data being used in research. Even if you anonymize the users you quote, many can still be identified in the networked online environment.

There are, however, limits of informed consent in critical research. It can act a censorship of critical research. Imagine you study online fascism or online harassment of women. In most of such cases, it is not feasible but rather dangerous for the researcher to ask for informed consent. "Dear Mr. Misogynist/Nazi, I am a social researcher gathering data from Twitter. Can you please give me the informed consent that I quote your violent threat against X?". Asking for informed consent in critical research can result in the circumstance that the researcher herself/himself becomes subject to violence or threats.

Some observers recommend to only use aggregated data and not to quote from social media data. Such an approach has, however, a bias towards quantitative methods, and critical social media discourse analysis thereby becomes impossible to conduct. In social media analysis, privacy's context matters (Nissenbaum 2010). We cannot assume that social media data analysis can never cause harm and that therefore anything goes in data analytics. At the same time, privacy fundamentalism risks to paralyse critical social media analysis. A realistic approach is needed. We need critical-realist social media research guidelines that go beyond research ethics fundamentalism and beyond big data positivism.

The British Psychological Society (2009) argues that online observation should only take place when and where users "reasonably expect to be observed by strangers" (p. 13). This criterion is feasible in many contexts. It implies, for example, that the use of a popular Twitter hashtag during specific mass events (e.g. the use of the hashtag #BBCDebate during the EU referendum campaign's first televised TV debate) is aimed at public outreach, so that the user cannot reasonably expect to remain unobserved. It would therefore be acceptable to quote these tweets without asking for informed consent. Whether to obtain informed consent or not in critical social media research depends on the specific contexts of data.

For Roy Bhaskar, critical moral realism is part of the philosophy of critical realism. It assumes that "moral propositions can be known; and, in particular, social-scientifically vindicated" (Bhaskar 2008, 242). In critical social media research, the user expresses moral values online, and the researcher has a critical attitude towards power structures. The morality and ideologies underlying the online expression can be laid open:

> Now the subject-matter of social science is composed not just by social objects but by beliefs about social objects, and if such beliefs are false (a judgment which is within the remit of social science), and one can explain the falsity, then, subject to a ceteris paribus clause, in virtue of the openness of the social world and the multiplicity of determinations therein, one can move without further ado to a negative evaluation of the explanans and a positive evaluation of any action rationally designed to absent it. (Bhaskar 2008, 244)

Critical moral realism in social media research means that the research tries to create knowledge about social media that helps understanding what is absent in the world and needs to be created (absenting absences), in order to foster participatory democracy, freedom, justice, fairness, and equality. This approach neither overdoes nor underdoes research ethics.

7.6 Conclusion

Digital media has become an important topic of study, as the emergence of the field of Internet research shows. It is, however, not just a research topic but has influenced the social sciences in general. Big data analytics and computational social science are the newest developments in this respect. Their emergence is a reflection of the general tendency that critique and theory have in the past decades become less of a focus in academia, which may be one of the consequences of the pressures exerted by neoliberalism, managerialism, and political pragmatism on academia. Effects of instrumental reason in the social sciences include high-level specialisation that is blind for society's big picture, a disregard for social philosophy, and management and business studies' influence on the social sciences. The search for a computational social science paradigm is another effect of the diminishing relevance of critique. The danger is that computer science colonises the social sciences and tries to turn them into a subdomain of computer science. There should certainly be co-operations between computer scientists and social scientists in solving societal problems, but co-operation is different from a computational paradigm. Turning social scientists into programmers as part of social science methods education would almost inevitably leave no time for engagement with theory and social philosophy, except if one radically increased the duration of study programmes. Programming is not something you learn overnight, but is a time-consuming field of education. Computer science's quantitative logic threatens to undermine critical social science. An alternative paradigm that does not reject, but critically scrutinise the digital, is needed. Critical theory is an alternative interdisciplinary approach that is of importance for both the social sciences and computer science.

Money is an important means for distributing power, positions, reputation, and influence in academia. Research funding is the academic system's key monetary resource. In social media research, we can find a distributional inequality of funding: There tend to be special programmes focused on funding big data analytics. This approach is a form of digital positivism and administrative research.

I have, in this chapter, argued for a paradigm shift from administrative, positivist big data analytics towards critical digital/social media research that combines critical social media theory, critical digital methods, and critical-realist social media research ethics. Advancing such a paradigm is a material question whose solution requires not just changes of attitudes but also institutional transformations and a change of funding practices.

Acknowledgement

This chapter has benefited from the discussion at the *European Journal of Communication* (EJC) symposium on social media (University of Minho, Braga, Portugal, 26–27 May 2016). I thank the editors for the invitation and organisation and all participants for interesting discussions.

References

Aouragh, Miriyam. 2016. Social Media, Mediation and the Arab Revolutions. In *Marx in the Age of Digital Capitalism*, eds.Christian Fuchs and Vincent Mosco, 482–515. Leiden: Brill.

Berners-Lee, Tim, Wendy Hall, James A. Hendler et al. 2006. A Framework for Web Science. *Foundations and Trends in Web Science* 1 (1): 1–130.

Bhaskar, Roy. 2008. *Dialectic: The Pulse of Freedom*. London: Routledge.

British Psychological Society. 2009. *Code of Ethics and Conduct*. Leicester: BPS.

British Sociological Association. 2002. Statement of Ethical Practice. Available at: https://www.britsoc.co.uk/equality-diversity/statement-of-ethical-practice

Fairclough, Norman. 2015. *Language and Power*,3rd edn. Abingdon: Routledge

Fuchs, Christian. 2017. *Social Media: A Critical Introduction*, 2nd edn. London: SAGE.

Fuchs, Christian. 2016a *Critical Theory of Communication: New Readings of Lukács, Adorno, Marcuse, Honneth and Habermas in the Age of the Internet*. London: University of Westminster Press.

Fuchs, Christian. 2016b. *Reading Marx in the Information Age: A Media and Communication Studies Perspective on 'Capital Volume I'*. New York: Routledge.

Fuchs, Christian. 2015a. *Culture and Economy in the Age of Social Media*. New York: Routledge.

Fuchs, Christian. 2015b. Left-Wing Media Politics and the Advertising Tax. *tripleC: Communication, Capitalism & Critique* 13 (1): 1–4.

Fuchs, Christian. 2014a. *Digital Labour and Karl Marx*. New York: Routledge.

Fuchs, Christian. 2014b. *OccupyMedia! The Occupy Movement and Social Media in Crisis Capitalism*. Winchester: Zero Books.

Fuchs, Christian. 2014c. *Social Media: A Critical Introduction*. London: SAGE.

Fuchs, Christian. 2014d. The Dialectic: Not Just the Absolute Recoil, but the World's Living Fire that Extinguishes and Kindles Itself. Reflections on Slavoj Žižek's Version of Dialectical Philosophy in "Absolute Recoil: Towards a New Foundation of Dialectical Materialism". *tripleC: Communication, Capitalism & Critique* 12 (2): 848–875.

Fuchs, Christian. 2012. Towards Marxian Internet Studies. *tripleC: Communication, Capitalism & Critique* 10 (2): 392–412.

Fuchs, Christian. 2011. *Foundations of Critical Media and Information Studies*. London: Routledge.

Fuchs, Christian. 2008. *Internet and Society: Social Theory in the Information Age*. New York: Routledge.

Fuchs, Christian and Vincent Mosco, eds. 2016a. *Marx and the Political Economy of the Media (Studies in Critical Social Sciences Volume 79)*. Leiden: Brill.

Fuchs, Christian and Vincent Mosco, eds. 2016b. *Marx in the Age of Digital Capitalism (Studies in Critical Social Sciences Volume 80)*. Leiden: Brill.

Gerbaudo, Paolo. 2012. *Tweets and the Streets: Social Media and Contemporary Activism*. London: Pluto Press.

Habermas. Jürgen. 1971. *Knowledge and Human Interest*. Boston, MA: Beacon Press.

KhosraviNik, Majid. 2013. Critical Discourse Analysis, Power, and New Media Discourse. In

References

Why Discourse Matters: Negotiating Identity in the Mediatized World, eds. Yusuf Kalyango Y and Monika W. Kopytowska, 287–305. New York: Peter Lang.

Lazarsfeld, Paul F. 2004 [1941]. Administrative and Critical Communications Research. In *Mass Communication and American Social Thought: Key Texts, 1919–1968*, ed. John Durham Peters, 166–173. Lanham, MD: Rowman & Littlefield.

Lupton, Deborah. 2015. *Digital Sociology*. London: Routledge.

Manovich, Lev. 2009. Cultural Analytics: Visualising Cultural Patterns in the Era of "More Media". Available at: http://manovich.net/content/04-projects/063-cultural-analytics-visualizing-cultural-patterns/60_article_2009.pdf

Marx, Karl. 1867. *Capital, Volume I*. London: Penguin Books.

Mosco, Vincent. 2016. Marx in the Cloud. In *Marx in the Age of Digital Capitalism*, eds. Christian Fuchs and Vincent Mosco, 516–535. Leiden: Brill.

Mosco, Vincent. 2014. *To the Cloud: Big Data in a Turbulent World*. Boulder, CO: Paradigm.

Nissenbaum, Helen. 2010. *Privacy in Context*. Stanford, CA: Stanford University Press.

O'Reilly, Tim. 2005a. Web 2.0: Compact Definition? Available at: http://radar.oreilly.com/2005/10/web-20-compact-definition.html

O'Reilly, Tim. 2005b. What is Web 2.0. Available at: http://www.oreilly.com/pub/a/web2/archive/what-is-web-20.html

O'Reilly, Tim and Battelle, John. 2010. Web Squared: Web 2.0 Five Years On. Available at: http://www.cs.mun.ca/~yzchen/papers/papers/web/web2009_websquared-whitepaper.pdf

Peng Tai-Quan, Lun Zhang, Zhi-Jin Zhong et al. 2013. Mapping the Landscape of Internet Studies: Text Mining of Social Science Journal Articles 2000–2009. *New Media & Society* 15(5): 644–664.

Reisigl, Martin and Ruth Wodak. 2001. *Discourse and Discrimination: Rhetorics of Racism and Antisemitism*. London: Routledge.

Rice, Roland E. and Ryan Fuller. 2013. Theoretical Perspectives in the Study of Communication and the Internet. In *The Oxford Handbook of Internet Studies*, ed. William H. Dutton, 353–377. Oxford: Oxford University Press.

Rogers, Richard. 2013. *Digital Methods*. Cambridge, MA: The MIT Press.

Terras, Melissa, Julianne Nyhan, and Edward Vanhoutte, eds. 2013. *Defining Digital Humanities: A Reader*. Farnham: Ashgate Publishing.

Townsend, Leanne and Claire Wallace. 2016. Social Media Research: A Guide to Ethics. Available at: http://www.gla.ac.uk/media/media_487729_en.pdf

Zimmer, Michael and Nicholas J. Proferes. 2014. A Topology of Twitter Research: Disciplines, Methods, and Ethics. *Aslib Journal of Information Management* 66 (3): 250–261.

Chapter Eight
Social Media, Big Data, and Critical Marketing

8.1 Introduction

Social media and big data have become ubiquitous keywords in everyday life. The term social media is commonly used for social networking sites (e.g. Facebook, Weibo), blogs (e.g. WordPress, Tumblr), micro-blogs (e.g. Twitter), user-generated content sharing sites (e.g. YouTube, Flickr, Instagram), or wikis (e.g. Wikipedia) (Fuchs 2017, chapter 2). Big data refers to the collection and analysis of data in such vast quantities that humans are incapable of processing them — only algorithms can (Fuchs 2017, chapter 2). There are diverse sources of big data, one example being credit and debit card transactions. So the term big data is not limited to social media. At the same time, given that Facebook has about 1.8 million monthly active users[1] and Google processes more than 100 billion searches per year on average,[2] these two US Internet companies are probably the largest data processors in the world. This tells of an inherent link between big data and social media. While social media characterise the techno-social systems enabling human interaction on the Internet, big data are the digital results of human activities. Google, Facebook, and other online platforms tend to store all data and meta-data for long periods of time and therefore require huge server farms consisting of numerous supercomputers.

Google and Facebook are two of the world's largest companies. In the 2016 Forbes ranking of the world's 2000 largest transnational corporations, Google (the holding company Alphabet Inc. is now the parent company of Google) occupied rank 27 with its annual profits of US$ 17 billion. Facebook was on rank 188 with annual profits of US$

---

1 Data source: Facebook, SEC Form 10-Q, November 2016
2 Data source: http://www.internetlivestats.com/google-search-statistics/, accessed on November 10, 2016.

DOI: 10.4324/9781003222149-8

3.7 billion. One should not be mistaken: Google and Facebook are not communications companies. They do not sell the ability to communicate. Rather, they are the world's largest advertising agencies. Their profits almost exclusively derive from targeted advertising. Understanding social media and big data therefore requires that we contextualise these phenomena through the critical study of marketing and advertising.

Critical marketing studies are based on the insight that "marketing has devoted too much attention to refining itself as an instrumental science, with the corollary emphasis on the production of knowledge for the 'marketing organisation', not for wider stakeholders" (Tadajewski 2010, 776). Further, it is a "systematic critique of marketing theory and practice" that uses "some form of critical social theory [...] whether this is drawn from the neo-Marxist critical theory tradition, some variant of humanism, feminism", or other approaches (Tadajewski 2010, 774). As a consequence, critical marketing does not mean conducting marketing critically or studying how to make marketing critical. Rather, critique and marketing are polar, dialectical opposites, just like socialism and capitalism. Critical marketing is a critique of marketing that aims at creating knowledge that helps us overcome both capitalism and marketing. Critical marketing studies as a discipline understands itself as being part of an emancipatory social science (Tadajewski and Brownlie, 2008). Taking a critical marketing perspective on social media means to apply critical social theory for understanding social media's power structures.

The task of this chapter is to critically understand social media and big data's political economy. It outlines key classical texts (section 8.2), contemporary texts (section 8.3), and future research directions (section 8.4) that can help us achieve this goal.

8.2 Key Theoretical Approaches

There are many critical approaches that matter for critically understanding the Internet and social media. In a text like this chapter, one is necessarily limited to the number of key texts and thinkers one can introduce. I will here focus on four classical thinkers and one text by each of them: Dallas Smythe, Karl Marx, Raymond Williams, and Sut Jhally.

8.2.1 Dallas Smythe: *Communications: Blindspot of Western Marxism*

Dallas Smythe's (1977) article *Communications: Blindspot of Western Marxism* has become a key text in the political economy of communication and when it comes to understanding advertising's political economy. Smythe's starting point is a critique of many Marxists' understanding of communications as transmitters of ideology and of advertising as belonging to an unproductive sphere of capital circulation. "The mass media of communications and related institutions concerned with advertising, market research, public relations and product and package design represent a blindspot in Marxist theory in the European and Atlantic basin cultures" (Smythe 1977, 1). Smythe criticised that a lot of critical and administration scholars analyse commercial media in terms of messages, information, images, meaning, entertainment, orientation, education, manipulation, and ideology. He argues for a perspective that gives a stronger role to the category of labour in the critical study of communication and culture.

Smythe bases his analysis on Karl Marx's (1867) insight that the commodity is capitalism's elementary form and that abstract labour produces the commodity's value. Smythe asks in the *Blindspot* essay: What is the advertising-based commercial media's commodity? Who produces the commercial media's commodity? Given that advertising-based media tend to provide their content gratis as a gift, the information cannot be the commodity.

Smythe gave the following answer:

> I submit that the materialist answer to the question – What is the commodity form of mass-produced, advertiser-supported communications under monopoly capitalism? – is audiences and readerships (hereafter referred to for simplicity as audiences). [...] Of the off-the-job work time, the largest single block is time of the audiences which is sold to advertisers. (Smythe 1977, 3)

Audiences would work to create the demand for monopoly capital's commodities (Smythe 1977, 6).

Audiences produce attention that is sold as audience commodity to advertisers. Therefore, according to Smythe, audiences conduct unpaid audience labour that produces the audience commodity and is exploited by advertisers. Smythe stressed that in capitalism, also unpaid labour is exploited and produces value. This focus was in line with developments in autonomous Marxism and Marxist feminism in the 1970s: Autonomous Marxists such as Antonio Negri (1988) stressed that there is a collective social worker who creates value inside and outside the factory and the office. They argued that society in capitalism is a social factory. Marxist feminists stressed that housework (re)produces labour-power as a commodity and is therefore exploited by capital (see, e.g. Dalla Costa and James 1973). Smythe's work, autonomous Marxism,

Key Theoretical Approaches

and Marxist feminism have in common that they stress the importance of the exploitation of unpaid labour for capitalism's existence.

In the age of digital media, there has been a resurgence of interest in Smythe's works. My contribution has in this respect been the linking of the notions of audience labour and the audience commodity to targeted online advertising (Fuchs 2012). How does Smythe's work matter for understanding social media? On social media, we are partly audiences watching, reading, and listening and partly producing consumers (prosumers) creating content ourselves. So for example on YouTube, most of us tend to predominantly watch videos. Many of these videos have in-video advertisements. So we not just consume the free content, but also provide attention to advertisements. And Google sells this attention to advertisers as a commodity. One difference to television is that on YouTube, users can produce and publish videos. So some users upload their own videos from time to time. And a smaller group of professional YouTubers tries to earn a living from creating YouTube content. By browsing videos on YouTube, searching on Google, and visiting websites, we produce a lot of meta-data that reveals a lot about our personal interests and tastes.

Google stores all of this data on its servers and identifies it with the IP address with which we access the Internet. Google also gains access to various other online data sources and thereby builds personal profiles of interests. Therefore, we do not simply find an audience commodity on social media, but also a big data commodity. In order to find out more about consumers' tastes and interests, advertisers and media organisations no longer need to conduct consumer surveys. The constant real-time surveillance of online behaviour and long-time storage of personal data allow for targeting advertisements based on individual profiles. The big data commodity allows an advertiser to, for example, target an ad for a soft drink to all users in London in the age group 16–30 years who have, at some point in time, googled the soft drink's name. The creation of big data commodity is a sophisticated form of surveillance and exploitation of user labour.

8.2.2 Karl Marx: *The Fetishism of the Commodity and its Secret*

The Fetishism of the Commodity and its Secret forms the fourth section of the first chapter in Karl Marx's main work *Capital Volume I* (Marx 1867, 163–177). In *Capital Volume I*'s first chapter, Marx shows that in capitalism both economic and ideological dimensions play an important role: a commodity has an economic dimension because it is produced by labour within class relations. The section on the commodity fetishism adds to the analysis that a commodity also has an ideological and aesthetic dimension that tries to deceive and manipulate humans. Marx here returns to the analysis of ideology that he advanced in an earlier work, *The German Ideology*, where he defined ideology as a *camera obscura* that makes humans and their social relations "appear upside-down" (Marx and Engels 1845, 42).

The social relations between workers' labour appear not "as direct social relations between persons in their work, but rather as material relations between persons and social relations between things" (Marx 1867, 166). Marx calls this phenomenon "the fetishism which attaches itself to the products of labour as soon as they are produced as commodities" (p. 165). He summarises the causes of the commodity's fetish character in the following words:

> Objects of utility become commodities only because they are the products of the labour of private individuals who work independently of each other. [...] Since the producers do not come into social contact until they exchange the products of their labour, the specific social characteristics of their private labours appear only within this exchange. (p. 165)

The notion of commodity fetishism points out that phenomena such as commodities and money are ubiquitous in our everyday lives in capitalist society. Given their thing-like status, we cannot directly see where they are coming from and how they have been produced. Therefore capitalism, commodity exchange, and money appear to be natural forms of the organisation of society, to which no alternatives exist. Fetishism de-historicises society. Fetishism is on the one hand a particular aesthetic of the commodity. On the other hand, all ideology is fetishistic in character as it attempts to legitimate, naturalise, and justify specific forms of domination and exploitation.

The most influential theoretical take-up of Marx's notion of commodity fetishism can be found in Georg Lukács' (1971) book *History and Class Consciousness*. Commodity logic conceals "every trace of its fundamental nature: the relation between people" so that "a relation between people takes on the character of a thing and thus acquires a 'phantom objectivity'" (Lukács 1971, 83). Lukács coined the notion of reification. Generally speaking, reification (another term for it is alienation) means conditions under which humans are not able to control and determine the structures that shape their lives. Reification therefore can exist in all realms of life (Fuchs 2016, chapter 5).

Lukács was particularly interested in economic and cultural reification. "Reification requires that a society should learn to satisfy all its needs in terms of commodity exchange" (Lukács 1971, 91), which includes "the separation of the producer from his means of production" (Lukács 1971, 91). Lukács added another important dimension to the theory of commodity fetishism: His notion of reified consciousness stressed the subjective dimension of ideology and fetishism. Ideology and fetishism are not just objective structures and strategies, they are also experienced and lived. Ideology aims at influencing human consciousness. Lukács' works have had major influence on Marxist ideology critique, including the approach of the Frankfurt School.

We can learn from Chapter 1 of Marx's *Capital* that when analysing capitalist phenomena such as advertising and targeted advertising on social media, there are always an economic and a cultural dimensions, as well as aspects of labour and ideology. Dallas Smythe's notions of audience labour stresses advertising's labour dimension. Given that, as Marx shows, any commodity also has a fetishistic and ideological dimension, one also needs to look at the ideological dimension of the audience commodity. The works of Sut Jhally and Raymond Williams can help us better understand commodity fetishism in the context of advertising.

8.2.3 Sut Jhally's "Advertising as Religion" and Raymond Williams's "Advertising: The Magic System"

Sut Jhally's (2006) essay *Advertising as Religion: The Dialectic of Technology and Magic* analyses advertising's fetishistic and ideological structure. Jhally points out that in capitalism, the division of labour ensures that people only work on one part of a product. As a result of the division between mental and physical labours, and the fact that goods come to us through markets, we do not understand their origins. "The social relations of production embedded in goods are systematically hidden from our eyes. The real meaning of goods, in fact, is *emptied* out in capitalist production and consumption" (Jhally 2006, 88). Advertising taps into this void: commodity fetishism empties commodities of human meaning. We cannot understand the meanings of life and experiences of commodity producers, as these are all removed from the equation. In an artificial way, advertising creates ideological meanings that it bestows on commodities. "Into the void left by the transition from traditional to industrial society comes advertising [...] The function of advertising is to refill the emptied commodity with meaning. [...] Production empties. Advertising fills. The real is hidden by the imaginary" (Jhally 2006, 88–89). He adds that the "most important functions that advertising performs is to provide meaning for the world of goods in a context in which true meaning has been stolen" (Jhally 2006, 93).

Advertising is tremendously powerful because it tells stories and provides meanings about goods and the economy that are not presented in other forms. It uses various strategies for doing so, for example the strategy of black magic (Jhally 2006, 91): Humans suddenly transform in supernatural ways through commodity use. Advertising is a secular form of religion. Advertising is a system of commodity fetishism: It promises satisfaction and happiness through the consumption of things (Jhally 2006, 102). For Jhally, advertising is propaganda that promotes the ideology of human happiness through the consumption of commodities. By analysing advertising as ideological commodity propaganda and commodity consumption ideology, Jhally defies positivist definitions of advertising that describe it as useful information for consumers that helps them navigate commercial options in complex markets. A typical example of such an uncritical definition of advertising defines it as "a channel of information from manufacturers to Consumers" that merely "tells where to find what you want" (Kaptan 2002, 28).

In his essay *Advertising: The Magic System*, Raymond Williams (2000) analyses the history of advertising. He shows that in the early stages of capitalism, advertising was seen as harmful and was therefore limited by an advertising tax. The emergence of advertising, as we know it today, can be traced back to the emergence of monopoly capitalism in the late 19th century.

> Advertising was developed to sell goods, in a particular kind of economy. Publicity has been developed to sell persons, in a particular kind of culture. The methods are often basically similar: the arranged incident, the 'mention', the advice on branding, packaging and a good "selling line". (Williams 2000, 183)

Comparable to Jhally, who sees advertising as capitalism's secular religion, Williams analyses advertising as capitalism's commodity magic: advertising is capitalism's system of "organized magic" (Williams 2000, 186) and "organized fantasy" (p. 193).

> You do not only buy an object: you buy social respect, admiration, health, beauty, success, power to control your environment. The magic obscures the real sources of general satisfaction because their discovery would involve radical change in the whole common way of life. (p. 189)

Key Theoretical Approaches

Jhally and Williams's analyses of advertising as capitalism's religion and magic system correspond to Marx's analysis of commodity fetishism in general. Marx (1867) argued that a commodity is a peculiar thing; it is "strange" (p. 163), "metaphysical" (p. 163), "'mystical'" (p. 164), and "'mysterious'" (p. 164). As a consequence, the commodity "stands on its head", and "grotesque ideas" (p. 163) about the commodity's nature emerge.

Marx's notion of the commodity fetishism and Jhally and Williams's applications of this concept to the critical analysis of advertising also matter in respect to social media; firstly, in the context of social media advertisement's general structure, and secondly, in respect to social media's inverse commodity fetishism. McDonald's is one of the biggest advertisers on Facebook. One example posting shows a "Mexican burger" and says: "Get in the mood for Mexico with spicy Habanero chilli mayo in this week's #GreatTastesoftheWorld: the Mexican Stack!"

The ad presents a particular image of a burger as being tasty, multicultural, international, spicy, etc. McDonald's presents itself as fostering an international lifestyle and eating culture by adopting culinary influences from all over the world. This image is, however, fetishistic, illusionary, magic, and religious. It is a belief system that may not correspond to the actual reality of the production of the burger that is advertised. The consumer does not know where the meat and ingredients come from and under which conditions they are produced. The advertisement distracts attention from common criticisms of McDonald's relating to working conditions, possible health, and environmental impacts, the McDonaldisation of the world, etc. The advert is fetishistic because it tries to create a brand image that only presents the burger and the company in a positive light and disregards the actual social conditions of production. What is specific for commodity fetishism on social media? Advertising's commodity fetishism in print publications and broadcast media (radio, television) is standardised and unified, every consumer of these media receives the same advertising messages. In contrast, we find personalised and targeted commodity fetishism on social media. Advertisers like McDonald's can target its ads at users who, based on their previous online activity, for example appear to be fond of fast food.

Targeted commodity fetishism is a first feature of advertising on social media. A second feature is what I in various publications have termed the inverse commodity fetishism (Fuchs 2014, chapter 11; Fuchs 2015, chapter 5). In conventional commodity fetishism, one cannot experience the social context of commodity production but is directly confronted with the logic of money and the commodity. On Facebook and other targeted-advertising-based social media platforms, the commodity fetishism is in-verted: because access to the platform is free and the sale of the big data commodity is hidden, one does not experience monetary exchange or commodity purchase on Facebook. Instead, the social dimension of communication, sharing, and community is what is foregrounded and experienced. As an effect, the commodity form is hidden behind the social form so that commodity fetishism tends to take on an inverted form. For Facebook users, it is not directly experienceable that users produce a commodity for Facebook, that they actually work for Facebook, and they are the ones generating the company's profits. The inverse commodity fetishism makes it more difficult for users to perceive themselves as workers who are creating value and are being exploited.

The ideological effects of commodity fetishism are an immanent manipulative feature of online advertising. Social media also enable an algorithmically engineered form of manipulation, namely the manipulation of emotions and attention. This became evident when researchers from Princeton University conducted a large-scale experiment on Facebook (Kramer et al. 2014): The emotional tone of postings shown on the News feed of 689,003 users was manipulated. "Two parallel experiments were conducted for positive and negative emotion: One in which exposure to friends' positive emotional content in their News Feed was reduced, and one in which exposure to negative emotional content in their News Feed was reduced" (Kramer et al. 2014, 8788). The

> results suggest that the emotions expressed by friends, via online social
> networks, influence our own moods, constituting, to our knowledge, the first
> experimental evidence for massive-scale emotional contagion via social
> networks [...], and providing support for previously contested claims that
> emotions spread via contagion through a network. (Kramer et al. 2014, 8789)

Such research has implications for advertising and marketing: if negative messages are kept from the News feed, then users are more likely to positively engage with content, including advertisements and the company's postings. The experiment that was sup-ported by Facebook also shows that technically it is easy to manipulate what is seen and not seen on the News feed. It is just a small step from research about manip-ulating emotions to practically conducting such manipulation. The effect would be that social media platforms would become purely positivist, suppressing attention to critical content, possibly also including the critique of politics and corporations. Facebook is a targeted advertising machine and one of the world's largest advertising corporations. Manipulation for the sake of keeping users and advertising clients happy can easily

Key Theoretical Approaches

result in the filtering out of critical postings. The result is then a platform that is an instrument of capitalist interests and censors everything that does not adhere to the logic of commodities.

Engineering and manipulating emotions and sociality on social media can easily result in one-dimensional social media. The Princeton researchers and Facebook were criticised for not obtaining the users' informed consent for the online experiment they participated in. Facebook apologised to its users[3]. The Electronic Privacy Information Centre demanded that Facebook makes its News feed algorithm public because the secrecy of algorithms enables and supports possible manipulation.[4]

8.3 Current Key Areas of Research

This section focuses on two key areas of current critical research about social media: digital labour and digital alienation.

8.3.1 Digital Labour

The notion of digital labour emerged in the context of the 2009 conference The Internet as Playground and Factory organised by Trebor Scholz at The New School in New York (see http://digitallabor.org). Later, also a collected volume of some of the presented contributions was published (Scholz 2013). The basic idea is that user activity on commercial digital media is unpaid labour that creates value and a digital commodity. Therefore social media companies such as Facebook and Google exploit users. My own contribution to the digital labour literature has been the combination of the digital labour concept with critical and Marxist theory (see Fuchs 2010, 2012, 2014, 2015).

If one wants to understand a particular aspect of capitalism, then one needs to look at how commodity production is organised. Marx has provided a framework for such an analysis (see Fuchs 2010):

$$M - C (c, v).. P.. C' - M'$$

3 https://www.theguardian.com/technology/2014/jul/02/facebook-apologises-psychological-experiments-on-users
4 https://www.theguardian.com/technology/2014/jul/04/privacy-watchdog-files-complaint-over-facebook-emotion-experiment

A capitalist corporation invests monetary capital M for purchasing specific commodities C as means of production. This includes labour-power (variable capital v) as well as resources and instruments (constant capital c). Labour-power is the subjective dimension of the means of production. Resources and instruments form the means of production's objective dimension. In the production process P workers transform the objects in order to create a new commodity C', in which labour-time and a surplus-product are objectified. The new product is more than the sum of its elements. When the commodity C' is successfully sold then an increased capital sum M' is created. A part of C' is reinvested so that a new cycle of accumulation starts, while other parts are paid out as interest, dividends, bonuses, and rent. The point of capitalism is the accumulation of capital, production with a monetary profit. The commodity C' is sold at a price that is higher than the investment costs. The commodity C' and its value are created by labour. But the workers do not own the products they create. They are only remunerated for part of their work in the form of wages. The surplus-value and surplus-product they create remain unremunerated. The key aspect of capitalism is that capital accumulation can only work by exploiting workers, which means that part of their labour is unpaid and that capitalists own the products that workers create.

The question that arises in the context of social media is how Marx's framework can be used. The access to Facebook, Google, YouTube, Twitter, etc. is not a commodity. This also implies that these companies' paid employees do not create a commodity, but rather a gift. But all of these companies are for profit. So there must be a different commodity and a different kind of value-generating activity. Marx's framework can be modified for social media capitalism as follows (Fuchs 2010, 2012, 2014 [chapter 11], 2015 [chapter 5]):

$$M - C (c, v1).. P1 \text{ (social media platform), } v2.. P2.. C' - M'$$

v1 is the paid employees who create and maintain the social media platform. Access to the platform is a gift, a "free lunch" for the users, who form the unpaid labour force v2. Their online activities create in the second production process P2 the big data commodity C' that is sold to advertisers so that an increased sum of monetary capital M' can be accumulated. All labour-producing commodities for capitalists involve unpaid labour that creates surplus-value.

The difference between regular wage labour and unpaid digital labour is that in the latter case there is no wage, which means that all labour-time is surplus labour-time. This circumstance is a feature that social media's digital labour shares with housework

(Fuchs 2010, 2018). Kylie Jarrett (2016) uses the notion of the digital housewife for pointing out parallels between unpaid online labour and houseworkers' domestic, reproductive labour. "Consumer labour is akin to domestic labour [...] because it is a site of social reproduction: a site for the making and re-making of the social, affective, ideological and psychological states of being that (may) accord with appropriate capitalist subjectivities" (Jarrett, 2016, 71).

The implication of the notion of digital labour is that Google, Facebook, Twitter, and other online corporations that use the targeted-advertising capital accumulation model exploit users, usage of these platforms is labour-time, digital workers are part of the contemporary proletariat, value-production is not limited to factories and offices, and activities that might feel pleasurable and personal can nonetheless be forms of economic exploitation.

The Marxist notion of digital labour results in a theoretical discussion (see, e.g. Fisher and Fuchs 2015; Proffitt, Ekbia and McDowell 2015). The main criticisms can be summarised in the following ideal-type arguments:

1) "Marx is a 19th-century theorist. A 19th-century theory is not fit for explaining 21st-century phenomena. Marx's theory is outdated";
2) "Only wage workers are productive workers who are exploited by capital. Facebook users do not work and are not exploited because they do not earn a wage";
3) "Facebook users are not producers, but media consumers. Consumption does not create any value";
4) "Social media is part of the advertising economy that is situated in capitalism's sphere of circulation, in which commodities are not produced, but sold. Circulation labour is not productive, but rather unproductive. Facebook therefore is a rent-seeking corporation that consumes the profits and value created by wage workers in other parts of the economy";
5) "The focus on the exploitation of users as unpaid trivialises much worse forms of exploitation, such as Taylorist labour and slave work".

Such arguments tend to imply that there is no problem with Facebook and Google. Their logic is: "They do not exploit us and therefore nothing needs to be done against them". Counter-arguments can be summarised as follows (for a detailed discussion see Fuchs 2015, chapter 5; see also Fuchs 2018):

1) The 2008 crisis of capitalism and its consequences show that Marx was right and remains important. Marx was a historical and dialectical thinker. Just like capitalism remains the same by constantly changing, also the categories used for analysing capitalism undergo a dialectic of continuity and change. The transformation of the Marxian formula of capital accumulation from $M - C (c, v).. P.. C' - M'$ into $M - C (c, v1).. P1, v2.. P2.. C' - M'$ on social media shows that the online targeted-advertising economy is based on such a dialectic of continuity and change;

2) If you assume that only wage workers are exploited in capitalism and that only a wage worker can be a productive worker, then the implication is that house workers, who are still predominantly female, and the world's estimated 30 million slaves are also not exploited. Your assumption is politically problematic. Marx saw productive labour as value-generating labour. One can produce value for capital without being paid;

3) There is in general a dialectic of production and consumption. Production involves the consumption of the means of production. Consumption produces meanings, effects, and the need for more production. Social media is different from traditional communication technologies. On social media, there is not a clear differentiation between producers and consumers of content or between production, circulation, and consumption technologies. The computer is a convergence technology. Consumption on social media is better termed "usage". And usage is also the production of data, meta-data, and often user-generated content. Social media users are prosumers;

4) The reason why a commodity produced by a brand company is much more expensive than a standard commodity has to do with the fact that branding involves advertising and marketing labour. In the contemporary economy, advertising forms an important industry in itself. It is therefore unrealistic to dismiss this part of the economy as unproductive. One can charge rent on a persistent product that was only created once but does not need constant labour input for being re-produced. But the big data commodity is frequently updated and renewed, so there is an actual labour input and a renewal of the commodity. It is therefore not feasible to argue that Facebook is a rentier. A rentier is a monopolist who controls a specific resource (usually land or real estate) and charges money to tenants, users, or leasers. Marx argued that transport labour is a form of productive circulation labour. Transport labour is the labour that is needed for transporting a commodity from the place where it is produced to the places where it is sold and consumed. Audience labour and social media users' digital labour is ideological transport labour that helps transporting advertisements that are commodity ideologies and product propaganda to users;

5) The logic of the argument "A is not exploited because the exploitation of B is more violent" disregards how different forms of exploitation are united in an international division of labour, from which transnational corporations benefit. They exploit a diverse range of workers in order to accumulate capital. The production of digital media and data is based on an international division of digital labour, in which we find slave workers extracting minerals, Tayloristic assemblage workers, low-paid software engineers and call centre agents, highly paid and highly stressed software engineers, precarious freelancers, user labour, etc. The notion of the international division of digital labour stresses that digital capital exploits all of these digital workers and that they therefore have a common interest to struggle against capital and to organise across national boundaries in the form of a digital labour union. The notion of digital labour is not limited to the users of targeted-advertising-based social media platforms. Marx stressed the connectedness of diverse forms of labour with the notion of the collective worker. In the international division of digital labour, there is collective digital labour.

Not all digital labour is unpaid and based on advertising. YouTube has introduced YouTube Red in the USA and is also rolling out the same programme in other countries: Members of YouTube Red pay a subscription fee for access to ad-free premium videos (including music, series, and vloggers' content).

> Our new paid membership, YouTube Red, lets members enjoy any video on YouTube without ads while still supporting creators. [...] New revenue from YouTube Red membership fees will be distributed to video creators based on how much members watch your content.[5]

YouTube celeb vloggers such as Lilly Singh (who had 11 million followers on her YouTube Channel in January 2017), PewDieDie (53 million), MatPat (8 million), Toby Turner (2 million), and Joey Graceffa (7.5 million)[6] have produced series and movies for YouTube Red. YouTube stars are a labour aristocracy, who can earn some money from their profiles because they managed to accumulate a large number of subscribers. Whereas there is a small number of labour-aristocratic YouTube-Vloggers, the vast number are proletarianised digital workers, working precariously and struggling to earn

5 https://support.google.com/youtube/answer/6306276?hl=en-GB
6 http://uk.businessinsider.com/youtube-red-original-movies-and-shows-2015-10?r=US&IR=T/#youtuber-joey-graceffa-will-star-in-a-new-youtube-murder-mystery-series-10

a living online. YouTube only enables this YouTube aristocracy to produce premium content that is paid for by YouTube Red subscribers. In this model, YouTube can be seen as a temporary employer of these YouTube celebs that pays them a wage for the creation of specific content. YouTube Red subscribers are consuming audiences paying for access to premium content. With the introduction of YouTube Red, Google has diversified its capital accumulation model. It continues to use targeted advertising as main revenue source and has in addition introduced a subscription service. YouTube is therefore based on two forms of digital labour: (a) Users' digital labour of watching and creating in the case of advertising sponsored part of the platform; and (b) The YouTube labour aristocracy's paid labour that creates premium content for YouTube Red.

8.3.2 Digital Alienation

Alienation (Entfremdung) is a term that Marx used for characterising conditions that humans are not in control of and under which they live. Alienation not just signifies an objective structural condition, but also a subjective feeling of dissatisfaction. In discussions about digital labour, there have been different approaches about how to think of alienation in the context of social media.

Mark Andrejevic argues that commercial social media only have an appearance of being non-alienating because they foster play and sociality. But in reality, using them means a form of digital alienation, "a form of the enclosure of the digital commons" (Andrejevic 2012, 84). "Users have little choice over whether this [surveillance] data is generated and little say in how it is used" (Andrejevic 2012, 85). Such "external, storable, and sortable collection of data about" users' "social lives" is "separated from us and stored in servers owned and controlled by, for example, Facebook" (Andrejevic 2011, 88). "Algorithmic alienation" (Andrejevic 2014, 189) determines users' lives by data mining, big data analysis, and statistical correlations.

Eran Fisher (2012) understands digital alienation in a different way. For him, it "signals an existential state of not being in control over something (the labour process, the product, etc.)" (Fisher 2012, 173). Less "alienation refers to a greater possibility to express oneself, to control one's production process, to objectify one's essence and connect and communicate with others. Thus, for example, working on one's Facebook page can be thought of as less alienating than working watching a television program" (Fisher 2012, 173). Social media

> establish new relations of production that are based on a dialectical link between exploitation and alienation: in order to be de-alienated, users must

Current Key Areas of Research

> communicate and socialize: they must establish social networks, share information, talk to their friends and read their posts, follow and be followed. By thus doing they also exacerbate their exploitation. (Fisher 2012, 179)

Fisher's conclusion is that on social media, low alienation creates high exploitation.

Andrejevic and Fisher have two different understandings of digital alienation. For Andrejevic, it is an objective condition, while for Fisher it is a subjective feeling. We do, however, not have to categorically separate subjective and objective alienation. Alienation is both an objective condition and something that is or is not felt. In the book *Critical Theory of Communication* (Fuchs 2016), I have suggested a matrix of alienation that distinguishes three types and three dimensions of alienation. We can discern between economic, political, and cultural alienations. Each of these types is organised on the subjective level (attitudes and feelings), the intersubjective level (social agency and interaction), and the objective level (structures and products of activity). Combining these types and levels results in a matrix with nine forms of alienation (Fuchs 2016, 167). The alienation matrix can be applied to Facebook and other commercial social media platform (see Table 8.1).

One important aspect of the matrix of digital alienation is that it goes beyond the economic realm. It also covers forms of political control and cultural disrespect. Social media is also a realm of the accumulation of political and cultural power that produces winners and losers. Another important aspect of the matrix is that objective digital alienation does not automatically imply subjective digital alienation. Although Facebook users are objectively exploited, they do not necessarily feel exploited, seeing that there is inverse commodity fetishism on corporate social media platforms. We therefore have to distinguish between feelings of digital alienation and non-alienation. In general, there is only an opportunity for societal change when conditions and the collective structure of feelings of alienation coincide. There is, however, also no guarantee that such change will automatically or necessarily be politically progressive in character.

8.4 Directions for Future Research

Studying social media and big data from a critical marketing perspective is interesting but also complex. It involves multiple dimensions, topics, questions, and approaches. This section identifies possible research questions that remain fairly unexplored and could be taken up by PhD students and other scholars. The list that follows is not complete, rather, it provides some examples.

TABLE 8.1 The matrix of digital alienation.

Forms of alienation/ reification	Subjects' attitudes and feelings		Intersubjectivity (social agency and interaction)	Object (structures, products)
Economic reification	Feeling of alienation:"Facebook exploits me!"	Feeling of non-alienation:"Facebook is fun and voluntary and gives me social advantages. Therefore I do not feel exploited".	Exploitation of users' digital labour;users' non-ownership of platforms	Users' lack of control over the use of personal data
Political reification	Feeling of alienation:"The surveillance-industrial complex that Facebook is part of threatens freedom".	Feeling of non-alienation:"For greater security, we have to give up some privacy. I therefore don't mind state surveillance of social media".	Political control and surveillance of citizens' communication	Citizens' lack of control over how political institutions regulate the Internet, establishment of a surveillance-industrial complex
Cultural reification	Feeling of alienation:"Facebook is mindless babble, narcissistic self-presentation and showing off".	Feeling of non-alienation:"Facebook is a great form of socialising with other people".	Asymmetric visibility of users that favours celebrities, corporations, and powerful institutions	Asymmetric influence on public meaning making, centralised online attention structures, and online visibility

Source: Fuchs (2016, 171).

- What are commonalities and differences between users' attitudes towards targeted advertising in Western countries and non-Western countries in Asia, Africa, and Latin America?
- How do traditional trade unions use social media and what do they think of the possibility of the creation of digital labour unions?
- What have workers' and users' experiences been in the digital sharing economy (including Airbnb, Uber, and online freelancing platforms such as Amazon Mechanical Turk and Upwork)?
- What are the experiences and political attitudes of digital workers in the international division of digital labour? What do they think of the perspective of the world's digital workers uniting in a global movement or union?

- What have been the experiences of people who have tried to establish alternatives to Facebook, Google, YouTube, Twitter, etc.? What problems have they faced? What challenges, limits, and problems do platform co-operatives face? Are there ways for such limits to be overcome?
- What kind of class are professional YouTubers? What kind of class consciousness do they have? How do they think about capitalism, entrepreneurship, neo-liberalism, freelancing, and precarious labour?
- How has marketing and advertising based on big data and social media changed the film and music industries? What do artists think about these changes? What is the role of precarious labour among artists in the social media age?
- How do right-wing parties and social movements (Trumpism, pro-Brexit movement, Front National, nationalists, racists, xenophobes, etc.) use targeted advertising, big data, and social media to advance their ideologies? How do they use social media as forms for political communication? What do everyday users think about such advertisements and right-wing online communication?
- How does marketing and targeted advertising change with the rise of the Internet of Things? What dangers do such forms of advertising entail? What do actual or potential users think about these dangers?
- What are the limits and problems of big data? How do users think about big data based advertising and targeted advertising? How do they think about non-commercial, commons-based, non-profit alternatives?
- How can an alternative paradigm to big data positivism and computational social science be established? What critiques can be levelled at these largely quantitative approaches? What alternative critically oriented social media research methods do we need to develop and how can they be applied to ideology critique?
- How are specific forms of ideologies expressed on social media?
- What policies are needed for advancing non-commercial, non-profit, commons-based social media?
- How can the logic of social media and online communication be decelerated and the political public sphere thereby be best advanced? What are slow media 2.0? What are the potentials of slow media 2.0?
- What are the dangers of branded online content and native online advertising? How does branded online content and native online advertising make use of big data? What do users think of branded online content? What are the dangers for journalism stemming from these forms of content?

- What problems does labour face in the context of crowdfunding? What power asymmetries and ideologies can we find in the world of crowdfunding? What have been experiences of actual project co-ordinators on crowdfunding platforms such as Kickstarter? How does crowdfunding relate to neo-liberalism and the ideology of entrepreneurship?
- What controversies develop when digital advertising gurus meet digital labour activists in focus groups to debate digital capitalism?

8.5 Conclusion

Social media and big data are relatively new phenomena. At the same time, they reflect old power structures, but in new ways. This chapter focused on the analysis of social media's political economy based on various critical theory approaches. It used classical concepts such as the audience commodity, audience labour, and commodity fetishism to show that critical analysis of advertising and targeted advertising needs to look at both economic and ideological dimensions. Facebook and Google are not communications corporations but the world's largest advertising agencies. Current research in critical social media studies focuses on issues such as digital labour and digital alienation. Given that social media and big data will not disappear overnight, the critical study of these phenomena remains an important task.

References

Andrejevic, Mark. 2014. Alienation's Returns. In *Critique, Social Media and the Information Society*, eds. Christian Fuchs and Marisol Sandoval, 179–190. New York: Routledge.

Andrejevic, Mark. 2012. Exploitation in the Data Mine. In C. Fuchs, K. Boersma, A. Albrechtslund and M. Sandoval, *Internet and Surveillance: The Challenges of Web 2.0 and Social Media.* New York: Routledge, pp. 71–88.

Andrejevic, Mark. 2011. Social Network Exploitation. In *A Networked Self*, ed. Zizi Papacharissi, 82–102. New York: Routledge.

Dalla Costa, Maria and Selma James. 1973. *The Power of Women and the Subversion of the Community.* Bristol: Falling Wall Press. Seceond Edition

Fisher, Eran. 2012. How Less Alienation Creates More Exploitation? Audience Labour on Social Network Sites. *tripleC: Communication, Capitalism & Critique* 10 (2): 71–183.

Fisher, Eran and Christian Fuchs, eds. 2015. *Reconsidering Value and Labour in the Digital Age.* Basingstoke: Palgrave Macmillan.

Fuchs, Christian. 2018. Capitalism, Patriarchy, Slavery, and Racism in the Age of Digital Capitalism and Digital Labour. Critical Sociology 44 (4-5): 677–702. 10.1177%2F08969205176911108

Fuchs, Christian. 2017. *Social Media: A Critical Introduction,*3rd edn. London: Sage

Fuchs, Christian. 2016. *Critical Theory of Communication: New Readings of Lukács, Adorno, Marcuse, Honneth and Habermas in the Age of the Internet.* London: University of Westminster Press.

Fuchs, Christian. 2015. *Culture and Economy in the Age of Social Media.* New York: Routledge.

Fuchs, Christian. 2014. *Digital Labour and Karl Marx.* New York: Routledge.

Fuchs, Christian. 2012. Dallas Smythe Today – The Audience Commodity, the Digital Labour Debate, Marxist Political Economy and Critical Theory. Prolegomena to a Digital Labour Theory of Value. *tripleC: Communication, Capitalism & Critique* 10 (2): 692–740.

Fuchs, Christian. 2010. Labor in Informational Capitalism and on the Internet. *The Information Society* 26 (3): 179–196.

Jarrett, Kylie. 2016. *Feminism, Labour and Digital Media. The Digital Housewife.* New York: Routledge.

Jhally, Sut. 2006. *Advertising as Religion: The Dialectic of Technology and Magic.* In Sut Jhally: *The Spectacle of Accumulation: Essays in Culture, Media, & Politics,* 85–97. New York: Peter Lang.

Kaptan, S. S. 2002. *Advertising: New Concepts.* New Delhi: Sarup & Sons.

Kramer, A.D.I. et al. 2014. Experimental Evidence of Massive-Scale Emotional Contagion Through Social Networks. *Proceedings of the National Academy of the Sciences of the United States of America* 111 (24): 8788–8790.

Lukács, Georg. 1971 [1923]. *History and Class Consciousness.* London: Merlin.

Marx, Karl. 1867. *Capital Volume I.* London: Penguin.

Marx, Karl and Engels, Friedrich. 1845. *German Ideology.* Amherst, NY: Prometheus.

Negri, Anotonio. 1988. *Revolution Retrieved. Selected Writings on Marx, Keynes, Capitalist Crisis & New Social Subjects 1967-83.* London: Red Notes.

Proffitt, Jennifer M., Hamid R. Ekbia, and Stephen D. McDowell, eds. 2015. Special Forum on Monetization of User-Generated Content – Marx Revisited. *The Information Society* 31 (1): 1–67.

Scholz, Trebor, ed. 2013. *Digital Labor: The Internet as Playground and Factory.* New York: Routledge.

Smythe, Dallas Walker. 1977. Communications: Blindspot of Western Marxism. *Canadian Journal of Political and Social Theory* 1 (3): 1–27.

Tadajewski, Mark. 2010. Towards a History of Critical Marketing Studies. *Journal of Marketing Management* 26 (9–10): 773–824.

Tadajewski, Mark and Brownlie, Douglas, eds. 2008. Critical Marketing: A Limit Attitude. I *Critical Marketing: Issues in Contemporary Marketing,* 1–28. Chicester: John Wiley.

Williams, Raymond. 2000. Advertising: The Magic System. In Raymond Williams: *Culture and Materialism,* 170–195. London: Verso.

Chapter Nine
Social Media and the Capitalist Crisis

9.1 Introduction

In this work, I focus on discussing selected aspects of the relationship between social media and the capitalist crisis. Detailed critical analyses of political, economic, and ideological aspects of social media can be found in associated publications (Fuchs 2014a, 2014b, 2014c, 2015, 2016a, 2016b, 2016c, 2017; Fuchs and Mosco 2016; Fuchs and Sandoval 2014; Fisher and Fuchs 2015; Trottier and Fuchs 2014; Fuchs et al. 2012). I first summarise my analysis of the crisis (section 9.2), then discuss aspects of targeted advertising (section 9.3), the ideology of Twitter revolutions (section 9.4), and anti-socialist ideology on Twitter (section 9.5). The basic point the chapter makes is that capitalist development is an important factor that has conditioned the emergence of social media, social media's economy, and ideology on social media.

9.2 The Capitalist Crisis

The profit rate is a key category of Marxist political economy (Marx 1867, chapter 17; for a discussion see: Fuchs 2016b, chapter 17).

The rate of profit is the relationship of profit and investment or of the monetary expression of surplus-value and the value of the means of production (constant and variable capital).

$$ROP = \frac{s}{c + v}$$

DOI: 10.4324/9781003222149-9

If we divide the numerator and the denominator by v, then we get:

$$ROP = \frac{\frac{s}{v}}{\frac{c}{v} + 1}$$

This formula shows that the rate of profit depends: (a) on the rate of surplus-value that Marx also calls the rate of exploitation because it described the relationship of unpaid and paid labours; and (b) the organic composition of capital that represents the relationship of dead and living labour, constant and variable capital, the value of machinery/resources, and labour-power. The organic composition is a measure of an economy's technological intensity. The rate of profit is directly proportional to the rate of surplus-value and indirectly proportional to the organic composition of capital.

New technology has the potential to increase both the rate of surplus-value and the organic composition of capital. The effects of new technology on the rate of profit depend on the relationship between the rate of surplus-value and the organic composition. If the organic composition increases more than the rate of surplus-value, then a fall of the rate of profit emerges. Vice versa, if the rate of surplus-value increases more than the organic composition, then the rate of profit rises. An important factor in this respect is class struggle that influences the absolute value of variable capital v. In any case, the formula for the rate of profit shows that technification has contradictory potentials: it can increase productivity and the exploitation of labour.

The increase of the organic composition as structural tendency of capital stands in a contradiction with class struggles. The outcomes of this contradiction cannot be predicted in advance, but depend on historical circumstances. If the organic composition increases and there are no or unsuccessful workers' struggles so that the wage sum decreases, then the rate of profit can increase. If however workers' struggles are successful and they resist lay-offs and achieve wage-increases, the profit rate is more likely to fall.

Figures 9.1 and 9.2 show the development of the rate of profit, the organic composition, and the rate of surplus-value in the USA and the EU15 countries.

The rate of surplus-value, that is, the degree of exploitation, has decreased in the 1960s and was relatively low in the 1970s in both the USA and the EU15. This is an indication that the working class' struggles were relatively successful in this time period and resulted in relative wage increases. In the early 1980s, the time of the rise

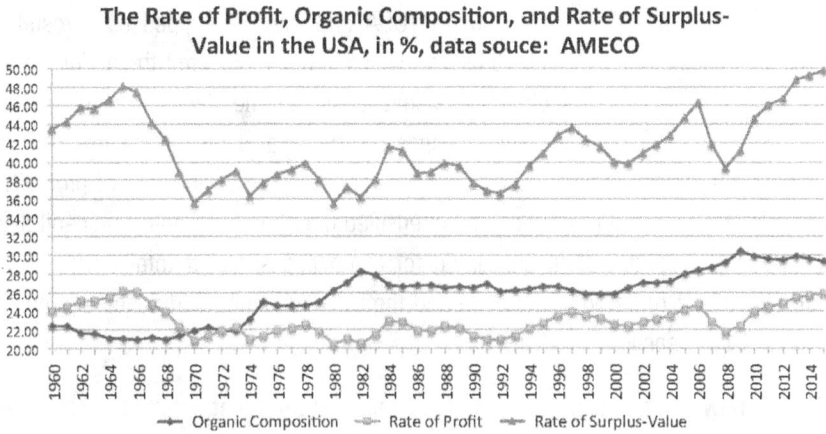

FIGURE 9.1 Economic development in the USA

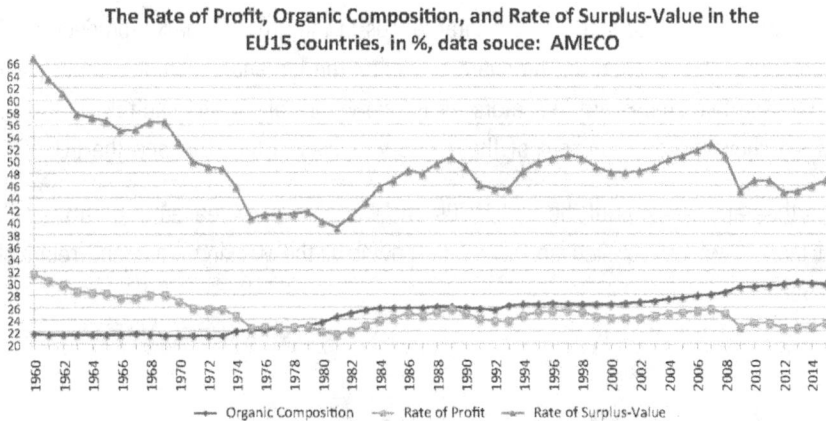

FIGURE 9.2 Economic development in the EU15 countries

of neoliberal politics such as Reagonomics and Thatcherism, the degree of exploitation started a long-term increase caused by wage repression.

The time period 1960–2015 is one, in which the computer has arisen, shaped, and transformed capitalist economies. As a result, both in the USA and the EU15 countries the organic composition has, in this period covering 55 years, increased from around 20% to almost 30%, which confirms Marx's analysis that there is a tendency of the organic composition to rise that results from the technification and scientification of production. The rate of profit in both the USA and the EU dropped as a result of increasing wages and the working class' struggles in the 1960s until the middle of the 1970s, the time of a large global economic crisis. In the decades following the mid-1970s, the increasing organic composition puts a downward pressure, and the increasing rate of surplus-value put an upward pressure on the rate of profit. The microelectronic revolution extended and intensified the role of technology in capitalism and financing computerisation accounted for a growing share of total capital. As a result, the rate of profit both in the EU and the USA fluctuated and never returned to the rates it had reached in the 1960s.

In 2008, a new world economic crisis of capitalism started that resulted in significant drops of the rate of profit in both the USA and the EU. In the USA, the effect was that the capitalist class heavily intensified exploitation in order to drive up the rate of profit. In the EU, the economy stagnated and the rate of profit remained at a low rate in the years after the crisis started in 2008.

The wage share is the share of the total wages in the gross domestic product (GDP), whereas the capital share is the share of capital (profits and constant capital) in the GDP. These two shares are indicators for the power of labour and capital. Figures 9.3 and 9.4 show the development of these two variables in the USA and the EU.

From the early 1960s until the mid-1970s, the wage share increased in both the USA and the EU, which signified an increasing power of the working class and relatively

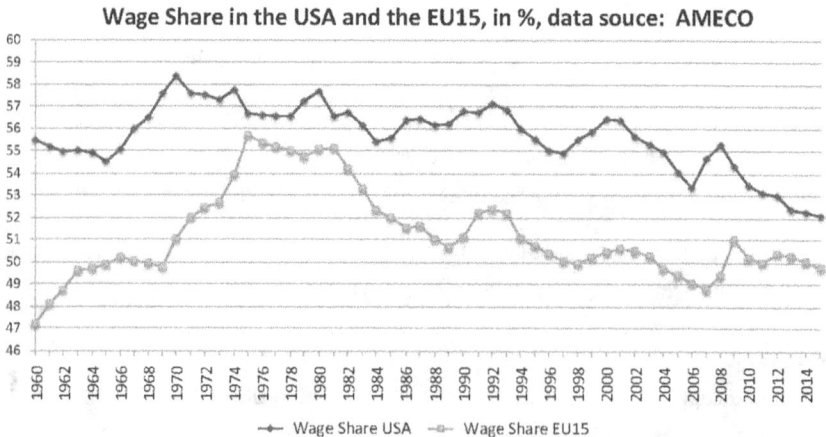

FIGURE 9.3 The wage share in the USA and the EU

Capital Share in the USA and the EU15, in %, data souce: AMECO

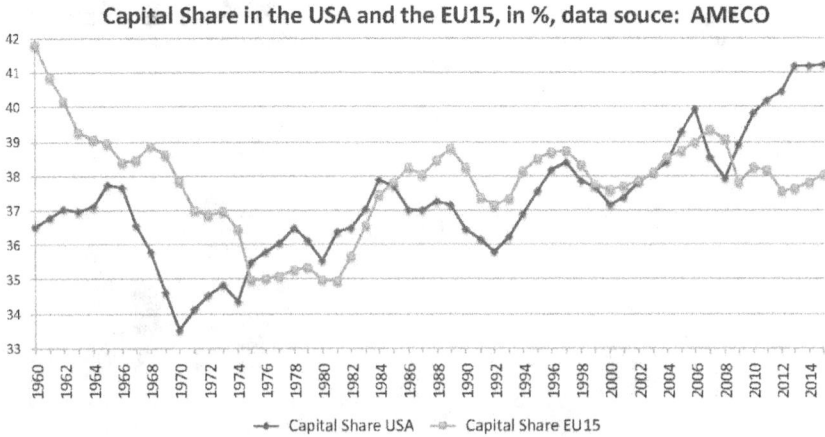

FIGURE 9.4   The capital share in the USA and the EU

successful class struggles during this period that compelled capital to increase wages. In the mid-1970s a period of wage repression started in both the EU and the USA, which result in significant drops of the wage share. At the same time, the share of capital in the total economy increased.

Since the mid-1970s, two contradictory tendencies have shaped capitalism: (a) computerisation's increase of the organic composition that resulted in increasing constant capital costs; and (b) top-down capitalist class struggle that decreased the wage share. As a result, the profit rate remained relatively constant and never returned to the levels of the 1960s. Capital was therefore searching for other ways for making profits, which resulted in an increased financialisation of capitalism. Significant shares of profits were invested in finance because capital is driven by the need to accumulate ever more profits and financial speculation promised high returns. The volatility of the economy steadily increased.

The share of the finance industry in the total value added has in many countries significantly increased. A general increase can be observed that has been especially strong in the USA, where the share has doubled from 1970 until 2005, when it made up 8.1% of the USA economy's total value added (data source: OECD iLibrary, STAN, financial industry=ISIC Rev. 3, C65-C67). There has been an increasing financialisation of capitalism.

Derivatives are relatively high-risk financial instruments that derive their value from other assets. Over-the-counter derivatives are traded directly between two partners. They include instruments such as foreign exchange contracts, forwards and forex

Share of gross market value of over-the-counter derivatives in world GDP
(data sources: derivates - Bank for International Settlements, GDP - IMF
World Economic Outlook), in %

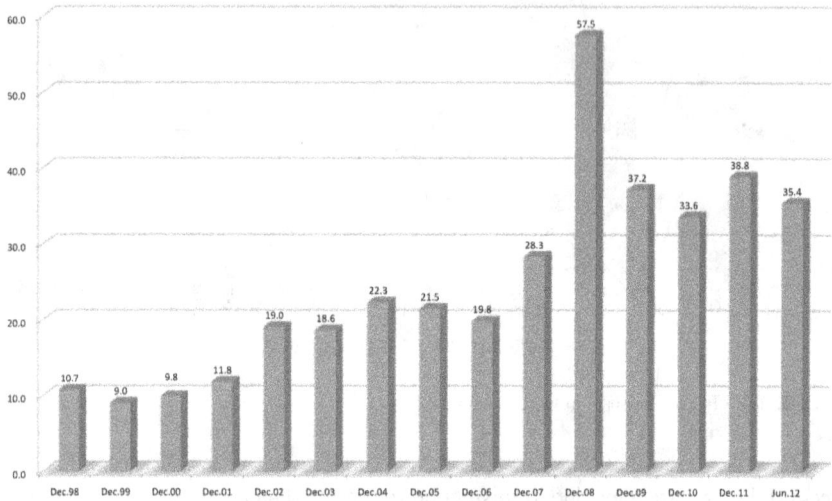

FIGURE 9.5   Share of the global gross market value of over-the-counter derivatives in world GDP (in %)

swaps, currency swaps, interest rate contracts, forward rate agreements, interest rate swaps, equity-linked contracts, or credit default swaps. They are high-risk because they are not direct ownership titles, but derived from the value of other assets. Figure 9.5 shows the development of the share (in %) of the global gross market value of over-the-counter derivatives in world GDP.

The rise of neoliberalism resulted in relative stagnation and wage losses, whereas profits rapidly increased. Neoliberalism therefore is a class struggle project of the ruling class aiming at increasing profits by decreasing wages with the help of strategies such as deregulation of labour laws, precarious labour conditions, welfare and public expenditure cuts, tax cuts for the rich and companies, the privatisation of public goods, the global offshoring and outsourcing of labour, etc. Many working families had to take out loans, consumer credits, and mortgages in order to be able to pay for their everyday life requirements. At the same time, capital investment into high-risk financial instruments boomed because the growing profits needed to be reinvested. Workers' debts were packaged into new financial instruments, so-called asset-backed securities, mortgage-backed securities, collateralised debt obligations, and credit default swaps. The financial market promised high financial gains, but the profits in the non-financial economy could in long run not fulfil these growth expectations, which created a mismatch between financial values and the profits of corporations and the expectations of shareholders and the reality of capitalist accumulation. The results were financial bubbles that burst in the 2008 crisis.

The data show that the capitalist economy has since the middle of the 1970s been shaped by the capitalist class' neoliberal struggle against the working class, increasing inequality between capital and labour, an increase of household debts, a decrease of capital taxation, a rising financialisation of the economy, and as a consequence an increased crisis volatility. The contradictions between capital and labour, fictitious value and actual profit, the production and consumption/investment of capital were heightened by the development dynamics of neoliberal capitalism and finally resulted in a new world economic crisis and a crisis of capitalist society.

Sections 9.3–9.5 aim to show that capitalism and its crisis are an important factor that has shaped social media. One aspect is that capitalism's crisis has favoured the expansion of targeted online advertising.

9.3 Targeted Advertising and the Crisis

Table 9.1 shows the development of the global advertising revenues. Whereas the share of broadcast advertising (radio and television) has, in the years from 2009 until 2013, slightly declined from 43.6% to 42.0%, the decline was more drastic in the print industry, where the share went from 32.4% to 25.2%. At the same time, the share of Internet advertising increased from 15.7% to 24.8%. These statistical data give grounds to the assumption that advertisers find online advertising more secure than other forms of advertising because it can be targeted, personalised, and it is based on consumer- and user-surveillance. The new capitalist crisis may have accelerated this shift from traditional advertising to online advertising because corporations are then especially afraid of bankruptcy and making losses. The crisis of journalism and the print news media stands in the context of the commercialisation of the media and the changes of advertising. In the United Kingdom, 37.1% of the advertising revenue was spent in the online industry, 28.3% in broadcasting, 18.7% in the print industry, 9.5% on direct mail advertising, 5.3% on outdoor ads, and 1.0% in the movie industry (Ofcom 2015, 375).

In 2014, Google had a share of 31.10% in the global digital ad revenue, Facebook 7.75%, Baidu 4.68%, Alibaba 4.66%, Microsoft 2.72%, Yahoo! 2.36%, IAC 1.00%, Twitter 0.84%, Tencent 0.83%, AOL 0.81%, Amazon 0.70%, Pandora 0.50%, LinkedIn

TABLE 9.1   The development of global advertising revenue, in £ billion and % of total ad revenue

	2009	2010	2011	2012	2013
Television	84.5	93.9	98.0	102.8	105.2
Internet	37.5	44.7	54.6	63.8	75.0
Newspapers	55.0	54.8	54.3	53.0	52.2
Magazines	22.6	23.4	24.0	23.9	23.9
Outdoor	18.6	20.0	21.0	21.6	22.6
Radio	20.0	20.4	20.9	21.3	21.8
Cinema	1.3	1.4	1.5	1.6	1.7
Total	239.5	258.6	274.3	288	302.4
Television	35.3%	36.3%	35.7%	35.7%	34.8%
Internet	15.7%	17.3%	19.9%	22.2%	24.8%
Newspapers	23.0%	21.2%	19.8%	18.4%	17.3%
Magazines	9.4%	9.0%	8.7%	8.3%	7.9%
Outdoor	7.8%	7.7%	7.7%	7.5%	7.5%
Radio	8.4%	7.9%	7.6%	7.4%	7.2%
Cinema	0.5%	0.5%	0.5%	0.6%	0.6%

Source: Ofcom (2014, 22)

0.49%, SINA 0.38%, Yelp 0.24%, and Millennial Media 0.08%.[1] Such data indicate that Google, Facebook, and Baidu are the key beneficiaries of Internet advertising's growth. One should not be mistaken: Google, Facebook, and Baidu are not communications companies. They do not sell digital content or access to online platforms. They are some of the world's largest advertising companies. They sell user data as commodity to advertisers, who in return can present targeted ads to users: in 2014, 89% of Google's revenues came from advertising (data source: SEC-Filings Google, Form 10-K 2014). In the case of Facebook this figure was 92% in 2014 (data source: SEC-Filings Facebook, Form 10-K 2014), for Baidu it was in the same year 98.9% online marketing services (data source: SEC-Filings Baidu, Form 20-F 2014).

Google and Facebook are very profitable companies (see figures 9.6 and 9.7). They not just monopolise online search and online social networking, but are also key players in the business of targeted advertising. In 2015, Google was the world's 39th largest transnational company and Facebook the 28th largest (data source: Forbes 2000 [2015]).

1 China's leading ad sellers to take 10% of the worldwide digital market this year. *eMarketer*, 16 December 2014.

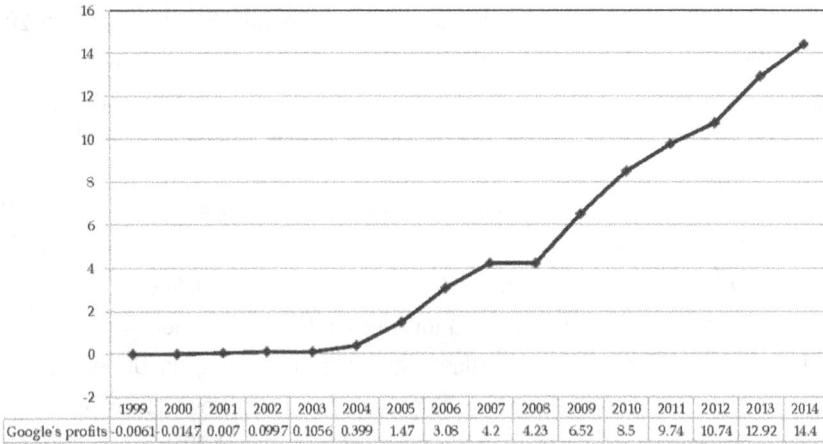

Google's profits	1999	2000	2001	2002	2003	2004	2005	2006	2007	2008	2009	2010	2011	2012	2013	2014
	-0.0061	0.0147	0.007	0.0997	0.1056	0.399	1.47	3.08	4.2	4.23	6.52	8.5	9.74	10.74	12.92	14.4

FIGURE 9.6   The development of Google's profits, in billion US$. Data source: SEC-Filings, From 10-K, various years

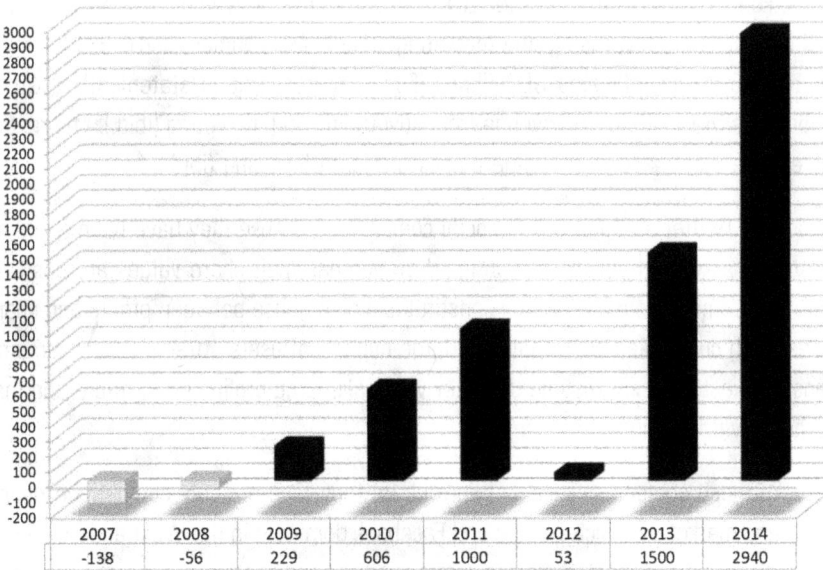

	2007	2008	2009	2010	2011	2012	2013	2014
	-138	-56	229	606	1000	53	1500	2940

FIGURE 9.7   The development of Facebook's profits, 2007–2014, in million US$

Twitter has been struggling financially, it became a stock-traded public company in November 2013, although its annual net losses were US$ 645.32 million in 2013 (Twitter SEC-Filings, Form 10-K 2013). Weibo – a subsidiary of Sina – made losses of US$ 116.74 million in 2011, 102.47 million in 2012, 38.12 million in 2013, and 62.7 million in 2014 (Weibo SEC-Filings, Form F-1 registration statement).

Just like Twitter in 2013, Weibo became a stock-marketed listed corporation in April 2014 when it made its initial public offering (IPO) on the NASDAQ stock exchange. And also like Twitter it made this move although it had made significant losses in the previous years and continued to make a total loss of US$ 62.6 million in financial year 2014. Weibo and Twitter's share values have been fluctuating. In December 2014, eight months after its IPO, Weibo's share value dropped below its initial value of US$ 17. The same happened to Twitter's share value in August 2015, when it dropped below the initial value of US$ 26. Both shares have been fluctuating and volatile. They have until late 2015 not seen large increases.

Twitter and Weibo are not communications companies, but predominantly large advertising agencies. Targeted advertising is their main revenue source. Around 85% of Twitter's revenues came from advertising in 2012 and 89% in 2013 (Twitter SEC-Filings, Form 10-K, annual report for 2013). About 78.8% of Weibo's revenues were in 2013 derived from advertising and marketing, 12.2% from games, and 5.9% from VIP membership services (Weibo SEC-Filings, Form F-1, registration statement). In 2014, Weibo generated 79% of its revenue from advertising and marketing (ibid.). The rest of the revenue was made from online games and data licencing (ibid.).

Weibo and Twitter are high-risk financial companies because they have been listed on the stock market without making profits. So, whereas their share values are positive, their net income is negative, which constitutes a divergence between profits and share values. Both companies hope that their large number of users attracts advertisers and financial investors. They assume that they will make large profits in the future and that this hope will keep investors confident.

The risks these companies face is two-fold: (a) they face a highly competitive online advertising market, in which Google and Facebook dominate in the West and Baidu is a big player in China; and (b) microblog communication has an immensely high speed and short attention span. It is difficult to place targeted ads on them and make users klick on them. It is not easy to make profits with targeted advertising because the average click-through-rate is around 0.1% (Comscore 2012); users only click on every 1000th online ad presented to them. And even then it is not sure if such clicks on targeted ads tend to result in purchases or not.

Twitter and Weibo's political economy is an indication that the social media economy is highly financialised and that investments in it are insecure. Financial crises can start if finance bubbles burst because there is a large divergence between actual profits and stock market valuation and investors lose confidence. The dot.com crisis in 2000 was an earlier expression of the high financialisation of the Internet economy, in which actual profits could not keep up with the promises of high stock market values. A new round of financialisation in the Internet industry has enabled the rise of social media while the ongoing world economic crisis showed us how crisis-prone financial markets are. Targeted advertising is a high-risk business. Users only klick on a small amount of ads and it is uncertain if and how often they purchase something on the landing pages to which they are transfered.

The future of the social media economy in China and the West is uncertain. It is clear that it is both in China and the West a highly financialised capitalist industry that depends on the influx of investments on finance markets and the confidence of advertisers that advertising works. There are many uncertainties associated with advertising capital accumulation models, especially concerning users' privacy concerns, the use of ad-block technologies and other limits to advertising, and the question if targeted ads are effective or not. The possibility of a dwindling confidence of investors after some trigger event and a resulting social media crisis cannot be ruled out because financialising and corporatising the Internet is accompanied by huge risks that both China and the West are facing.

Social media also has cultural, political, and ideological dimensions. One question that arises in this context, that is in the context of political crisis, is what social media's role is in revolutions.

9.4 Social Media Ideology #1: "Twitter and Facebook Revolutions"

Times of economic crisis tend also to be times of a crisis of the state. In such situations, protests and revolutions do not necessarily emerge, but are more likely. In the course of the protests and revolutions that took place since 2008, the techno-determinist ideology that Twitter, Facebook, and other social media caused such

TABLE 9.2 Frequency of usage per month of specific forms of communication in the mobilisation of protest

	Infrequently (0 per month)	Medium (1–6 times per month)	Frequently (> 6 times per month)
Face-to-face communication	15.0%	37.60%	47.40%
E-mail	29.8%	40.40%	29.80%
Phone	36.9%	39.50%	23.60%
SMS	49.7%	27.00%	23.30%
E-Mail list	46.2%	29.90%	23.90%
Facebook	25.2%	32.40%	42.00%
Twitter	52.0%	15.90%	32.10%

Source: Fuchs (2014c)

collective political action could often be heard. Even the *New York Times* wrote that the "Egyptian revolution began on Facebook".[2]

There is very little serious empirical research about the actual role of social media in protests and revolutions. Most published academic works are speculative or big data analyses that can say nothing about how prevalent social media use was among actual activists who occupied squares.

The *OccupyMedia! Survey* studied the role of social media in Occupy movements. I published its results in the book *OccupyMedia! The Occupy Movement and Social Media in Crisis Capitalism* (Fuchs 2014c). About 429 respondents, who participated in the Occupy movement, took part in the survey. One question was what the role of specific media was in protest mobilisation (see table 9.2).

The data indicate that face-to-face communication, Facebook, e-mail, phone, SMS, and Twitter are the most important media that occupy activists employed for trying to mobilise others for protests. Activists use multiple media for mobilisation-oriented communication. These include classical interpersonal communication via phones, e-mail, face-to-face, and private social media profiles as well as more public forms of communication such as Facebook groups, Twitter, and e-mail lists.

2 Spring awakening. How an Egyptian revolution began on Facebook. *New York Times Online.* 17 February 2012. http://www.nytimes.com/2012/02/19/books/review/how-an-egyptian-revolution-began-on-facebook.html?pagewanted=all&_r = 0

I also conducted a correlation analysis of the variables that cover protest mobilisation communication (Fuchs 2014c): the frequency of activism tends to positively influence the frequency of media use for informing oneself about the movement, sharing user-generated content online, communication between activists using various media, and using media for protest mobilisation communication. The use of face-to-face communication and online communication tend to mutually reinforce each other. The use of various online media for information, the sharing of user-generated content, and protest mobilisation also tends to mutually reinforce each other. We can therefore not say that online communication either determines protest or is unimportant. There is a *dialectic of online and offline protest communication*: activists use multiple online and offline channels for obtaining information, discussing protests, and trying to mobilise others. Online communication and face-to-face communication for these purposes tend to mutually reinforce each other.

The next section will show how right-wing ideology has in the contemporary crisis not just shaped society, but as a consequence also social media.

9.5 Social Media Ideology #2: Red Scare 2.0[3]

Anti-socialist ideology is at least as old as capitalism. After Marx's death, British right-wing media described *Das Kapital* as being "repellent in its cold formalism" and called Marx the "cold and methodical organiser of the International Association of Workers" (*The Morning Post*, March 19, 1883). The "English working men would not care to be identified with these principles [of communism] in their bald form" (*Leicester Chronicle and the Leicestershire Mercury*, 24 March 1883). *The Times* (18 January 1919) wrote three days after Rosa Luxemburg and Karl Liebknecht had been assassinated about Luxemburg: "Had power in Germany fallen into her hands, she would have surpassed the reign of terror of the Russian Bolshevists". This statement indirectly welcomes her murder and implies that not her assassination is a form of terror, but that her politics were terroristic and that she therefore deserved to be killed.

In the 1980s, right-wing British news media characterised the Labour Party-left and especially the Greater London Council, local London councils, Ken Livingstone, and Tony Benn as the "loony Left". The term "loony Left" "combines two concepts, insanity and left-wing politics, with a subtext that suggests irrational authoritarianism" (Curran, Petley and Gaber 2005, 229).

---

3 This section is a short summary of some aspects presented in Fuchs (2016c).

In respect to Tony Benn, the tabloid press spoke of "Dictatorship under Führer Benn" (*Daily Express*, 1 Februrary 1975), "Benn The Dictator" (*Daily Express*, 28 May 1981), "Citizen Benn who shouts from the rooftops the debt we owe to a man called Joseph Stalin" (*News of the World*, 13 September 1981), "the Bennite monster" (*Daily Mail*, 16 January 1984), or wrote that "some say Tony Benn is raving bonkers" (*The Sun*, 1 March 1984) (cited in: Hollingsworth 1986). Jeremy Corbyn's win of the Labour leadership election in September 2015 was accompanied by the return of the loony Left- and anti-socialist ideology.

I conducted an empirical ideology critique of tweets about Jeremy Corbyn during the leadership election. General opinions presented without arguments formed an important discourse topic in the dataset. One general bias that was frequently encountered in this respect was that Corbyn is a "loony" left-winger:

> a wet handwringing leftie terrorist supporting anti Semite for Prime Minister?? Corbyn will Drive Brit off a cliff. (#242)

> the radical extreme left wing lunacy of Jeremy left wing lunacy left wing loony lefty extreme radical Corbyn. (#438)

> Dangerous communist (#1228)

> Bloody pinko (#1287)

> Corbyn is satan (#4927)

> socialist pig (#12741)

> When will everyone realise that #Corbyn is a communist bastard? He's gonna fuck this country up if he gets in power #Labour. (#17405)

> Corbyn is a radical left wing idiot (#17528)

> Corbyn is a left wing socialist scumbag (#20456)

Single tweets even expressed the wish that Corbyn is killed because he is left-wing:

> Jeremy Corbyn.... A communist fraud .... hope he goes the way of Trotsky #Mexico1941 #NeverForget (#15440)

The sensationalist right-wing anti-Corbyn Twitter-discourse was not simply accepted, but contested. There were various strategies that Corbyn supporters used for

#Panorama cheap smear campaign against
Corbyn tonight trying to link him to terrorist
group short memory of this

116   52

FIGURE 9.8 A Twitter-critique of the BBC Panorama documentary on Corbyn that uses visual dialectical reversals by showing images of Gordon Brown and Tony Blair with Gaddafi, Blair with Assad, and Thatcher with Pinochet

challenging anti-socialist ideology online. One was that they associated Corbyn with positive general characteristics: "He seems to be about common sense and decency and so very normal/nice" (#422), "he is sensible, clear, knowledgeable & decent" (#606), "In my view he just preaches common sense" (#22591).

A second strategy was to use the strategy of discursive dialectical reversal: the argument made in this strategy is that not Corbyn, but the Tories are extremist, radical, violent, hard-right, and dangerous. Figure 9.8 shows an example.

A third strategy was to use satire and humour to ridicule anti-socialist ideology. It is based on the insight that ideologies are often irrational and emotional. They are difficult to challenge by rational arguments. The hashtag #suggestacorbynsmear that emerged on Twitter on 31 August 2015, and was used within 24 hours more than 11,000 times[4] is an example. Examples are: "Jeremy Corbyn shares the letter 'n' with Stalin and Satan, and the letters 'e' and 'r' with Hitler! #suggestacorbynsmear" (#5229); "Jeremy Corbyn was born in 1949. Stalin was alive in 1949. Coincidence? I think not. #suggestacorbynsmear" (#5251).

Ideologies are semiotic structures that justify domination. Twitter limits linguistic expression to 140 characters. User-generated ideology such as online redbaiting therefore has to compress ideology. User-generated ideology is the use of digital media for

Social Media Ideology #2: Red Scare 2.0[3]

---

4 http://www.telegraph.co.uk/news/politics/Jeremy_Corbyn/11836904/Twitters-funniest-smear-attacks-on-
  Jeremy-Corbyn-as-suggestacorbynsmear-goes-viral.html

producing and spreading semiotic structures that justify domination by distorting reality, misrepresenting it, or inventing false representations of reality. By making claims, insults, and personal attacks without underlying arguments and justifications, users compress ideology on Twitter into 140 characters. A feature of many anti-socialist tweets was that they made claims about Corbyn without arguments and proof.

Users are not the helpless victims of anti-socialist and other ideologies, but can contest, oppose, and struggle against ideologies. Social media is a communication space where ideologies are expressed and challenged. Studying user-generated ideologies online therefore allows identifying and analysing the structure of anti-socialist and anti-Corbyn ideologies and how they can best be challenged.

Left-wing social media users have developed intelligent strategies of how to react to ideological smear campaigns. Studying counter-discourses to anti-socialist ideology can inform political campaigns at a time when redbaiting is again omnipresent in politics.

9.6 Conclusion

Society shapes and is shaped by communications technologies and society. There is a dialectic of media and society. In an antagonistic society, new information and communication technologies will therefore display an antagonistic logic. A critical theory and critique of the political economy of communications and the media tries to understand the contradictions of society and communications.

This chapter has investigated causes of the crisis of capitalism. This crisis is not a crisis of regulation, but a fundamental economic crisis that has emerged from capitalism's inherent contradictions. The economic crisis has also turned into political and cultural crises, for example a crisis of the European idea and European politics. On the level of communications, crises tend to manifest themselves in various ways. The focus of this chapter was social media in the context of capitalism's crisis: capitalism's crisis has favoured the expansion of targeted online advertising. In the realm of politics, social media communication and offline communication are two interacting forms of protest communication. The strengthening of right-wing extremism has resulted in various forms of far-right ideology and nationalism online (see Fuchs 2016a, 2016b, for two detailed studies of ideology 2.0).

Social media is in complex ways embedded into the contradictions of capitalist society, economy, politics, and ideology. As a consequence, social media is incompletely social and is shaped by the logic of instrumental reason that turns such communications into forms of domination and exploitation. Only social struggles can develop potentials of communications and society that communalise both society and the media so that social media and society can become truly social.

References

Curran, James, Julian Petley, and Ivor Gaber. 2005. *Culture Wars*. Edinburgh: Edinburgh University Press.

Comscore. 2012. The Power of Like2: How Social Marketing Works. White Paper. https://www.comscore.com/ger/Insights/Praesentationen-und-Whitepapers/2012/The-Power-of-Like-2-How-Social-Marketing-Works(accessed on 23 July 2021).

Fisher, Eran and Christian Fuchs, eds. 2015. *Reconsidering Value and Labour in the DigitalAage*. Basingstoke: Palgrave Macmillan.

Fuchs, Christian. 2017. Fascism 2.0: Twitter Users' Social Media Memories of Hitler on His 127th Birthday. *Fascism: Journal of Comparative Fascist Studies* 6 (2): 228–263.

Fuchs, Christian. 2016a. Racism, Nationalism and Right-Wing Extremism Online: The Austrian Presidential Election 2016 on Facebook. *Momentum Quarterly – Zeitschrift für sozialen Fortschritt (Journal for Societal Progress)* 5 (3): 172–196.

Fuchs, Christian. 2016b. *Reading Marx in the Information Age: A Media and Communication Studies Perspective on "Capital Volume I"*. New York: Routledge.

Fuchs, Christian. 2016c. Red Scare 2.0: User-Generated Ideology in the Age of Jeremy Corbyn and Social Media. *Journal of Language and Politics* 15 (4): 369–398.

Fuchs, Christian. 2015. *Culture and Economy in the Age of Social Media*. New York: Routledge.

Fuchs, Christian. 2014a. *Digital Labour and Karl Marx*. New York: Routledge.

Fuchs, Christian. 2014b. *OccupyMedia! The Occupy Movement and Social Media in Crisis Capitalism*. Winchester: Zero Books.

Fuchs, Christian. 2014c. *Social Media: A Critical Introduction*. London: Sage.

Fuchs, Christian and Vincent Mosco, eds. 2016. *Marx in the Age of digital capitalism (Studies in Critical Social Sciences Volume 80)*. Leiden: Brill.

Fuchs, Christian and Marisol Sandoval, eds. 2014. *Critique, Social Media and the Information Society*. New York: Routledge.

Fuchs, Christian, Kees Boersma Anders Albrechtslund, and Marisol Sandoval, eds. 2012. *Internet and Surveillance. The Challenges of Web 2.0 and Social Media*. New York: Routledge.

Hollingsworth, Mark. 1986. *The Press and Political Dissent*. London: Pluto.

Marx, Karl. 1867. *Capital Volume I*. London: Penguin.

Ofcom. 2014. *International Communications Market Report 2014*. Available at: https://stakeholders.ofcom.org.uk/binaries/research/cmr/cmr14/icmr/ICMR_2014.pdf (accessed on 21 October 2016)

Ofcom. 2015. *The Communications Market Report 2015* [UK]. Available at: https:// stakeholders.ofcom.org.uk/binaries/research/cmr/cmr15/CMR_UK_2015.pdf (accessed on 21 October 2016).

Trottier, Daniel and Christian Fuchs, eds. 2014. *Social media, Politics and the State: Protests, Revolutions, Riots, Crime and Policing in the Age of Facebook, Twitter and YouTube*. New York: Routledge.

Chapter Ten
Capitalism, Patriarchy, Slavery, and Racism in the Age of Digital Capitalism and Digital Labour

10.1 Introduction

This chapter asks: how can understanding the relationship of exploitation and oppression inform the study of digital capitalism? To answer this question, the chapter re-visits and updates the discussion of how capitalism, patriarchy, and racism are connected.

One important question that arises in this context is how the economic and the non-economic are related to each other. This question is not just of theoretical relevance but also matters politically. It focuses on how class politics that struggle for redistribution of resources and identity politics that struggle for the recognition of oppressed identities are related (Fraser and Honneth 2003). Reductionist politics privilege either class or identity politics, whereas dualist politics say that both realms and demands are important without relating them (Fuchs 2011, section 2.3).

In Marxist feminism, patriarchy has not just been seen as a form of sexist oppression but as the exploitation of houseworkers in capitalism. Given that in the world of digital capitalism new unpaid forms of labour (Fuchs 2014; Lambert 2015), such as the use of Facebook or crowdsourced labour, have emerged, the question arises: what can we learn from studies of the relationship of exploitation and oppression that helps us to better understand unpaid digital labour?

The media's commodity has a peculiar character because information is not used up in consumption and it is difficult to exclude others from its use and copying. The labour involved in producing media therefore also takes on peculiar forms. Targeted

DOI: 10.4324/9781003222149-10

advertising is a very important capital accumulation model in the realm of Internet capitalism (Fuchs 2017b). Dallas Smythe (1977) and Sut Jhally (1987) have argued that not media workers but audiences produce the advertising-funded media's commodity. The access to such media is provided as a gift to the users and the audience's attention is sold as a commodity to advertisers. Smythe therefore speaks of audience labour and the audience commodity. In the context of targeted-advertising-based capital accumulation on social media platforms such as Facebook, YouTube, and Google, we find user labour that produces a data commodity and attention commodity. Based on constant surveillance and big data analytics, online advertising is personalised and interest based (Fuchs 2014, 2015, 2017b). Such user labour is yet another form of unpaid labour in capitalism. Therefore, the question arises as to what the role of unpaid labour is in the capitalist mode of production, what types there are, and what their commonalities and differences are.

Section 10.2 focuses on the relationship of housework and digital labour. Section 10.3 analyses the relationship of racism, slavery, and digital labour. Section 10.4 generalises the discussion and provides a typology that outlines the commonalities and differences of wage-labour, slave-labour, housework, and users' digital labour. Section 10.5 draws some conclusions.

10.2 Housework and Digital Labour

The task of this section is to explore commonalities and differences between housework and users' digital labour. This will be done in two steps: section 10.2.1 revisits the debate on reproductive labour and identifies two basic positions. The first holds that reproductive labour is productive labour, the second that reproductive labour is excluded from productive labour. Especially the first position is relevant in the digital age. Based on this discussion, section 10.2.2 updates debates about reproductive labour by engaging with the notion of digital housework that was introduced by the Marxist-feminist scholar Kylie Jarrett (2016).

10.2.1 The Debate on Housework and Reproductive Labour

Women have historically carried out the dominant part of reproductive labour, such as child-rearing, care, education, cooking, laundry, shopping, cleaning, etc. In contemporary capitalism, many more women are active in the paid labour force than 100 or 200 years ago, but housework is still predominantly women's concern, which creates multiple responsibilities and less free time for them.

10.2.2 Digital Housework and Reproductive Labour

The crucial difference in the analysis of different forms of labour is the one between wage-labour and unwaged labour. Slave-labour, reproductive labour, and unpaid Facebook labour have in common that they are unwaged, but by being integrated into capitalist society nonetheless they create surplus-value. They are therefore productive labour. Not all online activities are labour. For example, listening to music on Spotify based on a monthly subscription is advertising-free. The consumers do not create but consume a commodity. Not all digital labour is unpaid. For example, gold farmers on World of Warcraft or online freelancers tend to conduct their labour via Internet and to produce digital outputs, but are mostly paid. In this section, we focus on Facebook usage when speaking of digital labour.

Kylie Jarrett (2016) uses the notion of the digital housewife for pointing out parallels between unpaid online labour and houseworkers' domestic, reproductive labour. She argues that the social worker has not emerged in contemporary capitalism but has, in the form of houseworkers, always been an essential part of surplus-value production in capitalism.

Parallels between housework and Facebook labour include that both are unwaged and produce two use-values, of which only one is a commodity (wage-labour in the case of the houseworker, data in the case of the Facebook worker). Affects and social relations form the second use-value. The "Digital Housewife can have real friends on Facebook" (Jarrett 2016, 4). Jarrett argues that both the houseworker and the Facebook worker produce alienable and inalienable objects (p. 123). The first are "inalienable use-values such as pleasure, social solidarity and the general intellect" (p. 98).

> Consumer labour is akin to domestic labour not only because it is unpaid and occurs outside of formal factory walls in what is ostensibly free time. It is also akin to it because it is a site of social reproduction: a site for the making and re-making of the social, affective, ideological and psychological states of being that (may) accord with appropriate capitalist subjectivities. (p. 71)

Digital housewives "express themselves, their opinions and generate social solidarity with others in commercial digital media while, at the same time, adding economic value to those sites" (p. 4).

Nancy Fraser (1989, 116) argues that child-rearing is a dual aspect activity and at the same time an activity of material and symbolic reproductions, economic and cultural. One must caution in this respect that the symbolic and cultural realms are not immaterial because materiality in society means that humans socially produce results. So, it is better to speak of physical reproduction. Fraser (1989, 116) says that all work, including industrial food production and software engineering, reproduces social identities and physical existence. The difference is that both in reproductive labour and Facebook labour humans directly produce two use-values, whereas in software engineering and industrial food production conducted as paid jobs there is one main use-value, and sustained social relations between colleagues may or may not result as an indirect by-product of the labour process. Humans have a family and use Facebook for sustaining their social relations, whereas they have to have a paid job in order to earn money to be able to survive.

One should stress that the two use-values (created by both reproductive labour and Facebook labour) are not independent. Social relations and affects are key resources for the reproduction of labour-power in the case of housework and the creation of personal relations data in the case of Facebook. Social relations are the means of subsistence for houseworkers and Facebook workers.

Both housework and Facebook labour have a relation to commodity consumption: purchased consumer goods are part of the goods that housework transforms into the means of subsistence that sustain life and labour-power. In consumer capitalism, consumers learn about the existence of particular commodities via advertisements by looking at shelves in a shop. Audience labour and user labour generate attention and data that are used for presenting and targeting ads and selling commodities. Audience labour and commercial digital labour are therefore that part of reproductive labour that generates commodities that help advertisers to make profits so that consumer goods are sold and consumed. Housework transforms consumer goods into the means of subsistence that enable survival and the saleability of labour-power.

Marx argues that capital has aspects of living and dead labour. He therefore introduces the distinction between variable and constant capital. Both are key factors in the capitalist production process, but it is only living labour that creates value. The organic composition of capital is the relationship of constant to variable capital: "As value, it is determined by the proportion in which it is divided into constant capital, or the value of the means of production, and variable capital, or the value of labour-power, the sum total of wages" (Marx 1867, 762). Marx describes a tendency of the organic composition of capital to increase, that is an expression of the automation and technification of capitalism, by which the capitalist class tries to replace labour by technology. To offset increasing costs for constant capital, capital tends to be forced to also increase the exploitation of unpaid labour. Marx (1867, chapter 9) introduced for this purpose the rate of surplus-labour. It is the ratio of profit to wages, typically calculated at the level of monetary prices, not labour-time, and thereby leaving out forms of un-remunerated labour such as reproductive labour. It operates in respect to waged labour. The organic composition of labour is a new complementary variable that operates at the level of labour-time. It calculates the relationship of the total of unpaid labour hours to paid labour hours. Unpaid labour-time includes both unwaged labour-time and surplus-labour-time in waged labour.

Table 10.1 provides approximations for what can be termed the organic composition of labour that can be calculated as the ratio of unpaid labour-time (including both re-productive labour-time and wage-labour's surplus-labour-time) in an economy over the time period of one year. The data show that in the USA, the organic composition of labour is around 5.8. This means that per waged hour, there are 5.8 hours of unpaid labour. American capital only pays for one in seven labour hours. The rate of re-productive labour measures the share of both components of unpaid labour (table 10.1). It indicates that in the USA, reproductive labour accounts for around 83.7% of all unpaid labour-time and wage-labour's surplus-labour-time for about 16.3%.

The total production time includes the reproductive labour-time that reproduces the labour-power as a commodity. Reproductive labour is productive because it is surplus-labour-time unremunerated by capital. Capital not just exploits wage-labour, but also the reproductive labour required for the existence and reproduction of labour-power. Based on Marx's analysis, we can say that the exploitation of labour entails not a dual separation but a dialectic of reproductive labour and wage-labour.

Table 10.2 presents further estimates. It indicates that, on average, for each paid hour of labour, there are 5.8 hours of unpaid labour. I call the ratio of unpaid to paid labour-time the organic composition of labour. Unpaid labour includes both unpaid re-production labour as well as wage-labour's surplus-labour-time.

Housework and Digital Labour

TABLE 10.1 Reproductive labour in the USA

Variable	Average number of hours per week	Data source
Grooming	4.83	US Census Bureau, American Time Use Survey 2015
Health-related self care	0.70	US Census Bureau, American Time Use Survey 2015
Housework	3.99	US Census Bureau, American Time Use Survey 2015
Food preparation and cleanup	4.20	US Census Bureau, American Time Use Survey 2015
Lawn and garden care	1.40	US Census Bureau, American Time Use Survey 2015
Household management	0.91	US Census Bureau, American Time Use Survey 2015
Interior maintenance, repair, and decoration	0.42	US Census Bureau, American Time Use Survey 2015
Exterior maintenance, repair, and decoration	0.42	US Census Bureau, American Time Use Survey 2015
Vehicles	0.04	US Census Bureau, American Time Use Survey 2015
Appliances, tools, and toys	0.14	US Census Bureau, American Time Use Survey 2015
Travel related to household activities	0.35	US Census Bureau, American Time Use Survey 2015
Consumer goods purchases	2.52	US Census Bureau, American Time Use Survey 2015
Medical and care services	0.35	US Census Bureau, American Time Use Survey 2015
Personal care services	0.14	US Census Bureau, American Time Use Survey 2015
Travel related to purchasing goods and services	1.96	US Census Bureau, American Time Use Survey 2015
Caring for and helping household members	3.57	US Census Bureau, American Time Use Survey 2015
Caring for and helping nonhousehold members	1.33	US Census Bureau, American Time Use Survey 2015
Use of commercial TV and commerical social media	17.26	US Census Bureau, American Time Use Survey 2015
Watching television	19.46	2016 data, statista.com
Being online	2.18	http://time.com/96303/tv-commercials-increasing/
Watching ads (25% of watching time)	4.87	GlobalWebIndex, http://www.globalwebindex.net/hubfs/Reports/GWISocialReport-Q32015Summary.pdf
Using commercial social media	12.39	
Average reproductive labour-time per week per person	44.53	
Percentage share of commercial media use in reproductive labour-time	38.75	

If reproductive labour were paid at the average wage, then profits would dwindle and capitalism would not be able to survive. This fact shows on the one hand the importance of reproductive labour in capitalism. On the other hand it also indicates capitalism's inherent drive and need to create milieus of unpaid labour in order to survive. Another measure is the rate of reproductive labour. It measures the ratio between unpaid reproductive labour-time and wage-labour's surplus-labour-time. For the analysed data, the rate of reproductive labour is 5.14, which means that reproductive labour-time in the total economy is 5.14 times as large as wage-labour's surplus-labour-time.

Table 10.1 indicates that, on average, each person in the USA engages in 44.53 hours of reproductive labour per week. Commercial media use accounts for 38.75% of this time, which shows that advertising dominates a very significant portion of our lifetime. In 2015, global advertising revenue was £308 billion (Ofcom 2016, figure 1.21). Television advertising totalled £106 billion (34.4%) and online advertising £102 billion (33.1%) (Ofcom 2016, figure 1.21). So TV and the Internet are the two most profitable realms of advertising. At the level of human activities, this results from the fact that we spend large amounts of our free time watching television and using social media: On average, Americans watch 19.5 hours of television per week and spend 12.4 hours on social media (see table 10.1). A significant share of reproductive labour is television audience labour and social media digital labour.

A very important part of housework is made up by household activities such as food preparation, cleaning, lawn and garden care, and household management. According to statistics, US women in 2015 spent on average 48 minutes more time on such activities than men (men: 1.43 hours per day, women: 2.23 hours per day)[1]. Another important activity is caring for and helping others. Whereas, US men spent 0.47 hours per day on caring for and helping others, the amount for women was 0.91 hours. Shopping took up 0.6 hours per day for men and 0.88 hours for women. Taking the averages of these three types of activities allows us to estimate that US women tend to be responsible for, on average, 60% of reproductive labour and men 40%. Reproductive labour is both gendered and racialised. It is predominantly a realm of women, and in the case of paid reproductive labour, low-paid migrant workers and workers of colour form a proportionally very large share of the workforce. Capitalism is inherently connected to patriarchy and racism. The next section further explores this connection in the context of digital labour.

---

1 Source: http://www.bls.gov/news.release/atus.t01.htm (accessed on 29 October 2016).

TABLE 10.2 Reproductive labour in the USA

Variable	Value	Data source
Average reproductive labour hours per year per person	2315.3	US Census Bureau
Average total annual reproductive labour-time in the USA	578,878,251,900	578.9 billion unwaged hours per year
US population aged 15 or over (2013)	250,023,000	OECD Stats
Average annual hours worked (2010)	1,778	OECD Stats
Full time equivalents of total economic population (2010)	130,602,000	
Total annual hours worked (2010)	232,210,356,000	OECD Stats
Total wages and salaries in US $ (2010)	6,417,482,000,000	OECD Stats
Value added at current prices, US $ (2010)	14,526,547,000,000	OECD Stats
Gross fixed capital formation, US $ (2010)	2,061,800,000,000	
Profits, US$ (2010)	6,047,265,000,000	
Monetary rate of surplus-value	0.942	
Total annual hours of wage-workers' surplus-labour	112,656,723,676	= 48.5% of total annual hours worked by wage-labourer
Total annual hours of wage-workers' necessary labour	119,553,632,324	= 51.4% of total annual hours worked by wage-labourer
Monetary expression of labour-time (=profit created per paid working hour) in US $ (2010)	26.04	

TABLE 10.2 (Cont.)

Variable	Value	Data source
Average hourly wage/salary (2010), US$	27.64	
Monetary value of unpaid reproductive labour-time (calculated at average hourly wage)	15,998,170,046,127	
Organic composition of labour (OCL; relationship of unpaid/paid labour-time)	5.78	OCL = (Unpaid reproductive labour-time + Surplus wage-labour-time)/Paid labour-time = (578,878,251,900 + 112,656,723,676)/119,553,632,324
Rate of reproductive labour (RRL)	5.14	RRL = unpaid reproductive labour-time/wage-labour's surplus-labour-time = 578,878,251,900 / 112,656,723,676

10.3 Slavery and Racism in the Age of Digital Labour

Capitalism is not just connected to patriarchy but also to racism. When analysing digital capitalism, it is therefore also important to have a look at what forms racism takes in respect to digital media. This section explores this topic in two steps. The first sub-section of this part re-visits debates on the connection of capitalism and racism. The second sub-section builds on this discussion and discusses aspects of racism in the context of digital labour.

10.3.1 Slavery in the Age of Facebook

One of the most important differences between wage-labour, slave-labour, re-productive labour, and Facebook labour concerns their legal status and what makes the workers conduct labour. Slave-workers' bodies and minds are a private property that the slave-master owns at all time. Slavery is the most reified form of labour, which means that slaves have no rights so that the slave-master can treat them as he pleases and is legally allowed to kill them. So what makes the slave work is in the final instance the fear of being killed or experiencing physical violence. In slavery, "the worker is distinguishable only as *instrumentum vocale* [vocal instrument] from an animal, which is *instrumentum semi-vocale* [semi-vocal instrument], and from a lifeless implement, which is *instrumentum mutum* [silent instrument]" (Marx 1867, 303, footnote 18).

Whereas, the slave constantly faces the threat of death, wage-labour only does so in particular cases, for example when workers are being asked to conduct life-threatening work, such as cleaning up nuclear waste. Other than the slave, the wage-worker owns him-/her-self. In *Capital* (Volume 1, chapter 6) Marx (1867) formulates the unfreedom of wage-labour as the double freedom of labour. Modern labour is free because it is better off than slaves (although slavery has continued to exist in global capitalism), but it is also unfree because it is compelled to be exploited by capital and to having to enter class relations in order to be able to survive. Proletarians' minds and bodies are not the private property of the dominant class, as slaves are, they are rather compelled by the "silent compulsion of economic relations" (Marx 1867, 899), the violence of the market that makes ordinary people die if they do not obtain money that allows them to buy commodities, which compels many to become wage-workers.

A specific share of women experience domestic violence and economic dependence that force them to conduct reproductive labour against their will and create their fear to leave their partner. So, direct violence can be a means of coercion in the case of housework. But also commitment, solidarity, and love are important driving forces of reproductive labour. Housework can frequently involve hybrids of love and hatred, pain and pleasure, play and toil, care and violence, feelings of self-fulfilment, and aliena-tion. Facebook labour is normally not coerced by physical and psychological violence but by monopoly power, which is a specific form of structural violence. Facebook's and Google's absolute market dominance and their restrictive terms of use and privacy policies force users to use these platforms if they do not want to suffer from social and informational disadvantages.

It would be a mistake to assume that the rise of capitalism and wage-labour has brought an end to slavery. Although slavery is older than wage-labour, it continues to exist in specific forms in capitalism. Jack Qiu (2016) speaks of iSlavery in his book *Goodbye iSlave: A Manifesto for Digital Abolition*, to indicate that slavery is still a reality in the 21st century, where the iPhone has become one of the dominant tools for the organisation of life. Qiu bases his understanding of slavery on the 1926 UN Slavery Convention that foregrounds the ownership of a person by another as the key feature of slavery. The Bellagio-Harvard Guidelines on the Legal Parameters of Slavery (Qiu 2016, 189–196) specify that the ownership of a person can entail buying, transferring, or selling her; exploiting her labour or sexuality; managing such exploitative use; profiting from the use of a person; transferring the slave to another person (e.g. a heir or successor); or physical or psychological mistreatment. These definitions are in line with Marx's understanding of slavery that foregrounds the unfree character of a slave so that s/he is not in possession of his/her own body and mind.

According to estimates, in the year 2016 there were 45.8 million slaves in the world (Walk Free Foundation 2016), including high numbers in India, China, Pakistan, Bangladesh, Uzbekistan, North Korea, Russia, Nigeria, the Democratic Republic of Congo (DRC), Indonesia, Egypt, and Myanmar (Walk Free Foundation 2016, 30). The same report provides a concise definition of slavery as "situations of exploitation that a person cannot refuse or leave because of threats, violence, coercion, abuse of power or deception, with treatment akin to a farm animal" (p. 158).

Digital technologies are based on minerals such as cassiterite, coltan, gold, cobalt, or wolframite. Large amounts of it are extracted in conflict-ridden regions in the Congo. As a result, rebels and warlords that enslave villagers control some of the mines. Parts of the minerals used in mobile phones, laptops, etc. are based on slave-labour and child labour. This phenomenon has come to be known as conflict minerals (Fuchs 2014, chapter 6). Cobalt is an important mineral for the production of batteries used in phones and laptops. More than half of the world's supply comes from the Democratic Republic of the Congo.

> Amnesty International and Afrewatch conducted research in artisanal mining areas in southern DRC in April and May 2015, visiting five mine sites. [...] Chronic exposure to dust containing cobalt can result in a potentially fatal lung disease, called 'hard metal lung disease'. [...] Many of the miners complained that they coughed a lot or had problems with their lungs. [...] UNICEF estimated in 2014 that approximately 40,000 boys and girls work in all the mines across southern DRC, many of them involved in cobalt mining. The children interviewed by researchers described the physically demanding nature of the work they did. They said that they worked for up to 12 hours a day in the mines, carrying heavy loads, to earn between one and two dollars a day. (Amnesty International 2016, 5–6)

One can be a slave for a limited time period (Qiu 2016, 41)? Qiu documents how Foxconn workers, who manufacture iPhones, iPads, and other digital gadgets, faced "tremendous difficulty [...] to quit" and how "student interns were used as inexpensive and involuntary labor on a massive scale" (p. 47). He shows how forced labour and the lack of freedom to quit employment, two types of slavery, exist within the manufacturing domain of the international division of digital labour (IDDL) (see also Fuchs 2014, 2015, 2016, for a detailed discussion of the IDDL). Qiu also documents Foxconn's refusal to pay out wages to workers, violent and abusive factory guards, and the control of Foxconn workers' leisure and sleeping time. The example also shows that wage-labour can be a form of slavery. Qiu concludes that Foxconn's management system should be seen as "institutions and practices similar to slavery" (p. 82). The forms of control exercised include physical violence and structural, bureaucratic violence (forced internships, wage restraint, contracts that cannot be broken, etc.), so that any control of labour-time (its start and end) is forcefully removed from workers' decision-power.

Jack Qiu (2016, chapter 4) also identifies free consumer labour as a form of slavery that he calls manufactured iSlavery. The implication of his analysis is that users of advertising-funded online platforms are Facebook slaves, Google slaves, etc., who are coerced by advertising, monopolies, play and the addiction to commodity and media consumption into working without payment for advertising-based media. Qiu writes that the manufactured iSlave shows "voluntary servitude", in which "[a]ddiction becomes enslavement" (p. 111). The manufactured iSlave is a mind-slave – her or his mind is enclosed by the dominant class's logic.

Slavery can be used as a more restrictive or more expansive term. Marx did both at once. He on the one hand saw the differences between slave-labour and wage-labour by stressing that slavery is the most unfree and life-threatening form of labour. He however also stressed certain parallels between pure slavery and other class relations. So, for example, he characterised patriarchy as a system in which "the wife and children are the slaves of the husband" (Marx and Engels 1845, 52) and spoke of capitalism's "two poles of Capital and Wage-slavery" (Marx 1871, 335). Every class relation at least bears traces and has certain features of slavery because it always entails some form of unfreedom and coercion. There are historical dialectics of slavery.

But there are also reasons for not expanding the term slavery to every form of exploitation. There is a tendency for commonality in that slave-labour, reproductive labour, and Facebook labour are highly exploited and are unpaid forms of labour, in which all labour-time tends to be surplus-labour-time. But there is also a difference in respect to the difficulty of refusing labour, that is in respect to the political dimension of political economy that governs human activity, labour-power, and labour-time. Regular wage-workers because of their double freedom can leave their employer's factory or office at the end of the working day. They have to return in order to earn a wage, but they can also choose to search for another job, which is a relative freedom within unfreedom. In contrast to the wage-worker, the Congolese miner extracting coltan at gunpoint cannot leave the mine without being shot. He is a slave. Some Foxconn workers cannot leave the factory because they are locked into their contracts and into the factory walls all day and night. They too are slaves.

And what about the Facebook user? Is s/he a slave too? S/he may spend lots of time on the platform, but can also choose to log-off, to deliberately turn off the computer and phone in order to sleep, spend some time talking to friends and family, make love, enjoy an uninterrupted walk in nature, etc. The Facebook user's refusal of labour in the social factory is much easier to achieve than the Congolese miner's refusal. They are both highly exploited, but only the latter is a slave. Nonetheless, all labour and all class relations have certain dimensions of slavery because they are all coerced into labour in particular ways. The exploitation of the wage-worker, the slave, the houseworker, and the Facebook worker are in certain respects different as well as in certain other respects comparable. Only the collective revolt of slaves and other workers exploited by transnational corporations, their collective refusal to labour and search for alternatives, can put an end to capitalism and slavery.

Slaves can be houseworkers and digital workers, but not all houseworkers and digital workers are slaves in the classical sense of the term. A houseworker is a slave if s/he experiences violence that makes her afraid of leaving an abusive relationship. A digital worker is a digital slave if s/he, for example, is by debt bondage forced to work as a gold farmer for a game company and can therefore not choose to leave the job.

Slaves do not have political and social rights. Wage-workers have specific social rights in respect to wages, social security, and trade union representation. Houseworkers only have limited social rights in respect to, for example, child benefits. Being a Facebook worker does not give you particular social rights and mostly very limited legal rights in respect to privacy and data protection. Whereas, the wage-worker has a contractual and legally enforceable right to be paid a wage for the performed labour, slaves, houseworkers, and Facebook workers do not have such a right, which enables their exploitation as unpaid workers. But not all of digital labour and housework are unpaid. Parts of it are conducted as contractual labour. Paid carers and cleaners are an example. These are typically low-paid types of labour, often conducted by migrants and women. The intersection of reproductive labour and wage-labour tends to have a racialised and patriarchal character.

10.3.2 Racist Ideology and Digital Labour

Africans and Asians are employed in the most exploitative and precarious jobs in the IDDL. In contrast, high paid software engineers – the digital labour aristocracy – in the Western world tend to be predominantly male and white (Fuchs 2014). A structural form of racism operates in the IDDL.

Racism and challenges to racism also operate in the world of social media. On the one hand, racism makes use of social media. Here are two example tweets that were posted one day after Donald Trump won the 2016 presidential election:

> #Trump 卐 The end of #WhiteGenocide in America. #Nazi #SiegHeil

> President Trump wants to know if you have any last words Mr Soros? #RevengeWillBeSweet #WhiteGenocide #RapeJIhad #RWDS #Trump #Trump16 [+ image of a Nazi shooting a Jewish person]

On the other hand, anti-racism is also present on social media: In December 2016, the Twitter account of Black Lives Matter (@blklivesmatter) had around 195,000 followers and its Facebook group around 240,000 followers.

Commodity fetishism makes capitalism and wage-labour appear as natural properties of society, which tends to ideologically sustain both capitalism and class. Racism is an ideology that often justifies slavery and discriminatory labour practices. Sexism is an ideology that tries to chain women to the household and to create a gender pay gap. On Facebook and in housework, there is inverse commodity fetishism (Fuchs 2014, chapter 11; Fuchs 2015, chapter 5). The workers' immediate experience is not the production of commodities but the creation of social relations. Digital workers have, as Jarrett (2016, 104) says, friends online. And houseworkers tend to care for those they love. The commodity form is hidden behind the social form so that commodity fetishism tends to take on an inverted form. For houseworkers and Facebook workers, it is not directly experienceable that they produce a commodity for Facebook.

Racism, nationalism, sexism, and other ideologies can create economic, political, and cultural advantages for specific groups in society, typically white men. How does this approach relates to the realm of digital labour? Eileen Meehan (2002) introduced the notion of the gendered audience commodity. The advertising industry tends to base advertising on sexism and to "discriminate against anyone outside the commodity audience of white, 18 to 34-year-old, heterosexual, English-speaking, upscale men" (Meehan 2002, 220).

According to the UN Human Development Report (United Nations Development Programme 2015), Norway and the USA are two of the world's richest and most developed countries, whereas the Central African Republic (CAR), the DRC, and Malawi are three of the poorest. In 2014, the gross national income per capita was US $ 52,947 in the USA, US$ 64,992 in Norway, US$ 581 in the CAR, US$ 680 in the DRC, and US$ 747 in Malawi. Based on this variable, CAR, DRC, and Malawi were the world's three poorest countries. Table 10.3 suggests that Facebook calculates and provides for the maximum cost-per-click bid they should offer when presenting ads to users of a specific gender in a specific country.

The data indicate that Facebook's algorithm is based on sexist and racist logic by assuming that users in poorer countries and poorer users are less valuable consumers, that is less likely to click on ads and to purchase advertised commodities, than male users and users in rich countries. The Facebook data commodity is both gendered and racialised. The digital housewife is not just exploited, but this exploitation is combined with patriarchal and racist algorithmic discrimination that assumes that the poor and the female digital housewife are inferior to the male, rich digital housewife. Therefore,

TABLE 10.3 Facebook's suggested cost-per-click bid for users aged 18+ based on location and gender

Country	Gender	Suggested bid for a cost-per-click, in US$
USA	Male	3.59
USA	Female	3.55
Norway	Male	4.48
Norway	Female	4.27
Central African Republic	Male	0.23
Central African Republic	Female	0.17
Democratic Republic of Congo	Male	0.23
Democratic Republic of Congo	Female	0.20
Malawi	Male	0.35
Malawi	Female	0.26

Source: Facebook adverts manager, accessed 30 October 2016

it assumes that the price for one click by the "inferior audience" should be less than one of the "superior audience".

10.4 Capitalism, Racism, and Patriarchy

Sections 10.2 and 10.3 have shown that class, patriarchy, and racism are important dimensions in the age of Facebook and digital labour. Digital housework is one particular form of audience labour and reproductive labour that constitutes significant everyday life. It is just like housework–unpaid, exploited, and producing a peculiar commodity. Slavery and racism also play an important role in digital capitalism. Digital capitalism and phenomena such as social media, digital labour, mobile communication, and big data that are associated with it are part of the latest developments in advanced capitalism. Meta-racism takes on a specific form in it. Forced labour and child labour form an important dimension of the IDDL. It especially concerns African and Asian miners and assemblage workers. Structural racism and sexism shape the IDDL. Whereas, people of colour in developing countries conduct the most exploited, unfree, and precarious types of labour in the IDDL, the digital labour aristocracy of highly paid software engineers is predominantly white and male. Whereas, highly skilled and highly paid managerial and knowledge work tend to be primarily dominated by white people, low-paid precarious service jobs in the USA tend to be the domain of black people. Algorithms tend to reproduce racist ideologies that discriminate against people of colour based on the assumption that they are poor and therefore less valuable consumers than white users. Contemporary racism is both communicated and challenged on social media.

The question arises as to how we can make sense of the relationship of capitalism, patriarchy, and racism today. In digital capitalism, we can find an intersection of different forms of labour in the IDDL – paid labour, unpaid labour, reproductive labour, and users' digital labour. The economic dimension of the interrelation of these forms of labour is that capitalism requires and creates milieus of exploitation in order to sustain profitability. It strives to maximise capital accumulation by minimising labour costs. The diversification of labour is a result of the profit imperative. Non-standard forms of labour, such as slavery, precarious labour, freelancing, unpaid user labour, or housework are an expression of this diversification. The result of it is that transnational digital media corporations are achieving high profits. In 2016, Apple made profits of US$ 53.7 billion and was the world's ninth largest transnational corporations. AT&T was the 12th largest (profit: US$ 13.2 billion), Verizon the 15th largest (US$ 18 billion), Microsoft the 23rd largest (US$ 10.2 billion), and Google/Alphabet the 27th largest (US$ 17 billion).[2]

Capitalism is based on the capitalist class's appropriation of surplus-labour and surplus-value. Given that the working day consist of two parts, necessary labour and surplus-labour, that is paid labour and unpaid labour, all labour in capitalism contains unpaid labour. It is in the capitalist class's interest to maximise unpaid labour-time. Étienne Balibar (2013) argues in this context that "what characterises capitalism is *a normalisation of overexploitation*. The reverse side of this is a class struggle that tends to impose limits". The sustenance and creation of forms of labour that are completely unpaid or have a high degree of unpaid labour-time should therefore be understood as being part of this capitalist tendency to normalise over-exploitation. Unpaid digital labour is one of the newest manifestations of this tendency. Balibar concludes that "we should question the axiom" of "the distinction of *productive and unproductive labor*". *Theories of digital labour, just like theories of reproductive labour, are a contribution to this endeavour.*

Sandoval (2013) provides a typology with 14 dimensions that are relevant for a systematic analysis of labour in capitalism. These dimensions can be grouped into the categories of means of production, workforce, relations of production, production process, results of production, and the role of the state. Table 10.4 builds on Sandoval's typology. It uses a compressed version of her typology and adds to it the dimension of ideology that focuses on how justifications for the exploitation of specific forms of labour appear and are presented in public. The typology used in table 10.4 focuses on economic, political, and cultural/ideological dimensions of labour. It summarises the discussion of this chapter.

The control and coercion of labour works with both political-economic and ideological means. Political-economic means include physical violence, sexual violence, monopoly power, social violence, and the labour market's structural violence. The discussion has shown that in the IDDL, we can find all of these forms of violence. Ideological repression takes on specific forms in the IDDL.

Classical commodity fetishism does not allow workers and consumers to immediately experience all the forms of exploitation that are underlying the IDDL. In the usage of social media, there is just like in housework an inverse form of commodity fetishism

Capitalism, Racism, and Patriarchy

---

2 Source: Forbes 2000, 2016 list; http://www.forbes.com/global2000/list/ (accessed 17 December 2016).

TABLE 10.4 Characteristics of four types of labour

Dimension	Aspect	Wage-labour	Slave-labour	Reproductive labour	Users' unpaid digital labour on Facebook
1) Economy	Means of production	Brain, body, tools	Brain, body, uterus and genitals (women slaves), tools	Brain, body, uterus (women), genitals, tools	Brain, body, computers, online platforms
	Product of labour	Use-values and commodities owned by capitalist	Use-values and commodities owned by the slave-master, slaves (women slaves), workforce/labour-power (house slaves)	Commodity/use-value for capital: workforce and labour-power; use-value: affects, social relations, means of subsistence	Commodity/use-value for capital: data commodity, attention; use-value: social relations, affects
	Spaces of labour	Factory, office, social factory	Plantation (including contemporary plantations such as for-profit prisons)	Household, social factory	Internet
	Labour-time	Legal division between labour-time and leisure time, necessary labour-time (paid) and surplus-labour-time (unpaid)	Slave-master controls all time and can turn all life-time of slaves into labour-time, all labour-time is unpaid, slave-master has the legal power to end a slave's life-time by killing her/him	a.) All labour-time is unpaid; wages of the household's wage labourers are used for buying the household's means of consumption as means of production; b.) Paid reproductive workers are freelancers or work for the state or for-profit companies	Online time as unpaid labour-time
2) Politics	Wages and benefits	Wages and salary, legally guaranteed social benefits (unemployment insurance, health insurance, pension system)	No wages/salary, unpaid labour; no legally guaranteed social benefits	a.) No wages/salary, unpaid labour, limited legally guaranteed social benefits (child benefits)	No wages/salary, unpaid labour; no legally guaranteed social benefits

			b.) Low-paid labour (paid cleaners, babysitters, and carers)	
Legal aspects of labour	Double free labour: Labour-contract and labour legislation, freedom of the person, "wage-slave"	Double unfree labour: no labour-contract and legislation, no human rights, no freedom of the person: slave's body is owned by the slave-master	Unfree labour: no labour-contract and no labour legislation, family law, full or partial or no freedom of the person	Corporate self-regulation (terms of use and privacy policies as labour contracts that provide no rights to users), data protection legislation
Political representation of labour	Trade unions, labour parties	Abolition movement, anti-racist movement	Feminist movement	Privacy advocacy movements, consumer protection groups, digital labour unions (?)
Labour struggles and demands	Strikes, sabotage, occupations, worker co-operatives; wage-demands, shortening of the working day, better working conditions	Slave rebellions, political freedom, equality	Protests, equality, wages for housework, equal pay for equal work, abolishment and socialisation of housework	Protests, ad blocking, platform co-operatives, participatory media fee, online advertising tax, public service Internet, wages for use of Facebook, Google, etc.
Coercion and control of labour	Dull compulsion and structural violence of the labour-market	Physical violence, death threats, rape	Physical and sexual violence, social commitment (social violence)	Monopoly power, social disadvantages (social violence)
3) Culture and ideology — Ideology of labour repression	Commodity fetishism, wage-labour fetishism	Racism	Sexism, inverse commodity fetishism	Inverse commodity fetishism

Capitalism, Racism, and Patriarchy

that veils the role of the commodity by foregrounding sociality. Social media use does not feel like labour, but is unpaid labour that creates profits. Users' digital labour creates a big data commodity that digital media corporations sell to advertisers. The big data commodity is both gendered and racialised. Algorithms are based on the assumption that white, male users in the West are bona fide consumers potentially buying many commodities and spending lots of money, whereas others are considered to be inferior consumers. "The categorisations of targeted ad groups based on gender (and also other stereotypical features of class, race, ethnicity, and age) function as a kind of discrimination by assigning differential value to these different target markets" (Shepherd 2014, 164).

Classical and algorithmic ideologies create a paradoxical situation: in paid digital labour, white men dominate the employment structure and can obtain gendered and racialised wages of whiteness. People of colour (child labour and slaves in the Congo, predominantly female assemblage workers in China, etc.) in contrast have the most highly exploited and most precarious jobs in the international division of labour. At the same time, white men are also the privileged objects of exploitation in online advertising and unpaid digital labour based on racist and sexist ideologies designed into algorithms. New racism justifies the exploitation, exclusion, domination, or annihilation of an out-group. One can draw a "distinction between a racism of extermination or elimination (an 'exclusive' racism) and a racism of oppression or exploitation (an 'inclusive' racism)" (Balibar and Wallerstein 1991, 39). In the IDDL, one can both find the exclusive and the exploitative type of racism.

10.5 Conclusion

This chapter has studied the connection of capitalism, patriarchy, and racism in the digital age. Capitalism is inherently patriarchal and racist in character and uses ideology and discrimination for deepening exploitation and domination. Unpaid labour is not unproductive, but rather constitutes a super-exploited form of productive labour that generates surplus-value without wage. Racism, nationalism, sexism, and other ideologies can create economic, political, and cultural surplus-"wages" or, better expressed, Bourdieuian forms of economic, political, and cultural capital for dominant groups.

I took up Kylie Jarrett's notion of the digital houseworker in order to show commonalities and differences between three forms of unpaid labour, namely slave-labour, reproductive labour, and Facebook labour. These three forms of labour were also compared to wage-labour. Combining the notion of the digital houseworker with Eileen Meehan's concept of the gendered audience commodity allows us to understand that Facebook's data commodity is both gendered and racialised, which shows that digital capitalism instrumentalises both sexism and patriarchy by building their logic into algorithms that determine the data commodity's price by assuming that the price for one hour of labour should be based on gender and country.

Capitalism requires what Rosa Luxemburg (2003 [1913]) termed milieus of primitive accumulation in order to survive. Forms of unpaid labour constitute such territories. Housework has traditionally been such a milieu of exploitation that has sustained capitalism and wage-labour. Housework means "superexploitation of non-wage labourers [...] upon which wage labour exploitation then is possible" (Mies 1986, 48) because it involves the "externalization, or ex-territorialization of costs which otherwise would have to be covered by the capitalists" (p. 110). Housewifisation means the extension of super-exploitation and unpaid labour into realms beyond housework so that work or labour is transformed in such ways that it shows some parallels with the conditions of housework (Mies et al. 1988; Mies 1986; Fuchs 2014). Housewifised labour "bears the characteristics of housework" (Mies et al. 1988, 10).

Facebook labour is just like unpaid internships and the precariat's labour a form of housewifised labour. Unpaid forms of labour are differently exploited than wage-labour in that they form super-exploited milieus of primitive accumulation. How can unpaid labour today best be made visible in order to resist and overcome it? All labour is based on a specific degree of surplus-labour. In unwaged labour, surplus-labour-time is extended to a maximum. A universal basic income guarantee that is funded out of capital taxation is a progressive demand that builds on and extends the demand of wages for housework. That the organic composition of labour is around 5.8 in an advanced country like the USA shows the role that unpaid labour-time plays in capitalism. Socialist universal basic income does not aims at reforming or improving capitalism, but to provide humans with autonomous space and time beyond capitalism, so that foundations for thinking, living, producing, consuming, and usage beyond the logic of capital can be strengthened.

References

Amnesty International. 2016. *"This Is What We Die For": Human Rights Abuses in the Democratic Republic of the Congo Power the Global Trade in Cobalt.* London: AI.

Balibar, Étienne and Immanuel Wallerstein. 1991. *Race, Nation, Class. Ambiguous Identities.* London: Verso.

Balibar, Étienne. 2013. Exploitation. *Political Concepts* 3 (3). Available (consulted 25 December 2016) at: http://www.politicalconcepts.org/balibar-exploitation/

Fraser, Nancy, 1989. *Unruly Practices: Power, Discourse, and Gender in Contemporary Social Theory.* Minneapolis, MN: University of Minnesota Press.

Fraser, Nancy and Axel Honneth. 2003. *Redistribution or Recognition?* London: Verso.

Fuchs, Christian. 2017a. Donald Trump: A Critical Theory-Perspective on Authoritarian Capitalism. *tripleC: Communication, Capitalism & Critique* 15 (1): 1–72.

Fuchs, Christian. 2017b. *Social Media: A Critical Introduction,* 2nd edn. London: SAGE.

Fuchs, Christian. 2016. Digital labor and imperialism. *Monthly Review* 67 (8): 14–24.

Fuchs, Christian. 2015. *Culture and Economy in the Age of Social Media.* New York, NY: Routledge.

Fuchs, Christian. 2014. *Digital Labour and Karl Marx.* New York, NY: Routledge.

Fuchs, Christian. 2011. *Foundations of Critical Media and Information Studies.* London: Routledge.

Jarrett, Kylie. 2016. *Feminism, Labour and Digital Media: The Digital Housewife.* New York, NY: Routledge.

Jhally, Sut. 1987. *The Codes of Advertising.* New York, NY: Routledge.

Lambert, Craig. 2015. *Shadow Work: The Unpaid, Unseen Jobs That Fill Your Day.* Berkeley, CA: Counterpoint.

Marx, Karl. 1844. Introduction to a Contribution to the Critique of Hegel's Philosophy of Law. In *Marx & Engels Collected Works (MECW) Volume 3,* 175–187. London: Lawrence & Wishart.

Marx Karl 1867. *Capital Volume I.* London: Penguin.

Marx Karl 1871. The Civil War in France. In *Marx & Engels Collected Works (MECW) Volume 22,* 307–359. London: Lawrence & Wishart.

Marx, Karl and Friedrich Engels. 1845. *The German Ideology.* Amherst, NY: Prometheus.

Meehan, Eileen. 2002. Gendering the Commodity Audience: Critical Media Research, Feminism, and Political Economy. In *Sex & Money: Feminism and Political Economy in the Media,* eds. Eileen Meehan and Ellen Riordan, 209–222. Minneapolis, MN: University of Minnesota Press.

Mies, Maria. 1986. *Patriarchy & Accumulation on a World Scale: Women in the International Division of Labour.* London: Zed Books.

Mies, Maria, Veronika Bennholdt-Thomsen, and Claudia von Werlhof. 1988. *Women: The Last Colony.* London: Zed Books.

Ofcom. 2016. *The Communications Market Report 2016.* London: Ofcom.

Qiu, Jack L. 2016. *Goodbye iSlave: A Manifesto for Digital Abolition.* Urbana, IL: University of Illinois Press.

Sandoval, Marisol. 2013. Foxconned Labour as the Dark Side of the Information Age: Working Conditions at Apple's Contract Manufacturers in China. *tripleC: Communication, Capitalism & Critique* 11 (2): 318–347.

Shepherd, Tamara. 2014. Gendering the Commodity Audience in Social Media. In Carter C, Steiner L and McLaughlin L eds. *The Routledge Companion to Media and Gender* 157–167. London: Routledge.

Smythe, Dallas W. 1977. Communications: Blindspot of Western Marxism. *Canadian Journal of Political and Social Theory* 1 (3): 1–27.

United Nations Development Programme. 2015. *Human Development Report 2015*. New York, NY: UNDP.

Walk Free Foundation. 2016. *The Global Slavery Index 2016*. Available (consulted 25 December 2016) at: http://www.globalslaveryindex.org

Chapter Eleven
Digital Labour and Imperialism

11.1 Introduction

Lenin's *Imperialism, the Highest Stage of Capitalism*, Bukharin's *Imperialism and World Economy* that were both published in 1917 as well as Rosa Luxemburg's (1913) work *The Accumulation of Capital* spoke of capitalism as imperialism. It was a time of strikes for pay rises, Henry Ford's invention of the first assembly line that laid the foundations for Fordism, World War I, trusts and monopolies, antitrust laws, the October Revolution, the Mexican Revolution, the failed German Revolution, etc. It was a time of the extension and deepening of as well as of challenges to capitalism.

This chapter first reviews the notion of the role of the international division of labour in classical concepts of imperialism. It then uses these foundations for discussing the role of the international division of labour in the production of information and information technology today and introduces in this context the notion of the international division of digital labour. The overall task is to illuminate the relationship of digital labour and imperialism.

Lenin defined imperialism as

> capitalism at that stage of development at which the domination of monopolies and finance capital is established; in which the export of capital has acquired pronounced importance; in which the division of the world among the international trusts has begun: in which the division of all the territories of the globe among the biggest capitalist powers has been completed. (Lenin 1917, 266–267)

Bukharin and Preobrazhensky (1920 [2007], 119) gave the following definition of imperialism: "The policy of conquest which financial capital pursues in the struggle for

DOI: 10.4324/9781003222149-11

markets for the sources of raw material, and for places in which capital can be invested, is known as imperialism". Bukharin (1917), a contemporary of Lenin and editor of Pravda from 1917–1929, implicitly saw Lenin's five characteristics as constitutive for imperialism. He characterised imperialism as "a product of finance capitalism" and argued that "finance capital cannot pursue any other policy than an imperialist one" (Bukharin 1917, 140).

For Bukharin, imperialism is necessarily a form of a state capitalism, which is difficult to apply in the context of a neoliberal form of imperialism based on worldwide corporate domination. He saw countries as "state capitalist trusts" that stand in a "worldwide struggle", resulting in a world war (Bukharin 1917, 158). "Countries are state capitalist trusts that engage in world wars for centralizing and concentrating capital in their hands" (Bukharin 1917, 120–121). Imperialism is "the expression of competition between state capitalist trusts" (Bukharin 1917, 185) and a form of "state capitalism" (Bukharin and Preobrazhensky 1920 [2007], 127). Lenin (1917, 269) in contrast wrote that "an essential feature of imperialism is the rivalry between several great powers in the striving for hegemony, i.e. for the conquest of territory, not so much directly for themselves as to weaken the adversary and undermine *his* hegemony". The formulation of a competition between "great powers" is more careful than Bukharin's concept of state capitalist trusts because it encompasses both companies and states.

For Rosa Luxemburg, imperialism is the violent geographical and geo-political expansion of the accumulation of capital:

> Imperialism is the political expression of the accumulation of capital in its competitive struggle for what remains still open of the non- capitalist environment. [...] With the high development of the capitalist countries and their increasingly severe competition in acquiring non-capitalist areas, imperialism grows in lawlessness and violence, both in aggression against the non-capitalist world and in ever more serious conflicts among the competing capitalist countries. But the more violently, ruthlessly and thoroughly imperialism brings about the decline of non-capitalist civilisations, the more rapidly it cuts the very ground from under the feet of capitalist accumulation. (Luxemburg 1913, 426–427)

Luxemburg argues that capital wants to globally extend capital exploitation, it wants to "mobilise world labour power without restriction in order to utilise all productive forces of the globe" (p. 343).

Formulations such as the one that imperialism is "the final phase of capitalism" (Luxemburg 1913, 427), "decaying capitalism" (Lenin 1917, 300), and that in it the "ruin of the bourgeoisie is inevitable" (Bukharin and Preobrazhensky 1920 [2007], 143) not just show a certain political optimism of the revolutionaries of the time, but also a certain for the time common structuralism that assumes an inevitable breakdown of capitalism. Around 100 years later, capitalism can still be characterised as imperialism and continues to experience major outbreaks of its inherent crisis tendencies, although it has taken on new qualities, which allow characterising it as a new imperialism (cp. Foster and McChesney 2012; Harvey 2003; Wood 2003). Classical concepts of imperialism also can be used for analysing that in the new imperialism the information industries form one of the highest concentrated economic sectors, that hyperindustrialism, finance and informationalism belong together, that transnational informational corporations are grounded in nation states, but operate globally, capitalism dominates the information sector globally, and information technology plays a role as a means of war (for detailed analyses, see: Fuchs 2012, 2010a, 2010b, 2010c).

11.2 Imperialism and the Division of Labour

Lenin (1917, 221–222) uses the notion of the division of labour as meaning a division between industries, on which certain banks focus their investment activities. He sees the export of capital in contrast to the export of goods as a crucial feature of imperialism:

> As long as capitalism remains what it is, surplus capital will be utilised not for the purpose of raising the standard of living of the masses in a given country, for this would mean a decline in profits for the capitalists, but for the purpose of increasing profits by exporting capital abroad to the backward countries. In these backward countries profits are usually high, for capital is scarce, the price of land is relatively low, wages are low, raw materials are cheap. (Lenin 1917, 241)

Bukharin (1917, 18 and 21) argued based on Marx that a social division of labour between town and country, enterprises, branches, economic subdivisions, and countries is a feature of capitalism. He calls the latter the international division of labour (Bukharin 1917, 18). It would partly have natural causes – "Cocoa can be produced only in tropical countries" (p. 19) – and partly social causes: "the unequal development of productive forces creates different economic types and different production spheres, thus increasing the scope of international social division of labour" (p. 20).

The "labour of every individual country becomes part of that world social labour through the exchange that takes place on an international scale" (p. 22). "[W]orld division of labour and international exchange presuppose the existence of a world market and world prices" (p. 23). Given a world market and unequal productivity, less productive countries have to sell commodities at prices below their values in order to compete, which results in unequal exchange.

Rosa Luxemburg (1913, 432) focused in her concept of imperialism on the "relations between capitalism and the non-capitalist modes of production which start making their appearance on the international stage".

> Its predominant methods are colonial policy, an international loan system – a policy of spheres of interest – and war. Force, fraud, oppression, looting are openly displayed without any attempt at concealment, and it requires an effort to discover within this tangle of political violence and contests of power the stern laws of the economic process. (p. 432)

For Luxemburg, the international relations of imperialism have to do with robbery and the exploitation of labour: "Capital needs the means of production and the labour power of the whole globe for untrammelled accumulation; it cannot manage without the natural resources and the labour power of all territories" (pp. 345–346). "'Sweating blood and filth with every pore from head to toe' characterises not only the birth of capital but also its progress in the world at every step" (p. 433).

Although there were political differences in questions about imperialism between Lenin, Bukharin, and Luxemburg, especially concerning the role of the national and international level in class struggles and liberation, the question of national self-determination, the causes of crises, organisation and spontaneity in class struggles and revolutions, and the role of foreign markets in capitalism (cp. Mattick 1935), the discussion shows that in all three concepts of imperialism, the periphery is not just a source of resources and a market for selling commodities, but is also embedded into an international division of labour, as part of which workers in the periphery produce relatively cheaply in such a manner that their exploitation results in the export of surplus-value and the appropriation of this value by large companies.

11.3 The International Division of Digital Labour

International communications in the form of the telegraph and international news agencies already played a role in the imperialism of the time of World War I. They helped organising and co-ordinating trade, investment, accumulation, exploitation, and war at the international level. Around 100 years later, qualitatively different means of information and communication, such as the computer, the laptop, tablets, the Internet, mobile phones, and social media, have emerged. The production of information and information technology is embedded into an international division of information labour. There are new technologies, but capitalism, imperialism, class, and exploitation continue to form the heart of society and international relations and shape the modes of information production, distribution, and consumption that have become so important in the 21st century.

All work is a dialectic of subject and object, in which human subjects use objects (resources, technologies) to produce a new subject-object, a product of work (Fuchs 2014). Work is organised in specific social relations that determine the mode of ownership, organisation of work, the mode of allocation and distribution, and forms of consumption. Classical slavery, serfdom, and wage-labour are three important historical forms of class relations that are at the heart of specific modes of production (Engels 1884). Table 11.1 provides a classification of modes of production based on the dominant forms of ownership and class relations (self-control, partly self-control and partly alien control, full alien control).

Capitalism as the dominant mode of production has not brought older modes to an end, but has rather subsumed them. Slavery and patriarchy continue to exist and to be modes of organisation for the super-exploitation of labour. In 2014, 35.8 million people lived in modern forms of slavery (Global Slavery Index 2014). Modern slavery includes slavery, debt bondage, forced marriage, sale and exploitation of children, forced labour, and human trafficking (ibid.). Slaves in the Democratic Republic of Congo (DRC) mine a specific portion of the minerals (such as cobalt, coltan, and tin) needed for

TABLE 11.1 The main forms of ownership in various modes of production

	Owner of labour power	Owner of the means of production	Owner of the products of work
Patriarchy	Patriarch	Patriarch	Family
Slavery	Slave master	Slave master	Slave master
Feudalism	Partly self-control, partly lord	Partly self-control, partly lord	Partly self-control, partly lord
Capitalism	Worker	Capitalist	Capitalist
Communism	Self	All	Partly all, partly individual

The International Division of Digital Labour

creating electronics and computing equipment (Fuchs 2014, chapter 6). In 2014, the DRC was ranked 186 out of 187 countries in human development, 87.8% lived in extreme poverty on less than US$ 1.25 per day, and 38.8% of the population aged 15 years or older were illiterate.[1] War and neo-imperialist exploitation of labour and the country's resources that does not benefit local people, but primarily Western companies, have created the paradox typical for capitalism that one of world's countries that is richest in natural resources is socially the world's poorest country. Also in 2014 the political situation in the DRC saw continued fights involving government forces, rebels, and fighters from Uganda and Rwanda. The country's inhabitants experienced war crimes, crimes against humanity, forced recruitment of children as soldiers, mass rapes, and the killing, mutilation and torture of civilians.[2] According to estimations, more than 760,000 people in the DRC were slaves in 2014.[3] Following Nigeria, it is the country of the world with the second largest absolute number of slaves.

Critical scholars introduced the notion of the new international division of labour (NIDL) in the 1980s in order to stress that developing countries had become cheap sources of manufacturing labour and the rise of transnational corporations (TNCs) (Fröbel, Heinrichs and Kreye 1981). Foster and McChesney (2012) situate the rise TNCSs in capital's attempt to overcome long-term economic stagnation. They see transnationalisation as an attempt of capital to attain global monopoly profits. TNCs aim to drive down the wage share globally in order to try to increase their profits by installing a system of global competition between workers. The consequence is a worldwide increase of the rate of exploitation (Foster and McChesney 2012, 114–115 and 119) that based on Stephen Hymer Foster and McChesney terms TNC's "strategy of divide and rule" (pp. 119 and 126).

Table 11.2 shows comparative data for the world's 2000 largest TNCs in the years 2004 and 2014. These companies' revenues accounted for more than 50% of the worldwide gross domestic product, which shows that TNCs operate at the global level for trying to obtain monopoly status. In both years almost three quarters of the capital assets of these companies were located in the FIRE sector (finance, insurance, real estate), which confirms Foster and McChesney's (2012) assumption that we can speak of global monopoly-finance capitalism. There are however also significant shares of the

---

1 Data source: Human Development Indicators, http://hdr.undp.org/, accessed on 26 October 2014.
2 Source: Human Rights Watch 2014 Report: Democratic Republic of Congo: http://www.hrw.org/world-report/2014/country-chapters/democratic-republic-congo, accessed on 22 December 2014.
3 Ibid.

mobility industries (transportation, oil and gas, vehicles), the manufacturing industry, and the information industries (telecommunication, hardware, software, semi-conductors, advertising, Internet, publishing, and broadcasting), which indicate that to specific degrees global capitalism is, besides finance capitalism, also a global monopoly mobility capitalism, a global monopoly hyperindustrial capitalism, and a global monopoly information capitalism (Fuchs 2014, chapter 5). Furthermore, these capitalisms in an interconnected manner form one overall global capitalist whole, a capitalist world system.

A significant change within these ten years was that Chinese TNCs increased their shares of assets, revenues, and profits. European and North American TNCs now no longer control around three quarters, but two-thirds of global capital, which means that they continue to be dominant. That Chinese TNCs play a more important role does not signify a fundamental break, but is rather an indication that China imitates Western-style capitalism so that a capitalism with Chinese characteristics has emerged.

The NIDL is at the heart of the information and digital economy that produces in-formation and information and communication technologies (ICTs). Specific forms of physical work produce information technologies that are then used by workers in the media and cultural industries for creating informational content (music, movies, data, statistics, multimedia, images, videos, animations, texts, articles, etc.) in digital form. Informational content is produced, disseminated, and consumed with the help of in-formation technologies. Technology and content are dialectically interconnected so that the information economy is both physical and non-physical at the same time. The information economy is neither a superstructure nor immaterial, but rather a specific form of the organisation of the productive forces that cuts across the base/super-structure divide and makes information and information technology an immediate productive force.

Figure 11.1 shows a model of the major production processes that are involved in the international division of digital labour. Each production step/labour process involves human subjects (S) using technologies/instruments of labour (T) on objects of labour (O) so that a new product emerges. The very foundation of digital labour is an agri-cultural labour cycle in which miners extract minerals. These minerals enter the next production process as objects so that processors based on them in physical labour processes create ICT components. These components enter the next labour cycle as objects: assemblage workers build digital media technologies and take ICT components

TABLE 11.2 Data on the world's 2000 largest TNCs, own calculations based on the following data sources: Forbes 2000 (2004 and 2014 lists), in billion US$, data refer to 2003 and 2013; data source for world GDP: IMF World Economic Outlook Database (2003 and 2013, world GDP in billion US$)

	2004	2014
Total revenues (billion US$)	19,934	38,361
Total capital assets (billion US$)	68,064	160,974
Share of revenues in world GDP	50.8%	51.4%
Total profits (billion US$)	760.4	2927.5
Total market value (billion US$)	23,755	44,410
Share of FIRE in total assets	70.8%	73.6%
Share of FIRE in total profits	32.7%	33.5%
Share of FIRE in total revenues	20.2%	19.8%
Share of information in total assets	5.9%	5.5%
Share of information in total profits	−0.8%	17.3%
Share of information in total revenues	11.3%	13.1%
Share of mobility industries in total assets	7.5%	6.9%
Share of mobility industries in total profits	22.4%	19.0%
Share of mobility industries in total revenues	21.4%	24.0%
Share of manufacturing in total assets	7.1%	6.9%
Share of manufacturing in total profits	28.3%	18.6%
Share of manufacturing in total revenues	21.1%	21.7%
Number of Chinese TNCs	49	207
Number of US TNCs	751	563
Share of US assets	33.5%	23.0%
Share of US revenues	38.9%	30.0%
Share of US profits	64.1%	39.0%
Share of Chinese assets	1.1%	13.7%
Share of Chinese revenues	1.0%	10.8%
Share of Chinese profits	3.6%	14.3%
North American + European assets	77.4%	63.1%
North American + European revenues	75.8%	62.3%
North American + European profits	82.9%	61.7%

as inputs. Processors and assemblers are industrial workers involved in digital production. The outcome of such labour are digital media technologies that enter various forms of information work as tools for the production, distribution, circulation, prosumption, and consumption of diverse types of information.

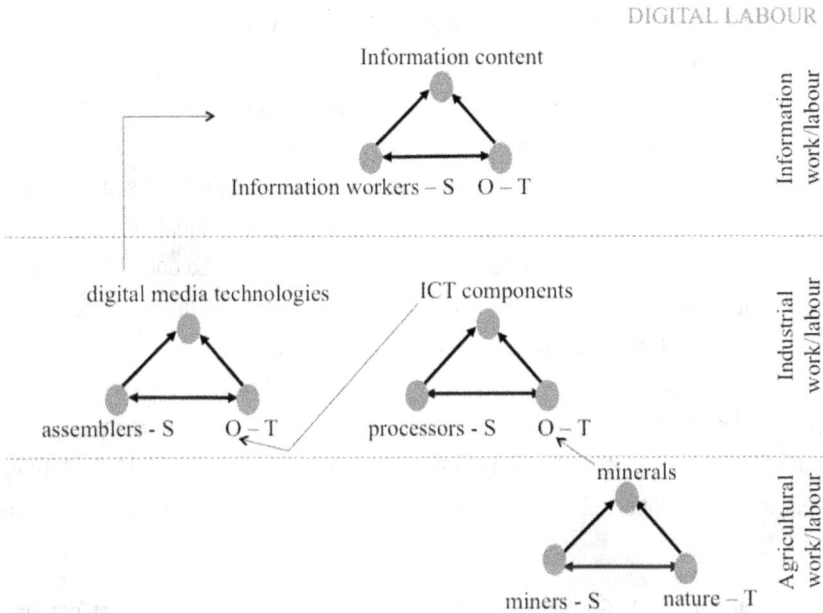

FIGURE 11.1   The international division of digital labour (cp. Fuchs 2014, 2015)

"Digital labour" is not a term that only describes the production of digital content. It is a category that rather encompasses the whole mode of digital production that contains a network of agricultural, industrial, and informational forms of work that enables the existence and usage of digital media. The subjects involved in the digital mode of production (S) – miners, processors, assemblers, information workers, and related workers – stand in specific relations of production that are either class relations or non-class relations. So what is designated as S in Figure 11.1 is actually a relationship S_1–S_2 between different subjects or subject groups. In contemporary capitalist society, most of these digital relations of production tend to be shaped by wage-labour, slave labour, unpaid, precarious, and freelance labours.

The international division of digital labour is a complex network that involves global interconnected processes of exploitation, such as the exploitation of Congolese slave-miners who extract minerals that are used as the physical foundation for ICT components that are manufactured by millions of highly exploited Fordist wage-workers in factories such as Foxconn, low-paid software engineers in India, highly paid and highly stressed software engineers at Google and other Western software and Internet corporations, or precarious freelancers in the world's global cities who are using digital technologies to create and disseminate culture, poisoned eWaste workers who dis-assemble ICTs and thereby come in touch with toxic materials, etc. (Fuchs 2014, 2015).

Let us look at an example form of digital labour. Apple has according to the Forbes' 2000 list of the largest transnational companies been the world's 15th largest company in 2014.[4] Its profits were US\$ 37.0 billion in 2013 and US\$ 39.5 billion in 2014.[5] In 2014, iPhones accounted for 56% of Apple's net sales, iPads for 17%, Macs for 13%, iTunes, software and services for 10%.[6] According to calculations, the Chinese labour involved in manufacturing an iPhone makes up only 1.8% of the iPhone's price, Apple's profits 58.5% (Chan, Pun and Selden 2013, 107) and Apple's suppliers, such as the Taiwanese company Hon Hai Precision that is also known as Foxconn, 14.3%. So the iPhone 6 Plus does not cost US\$ 299 because of labour costs, but rather because Apple on average earns US\$ 175 profits, Foxconn US\$ 43 profits, and the workers assembling the phone in a Foxconn factory in total US\$ 5. The high costs are a consequence of a high profit rate and a high rate of exploitation that are achieved by organising digital labour within an international division. China is "the world assembly hub" (p. 170) in a system of "global labor arbitrage and [...] superexploitation" (Foster and McChesney 2012, 172).

According to the CNN Global 500 2012 list,[7] Foxconn is the fifth largest corporate employer in the world. In 2011, Foxconn had enlarged its Chinese workforce to a million, a majority being young migrant workers coming from the countryside (Students & Scholars Against Corporate Misbehaviour, 2011). Foxconn assembles, for example the iPad, iMac, iPhone, the Amazon Kindle, and various consoles (by Sony, Nintendo, Microsoft). When 17 Foxconn workers attempted to commit suicide between January and August 2010 (most of them succeeded), the topic of bad working conditions in the Chinese ICT assemblage industry became widely known. This circumstance was followed up with a number of academic works that show that workers' everyday reality at Foxconn includes low wages, working long hours, frequent work shift changes, regular working time of over ten hours per day, a lack of breaks, monotonous work, physical harm caused by chemicals such as benzene or solder paste, lack of protective gear and equipment, forced use of students from vocational schools as interns (in agreement with the school boards) that conduct regular assembly work that does not help their studies, prison-like accommodations with 6–22 workers per room, yellow unions that are managed by company officials and whom the workers do not trust, harsh management methods, a lack of breaks, prohibitions that workers move, talk, or stretch

---

4 http://www.forbes.com/global2000/list, accessed on 22 December 2014.
5 Apple SEC-Filings, Form 10-K, 2014.
6 Ibid.
7 http://money.cnn.com/magazines/fortune/global500/2012/full_list/, accessed on 29 October 2013.

their bodies, workers that had to stand during production, punishments, beatings, and harassments by security guards, and disgusting food (Chan 2013; Chan, Pun and Selden 2013; Foster and McChesney 2012, 119–120, 139–140, 173; Fuchs 2014, chapter 7; Pun and Chan 2012; Qiu 2012; Sandoval 2013).

Apple claims in its *Supplier Responsibility 2014 Progress Report* that it drove its "suppliers to achieve an average of 95 percent compliance with our maximum 60-hour work week".[8] The International Labour Organization's Convention C030 – Hours of Work recommends that the working week should not last longer than 48 hours. That Apple defines itself a standard of 60 hours for labour in its supply chain and prides itself for this fact shows that imperialism's international division of labour is not just exploitative, but also racist in character: Apple assumes that for people in China 60 hours is an appropriate standard of working time.

Apple says that for its 2014 report it audited the working conditions of more than 1 million workers. It is however a fact that these audits are not conducted independently and that the results are also not reported independently. Apple does not rely on independent corporate watchdog organisations such as Students & Scholars Against Corporate Misbehaviour (SACOM), but rather conducts studies that one can only consider to be biased. Workers who are studied by their own employers will certainly not report what they think is wrong because they are afraid to lose their job. Apple's report is written in a style and language that conveys the impression that suppliers and local agencies that behave immorally are the problem: "Our suppliers are required to uphold the rigorous standards of Apple's Supplier Code of Conduct, and every year we raise the bar on what we expect. [...] We audit all final assembly suppliers every year". That such behaviour is however driven by TNCs' demand to produce cheaply and quickly is never mentioned. Apple uses the ideological strategy that it emphasises positive things about itself and negative things about suppliers in order to distort attention from its own responsibility for the exploitation of Chinese workers.

SACOM published in autumn 2014 a new report on working conditions at Apple's supplier Pegatron in Jinagsu,[9] where tens of millions of the iPhone 6 have been manufactured. Undercover scholars conducted the research.

8 https://www.apple.com/supplier-responsibility/pdf/Apple_SR_2014_Progress_Report.pdf, accessed on 22 December 2014.
9 See also the 2013 investigation by China Labor Watch: http://www.chinalaborwatch.org/report/68. A comparable case is the iPhone 6 assemblage at Jabi in Wuxi: http://www.chinalaborwatch.org/report/103

> Workers told SACOM researchers that they sometimes have to work very long hours till early morning, often 12 to 15 hours a day, and sometimes even up to 17 to 18 hours a day. In other words, the total amount of overtime hours can be up to 170 to 200 hours a month, which, in turn, means that workers have to work more than 360 hours a month. (Students & Scholars Against Corporate Misbehaviour 2014, 2)

Further issues at Pegatron included an unsafe and unhealthy working environment, illegal charges for health checks, insufficient health information, precarious dispatch labour, exclusion from social insurance, difficulties to resign from the job, scolding, fines, repressive management, and lack of trade unions. The report concludes:

> Pegatron and its buyer Apple have continuously engaged in poor labour practices and abuses of workers' rights. Even though the Apple Inc. has established its code of conducts since 2005, the working conditions in Apple's supply chain are still far from satisfactory. This report, along with the earlier investigative reports released by SACOM throughout the years, have continuously demonstrated that Apple and its suppliers in the Chinese mainland have never treated their workers with dignity. (Students & Scholars Against Corporate Misbehaviour 2014, 21)

A 2014 BBC undercover report unveiled that workers assembling iPhones 6 in Pegatron factories are so overworked that they fall asleep during work and in their breaks.[10]

An ideology is a claim that does not correspond to reality. SACOM's studies show that reality in the factories of Apple's Chinese suppliers is different than reported in the company's own reports. Apple tries to distort presentations of labour in its supply chain by ideology in order to forestall critique of capitalism.

The Foxconn example shows that the existence and usage of digital media not just depends on the labour of software engineers and content producers. Digital labour covers a broad range of labour working under different conditions, including slave-miners working in African conflict mines, smelters, hardware assemblers, software engineers, digital media content producers, eWaste workers, or users of commercial digital media (Fuchs 2014, 2015).

---

10 Apple "failing to protect Chinese factory workers". http://www.bbc.com/news/business-30532463 *BBC Online*, accessed on 18 December 2014.

11.4 Conclusion

Apple has marketed the iPhone 5 as being made "for the colourful" and the iPhone 6 as being "bigger than big". Such slogans communicate that the digital technological revolution has brought about a new and better society that benefits all. Similar ideological promises and claims can be found in the context of phenomena such as social media, cloud computing, big data, the sharing and like economy, crowdsouring, crowdfunding, the maker movement, etc. Such assertions are forms of technological fetishism that assume that technology inherently fosters a good society without analysing the social relations into which it is embedded. In technological fetishism, the "definite social relation between men themselves" assume "the fantastic form of a relation between things", technological things (Marx 1867, 165).

Confronting what some call the digital or information society with Lenin, Luxemburg, and Bukharin's classical concepts of imperialism helps us to unmask technological fetishism. The example of Apple shows that digital technology and the ideologies that often positively frame it in advertisements, the press, bourgeois politics, and the public are distorted by the fascination of the new that overlooks the continuities of exploitation in an international division of labour.

Apple achieves high profits in the international division of digital labour by outsourcing manufacturing labour to China, where the Western strategy of "exporting capital abroad" achieves high profits because "wages are low" (Lenin 1917, 241) and the rate of exploitation is high. The exploitation of workers at Foxconn, Pegatron, and other companies in the international division of digital labour shows that "'[s]weating blood and filth with every pore from head to toe' characterises not only the birth of capital but also its progress in the world at every step" (Luxemburg 1913, 433). Both these analyses by Lenin and Luxemburg are as true in the 21st century as they were 100 years ago.

The international division of digital labour involves diverse forms of the exploitation of labour, including the labour of slave-miners, Fordist hardware assemblers, highly stressed and highly paid aristocratic workers at playworkplaces in Silicon Valley tech companies, low-paid precarious data processors carrying out deskilled digital labour, highly skilled, creative, and precariously self-employed freelancers in the digital and cultural industries, users who become value-generating play-workers for targeted-advertising financed social media companies, etc. (Fuchs 2014, 2015). This division is organised in global space, which shows that also in digital capitalism capital "needs the means of production and the labour power of the whole globe for untrammelled accumulation" (Luxemburg 1913, 345–346).

To my knowledge, no mobile phone or laptop exists that has not been produced as part of the imperialist division of labour that characterises digital capitalism. The political task is to question the capitalist character of media, culture, communications, and the Internet and to find ways to transform them into and defend them as common and public goods. Given the global conditions of exploitation, the contradictions of the international division of digital labour result again and again result in class struggles.

Foster and McChesney argue that "capitalist contradictions with Chinese characteristics" (Foster and McChesney 2012, 157) feature the overinvestment in construction and urban real estate, weak consumption, extreme exploitation, rising inequality, unused infrastructure, discrimination of rural migrant labour, pollution, and environmental degradation. Media reports about China in the West tend to ignore the active political culture of working class and social struggles stemming from these contradictions. A better world can only be the result of social struggles. "The emancipation of the working class must be the work of the working class itself" (Marx and Engels 1879, 555). According to data by China Labour Bulletin, 1276 strikes took place in China during 2014.[11] China is not a monolithic society, but one with very active and vivid working class struggles against exploitation. One example is that in October 2014 1000 workers went after earlier labour unrest in June on strike for wage increases at Foxconn Chongqing.[12]

The short-term perspective for digital working class struggles should be the formation of worker-controlled companies in the digital and cultural industries at all levels of organisation and over the entire globe, no matter if it concerns social media organisations, software engineering, the cultural freelance economy, mineral extraction, or ICT assemblage. In the medium term the perspective should be to overcome the capitalist organisation of these spheres together with capitalist society. The question what role the national and/or the international dimension of social struggles against digital capitalism should have is in this context a matter for strategic political debates. In an address of the International Workingmen's Association, Marx argued that "in order to oppose their workers, the employers either bring in workers from abroad or

11 China Labour Bulletin Strike Map, http://www.numble.com/PHP/mysql/clbmape.html
12 China Labor Watch: Thousands of Foxconn workers strike again in Chongqing for better wages, benefits. http://www.chinalaborwatch.org/newscast/395, accessed on October 8, 2014.

else transfer manufacture to countries where there is a cheap labour force" (International Workingmen's Association 1867, 422). It is true today as it was true at the time of Marx that if "the working class wishes to continue its struggle with some chance of success", then the adequate response to global capitalist rule that "the national organisations must become international" (International Workingmen's Association 1867, 422).

References

Bukharin, Nikolai. 1917. *Imperialism and World Economy.* New York: Monthly Review Press.

Bukharin, Nikolai and Evgenii Preobrazhensky. 1920/2007. *The ABC of Communism.* Monmouth: Merlin Press.

Chan, Jenny. 2013. A Suicide Survivor: The Life of a Chinese Worker. *New Technology, Work and Employment* 28 (2): 84–99.

Chan, Jenny, Ngai Pun and Mark Selden. 2013. The Politics of Global Production: Apple, Foxconn and China's New Working Class. *New Technology, Work and Employment* 28 (2): 100–115.

Engels, Friedrich. 1884. The Origin of the Family, Private Property and the State. In *Marx Engels Collected Works (MECW) Volume 26*, 129–276. London: Lawrence & Wishart.

Foster, John Bellamy and Robert W. McChesney. 2012. *The Endless Crisis: How Monopoly-Finance Capitalism Produces Stagnation and Upheaval From the USA to China.* New York: Monthly Review Press.

Fröbel, Folker, Jürgen Heinrichs and Otto Kreye. 1981. *The New International Division of Labour.* Cambridge: Cambridge University Press.

Fuchs, Christian. 2015. *Culture and Economy in the Age of Social Media.* New York: Routledge.

Fuchs, Christian. 2014. *Digital Labour and Karl Marx.* New York: Routledge.

Fuchs, Christian. 2012. Media, War and Information Technology. In *Media & Terrorism. Global Perspectives*, eds.Des Freedman and Daya Kishan Thussu, 47–62. London: Sage.

Fuchs, Christian. 2010a. Critical Globalization Studies: An Empirical and Theoretical Analysis of the New Imperialism. *Science & Society* 74 (2): 215–247.

Fuchs, Christian. 2010b. Critical Globalization Studies and the New Imperialism. *Critical Sociology* 36 (6): 839–867.

Fuchs, Christian. 2010c. New Imperialism: Information and Media Imperialism? *Global Media and Communication* 6 (1): 33–60.

Global Slavery Index. 2014. *The Global Slavery Index 2014.* Dalkeith (Western Australia): Walk Free Foundation.

Harvey, David. 2003. *The New Imperialism.* Oxford: Oxford University Press.

International Workingmen's Association. 1867. On the Lausanne Congress. In *Marx Engels Collected Works (MECW), Volume 20*, 421–423. London: Lawrence & Wishart.

Lenin, Vladimir I. 1917. Imperialism, the Highest Stage of Capitalism. In Lenin Collected Works Volume 22: December 1915-July 1916, 185–304. London: Lawrence & Wishart.

Luxemburg, Rosa. 1913. *The Accumulation of Capital*. New York: Routledge.

Marx, Karl. 1867. *Capital Volume I*. London: Penguin.

Marx, Karl and Friedrich Engels. 1879. The Manifesto of the Three Zurichers. In *The Marx-Engels Reader*, 2nd edn , ed. Robert C. Tucker, 549–555. New York: W. W. Norton & Company.

Mattick, Paul. 1935. Luxemburg Versus Lenin. Available at: https://www.marxists.org/archive/mattick-paul/1935/luxemburg-lenin.htm

Pun, Ngai and Jenny Chan. 2012. Global Capital, the State, and Chinese Workers: The Foxconn Experience. *Modern China* 38 (4): 383–410.

Qiu, Jack L. 2012. Network Labor: Beyond the Shadow of Foxconn. In *Studying Mobile Media: Cultural Technologies, Mobile Communication, and the iPhone*, eds. Larissa Hjorth, Jean Burgess and Ingrid Richardson, 173–189. New York: Routledge.

Sandoval, Marisol. 2013. Foxconned Labour as the Dark Side of the Information Age: Working Conditions at Apple's Contract Manufacturers in China. *tripleC: Communication, Capitalism & Critique* 11 (2): 318–347.

Students & Scholars Against Corporate Misbehaviour. 2014. *The Lives of iSlaves: Report on Working Conditions at Apple's Supplier Pegatron*. Available at: https://sacom.hk/wp-content/uploads/2014/09/SACOM-The-Lives-of-iSlaves-Pegatron-20140918.pdf

Students & Scholars Against Corporate Misbehaviour. 2011. *iSlave Behind the iPhone. Foxconn Workers in Central China*. Available at: https://sacom.hk/wp-content/uploads/2011/09/20110924-islave-behind-the-iphone.pdf

Wood, Ellen Meiksins. 2003. *Empire of Capital*. London: Verso.

Chapter Twelve

The Information Economy and the Labour Theory of Value

12.1 Introduction

The question if and how Marx's labour theory of value applies to the information industries has been an important and contested issue in Marxist theory that has gained a
new impetus with the rise of so-called "social media" platforms such as Facebook,
Twitter, Weibo, and YouTube (Arvidsson and Colleoni 2012; Beverungen, Böhm and Land
2015; Bolaño 2015; Carchedi 2014; Comor 2014; Foley 2013; Fuchs 2010, 2012a, 2012b,
2014a, 2015, 2016b, 2017; Huws 2014; McGuigan and Manzerolle 2014; Perelman 2002,
2003; Proffitt, Ekbia and McDowell 2015; Reveley 2013; Rigi 2014; Rigi and Prey 2015;
Teixeira and Rotta 2012; Zeller 2008). As part of neo-liberal hypes of the "new economy",
the Internet and the "creative industries", the actual economic relevance of the Internet
and knowledge work has often been overestimated (Garnham 1998, 2005). But at the
same time it cannot be dismissed that these phenomena have some relevance and that
Marxist political economy therefore needs to consider and analyse them (Fuchs 2013). The
theoretical question that has been discussed within Marxist theory in recent time is what
Marxian categories, such as value, productive labour, rent, profit, commodification, reproductive labour, etc. can be used for understanding information and the Internet. This is
a complex theoretical debate that is not subject of this chapter.

Fisher and Fuchs (2015) as well as Fuchs (2015, chapter 5) provide overview discussions of various aspects of this theory's debate. Approaches used have, for example,
included Dallas Smythe's (1977) theory of the audience commodity and audience labour, rent theory, Autonomist Marxism, and Marxist feminism. A basic question is if
labour or specific labour conducted in the information economy is productive or unproductive? This question already goes back to Smythe's (1977) works. Claims that

DOI: 10.4324/9781003222149-12

labour in the information economy is unproductive are not new. They tend to reoccur within the contemporary political-economic debate about value in the Internet and information economy. They are often reformulations of Michael Lebowitz's (1986) criticism of Dallas Smythe's concept of audience labour. This chapter only discusses empirical aspects of the labour theory of value in the context of the information industries. The reader further interested in the theoretical foundations is therefore referred to the above-mentioned debate on this question.

Information, media, communication, and culture are connected terms. How do they relate to each other? Culture is the process and system, in which humans produce social meanings in society. This means that it is the system, where social information is produced. The term information has a broader meaning because information also exists in living systems, as the term genetic information indicates. For the purpose of this chapter, information is however understood as social information. Social information is often also termed knowledge. Information in society exists as cognitive thought patterns, communicated information, and information stored in objects. Communication is the process of symbolic interaction between humans. Mediation means a relation between interacting systems. A medium is therefore a system that enables interaction. Wherever humans communicate, there is a medium of communication. Culture therefore is a social information system, in which humans produce, communicate, and use information with the help of media. It is society's social information system. In this chapter, I will predominantly use the terms information economy and information industries.

The information economy is in this chapter defined as the realm of the production of information and technologies for the consumption and transmission of information.[1] This definition can be challenged on the ground of combining aspects of the production of physical and non-physical production, such an argument is however a form of cultural idealism that neglects the materiality of culture (Williams 1977). Raymond Williams' argument is that separating the economy and culture is idealist: culture is produced by information workers. The emergence of cultural work and the culture industry show the importance of the interconnection of culture and economy (Fuchs 2015, chapter 2). For Williams, culture is not a superstructure that sits on top of an economic base. Culture and ideas are just like all reality material.

---

1 In the International Standard Industrial Classification of All Economic Activities (ISIC Revision 4) these are the following categories: D18 printing and reproduction of recorded media; D26 computer, electronic, and optical products; D58T63 publishing, audiovisuals, broadcasting, telecommunications, IT; D72 research; D73 advertising and marketing research; D85 education; D90T93 arts, entertainment, and recreation.

In discussions about the contemporary information economy, one can find tendencies that categories such as information, the digital, knowledge, cultural/information/digital/virtual labour are separated from physical labour that produces information technology. The most extreme example is the concept of immaterial labour that implies that there are parts of society that are not material, which contradicts a materialist worldview. Raymond Williams' cultural materialism is an approach that allows us to see the dialectic of categories. So, for example, all work has mental and physical aspects (Fuchs 2015). But a specific concrete work has a specific degree of mental and physical aspects. Culture at the same time belongs to the economy and does not belong to it: humans produce all culture and information is created in concrete economic production processes. The created information however has effects in all parts of society. Information matters, makes a difference, and has meaning – not just in the economy. It has emergent effects when humans interpret the world based on existing information and with the help of information technology (Fuchs 2015).

In defining the information economy, there is a difference between industry and occupation approaches (Machlup 1962). Occupation approaches consider the information economy, the aggregate of the value created by all workers whose occupation is to produce information. Industry approaches in contrast define the information economy as the aggregated value produced by all companies creating information products. The occupation approach is methodological individualist, whereas the industry approach is in line with what Marx (1867, 643) termed the collective worker, "a combination of workers" jointly creating a product. In the contemporary corporation, this includes the value created together by a variety of workers. In an information corporation, this includes both occupations that create tangible and intangible outputs that contribute together to the production of information technologies and information content.

The OECD has in the fourth revision of the International Standard Industrial Classification of All Economic Activities (ISIC) introduced an information sector (sector J) that it defines in the following way:

> This section includes the production and distribution of information and cultural products, the provision of the means to transmit or distribute these products, as well as data or communications, information technology activities and the processing of data and other information service activities.[2]

Introduction

---

2 http://unstats.un.org/unsd/cr/registry/regcs.asp?CI=27&Lg=1&Co=J

It, however, also defines a separate arts, entertainment, and recreation sector (sector R) and defines scientific research, advertising, market research, consulting, accounting as part of sector M: professional, scientific, and technical activities. Given that science, art, entertainment, research, advertising, consulting, and accounting all produce some form of information, such a definition is confusing and results in a narrow understanding of the information sector.

Goodrige, Hasek and Wallis (2014) have measured the investment in intangible assets ordered by year, industries, and intangible asset types. In their conceptual framework, intangible assets are comprising reseach and development, mineral exploration, financial product innovation, design, training, artistic originals, organisational structure, software, and branding. They calculated that in 2011, intangible asset investment was significantly larger in the UK economy than tangible asset investment. The core distinction in this approach is the one between tangibles and intangibles. The basic question is however if this strict separation can be upheld in the contemporary economy. A computer clearly is a tangible machine. It however is an information technology, that is a data processing machine. So it has to do with a tangible form that processes an intangible asset. It is therefore unclear how the computer as asset should exactly be classified in this approach.

Higgs, Cunningham and Pagan (2007, 20) define the creative economy as "human activities related with the production, distribution, exchange, and consumption of creative goods and services". They say it is broader than the term cultural industries that focuses on artistic production and stresses the commercial use of "symbolic knowledge and skills" (p. 4). The authors understand the Creative Trident as the total of the creative occupations in the core creative industries as well as in other industries. The definition includes, in contrast to the ISIC's understanding of the information sector, a broad range of information industries (music, performing arts, film, TV, radio, advertising, marketing, software, online, publishing, architecture, design, and visual arts) in the core creative industries. It furthermore combines the industry and occupation approach.

Bakhshi, Freeman and Higgs (2013) take a comparable approach that suggests measurements of the creative intensity of creative occupations in any industry. They make creative talent the defining feature of a creative occupation. The defining qualities of creative activity are that it is a novel process, mechanisation resistant, non-repetitive, non-uniform, independent of context, and that it involves interpretation not mere transformation (p. 24).

This confers a unique and important quality on the creative worker within the creative process, namely that it is difficult to *mechanise* the creative process and hence to substitute machines or devices for the humans, reversing a trend that has dominated much of history. Implementing a creative decision is not really a creative role, we would argue, but making one is. (Bakhshi, Freeman and Higgs 2013, 22)

Based on this approach the authors calculated that in 2010, 8.7% of the UK workforce was part of the creative economy and that the majority of these workers were employed outside the core creative industries.

The two latter approaches have a strong focus on measuring occupations. However, in capitalism, "the commodity-form of the product of labour [...] is the economic cell-form" (Marx 1867, 90). The commodity is the economic form that objectifies value generated by humans and whose sale results in the realisation of monetary profit. Like Marx, it therefore makes sense to start economic analysis with the commodity form. Speaking about the information sector, this means that one must have a look at the commodity form of information as the economic cell-form of the information sector. The focus on creative occupations makes individual activities that generate novel information and are based on highly skilful and qualified labour the cell-form of this sector. The notions of creative labour, creative industries, and the creative economy overestimate the role of highly educated and qualified non-replaceable labour. Many information commodities are generated in a division of labour that involves occupations that produce information, services, and physical products, that have varying forms of qualification (low, medium, high skill), etc. The point is that for the production of certain information commodities, the labour-time of a diverse set of workers is needed. All of their labour-time is reflected in the commodity. A labour theory of value applied to information sector must therefore start with the information commodity produced by a collective (but diverse) information worker as the basic focus.

"Editing a film is a creative task – but operating a 6 plate 35 mm Steenbeck editing table under the direction of the editor is not" (Bakhshi, Freeman and Higgs 2013, 22). The point here is that both the editor and the operator's labour-time is objectified in the film as commodity and that they work in the same division of labour of the movie industry. To argue that the first's labour is creative and the second is not can easily create the impression that only skilled workers are creating surplus-value and unskilled ones do not. In the production of an information commodity such as a film both of them are however productive workers, that is the exploitation of their labour that is expended in time results in commodities that are sold in order to accumulate capital.

Introduction

There are certainly informational occupations that do not result in the production of an information commodity, but rather in different commodity types. They are part of a collective workforce outside the information sector. The distinction between the occupational and the industry definition of industries certainly is feasible and can be combined. The question however is which one fits best for a Marxist understanding of the economy.

To avoid an elitist definition of creativity, one can also resort to Marx (1867, 284), who argued that at the "end of every labour process, a result emerges which had already been conceived by the worker at the beginning, hence already existed ideally". All human labour requires mental planning and anticipation of the result, albeit with different qualities. All occupations have an information dimensions and are creative in the general understanding of the word that Marx hints at, namely that they *create* use-values that satisfy needs.

This brief non-exhaustive discussion shows why this chapter uses a framework, in which the information industry is defined as the realm of the production, circulation, and consumption of information products, both information goods and services. Many information products take on the form of commodities. There is however a growing sector of the information economy that transcends the commodity form and in which peer produced information takes on the form of an informational commons. Given this definition of the information economy, the share of the information industry in total national value added was in 2010 15.6% in Finland, 14.1% in France, 12.4% in Germany, 12.0% in Italy, and 10.6% in Norway (data source: OECD STAN).[3] The total employment share of this sector was in the same year 16.3% in Finland, 13.8% in France, 13.2% in Germany, 11.7% in Italy, and 14.2% in Norway (ibid.). One may now say these are significant, but not overwhelming shares. Let's, however, compare these data to the manufacturing sector:[4] it accounted in 2010 for 14.8% of value added in Finland, 9.7% in France, 14.8% in Finland, 20.0% in Germany, 17.1% in Italy, and 7.3% in Norway. Manufacturing comprised in the same year 13.4% of total employment in Finland, 10.2% in France, 15.9% in Germany, 15.1% in Italy, and 8.8% in Norway. Six

---

3 Comparable results can be obtained for other countries. OECD STAN at the moment of writing (January 2014) only provides data for 15 countries because ISIC Revision 5 is still a relatively new metric introduced in 2008 that has not been applied to older data and is not used for statistical purposes in all countries. No data are available for the United Kingdom. The data for the USA are not sufficiently disaggregated for use. See the appendix for a methodological discussion.
4 I calculated value added of manufacturing based on ISCI Revision 5 aggregated category D10T33 minus D18 and D26 that according I consider to be part of the information economy.

out of ten country-specific variables in these example calculations have higher values in the information than in the manufacturing sector.

In this chapter, section 12.2 studies an example case — the German information economy — with the help of the labour theory of value in order to formulate some assumptions. Section 12.3 tests based on the same case, the assumption that the labour theory of value cannot be applied to the information sector.

12.2 The Information Industry and Marx's Labour Theory of Value

Some representatives of Autonomist Marxist theory argue for example that the law of value does not apply to the information economy because it is networked and based on co-operation. Antonio Negri (1991, 172) writes for example that Marx in the *Grundrisse* argues for the death of the law of value. Paolo Virno (2004, 100) says that the development of capitalism refutes the law of value. Hardt and Negri (2004, 145) claim that the law of value in contemporary capitalism "makes no sense". Vercellone (2010, 90) speaks of capitalism's "crisis of measurement". But Marx (1857 [1858], 705), in the specific passage that these authors refer to, does not talk about the law of value in capitalism, but rather about the death of the law of value in a communist society (Rosdolsky 1977, 428). The law of value is a foundation of all forms of capitalism (Postone 2008, 126).

A comparable argument has been made by Nicholas Garnahm, who assumes that the labour theory of value is invalid in the information industries. Nicholas Garnham is one of these scholars. Garnham (1998, 103) says that the labour theory of value works if "labour time is largely a matter of energy and expended" and productivity rises due to saving of human energy expenditure based on technology. He questions whether this works in a "non-entropic economy of bits". The labour theory of value for Garnham works well "in an economy based [...] on the measurable increase in the productivity of human work-time and especially on the saving of human energy inputs through the substitution of natural energy sources" (Garnham 2000, 146). "In an economy dominated by information production any stable relation between labour and value breaks down" (Garnham 2000, 146). Garnham (2011, 47–48) writes that the economic concepts of productivity and efficiency cannot be applied to culture because of an "uncertain relationship between labour inputs and outputs" (Garnham 2011, 47). Information labour could not easily be automated and mechanised.

In a newer version of his argument, Garnham argues that the labour theory of value

> served a useful analytical function and within the relatively simple material
> economies of the day bore some relevant relationship to relative prices and
> the division of the surplus and thus to class relations. [...] In an economy
> based upon a complex division of labour, on a growing ratio of dead labour to
> living labour and on the application of knowledge, it made, and makes, less
> and less sense. (Garnham 2016, 295–296; for a response see Fuchs 2016a)

Garnham argues that Piero Sraffa (1960) in his book *Production of Commodities by Means of Commodities* has shown that "the inequalities of capitalism can be generated within the process of commodity production and exchange without recourse to an exploitation theory of labour" (Garnham 2016, 297; for a critique see Fuchs 2016a).

One should bear in mind that Cantabrigian economics (Pierro Sraffa, Joan Robins, John Eatwell, and others) has resulted in Marxist critique. In this approach, "people as human beings – and, more importantly, as historical social classes – are given no role in the process of production" (Roosevelt 1975, 7). The Cantabrigians separate "relations between things from relations between people" (Roosevelt 1975, 19), which results in a commodity-fetishistic model of capitalism, in which "things produce things" (p. 19). "However ingenious the Cantabrigians are in analyzing price phenomena, they never connect such phenomena with social relations in the way that Marx did in *Capital*" (p. 20). Sraffa and Robinson's approaches constitute a "[p]rice theory without value theory" (p. 19). Robinson (1966, 22) revises Marx theory and argues that "no point of substance in Marx's argument depends upon the labour theory of value". For Marx, distribution and production are intertwined social processes, for the Cantabrigians they are separate, production being technical in nature and distribution social. For Sraffa (1960, 9), surplus is not surplus-value, but a physical "surplus production" of commodities, "a surplus of some commodities" (p. 26). In contrast, for Marx surplus is surplus-value that stems from capital's exploitation of labour in class relations.

For Marx, there is a social production process, in which humans enter social relations of production and these social relations use means of production for creating new goods that are distributed in relations of distribution (Fuchs 2016b). Production and distribution are interrelated social processes grounded in human activity. For Marx, human creativity and activity sustain any economy. Capitalism is a mode of production that is based on the general production of commodities that reflects socially necessary labour-time, that is an average quanta of human labour that is exploited by capital. Production is a social process, in which humans work together in order to produce a good or service. In capitalism, this involves a division of labour. In addition, in complex economies there are multiple organisational units of production creating similar types of goods and services. In capitalism, this involves a social process of competition for productivity levels, price advantages, markets, customers, and profits. Marx's labour theory of value is a theory of time in capitalism (Fuchs 2016b; Fuchs 2015, chapter 4). It distinguishes between necessary labour-time and surplus labour-time. The first constitutes the value of labour-power and the value of the necessary means of production. The second is surplus-value that is unremunerated labour-time. Parts of the working day are not paid, which results in monetary profit and a surplus product owned by the capitalist class. Capitalism means a struggle focused on paid and unpaid labour-time. The working class has the interest that all of its time is remunerated, whereas the capitalist class has the interest that no labour-time is paid at all. The class struggles oscillates depending on the power of the involved forces somewhere between the poles of maximum wage and maximum profit that corresponds to the two extremes of the payment of all labour-time on the one end and the payment of no labour-time at all on the other end.

To argue that increasing importance of the information economy invalidates Marx's labour theory of value means that time and labour-time do no longer play any role in the economy. Consequently, the class conflict must have come to an end and the production of information must have become autonomous from humans. But none of the two can be observed today. There are several reasons why the labour theory of values continues to apply in information capitalism and digital capitalism (see Fuchs 2014a, 2015, 2016b, 2017 for details of these arguments):

- First, commercial software and other information goods are not just produced once and then copied, but there are often new versions, constant updates, and forms of support labour.
- Second, one has to see that large parts of the Internet's political economy are based on targeted advertising. Google and Facebook are not communications corporations. They are the world's largest advertising companies. Advertising is not just based on the labour-time of marketing professionals, but also on the attention time of audiences and on commercial Internet usage time that is (unpaid) labour time.
- Third, there is an international division of digital labour, in which various forms of labour are organised. It ranges from the exploitation of enslaved miners in the

Congo, Tayloristic information and communication technology (ICT) assemblers at Foxconn in China, or software engineers in India or the Silicon Valley to various forms of unpaid online labour (Fuchs 2014a, 2014b, 2015). The production of information technology is highly exploitative and time-consuming.

- Fourth, there are various forms of irregular, unpaid, precarious, outsourced, crowdsourced, and click-worked digital labours. Examples include the usage of Facebook, Google, YouTube, Weibo, LinkedIn, Pinterest, and Instagram; online customer reviews on Amazon or Yelp; work via freelancer platforms such as Upwork, PeoplePerHour, Amazon Mechanical Turk, and ClickWorker; the participation in customer surveys, installing software updates, deleting spam, unsubscribing from spam lists, the time spent on online daring platforms such as match.com or Tinder, answering professional e-mails via the mobile or tablet out of regular working hours, working on the train, tube, or in cafés; online travel booking, etc.

- Consumer and prosumer labour is shadow work because it does not in an obvious way feel like work, but creates value for corporations. It takes time. And it takes time away that could be used outside the commodity culture. It substitutes paid labour by precarious and unpaid labour and by reducing corporations' wage-sum helps increasing their profits. Consumers and users have become part of the working class.

The digital law of value has created new forms of exploitation as well as contradictions that allow the creation of new spheres of non-commercial, alternative, co-operative production and a solidarity, commons-based, and peer production economy outside the realm of capitalism that undermine the law of value. The political aim of destroying the law of value is not an automatism that flows from information and information technology. It can rather only be achieved in conscious political struggles for the decommodification of information, the economy, and the world. It requires the dialectical political unity of the social movement "crowd" and the party (Dean 2016).

In order to show that the labour theory of value applies to the information economy, I employ in this chapter the Temporal Single-System Interpretation (TSSI) of Marxian value theory for the analysis of the German information economy. One could certainly discuss if the TSSI is the right methodology or if another one should be used, which is a more scholastic discussion that I leave to others. One could simply in an equal manner apply other interpretations and check the feasibility of the results. The space of this chapter allows however to just apply one method of analysis and the TSSI seems to be an interesting approach.

The TSSI is a version of Marxian value theory. It assumes a dynamic character of accumulation. It has been created by a group of economists around Andrew Kliman and Alan Freeman. Some of the basic insights of this interpretation are:

- Marx's theory is not erroneous or inconsistent. It does not require a correction or revision with external assumptions, but is in itself consistent.

- Claims that Marx's theory is inconsistent or erroneous often serve the purpose to suggested that it should not be used today and that its political implications are wrong. The consequential assumption of such approaches is that capitalism and class should not be abolished.

- Critics of Marx's theory often either argue that his theory of the tendency of the rate of profit to fall, the labour theory of value, or his solution to the transformation problem (the transformation of labour values into prices) are false and therefore invalidate his theory.

- The TSSI shows that all three aspects are internally consistent on the grounds of Marx's theory.

- The TSSI assumes the existence of a single-system of labour values and prices. Values and prices are not seen as being independent, but standing in a relationship to each other. The monetary expression of labour-time (MELT) is a variable that can be calculated for an economic system and that allows the transformation of labour values (calculated in hours) into prices (calculated in monetary units) and vice-versa.

- The TSSI is temporal because it assumes a dynamic character of the capitalist economy. This means that the outputs of one time period (typically one full year) act as inputs into and influence the outputs of the next time period. This means that the total hours worked during one period of time create means of production that are typically used during the next period of time. One therefore does not have to assume that the values and prices of the economic inputs have to equal those of the outputs during a certain period of time.

Alan Freeman (2010, 592) argues that the price of a commodity "at time t1 must be equal to the sale price at time t0" (Freeman 2010, 592), that is there is a connection between output and input prices of one production period and the next. "In each period, new prices are established in circulation on the basis of the values arising thus from the immediately preceding phase of production" (Freeman 1998, 11). The TSSI also assumes, as Marx did, that commodities do not necessarily sell at their value, but can be sold above or below their value:

the production price of a commodity is not at all identical with its value. [...] It has been shown that the production price of a commodity may stand above or below its value and coincides with it only in exceptional cases. (Marx 1894, 892)

In the TSSI, the

value is quite distinct from the price, and the difference is a quantitative one. In exchange the values that have arisen in the manner we have just described will be exchanged against money and this money, in exactly the same way but with new proportions, will represent value, measurable in hours. Some will realize more hours than their value, and some will realise less. Conversely, since every amount of value may equally well be represented in money, we may assign a money magnitude to their value and we will find that their value, measured in money, is in general systematically different from their price. (Freeman 1998, 11)

Two main assumptions of the TSSI are that:

1) "valuation is temporal, so input and output process can differ";
2) "values and prices, though quite distinct, are determined interdependently" (Kliman 2007, 2).

As indicated in the introduction, there is an ongoing theory debate in Marxist political economy about value-creation in the information economy. This discourse has theoretical importance, but has remained on a purely philosophical and theory level devoid of applications to empirical economic analysis, especially mathematical and statistical political economy. This chapter takes a different approach and is especially interested in empirical analysis of available statistical data. The TSSI is an approach that is grounded in the labour theory of value and mathematical and statistical analysis. The TSSI is the most thorough and rigorous mathematical formulation of the relationship between labour and time, for which it uses the category of the MELT, a category introduced first by Ramos (1998 [1999]). Furthermore the TSSI allows conceiving the information economy as value-creating, which stands in contrast to some other contemporary approaches such as certain versions of Autonomist Marxism.

The TSSI implies that for calculating the value of a commodity (measured in hours or units of money) and how it differs from the commodity price (also measured in hours or units of money), the wage (variable capital) needs to be transformed into "the value of the money used to purchase that worker's labour power" (Freeman 2010, 595), which is done based on a ratio called the MELT; the MELT is obtained by calculation ratio of the whole economy's total money to total labour-time (measured in hours) during a specific period of time, such as one year (Freeman 1998, 13). It indicates the degree of value measured in money that workers create on average in one hour of labour. The MELT's unit of measurement is £/hour (or another currency). When Marx speaks about value, he mostly means units of labour-time, but sometimes also monetary values. The MELT is a way of connecting these two measures of economic value.

The TSSI implies that value is produced in the production process and not when the commodity is sold (Kliman 2007, 37). The latter interpretation has been given recently by Michael Heinrich (1999, 2012) in what can be characterised not as a labour theory of value, but a money theory of value that implies that the worker is not exploited if the commodity s/he produces cannot be sold on the market (for a critique, see Kliman et al. 2013).

I will outline how the labour theory of value can be mathematically applied to information industries with the help of an example. I have chosen data for specific industries in Germany for the years 2001–2011 that were obtained from the OECD's Database for Structural Analysis (STAN). I have chosen Germany because the required data are relatively complete for this country and the time period 2001–2011 because data are available for it based on the International Standard Industrial Classification of All Economic Activities (ISIC), Revision 4, that in contrast to ISIC Revision 3 provides more detailed data for the information industries. The appendix of this chapter discusses differences between the ISIC Revisions 3 and 4 in relation to the information economy and the classification codes used for defining the information sector in this chapter.

The empirical model used in this chapter follows the assumption widely spread in Marxist theory that finance, insurance, and real estate constitute unproductive realms of the capitalist economy. Marx argues that productive labour creates use-values that satisfy human needs and in capitalism take on the form of exchange-value and commodities. Real estate is an unproductive sector because rent can be generated without any labour. Once housing or a piece of land exists, it can be rented out. Financial capital's production process takes on the form M–M', money results in more money through financial instruments such as loans, mortgages, financial derivatives, shares, etc. There is no commodity separate from money. This becomes evident when you think of a loan: you receive a sum of money that a bank lends to you. Over a specific period of time, you pay back the whole sum plus an interest that you pay over time from your salary. Given that there is no commodity separate from money involved and productive labour is in Marxian theory tied to the production of a new commodity, the realm of finance is often considered as being unproductive. It is therefore often excluded from calculations of productive labour (see Shaikh and Tonak 1994). The theoretical assumption that financial capital is not the result of productive labour can also be observed practical in financial crises: they emerge from financial bubbles that build up through processes that constitute a difference between the monetary profits attained from the sale of commodities produced by labour and market values the same companies selling these commodities achieve on financial markets. Large divergences between financial capital values and profits constitute a source of financial crisis. Marx (1894) speaks of financial capital as fictitious capital because it takes on artificial values that are decoupled from labour-values. From "time to time [...] flows of fictitious capital got out of hand to form speculative financial and commercial bubbles" (Harvey 2014, 239). The 2008 US housing market crisis that triggered a larger international economic crisis was the result of "fictitious capital run wild" (Harvey 2014, 33) because mortgages had been bundled together into derivatives that were traded as high-risk financial instruments.

The method applied to this data was inspired by Freeman (1998) and Kliman (2007, 25–26) and included the following steps:

- The following data were obtained from OECD STAN and taken to represent as suggested by Shaikh and Tonak (1994) the following Marxian variables:

  INTI = intermediate inputs: corresponds to constant capital c,

  LABR = compensation of employees: corresponds to variable capital v,

  NOS = net operating surplus: corresponds to profit p,

  HRSE = hours worked by employees h

- All data were available in aggregated form at the level of industries as defined by ISIC Revision 4.
- Not all labour is productive. Therefore, there are industries that add no value to the economy in a Marxian framework. They are either unproductive or consume value. This question is contested in Marxist value theory and the empirical

results one obtains depend on the theoretical choices one makes. I am in favour of a relatively broad concept of productive labour (Fuchs 2014a, 2014b, 2015), but assume that the financial and insurance industry as well as real estate do not create value. Data for these industries are however included in STAN (categories D64–D66 Financial and insurance activities, D68 Real estate activities). I therefore transformed the obtained data in such a way that I excluded data for these categories and recalculated the totals for all variables. Finance produces interest and real estate creates rent. Interest and rent are paid for by wages and profits, they consume and do not create surplus and value.

- At a specific time t, the MELT can be calculated as (Freeman 1998):

$\text{MELT}(t) = (c_p(t) + v_p(t) + p_p(t) \text{ [in prices]}) / (c_h(t-1) + v_h(t-1) + p_h(t-1) \text{ [in years or hours]})$

where $c_p(t)$ stands for total constant capital at the price level at point of time t (measured in monetary units);

$v_p(t)$ is total variable capital at the price level at point of time t (measured in monetary units);

$p_p(t)$ is total profit at the price level at point of time t (measured in monetary units);

$c_h(t-1)$ is total constant capital at the level of labour-time at the point of time t-1 (measured in hours or years);

$v_h(t-1)$ is total variable capital at the level of labour-time at the point of time t-1 (measured in hours or years) (= necessary labour-time at the level of wages);

$p_h(t-1)$ is total profit at the level of labour-time at the point of time t-1 (measured in hours or years) (= surplus labour-time).

- I calculated the economy-wide MELT for the German economy for the years 2000–2011 (t=0, 1, 2….10). Table 12.1 gives an overview. The initial MELT (0) in the years 2000 was calculated as:

$\text{MELT}(0) = (c_p(0) + v_p(0) + p_p(0) \text{ [in prices]}) / (c_h(0) + v_h(0) + p_h(0) \text{ [in hours]})$

The total hours worked during a year (= h) in the economy represent the hours during which living labour creates the value of its labour power (wages, necessary labour-time) and new value (surplus-value, surplus labour-time):

$h(t) = v_h(t) + p_h(t)$

where $h(t)$ is total hours worked in year t;

$v_h(t)$ is necessary labour-time in year t;

$p_h(t)$ is surplus labour-time in year t.

Living value per hour: $lvph(t) = (v_p(t) + p_p(t)) / h(t)$ [€/hour]

where $v_p(t)$ is total wages in year t;

$p_p(t)$ is total profits in year t;

$h(t)$ is total hours worked in year t.

The value of constant capital has already been created at this point of time. It is transferred to commodities and represents specific amounts of value:

$c_h(t) = c_p(t) / lvph(t)$

where $c_h(t)$ is constant capital in year t, measured in hours;

$c_p(t)$ is constant capital in year t, measured in monetary units (€);

$lvph(t)$ is living value per hour in year t, measured in €/hour.

Given all these assumptions, MELT (t) can be calculated for t = 0 and then iteratively for all other points of time t = 1...n.

- I selected the following information industries and industry aggregates for analysis:

D58T63 Information and communication;

D58T60 Publishing, audiovisual, and broadcasting activities;

D58 Publishing;

D59T60 Audiovisual and broadcasting activities;

D61 Telecommunications;

D62T63 IT and other information services;

D73 Advertising and marketing research;

D90T93 Arts, entertainment, and recreation.

- In the next step of analysis, I calculated several measures for all time periods and for all of these industries:

Sum of commodity prices $pr_p(t) = c_p(t) + v_p(t) + p_p(t)$ [€]

$c_h(t) = c_p(t) / \text{MELT}(t)$ [hours]

$v_h(t) = v_p(t) / \text{MELT}(t)$ [hours]

Surplus-value: $s_h(t) = h(t) - v_h(t)$ [hours]

Surplus-labour: $s_p(t) = s_h(t) \times \text{MELT}(t)$ [€]

$pr_h(t) = pr_p(t) / \text{MELT}(t)$ [hours]

$p_h(t) = p(t) / \text{MELT}(t)$ [hours]

Value of output: $w_p(t) = c_p(t) + v_p(t) + s_p(t)$ [€]

Value of output: $w_h(t) = c_h(t) + v_h(t) + s_h(t)$ [hours]

Difference between value and price: $\Delta_p = pr_p(t) - w_p(t)$

Difference between value and price: $\Delta_h = p_h(t) - w_h(t)$

Value rate of exploitation: $e_v = s_h(t) / v_h(t) = s_p(t) / v_p(t)$ (surplus labour / necessary labour)

Price rate of exploitation: $e_p = p_h(t) / v_h(t) = p_p(t) / v_p(t)$

Organic composition of capital: $oc_v = c_h(t) / v_h(t) = c_p(t) / v_p(t)$ (constant capital / variable capital)

Value rate of profit: $rp_v = s_h(t) / (c_h(t) + v_h(t)) = s_p(t) / (c_p(t) + v_p(t))$ (surplus / (constant capital + variable capital))

Price rate of profit: $rp_p = p_h(t) / (c_h(t) + v_h(t)) = p_p(t) / (c_p(t) + v_p(t))$ (profit / (constant capital + variable capital))

In the presentation of the results that follows, I will use the following conventions for industries:

1) D58T63 Information and communication;
2) D58T60 Publishing, audiovisual, and broadcasting activities;

TABLE 12.1 The German economy's monetary expression of labour-time, 2000–2011 (in € per hour)

2000	2001	2002	2003	2004	2005	2006	2007	2008	2009	2010	2011
29.1	29.9	29.5	30.4	31.8	33.0	35.0	36.8	37.2	33.0	36.1	34.6

3) D58 Publishing activities;

4) D59T60 Audiovisual and broadcasting activities;

5) D61 Telecommunications;

6) D62T63 IT and other information services;

7) D73 Advertising and market research;

8) D90T93 Arts, entertainment, and recreation.

In order to make the results easier to understand, I converted labour hours into full-time-equivalent labour years, assuming a full-time working week of 35 hours and 48 working weeks per year. In Germany, the minimum statutory leave is four weeks, so 1 working year = 35 × 48 hours = 1680 hours.

Table 12.2 presents a comparison of the German information industries' output value in the years 2001–2011. Table 12.3 gives the same data, but not calculated in years, but in monetary units (€). The data show that in all analysed information industries, information tends to be sold at prices higher than values. Table 12.4 shows how much larger prices are than values. Prices tend to be between 1.3% and 47.0% higher than values. There is only one case, where the total value is higher than the total price (industry #6, 2008). The annual average differences vary between a minimum of 8.2% in 2008 and a maximum of 20.6% in 2002. The annual average price-value-difference for all information industries cumulated over the years 2001–2011 is around 13%. The price-value-difference is on average largest in the IT industry (26.3%) and lowest in the telecommunications industry (5.1%).

Table 12.5 shows the organic composition of capital – the relationship of constant to variable capital – in the German information industries in the years from 2001 until 2011. It ranges between 0.2 and 4.9. The annual average for all industries is 1.9, which means that on average constant capital tends to be almost twice as large as variable capital. The organic composition tends to be especially high in broadcasting and telecommunications and rather low in IT and information services as well as advertising and market research. This is an indication that broadcasting and telecommunications are particularly technology-intensive, whereas IT, advertising, and market research are particularly labour-intensive industries.

TABLE 12.2 Comparison of the value of output $w_h(t)$ and prices $p_h(t)$ in the German information industries, in thousand years

	2001	2002	2003	2004	2005	2006	2007	2008	2009	2010	2011
1											
w:	2458	2385	2471	2344	2393	2282	2345	2452	2758	2620	2773
p:	2896	2875	2792	2701	2672	2556	2575	2670	3252	2934	3105
2											
w:	1008	961	909	882	852	838	831	841	928	862	N/A
p:	1113	1036	973	942	923	896	905	950	1143	1021	N/A
3											
w:	N/A	N/A	N/A	N/A	N/A	N/A	N/A	N/A	N/A	N/A	N/A
p:	622	592	557	538	524	511	542	592	714	625	N/A
4											
w:	N/A	N/A	N/A	N/A	N/A	N/A	N/A	N/A	N/A	N/A	N/A
p:	491	444	416	404	398	385	363	359	428	396	N/A
5											
w:	700	710	852	770	814	725	750	777	938	840	N/A
p:	950	1043	1067	1043	996	929	896	900	1111	967	N/A
6											
w:	750	714	710	692	727	720	764	835	892	918	N/A
p:	833	796	752	716	753	730	774	820	998	945	N/A
7											
w:	N/A	N/A	N/A	N/A	N/A	N/A	N/A	N/A	N/A	N/A	N/A
p:	474	447	427	425	412	410	408	405	416	387	N/A
8											
w:	603	601	586	584	584	586	598	616	665	658	698
p:	690	697	675	665	649	635	627	646	741	701	772

The rate of profit is the relationship of output-surplus to input, the ratio of profit to investments. There is a difference between the price rate of profit and the value rate of profit (Kliman 2007, 26). The value rate of profit calculates the output-surplus based on total surplus-value, whereas the profit rate of profit uses total monetary profits:

value rate of profit $rp_v = s_h(t)/(c_h(t) + v_h(t)) = s_p(t)/(c_p(t) + v_p(t))$

price rate of profit $rp_p = p_h(t)/(c_h(t) + v_h(t)) = p_p(t)/(c_p(t) + v_p(t))$

The Information Industry and Marx's Labour Theory of Value

TABLE 12.3 Comparison of the value of output $w_p(t)$ and prices $p_p(t)$ in the German information industries, in billion €

	2001	2002	2003	2004	2005	2006	2007	2008	2009	2010	2011
1											
w:	123	118	126	125	133	134	145	153	153	159	161
p:	145	143	143	144	148	150	159	167	180	178	180
2											
w:	51	48	46	47	47	49	51	53	51	52	N/A
p:	56	51	50	50	51	53	56	59	63	62	N/A
3											
w:	N/A	N/A	N/A	N/A	N/A	N/A	N/A	N/A	N/A	N/A	N/A
p:	31	29	29	28	29	30	34	37	40	38	N/A
4											
w:	N/A	N/A	N/A	N/A	N/A	N/A	N/A	N/A	N/A	N/A	N/A
p:	25	22	21	22	22	23	22	22	24	24	N/A
5											
w:	35	35	43	41	45	43	46	49	52	51	N/A
p:	48	52	55	56	55	55	55	56	62	59	N/A
6											
w:	38	35	36	37	40	42	47	52	49	56	N/A
p:	42	39	39	38	42	43	48	51	55	57	N/A
7											
w:	N/A	N/A	N/A	N/A	N/A	N/A	N/A	N/A	N/A	N/A	N/A
p:	24	22	22	23	23	24	25	25	23	23	N/A
8											
w:	30	30	30	31	32	34	37	38	37	40	41
p:	35	35	35	35	36	37	39	40	41	43	45

Tables 12.6 and 12.7 show the value and price rates of profit for the German information industries in the years 2001–2011.

The average value rate of profit in the German information industries for the years 2001–2011 is 3%, the average price profit rate 30%. This means that in terms of value calculated as average socially necessary labour-time, the surplus tends to be around 3% of investments, whereas in terms of monetary prices it is around 30%. This difference derives from the previously presented result that there is a tendency that information commodities are sold above their values. In the German information

TABLE 12.4 Differences between prices $p_{p,h}(t)$ and values of output $w_{p,h}(t)$ in the German information industries, in %

	2001	2002	2003	2004	2005	2006	2007	2008	2009	2010	2011	Ø
1	17.8	20.6	13.0	15.2	11.6	12.0	9.8	8.9	17.9	17.8	12.0	*13.7*
2	10.4	7.8	7.0	6.8	8.2	7.0	8.9	13.1	23.1	18.5	N/A	*11.1*
5	35.8	47.0	25.3	35.4	22.4	28.2	19.4	15.9	18.5	15.3	N/A	*26.3*
6	11.0	11.5	5.8	3.5	3.6	1.5	1.3	-1.8	11.8	2.9	N/A	*5.1*
8	14.4	16.1	15.1	13.9	11.0	8.3	4.9	4.9	11.4	6.5	10.6	*10.7*
Ø	*17.9*	*20.6*	*13.2*	*14.9*	*11.4*	*11.4*	*8.9*	*8.2*	*16.5*	*11.0*	*11.3*	*≈13*

TABLE 12.5 Organic composition of capital c/v in the German information industries, 2001–2011, in %

	2001	2002	2003	2004	2005	2006	2007	2008	2009	2010	2011	Ø
1	1.7	1.5	1.7	1.7	1.8	1.7	1.7	1.8	2.0	2.0	2.0	1.8
2	2.6	2.4	2.4	2.4	2.4	2.4	2.5	2.9	3.0	2.8	N/A	2.6
3	2.1	2.0	1.9	1.9	1.9	2.0	2.2	2.7	2.9	2.7	N/A	2.2
4	3.5	3.1	3.1	3.1	3.1	3.3	3.1	3.2	3.1	3.1	N/A	3.2
5	2.4	2.5	3.5	3.3	3.7	3.3	3.5	3.8	4.8	4.9	N/A	3.6
6	0.8	0.6	0.6	0.6	0.7	0.7	0.7	0.7	0.8	0.8	N/A	0.7
7	0.2	0.2	0.2	0.2	0.2	0.2	0.2	0.2	0.2	0.2	N/A	0.2
8	1.1	1.1	1.1	1.1	1.2	1.2	1.3	1.3	1.3	1.3	1.4	1.2
Ø	*1.8*	*1.7*	*1.8*	*1.8*	*1.9*	*1.8*	*1.9*	*2.1*	*2.2*	*2.2*	*1.7*	*≈1.9*

TABLE 12.6 The value rate of profit rp_v in the German information industries, 2001–2011, in %

	2001	2002	2003	2004	2005	2006	2007	2008	2009	2010	2011	Ø
1	-2.1	-3.8	-3.4	-2.2	-1.0	0.5	2.2	1.8	-3.0	-0.6	-3.0	-1.3
2	0.0	-1.0	-0.6	0.5	1.6	2.6	3.5	3.4	-0.6	1.5	N/A	1.1
3	N/A	N/A	N/A	N/A	N/A	N/A	N/A	N/A	N/A	N/A	N/A	N/A
4	N/A	N/A	N/A	N/A	N/A	N/A	N/A	N/A	N/A	N/A	N/A	N/A
5	-0.4	-1.6	-1.1	-0.1	0.5	1.1	2.1	1.8	-1.1	0.1	N/A	0.1
6	-6.4	-9.3	-9.0	-7.5	-5.5	-2.5	1.0	0.2	-7.3	-3.2	N/A	-4.9
7	N/A	N/A	N/A	N/A	N/A	N/A	N/A	N/A	N/A	N/A	N/A	N/A
8	12.3	11.4	12.8	16.6	22.1	26.7	31.9	31.4	20.0	24.2	17.5	20.6
Ø	*0.7*	*-0.8*	*-0.3*	*1.5*	*3.5*	*5.7*	*8.2*	*7.7*	*1.6*	*4.4*	*7.2*	*≈3*

The Information Industry and Marx's Labour Theory of Value

TABLE 12.7   The price rate of profit rp_p in the German information industries, 2001–2011, in %

	2001	2002	2003	2004	2005	2006	2007	2008	2009	2010	2011	∅
1	24.4	26.4	14.5	20.3	16.5	20.0	19.4	16.8	21.4	17.0	12.9	19.1
2	14.4	9.6	9.1	10.3	14.2	13.7	17.9	22.8	29.9	27.4	N/A	16.9
3	14.5	12.3	12.8	15.1	16.0	17.2	22.8	33.6	41.7	40.1	N/A	22.6
4	14.4	6.5	5.0	5.1	12.3	9.9	11.6	8.1	13.6	11.3	N/A	9.8
5	49.7	62.4	30.7	46.0	29.1	38.5	28.1	22.6	20.8	18.5	N/A	34.6
6	9.0	3.1	-9.5	-11.1	-5.2	-2.6	5.9	-3.8	8.3	-0.7	N/A	-0.7
7	83.7	71.7	83.0	75.4	65.4	79.8	86.1	87.1	64.1	63.8	N/A	76.0
8	54.3	57.0	57.6	62.4	66.1	67.8	68.4	68.1	59.9	57.0	52.2	61.0
∅	33.0	31.1	25.4	27.9	26.8	30.6	32.5	31.9	32.5	29.3	32.6	≈30

industry, particularly high profit rates have continuously been achieved in the first decade of the 21st century in advertising and market research as well as arts, entertainment, and recreation.

In the case of information, because of a sunk-cost rule the initial copy or prototype tends to be cost-intensive. This means that the value measured as labour-time that is required for information production is high. But once information is created, the value for reproducing it is extremely small or almost zero. There are only costs and labour-time for reproducing and circulating information or for updating it, but not for originally creating it because it is not used up during consumption. A mechanism that is therefore of particular importance for achieving profit by selling information is to secure copyrights and to sell copies and licenced usage of information at prices that stand above labour-values. The difference between the low production price of a copy guaranteed by low labour inputs and in comparison a relatively high sales-price is an important principle of capital accumulation in the information industries.

This mechanism can be observed in the data presented in this section: I showed for the German information industries that on average during a period of ten years, the difference between commodity values and commodity prices was about 13%. The price/value difference reached an average maximum of 26.3% in telecommunications, where the peak difference was 47.0% in 2002. In publishing, audiovisuals, and broadcasting the average price/value difference was 11.1%, in IT/information services 5.1%, and in arts, entertainment, and recreation 10.7%. We can in comparison calculate the price/value difference for the entire German economy (excluding finance and renting that we consider as unproductive sectors) and the manufacturing sector (table 12.8). We can see that on average manufacturing goods tended to be sold 4.8% above their values. In the total economy, values on average roughly equalled prices. This is not a proof, but a potential indication that the information industries tend to be especially characterised by selling commodities above their average values and to accumulate surplus-profits. To substantiate this assumption, further research will be needed in the future with data from different countries. The assumption that the information industries use a special form of capital accumulation is further substantiated by the fact that the price profit rate in manufacturing was on average around 7% and in the total German economy (excluding finance and real estate) around 13% (table 12.9), whereas the average in the information industries was around 30% (table 12.7). In these data, profits tend to be quite higher in relation to investment costs in the information industries than both in the total German economy and the manufacturing industry.

The average organic composition of capital c/v was around 2 in the German information industries (table 12.5) and according to my calculations in the same time period (2001–2011) 1.8 in the entire economy (excluding finance and real estate). The average monetary profit generated per working hour was 9.0€ in manufacturing, 8.6€ in the total economy, and 10.7€ in the information industries. The average labour costs per hour were 30.9€ in manufacturing, 24.7€ in the total German economy, and 30.7€ in the information industries. So both labour costs and profit per hour were in the information industries somewhat higher than in the total economy. These differences are not striking, the German information industry overall is an average industry in terms of the average organic composition, monetary profit per hour, and wages per hour.

Tables 12.10 and 12.11 show the average differences between total prices and total investment costs in the information industries, manufacturing, and the total German economy:

TABLE 12.8 Differences between prices $p_{p,h}(t)$ and values of output $w_{p,h}(t)$ in the German manufacturing industry (= M) and the entire economy (= E; excluding finance and real estate), in %

	2001	2002	2003	2004	2005	2006	2007	2008	2009	2010	2011	Ø
M	3.3	4.1	4.4	4.5	4.4	5.3	5.1	3.6	4.1	5.6	8.0	4.8
E	−0.3	−1.8	−1.1	−0.3	0.3	1.0	2.1	2.5	−1.1	1.0	−1.9	0.1

TABLE 12.9 The price rate of profit rp_p in the German manufacturing industry (= M) and the entire economy (= E; excluding finance and real estate), 2001–2011, in %

	2001	2002	2003	2004	2005	2006	2007	2008	2009	2010	2011	Ø
M	5.0	4.9	5.5	6.5	7.1	8.4	9.1	7.2	3.8	7.8	8.5	6.7
E	11.5	11.8	11.6	12.4	13.0	14.0	14.5	13.4	11.0	12.4	11.8	12.5

TABLE 12.10 Rates at which prices are higher than investments in the German information industries, 2001–2011, in %

	2001	2002	2003	2004	2005	2006	2007	2008	2009	2010	2011	Ø
1	15.3	16.0	9.2	12.7	10.5	12.5	12.2	10.8	14.3	11.3	8.6	12.1
2	10.4	6.8	6.4	7.3	10.0	9.7	12.8	16.9	22.4	20.3	N/A	12.3
3	9.8	8.2	8.4	10.0	10.5	11.4	15.6	24.6	31.0	29.1	N/A	15.9
4	11.2	5.0	3.8	3.9	9.3	7.6	8.8	6.2	10.3	8.5	N/A	7.4
5	35.3	44.7	23.8	35.3	23.0	29.6	21.9	17.9	17.2	15.4	N/A	26.4
6	3.9	1.2	-3.7	-4.2	-2.1	-1.0	2.4	-1.6	3.6	-0.3	N/A	-0.2
7	62.7	53.1	59.6	55.1	48.4	58.7	62.8	62.0	46.2	46.2	N/A	55.5
8	28.4	29.2	29.9	32.8	35.6	37.3	38.3	37.8	33.7	32.3	30.0	33.2
Ø	N/A	N/A	N/A	N/A	N/A	N/A	N/A	N/A	N/A	N/A	N/A	20.3

TABLE 12.11 Rates at which prices are higher than investments in German manufacturing and the total economy (excluding finance and real estate), 2001–2011, in %

	2001	2002	2003	2004	2005	2006	2007	2008	2009	2010	2011	Ø
M	5.0	4.9	5.5	6.5	7.1	8.4	9.1	7.2	3.8	7.8	8.5	6.7
E	11.5	11.8	11.6	12.4	13.0	14.0	14.5	13.4	11.0	12.4	11.8	12.5

$$d = (prices/(c + v))-1$$

d measures to which percentage degree prices are on average higher than investment costs.

The data show significant differences in that in all except one industry (IT), d is on average quite higher than in manufacturing and the total economy. Whereas, prices are on average 12.5% higher than investments in the total economy and 6.7% in manufacturing, the price/investment ratio is on average 20.3% in the German information industries.

Selling information has high initial development and investment costs (sunk cost rule). It is also highly uncertain if audiences and users will have interest in a specific book, film, record, software, television series, advertisement, mobile phone because human tastes and cultural preferences are complex and cannot be calculated in advance (hit rule, nobody knows anything rule, see also Caves 2002). Initial labour costs and requirements are high, whereas the costs and hours for reproducing information goods (except live performances and unique pieces of art) are fairly low. The data presented in this section are empirical indications for the tendency that information companies try to set off the risks involved in their form of production by selling their commodities at prices above their output values (on average around 13% higher), at prices that are significantly higher than investment costs (on average around 20% higher) than in the total economy, which – given successful commodity sales – results in higher profit rates. The price rate of profit in the German information industries was in the observed data therefore on average around 30%, whereas it was on average only around 7% in the manufacturing industry and 12.5% in the total economy.

12.3 Labour Productivity in the Information Sector

The question arises whether it is possible or rather difficult to increase productivity in the information sector. From a theoretical perspective, the assumption of limited productivity increases seems to be only partly true for information, art, and culture: journalists can be made to work faster, that is to write more articles, cut and paste them online or from press releases, etc. Art and culture can be digitally reproduced and thereby become commodities that can be reproduced faster. Advertising is content that can be made more efficient by targeted advertising that allows presenting different advertisements at once to many people. Designers and architects can be made to work on more projects simultaneously. Freeman (2008, 3) argues in this context that "reproduction, transmission and recording" have "eroded handicrafts limits beyond the point at which the handicraft concept remain viable". The Internet is a medium enabling the creation, production, transmission, and consumption of information in one space as well as the convergence of these processes (prosumption). Freeman argues that in the Internet age service productivity "is free to expand without natural impediment" (Freeman 2008, 3).

The labour productivity index is an OECD statistical indicator that uses the following definition of labour productivity:

> Labour productivity is here calculated as the ratio of value added volumes to number engaged. Labour productivity represents the amount of output per unit of input, output being here defined as value added while the input measure used is total employment.[5]

So, it measures value added per employed person. The statistical definition acknowledges that it would be better to use hours worked data at the industry level, but says such data are thus far not available in the OECD STAN database. The number of employed persons is however a good approximation for the total hours worked in an industry so that the labour productivity index is a feasible measure for understanding the productivity development in the information economy.

The labour productivity index increased in printing and publishing in the USA from 68.9 in 1980 to 137.0 in 2007, in post and telecommunications from 44.8 in 1977 to 158.8 in 2007, in computing services (including software engineering) from 105.5 in 1998 to 173.7 in 2007 (data source: OECD STAN). It decreased from 101.8 to 99.6 in other community, social, and personal services that include recreational, cultural and sporting activities, such as film production, sound recording, motion picture projection, production, and broadcasting of television and radio programmes, live theatre, concerts, art production and exhibition, entertainment parks, etc. (data source: OECD STAN). In the United Kingdom, the same services increased their labour productivity index from 66.7 in 1980 to 102.0 in 2003, post and telecommunications increased the index from 29.3 in 1980 to 109.7 in 2003 (data source: OECD STAN). In Germany, the labour productivity index increased in printing and publishing from 69.0 in 1970 to 100.9 in 2007, in post and telecommunications from 21.5 in 1970 to 129.1 in 2007, in computing services from 47.2 in 1970 to 95.5 in 2007, etc. (data source: OECD STAN). In community, social, and personal services, it decreased from 106.9 in 1970 to 90.3 in 2008 (data source: OECD STAN). In France, the labour productivity index increased in printing and publishing from 69.7 in 1970 to 125.1 in 2007, in post and telecommunications from 13.8 in 1970 to 168.4 in 2008, and in community, social, and personal services from 80.6 in 1970 to 101.9 in 2007 (data source: OECD STAN).

Such service data are somewhat hard to interpret because they include besides broadcasting, arts, and live entertainment also sanitation, sewage, and refuse disposal, activities of membership organisations, hairdressers, funeral services, washing

5 http://stats.oecd.org/OECDStat_Metadata/ShowMetadata.ashx?Dataset=STANINDICATORS&Coords=[VAR]. [IPTY]&ShowOnWeb=true&Lang=en

and cleaning services, porters, shoeshiners, solariums, baths, etc. But overall they could be indicators that live entertainment and arts can have problems increasing labour productivity, whereas publishing, computing, and telecommunications seem to be doing better in this respect.

It is not straightforward to measure the productivity of some information sectors. So for example Microsoft constantly releases software updates of its Windows operating system, but only once in a while a new version such as Windows 10 and even more rarely a completely new type of software. So depending on if our unit of measure is the number of software updates, versions, or different software types, one will get very different productivity measures for Microsoft. A unified and standardised measure of productivity based on measuring the output of use-values per unit of time is therefore very difficult to obtain. However, all capitalist companies produce commodities that yield a specific amount of profit per year. So if one measures the monetary output per labour input (e.g. US$/hour), then one can arrive at a unified and standardised measure of productivity that can be applied to the information sector.

Such a measure can be obtained by combining two variables from OECD's STAN database, namely value added in current prices (national currency) (VALU) and total hours worked by employees (HRSE). I downloaded these data for six countries and then calculated:

labour productivity = VALU / HRSE [national currency/hour]

Tables 12.12 and 12.13 present the results.

TABLE 12.12 Labour productivity in the information and communication sector, in national currency per hour (G = Germany, AT = Austria, F = France, I = Italy, NL = Netherlands, S = Sweden)

	2000	2001	2002	2003	2004	2005	2006	2007	2008	2009	2010	2011	Av. growth (%)
G	53.8	56.2	57.4	52.0	56.7	55.8	58.2	60.2	57.9	62.1	62.3	61.4	14.0
AT	44.4	50.6	52.0	55.2	54.7	57.8	58.5	60.1	61.7	60.8	61.6	N/A	38.6
F	68.1	69.0	75.3	78.1	79.7	80.9	82.7	82.9	82.2	82.3	83.7	81.8	20.1
I	59.4	61.2	67.3	69.0	72.3	74.4	72.3	73.0	72.9	70.4	73.3	70.0	17.8
NL	46.6	48.8	57.2	64.4	67.4	68.2	69.2	71.2	69.4	67.1	71.0	70.2	50.5
S	398.2	412.9	457.7	503.4	533.5	560.3	568.8	574.4	588.0	591.1	619.4	667.1	67.5
													34.8

TABLE 12.13 Labour productivity in the arts, entertainment, and recreation sector, in national currency per hour (G = Germany, AT = Austria, F = France, I = Italy, NL = Netherlands, S = Sweden)

	2000	2001	2002	2003	2004	2005	2006	2007	2008	2009	2010	2011	Av. growth (%)
G	48.1	49.4	50.4	50.1	53.0	53.1	54.0	54.9	55.3	52.2	53.6	54.3	11.4
AT	34.0	33.8	36.1	37.9	37.9	39.8	41.9	43.0	45.9	46.0	48.0	N/A	41.0
F	29.9	30.1	32.3	34.2	35.2	37.2	38.2	38.6	38.8	39.4	40.2	N/A	34.4
I	44.5	45.3	47.8	48.8	50.0	51.1	48.9	50.7	50.1	48.6	50.5	53.3	19.9
NL	28.3	30.4	32.7	33.4	34.8	35.1	35.6	36.3	36.1	37.3	37.9	38.0	34.2
S	269.9	246.8	260.7	281.3	285.7	298.5	325.5	336.8	343.0	344.3	342.9	358.1	32.7
													28.9

The information and communication sector consists in the ISIC Revision 4 classification that OECD STAN uses of publishing, motion picture, video and television programme production, sound recording and music publishing activities, programming and broadcasting activities, telecommunications, computer programming, consultancy and related activities, information service activities. These are all sectors where computing, media, and information processing play a role. The growth of information storage capacity per integrated circuit with falling costs (Moore's Law), the growth of data transmission speed, and the possibility for mediation, digitisation, computerisation of outputs and labour activities can increase productivity in many of these sub-industries.

The arts, entertainment, and recreation sector consists in the ISIC Revision 4 classification of art, live entertainment and performance, libraries, archives, museums, gambling and betting activities, sports, and amusement. It is rather difficult to increase productivity in arts, live entertainment and in contrast easier in publishing, audiovisual, and broadcast media, telecommunications, IT. Live entertainment such as the operation of theatres, concert halls, museums, archives, libraries, exhibition sites, gambling and betting, sports clubs and facilities, sports events, amusement and team parks, discotheques and clubs include consumption at the moment of production, human co-presence, non-storage, and non-reproducibility. Such culture is just like art production that is also included in this sector based on highly original creativity. These characteristics make Baumol's disease – the assumption that it is difficult to increase productivity in the arts (Baumol and Bowen 1965) – more likely in this sector than in other information industries. Live events can certainly be recorded and then sold as commodities, but such activities then belong to and statistically enter the publishing, audiovisual and broadcast media sector.

The data in tables 12.12 and 12.13 indicate that in all analysed countries, absolute productivity is significantly higher in the information/communication sector than in the arts and live entertainment sector. Also the cross-country ten-year average productivity growth rate is with 34.8% higher in the first sector than in the second, where it is 28.9%.

The production and diffusion of content (radio, television, telecommunications, software, Internet, advertisements, newspapers, and print publications) is based on specific qualities of information, especially that it can be shared, easily copied, and is not used up in consumption. In this sector, productivity tends to rise, which is reflected in the empirical results presented for the information and communication sector in table 12.8. We have found empirical indications that productivity can rise in the information and communication sector. Therefore, his argument that the labour theory of value does not apply because of a productivity paradox does not hold. In contrast, the labour theory of value works wherever capital is accumulated and so profit is made.

12.4 Conclusion

This chapter has produced empirical example case data that could be interpreted as providing some indications that the information economy has peculiar characteristics that need to be taken into account when applying the labour theory of value to it. The high initial costs and the high uncertainty of popularity and possible audience rates seem to make *information companies try to set off the risks involved in their form of production by selling their commodities at prices way above their output values and at prices that are significantly higher than investment costs than in the total economy, which given successful sales results in higher profit rates.*

How can we interpret this phenomenon? Some observers argue that the information economy is in general based on rent and not on productive labour and profits and therefore consumes and robs the profits of other sectors (e.g. Foley 2013; Rigi 2014; Teixeira and Rotta 2012). I showed in this chapter that there are indications that productivity can be increased in the information-processing-based part of the information economy that uses computing and data transmission and is rather difficult to achieve in the live entertainment and the arts sectors. Storage growth and transmission acceleration are factors helping to increase productivity in these sectors that are themselves partly creating ICT innovations and are among the first to use them. As a result, the productivity level can be increased in this industry, which allows to produce more value per unit of labour-time in comparison to many other industries and to thereby gain surplus-profits. Table 12.14 provides empirical indications for selected countries and regions that productivity measures as monetary value per hour worked has in the information and communication (I&C) sector been growing significantly faster than in the total economy.

More productive companies and industries produce more commodities per hour than the average company or industry. Reasons can for example be specific organisation and management methods that make the workers produce faster, the use of more efficient machines, or more skilful workers. The value of the single commodity will therefore be lower than the average commodity. If the more productively produced commodity is sold at an average price, then more profit tends to be achieved. More use-values have then been created per hour and therefore yield more profit. More developed productive forces in one industry allow the workers in it or in a company

TABLE 12.14   Index of gross value added per hour worked, 2005 = 100, total economy = non-agriculture business sector excluding real estate (data source: OECD.Stat)

	1980	1990	2000	2010	Latest (2013 or 2014)
I&C EU28			80.8	114.5	117.2
Total EU28			9.2	104.4	107.9
I&C Germany		55.0	94.5	127.4	145.4
Total Germany		77.0	91.3	103.9	107.7
I&C France	46.8	61.6	79.0	110.2	120.3
Total France	53.0	71.3	93.2	102.4	106.2
I&C UK			80.1	115.7	112.4
Total UK			86.9	105.3	106.8
I&C Finland	34.2	51.2	82.9	110.2	120.3
Total Finland	41.8	58.4	87.3	98.7	103.8
I&C Ireland			47.5	162.2	165.2
Total Ireland			91.8	118.9	121.0
I&C Norway	28.3	43.1	69.6	124.5	139.6
Total Norway	48.1	66.2	89.4	92.2	91.3

Notes: I&C, information and communication.

belonging to it to produce more use-values in less time than others. Increasing productivity means the creation of more or qualitatively richer use-values and potentially also profit per hour. The more productive industries can reduce their labour costs and investment costs. As a consequence, they can increase the share of profit in the price and the share of surplus labour-time in the total labour-time. Companies producing less productively have problems to compete. In order to try to catch up, they have to reduce the labour costs so that their rate of surplus-value increases and they can still yield some profit when selling at the prices set by the more competitive companies.

> If, therefore, the capitalist who applies the new method sells his commodity at its social value of one shilling, he sells it for 3d. above its individual value, and thus he realizes an extra surplus-value of 3d. [...] Nevertheless, even in this case, the increased production of surplus-value arises from the curtailment of the necessary labour-time, and the corresponding prolongation of the surplus labour. [...] The exceptionally productive labour acts as intensified labour; it creates in equal periods of time greater values than average social labour of the same kind. [...] Hence the capitalist who applies the improved method of production appropriates and devotes to surplus labour a greater portion of the working day than the other capitalists in the same business. [...] On the other hand, however, this extra surplus-value vanishes as soon as the new method of production is generalized, for then the difference between the individual value of the cheapened commodity and its social value vanishes (Marx 1867, 434–436).

Empirical data provide indications that it is rather difficult to increase productivity in arts and live entertainment and in contrast easier in publishing, audiovisual, and broadcast media, telecommunications, and IT. We also have tried to show that the assumption that the labour theory of value is inapplicable to the information industries is not feasible.

The overall conclusion that we can draw is that we need approaches that combine the Marxian labour theory of value and empirical economic analysis of macro-economic data. Such approaches should also think of how to critically theorise and measure the information economy's value.

References

Arvidsson, Adam and Eleanor Colleoni. 2012. Value in Informational Capitalism and on the Internet. *The Information Society* 28 (3): 135–150.

Bakhshi, Hasan, Alan Freeman, and Peter Higgs. 2013. *A Dynamic Mapping of the UK's Creative Industries*. London: NESTA.

Baumol, William J. and William G. Bowen. 1965. On the Performing Arts. The Anatomy of their Economic Problems. *The American Economic Review* 55 (1/2): 495–502.

Beverungen, Armin, Steffen Böhm, and Chris Land. 2015. Free Labour, Social Media, Management: Challenging Marxist Organization Studies. *Organization Studies* 36 (4): 473–489.

Bolaño, César. 2015. The Political Economy of the Internet: Social Networking Sites and a Reply to Fuchs. *Television and New Media* 16 (1): 52–61.

Carchedi, Guglielmo. 2014. Old Wine, New Bottles and the Internet. *Work Organisation, Labour & Globalisation* 8 (1): 69–87.

Caves, Re. 2002. *Creative Industries: Contracts Between Art and Commerce*. Cambridge, MA: Harvard University Press.

Comor, Edward. 2014. Value, the Audience Commodity, and Digital Prosumption: A Plea for Precision. In *The Audience Commodity in a Digital Age. Revisiting a Critical Theory of Commercial Media*, eds. Lee McGuigan and Vincent Manzerolle, 246–266. New York: Peter Lang.

Dean, Jodi. 2016. *Crowds and Party*. London: Verso.

Doyle, Gillian. 2013. *Understanding Media Economics*. London: Sage. Second edition.

Fisher, Eran and Christian Fuchs, eds. 2015. *Reconsidering Value and Labour in the Digital Age*. Basingstoke: Palgrave Macmillan.

Foley, Duncan K. 2013. Rethinking Financial Capitalism and the "Information" Economy. *Review of Radical Political Economics* 45 (3): 257–268.

Freeman, Alan. 2010. Trends in Value Theory Since 1881. *World Review of Political Economy* 1 (4): 567–606.

Freeman, Alan. 2008. Culture, Creativity and Innovation in the Internet Age. MPRA Paper No. 9007. Available at: https://mpra.ub.uni-muenchen.de/9007/

Freeman, Alan. 1998. Time, the Value of Money and the Quantification of Value. MPRA Paper No. 2217. Available at: https://mpra.ub.uni-muenchen.de/2217/

Fuchs, Christian. 2017. *Social Media. A Critical Introduction*, 2nd edn. London: Sage.

Fuchs, Christian. 2016a. Against Theoretical Thatcherism: A Reply to Nicholas Garnham. *Media, Culture & Society* 38 (2): 301–311.

Fuchs, Christian. 2016b. *Reading Marx in the Information Age. A Media and Communication Studies Perspective on "Capital Volume 1"*. New York: Routledge.

Fuchs, Christian. 2015. *Culture and Economy in the Age of Social Media*. New York: Routledge.

Fuchs, Christian. 2014a. *Digital Labour and Karl Marx*. New York: Routledge.

Fuchs, Christian. 2014b. *Social Media. A Critical Introduction*. London: Sage.

Fuchs, Christian. 2013. Capitalism or Information Society? The Fundamental Question of the Present Structure of Society. *European Journal of Social Theory* 16 (4): 413–434.

Fuchs, Christian. 2012a. Dallas Smythe Today – The Audience Commodity, the Digital Labour Debate, Marxist Political Economy and Critical Theory. Prolegomena to a Digital Labour Theory of Value. *tripleC: Communication, Capitalism & Critique* 10 (2): 692–740.

Fuchs, Christian. 2012b. With or Without Marx? With or Without Capitalism? A Rejoinder to Adam Arvidsson and Eleanor Colleoni. *tripleC: Communication, Capitalism & Critique* 10 (2): 633–645.

Fuchs, Christian. 2010. Labor in informational Capitalism and on the Internet. *The Information Society* 26 (3): 179–196.

Garnham, Nicholas. 2016. Book Review: Christian Fuchs: Digital Labour and Karl Marx. *Media, Culture & Society* 38 (2): 294–300.

Garnham, Nicholas. 2011. The Political Economy of Communication Revisited. In *The Handbook of Political Economy of Communications*, eds. Janet Wasko, Graham Murdock and Helena Sousa, 41–61. Malden, MA: Wiley-Blackwell.

Garnham, Nicholas. 2005. From Cultural to Creative Industries. *International Journal of Cultural Policy* 11 (1): 15–29.

Garnham, Nicholas. 2000. "Information Society" as Theory or Ideology? A Critical Perspective in Technology, Education and Employment in the Information Age. *Information, Communication & Society* 3 (2): 139–152.

Garnham, Nicholas. 1998. Information Society Theory as Ideology: A cCitique. *Loisir et Société* 21 (1): 97–120.

Goodrige, Peter, Jonathan Haskel, and Gavin Wallis. 2014. *Estimating UK Investment in Intangible Assets and Intellectual Property Rights*. Newport: Intellectual Property Office.

Hardt, Michael and Antonio Negri. 2004. *Multitude*. New York: Penguin.

Harvey, David. 2014. *Seventeen Contradictions and the End of Capitalism*. Oxford: Oxford University Press.

Heinrich, Michael. 2012. *An Introduction to the Three Volumes of Karl Marx's Capital*. New York: Monthly Review Press.

Heinrich, Michael. 1999. *Die Wissenschaft vom Wert: Die Marxsche Kritik der politischen Ökonomie zwischen wissenschaftlicher Revolution und klassischer Tradition*, 2nd edn .Münster, Germany: Westfälisches Dampfboot.

Higgs, Peter, Stuart Cunningham, and Janet Pagan. 2007. *Australia's Creative Economy: Definitions of the Segments and Eectors*. Brisbane: ARC Centre of Excellence for Creative Industries & Innovation.

Huws, Ursula. 2014. The Underpinnings of Class in the Digital Age: Living, Labour and Value. *Socialist Register* 50: 80–107.

Kliman, Andrew. 2007. *Reclaiming Marx's "Capital". A Refutation of the Myth of Inconsistency*. Lanham, MD: Lexington Books.

Kliman, Andrew et al. 2013. *The Unmaking of Marx's Capital: Heinrich's Attempt to Eliminate Marx's Crisis Theory*. Available at: https://papers.ssrn.com/sol3/papers2.cfm?abstract_id=2294134

References

Lebowitz, Michael A. 1986. Too Many Blindspots on the Media. *Studies in Political Economy* 21: 165–173.

Machlup, Fritz. 1962. *The Production and Distribution of Knowledge in the United States.* Princeton, NJ: Princeton University Press.

Marx, Karl. 1894. *Capital Volume III.* London: Penguin.

Marx, Karl. 1867. *Capital Volume I.* London: Penguin.

Marx, Karl. 1857 [1858]. *Grundrisse. Foundations of the Critique of Political Economy.* London: Penguin.

McGuigan, Lee and Vincent Manzerolle, eds. 2014. *The Audience Commodity in a Digital age. Revisiting a Critical Theory of Commercial Media.* New York: Peter Lang.

Negri, Antonio. 1991. *Marx Beyond Marx. Lessons on the Grundrisse.* New York: Autonomedia.

Perelman, Michael. 2003. Intellectual Property Rights and the Commodity Form: New Dimensions in Legislated Transfer of Surplus Value. *Radical Political Economics* 35 (3): 304–311.

Perelman, Michael. 2002. *Steal this Idea: Intellectual Property Rights and Corporate Confiscation of Creativity.* New York: Palgrave.

Postone, Moishe. 2008. Rethinking *Capital* in the lLght of the *Grundrisse.* In *Karl Marx's Grundrisse,* ed. Marcello Musto, 120–137. London: Routledge.

Proffitt, Jennifer M., Hamid R. Ekbia and Stephen D. McDowell. 2015. Special Forum on Monetization of User-Generated Content – Marx Revisited. *The Information Society* 31 (1): 1–67.

Ramos, Alejandro M. 1998 [1999]. Value and Price of Production: New Evidence on Marx's Transformation Procedure. *International Journal of Political Economy* 28 (4): 55–81.

Reveley, James. 2013. The Exploitative Web: Misuses of Marx in Critical Social Media Studies. *Science & Society* 77 (4): 512–535.

Rigi, Jakob. 2014. Foundations of a Marxist Theory of the Political Economy of Information: Trade Secrets and Intellectual Property, and the Production of Relative Surplus Value and the Extraction of Rent-Tribute. *tripleC: Communication, Capitalism & Critique* 12 (2): 909–936.

Rigi, Jakob and Robert Prey. 2015. Value, Rent, and the Political Economy of Social Media. *The Information Society* 31 (5): 392–406.

Robinson, Joan. 1966. *An Essay on Marxian Economics.* London: Macmillan.

Roosevelt, Frank. 1975. Cambridge Economics as Commodity Fetishism. *Review of Radical Political Economics* 7 (4): 1–32.

Rosdolsky, Roman. 1977. *The Making of Marx's "Capital".* London: Pluto.

Shaikh, Anwar M. and E. Ahmet Tonak. 1994. *Measuring the Wealth of Nations.* Cambridge: Cambridge University Press.

Smythe, Dallas. 1977. Communications: Blindspot of Western Marxism. *Canadian Journal of Political and Social Theory* 3 (1): 1–27.

Sraffa, Piero. 1960. *Production of Commodities by Means of Commodities.* Cambridge: Cambridge University Press.

Teixeira, R. Alves and Tomas Nielson Rotta. 2012. Valueless Knowledge-Commodities and Financialization: Productive and Financial Dimensions of Capital Autonomization. *Review of Radical Political Economics* 44 (4): 1–20.

Vercellone, Carlo. 2010. The Crisis of the Law of Value and the Becoming-Rent of Profit. In *Crisis in the Global Economy*, eds. Andrea Fumagalli and Sandro Mezzadra, 85–118. Los Angeles, CA: Semiotext(e).

Virno, Paolo. 2004. *A Grammar of the Multitude: For an Analysis of Contemporary Forms of Life.* New York: Semiotext(e).

Williams, Raymond. 1977. *Marxism and Literature.* Oxford: Oxford University Press.

Zeller, Christian. 2008. From the Gene to the Globe: Extracting Rent on the Basis of Intellectual Property Monopolies. *Review of Radical Political Economic* 15 (1): 86–115.

References

Methodological appendix: the information sector and the International Standard Industrial Classification of All Economic Activities

Freeman (1998) uses input/output data from the UK National Office of Statistics that based on International Standard Industrial Classification of All Economic Activities (ISIC) Revision 3 uses a highly aggregated distinction between 11 industries that does not allow focusing on the information sector in particular. The information industries are in these data supplied by the UK Office of National Statistics subsumed under the categories "real estate, renting, and business activities", "transport, storage, and communication", "manufacturing", and "other community, social, and personal service activities". So in ISIC Revision 3 the category "72 Computer and related activities" is part of K Real estate, renting, and business activities. "642 Telecommunications" is part of "64 Post and telecommunications" that is again part of "I Transport, storage, and communications" so that physical transport, communications, and postal services are merged together into a mobility sector that includes both physical and data transport. "22 Publishing, printing, and reproduction of recorded media" (221 Publishing, 222 Printing and service activities related to printing, 223 Reproduction of recorded media) is part of the manufacturing sector "D Manufacturing". "743 Advertising" is a subcategory of "74 Other business activities" that belongs to "K Real estate, renting, and business activities". Broadcasting and entertainment are merged as "92 Recreational, cultural, and sporting activities" (921 Motion picture, radio, television, and other entertainment activities, 922 News agency activities, 923 Library, archives, museums, and other cultural activities, 924 Sporting and other recreational activities) are part of "O Other community, social, and personal service activities". Given that statistical data tend to be highly aggregated and that disaggregation down to more detailed statistical levels is rare, it is based on ISIC Revision 3 rather difficult to calculate data for the information industries.

The United Nations Statistics Division introduced the ISIC Revision 4 in August 2008.

The data that is available based on this classification is still limited in terms of countries and the available time period. At the time of analysis (January 2014), the UN's Structural Analysis Database (STAN) Statistics Database provided data for 15 countries from 2000 until 2011 based on ISIC Revision 4, whereas for Revision 3 it held data for 35 countries from 1970 until 2009. Using the ISIC Revision 3 data clearly pose advantages in terms of the available countries and time period, but it is impossible to disentangle the information sector data from other data. So for example for many countries there is only data for "C90T93 Other community, social, and personal data". The analysis of the information economy is interested in "C92 Recreational, cultural, and sporting activities" that is not available separately, but only aggregated together with "C90 Sewage and refuse disposal, sanitation, and similar activities", "C91 Activities of membership organizations", and "C93 Other service activities". Similarly telecommunications is merged with postal services as "C64 Post and tele-communications". If one is only interested in telecommunications, then no separate data are available.

ISIC Revision 4 poses advantages for the analysis of the information economy. Its limit is that thus far only data for a few countries are available, that economically powerful countries are missing (for example China, Japan, the UK, Brazil, Russia, India, Canada, Australia, Spain, Mexico, Indonesia, and Turkey), and that historical data have not been recoded. The advantage is however that the statistical aggregates are more user-friendly and ready to use for the analysis of the information economy. Another benefit is in this respect the introduction of a new sector "J Information and communication" that consists of the following statistical aggregates:

58 Publishing activities,

59 Motion picture, video and television programme production, sound recording and music publishing activities,

60 Programming and broadcasting activities,

61 Telecommunications,

62 Computer programming, consultancy and related activities,

63 Information service activities.

In addition, I have selected the following example sectors that are important for the analysis of the information economy:

73 Advertising and market research (part of 73 Professional, scientific and technical activities):

731 Advertising,

732 Market research and public opinion polling;

R Arts, entertainment and recreation:

90 Creative, arts and entertainment activities,

91 Libraries, archives, museums and other cultural activities,

92 Gambling and betting activities,

93 Sports activities and amusement and recreation activities.

Advertising is a communication service. Market research and public opinion are data collection services. Therefore, arguably these two categories could be part of the information and communication sector.

Part IV

Conclusion

Chapter Thirteen
Conclusion

This chapter draws conclusions from the twelve preceding chapters on a meta-level. This book has asked: what is digital capitalism? It has illuminated what it means to live in digital capitalism. It has presented analyses of economic, political, and ideological aspects of digital capitalist society. It has engaged with the thought of a variety of critical thinkers whose theories and approaches enable a critical understanding of digital capitalism, including Karl Marx, Theodor W. Adorno, Henri Lefebvre, Georg Lukács, Dallas Smythe, and Friedrich Engels.

13.1 Digital Capitalism

Capitalism is not simply an economic system, but a social totality, societal formation, and type of society. The economy plays an important role in capitalist society but the latter cannot be reduced to it. Each social system has its own economy, which means that social production plays an important role. In capitalism, the logic of accumulation, alienation, alienated labour, and class relations play a role in all aspects of life and society. Marx was aware of the dialectic of economy and society in capitalism, which is why he referred to capitalism as economic mode of production and as capitalist society. Class, labour, and exploitation are not the determining aspects of capitalist society, but all aspects of capitalist society stand in a relation to and are shaped by, conditioned by, and intertwined with class, labour, and exploitation.

The capitalist economy is a class system, in which workers produce commodities with the help of means of production that are the private property of members of the capitalist class. These commodities are sold on commodity markets so that profit is achieved and capital can be accumulated. Class relations where capital exploits labour are a key feature

DOI: 10.4324/9781003222149-13

of the capitalist economy. Workers are alienated from the conditions of production in class society because they do not own the means of production and the products of their labour.

The logic of accumulation is not limited to the realm of the economy but extends into the political and cultural realms. We can therefore speak of *capitalist society*. Capitalism is a type of society where the mass of humans is alienated from the conditions of economic, political, and cultural production, which means that they do not control the conditions that shape their lives, which enables privileged groups' accumulation of capital in the economy, decision-power in politics, and reputation, attention, and respect in culture. Alienation in the economy means the dominant class' exploitation of the working class' labour. Alienation in non-economic systems means domination, that is, one group's benefits at the expense of other groups via means of control such as state power, ideology, and violence. In capitalism, we find the accumulation of capital in the economy, the accumulation of decision-power and influence in politics, and the accumulation of reputation, attention, and respect in culture. The key aspect is not that there is growth, but that there is the attempt of the dominant class and dominant groups to accumulate power at the expense of others who as a consequence have disadvantages. Capitalist society is therefore based on an economic antagonism of exploitation between classes and social antagonisms of domination.

Digital capitalism is the dimension of capitalist society where processes of the accumulation of capital, decision-power, and reputation are mediated by and organised with the help of digital technologies and where economic, political, and cultural processes result in digital goods and digital structures. Digital labour, digital capital, the digital means of production, political online communication, digital aspects of protests and social struggles, ideology online, and influencer-dominated digital culture are some of the features of digital capitalism. In digital capitalism, the accumulation of capital and power is mediated by digital technologies. There are economic, political, and cultural-ideological dimensions of digital capitalism. Digital capitalism is an antagonistic dimension of society, a dimension that stands for how the economic class antagonism and the social relations of domination are shaped by and shape digitalisation. Digital capitalism's antagonisms are the class antagonism between digital labour and digital capital, the political antagonism between digital dictators and digital citizens, and the cultural antagonism between digital ideologues and digital humans.

Big data analytics and computational social science have emerged as a new paradigm in research. This paradigm is a form of digital positivism (see chapter 7) that fetishizes quantification. It is a type of instrumental reason, what Georg Lukács characterises as reification (see chapter 5), and what Engels criticises as naïve materialism (see section 3.2 in chapter 3). The danger is that computer science colonises the social sciences and leaves no space and time for critical theory, social theory, and philosophy. The main danger of the computational social science is that it makes the social sciences uncritical and turns them into administrative sciences. Ethics, morals, critique, theory, emotions, affects, motivations, worldviews, interpretations, political assessments, power, social struggles, contradictions love, sadness, happiness, (dis)respect, (in)justice, solidarity, etc. cannot be properly understood by purely or predominantly quantitative methods.

Critical digital and social media research is the alternative to digital positivism (see chapter 7). It combines critical digital theory, critical digital methods, and critical-realist social media research ethics. Critical theories of society play an important role as guiding approach of critical digital and social media research. The latter approach uses critical, creative, and experimental methods that combine aspects of quantitative data with a qualitative understanding of humans' motivations, experiences, interpretations, norms, and values; and it interprets the world with the help of critical theories and philosophy.

We can learn from critical theory and from critical theorists such as Marx, Engels, Lefebvre, Lukács, and Adorno that we should think dialectically about digital technologies in society. Digitalisation advances new potentials for the creation of a good, democratic, socialist, humanist society but under class and dominative relations often has negative impacts on society. For example, Henri Lefebvre sees on the one hand the potentials of computing to deepen class contradictions and on the other hand its potential to make the end of toil possible (see chapter 5).

13.2 Economic Aspects of Digital Capitalism

Digital capitalism's economy is the realm where digital commodities are produced and sold. Digital capital is produced and accumulated based on a variety of models that together form the digital culture industry (see chapter 4). These models are based on the commodity that is produced and sold. Digital commodities include digital content, software, digital finance, computing hardware, access to digital networks, targeted online ads, commodities sold in e-shops, services sold via online platforms, goods rented out via apps and online platforms, access to collections of digital resources such as entertainment, and the combination of various digital commodities.

Digital labour is organised as a class relation between digital workers and digital capitalism on a global scale, the international division of digital labour (see chapter 11). Capitalists aim to maximise their profits by minimising labour costs in the international division of labour.

Transnational digital corporations exploit a variety of digital labour that create different interacting digital goods and services. For example, Apple in its production of iPhones exploits mineral extractors in Africa, hardware assemblers at Foxconn and Pegatron in China, software and hardware engineers, and a variety of service workers (see chapter 11; section 2.3.3 in chapter 2). Other forms of digital labour we have encountered in this book are users' unpaid digital labour of using targeted-advertising-based online platforms such as Facebook and Google (section 2.3.6 in chapter 2; chapter 6; chapter 8), play labour at Google (section 2.3.4 in chapter 2), precarious platform labour performed by freelancers via apps and Internet platforms such as Uber, DiDi, Deliveroo, Fiverr, Upwork, or Freelancer (section 2.3.5. in chapter 2). Such forms of labour interact in the international division of labour. For example, software engineers and digital freelancers use computers that are created by the labour of miners in Africa and Chinese hardware assemblers. Freelancers make use of software and platforms programmed by software engineers. The international division of digital labour encompasses the whole mode of digital production that contains a network of agricultural, industrial, and informational forms of work that enables the existence and usage of digital media. The international division of digital labour is a complex network that involves global interconnected processes of exploitation, such as the exploitation of Congolese slave-miners who extract minerals that are used as the physical foundation for information and communication technology (ICT) components that are manufactured by millions of highly exploited Fordist wage-workers in factories such as Foxconn, low-paid software engineers in India, highly paid and highly stressed software engineers at Google and other Western software and Internet corporations, or precarious freelancers in the world's global cities who are using digital technologies to create and disseminate culture, poisoned eWaste workers who disassemble ICTs and thereby come in touch with toxic materials, etc.

Dallas Smythe's concepts of the audience commodity and audience labour help explaining how value-generation works on ad-financed social media platforms (see chapter 6). The difference between the audience commodity in broadcasting and on social media is that in the online world we find user-generated content (prosumption, productive consumption), constant surveillance of the Internet users that allows targeting and personalising ads, and algorithmic auctions (see chapter 6).

Unwaged labour plays an important role in digital capitalism. Kylie Jarrett argues that Facebook users are digital workers who are unwaged just like houseworkers (see chapter 10). Jack Qiu shows that slavery is not a past form of exploitation, but continues to exist in digital capitalism. For example, slavery can be found in African mines where slaves at gunpoint extract minerals that form the physical foundation of the hardware of computing and communication equipment (see chapter 10).

13.3 Political Aspects of Digital Capitalism

Social struggles in capitalism are organised around antagonisms between digital commodities and the digital commons in the economy, digital authoritarianism and digital democracy in politics, and digital hatred/division/ideology and digital friendship in culture (see table 1.4 in chapter 1 and section 5.4.2 in chapter 5 on Henri Lefebvre).

Digital socialism begins and develops through class struggles of digital workers. If the labour movement and trade unions do not succeed in engaging and organising on issues such as digital labour, domestic labour, unpaid labour, freelance labour, crowdsourcing, platform labour, consumer labour, the labour of Internet users, privacy, digital surveillance, consumer protection, slave labour, etc., and if they do not see these issues as key to labour struggles, these movements commit suicide. In digital capitalism, strikes need to add new digital dimensions of struggles in order to be effective. Unions and labour movements should be present on social media and should mobilise and organise via social media and communicate their goals using hashtags, video platforms, social networking sites, messenger apps, blogs, memes, digital images, digital animations, etc. Digital corporations such as Google, Facebook, and Amazon accumulate capital online, which is why digital strikes against such companies should make use of user-boycotts.

13.4 Ideological Aspects of Digital Capitalism

Theodor W. Adorno's F-scale and concept of authoritarianism help us to understand and analyse digital authoritarianism, the communication of authoritarianism on the Internet (see chapter 4). An example is the way of how Donald Trump used the social media platforms Twitter, Facebook, and Instagram (see chapter 4 on the use of Adorno use for analysing Trump and ideology online; section 3.2 in chapter 3 on Lukács) until his accounts were banned in January 2021 after his followers had stormed the US

Capitol. Digital right-wing authoritarianism involves the online communication of top-down leadership, nationalism, the friend/enemy-scheme, violence, and law-and-order politics. Digital authoritarianism is an ideology that helps distracting attention from the real causes of society's problems and the roles of class, exploitation, and domination in these problems.

Digital fascism means the communication of fascism online as well as fascist groups' and individuals' use of digital technologies as means of information, communication, and organisation. Fascism is a particular form of right-wing authoritarianism that aims at killing the identified enemies by the use of violence, terror, and war. In digital fascism, fascists make use of digital technologies for trying to advance violence, terror, and war as means for the establishment of a fascist society. The scapegoats that fascist ideology constructs and against whom it agitates online include, for example, immigrants, socialists, liberals, intellectuals, experts, and democrats (see section 9.5 in chapter 9).

Digital ideology not just means ideology on the Internet but also ideology of the digital, that is, the digital as ideology. Digital ideology conveys the impression that computing with necessity brings about certain changes of society that cannot be undone or stopped. As a consequence, digital ideology with is fetishistic aura of novelty, speed, and pseudo-radicalness that distracts attention from class, exploitation, domination, and other social relations. Big data fetishism is an example of digital ideology. The ideology of big data assumes that data is the new oil and is bringing about a radically novel society (see section 3.4 in chapter 3; see also section 9.4 in chapter 9). But big data is embedded into capitalist relations, into big data capitalism as aspect of digital capitalism.

Cultural, media, and creative digital labour *appears* to be less reified and alienated than manual labour, but is often organised as precarious labour that does not provide adequate social, job, and income securities. Such workers form a relatively new stratum of the working class that is highly exploited and confronted with the ideology that their labour is fun and self-determined. Luc Boltanski and Ève Chiapello have in this context coined the notion of the new spirit of capitalism, a kind of reified class consciousness of cultural, media, and digital workers in the age of digital capitalism (see section 3.3 in chapter 3 and section 2.3.4 in chapter 2).

Fake news online is another aspect of ideology in the age of digital capitalism. Fake news is as old as the tabloid press, but in the online world fake news can spread quickly, can be individually targeted, and it is often hard to distinguish if online be-haviour in the context of fake news is conducted by humans or algorithms. Right-wing movements try to make use of social media for spreading their propaganda and challenging socialist and liberal political positions and worldviews online. They not just use bots and traditional lobbying methods online, but often also resort to threats, bullying, and hate speech.

13.5 Alternatives to Digital Capitalism

There are two major alternatives to digital capital (see section 2.4 in chapter 2): on the one hand, the renewal of the movement of co-operatives and self-managed companies in the form of platform co-operatives, that is, Internet platforms that are self-managed by users and digital workers; and on the other hand, the creation of public Internet platforms through a network of public service media. Many platform co-operatives do not make it from concept to reality and many soon disappear again.

Digital socialism is the democratic and humanist alternative to digital capitalism. Digital capital is organised and acts globally. Workers, political regulation, and poli-tical groups are in contrast predominantly confined to the national level. Marx and Engels argued that struggles for alternatives require internationalism and called for the workers of all lands to unite in a political movement. In order to establish democratic digital socialism as alternative to digital capitalism, the digital workers of all countries have to unite in an international trade digital labour union and a political movement.

Index

For Product Safety Concerns and Information please contact our EU
representative GPSR@taylorandfrancis.com
Taylor & Francis Verlag GmbH, Kaufingerstraße 24, 80331 München, Germany